FOR
SAMUEL AND RUTH RIMLER

A Gershwin COMPANION

A Critical Inventory & Discography, 1916-1984

by
Walter Rimler

Popular Culture, Ink.
1991

Book design and layout by Tom Schultheiss and Alex Przebienda.
Cover design by Diane Bareis.
Computer programming by Alex Przebienda.

Cover musical notation and lyrics from "HI HO"
(George Gershwin, Ira Gershwin) © 1967 Chappell & Co.
All Rights Reserved. Used by Permission.

Cover photograph and frontispiece courtesy of the Gershwin Family.
All Rights Reserved. Used by Permission.

All other cover art is copyright © 1991 by Popular Culture, Ink.

ISBN 1-56075-019-7 (hardcover)
LC 91-61884

Published by Popular Culture, Ink.
P.O. Box 1839 Ann Arbor, MI 48106 U.S.A.

PCI Collector Editions
are published especially for discerning collectors and libraries.
Each Collector Edition title is released in limited quantities
identified by edition, printing number, and number of copies.
Unlike trade editions, they are not generally available in bookstores.

10 9 8 7 6 5 4 3 2 1
(First edition, first printing: 1000 copies)

Contents

INTRODUCTION

Some years ago I wrote a short novel entitled *Old Friends*. In it, the narrator described how his life was forever changed when, as a boy, he inadvertently found himself in a room in which a recording of the *Rhapsody in Blue* was playing. "The *Rhapsody in Blue*," he said somewhat grandly, "breathed music into my nostrils." Needless to say, he was speaking those words for me. And I, in the phrase "Old Friends," was, in turn, referring, if a bit presumptuously, to myself and the composer of the *Rhapsody in Blue*.

After months of listening to that first recording of the *Rhapsody*, I was finally sated enough to turn the disk over, whence I spent the next several months spellbound by the *Concerto in F*. And then the same thing happened when I listened to recordings of *An American in Paris* and the *Preludes for Piano* and the *Cuban Overture* and *Porgy and Bess* and the two dozen or so songs that were in circulation. This was interest compounding at a furious rate and I did not want it to stop; I wanted to hear every Gershwin piece—for, so far, each note had either contributed to the magic of the Gershwin name or had sported a magical aura for his having written it. But there was a problem. I knew, from having read biographies of the man, that he had produced hundreds of compositions. Yet, only a small sampling of his work was available in sheet music or on recordings. What were the other pieces like? If I were to hear them, would they too make me drunk?

Eventually, when I realized that I was not going to be able to get hold of this lost music, I hoped that I could at least find a book—a critical inventory—that would describe it. But no such book was available. Nor, in the intervening years, did one appear. Although an ever wider variety of Gershwin compositions was being recorded and published, there was still no way for a devotee to satisfy his or her curiosity about the rest of this composer's oeuvre without coming up with the time and money to hunt down rare records and sheet music.

It was and is an odd situation. Gershwin published nearly 300 works in his lifetime but most of them have been forgotten or were never known. And that is not even counting the several hundred that never made it into print. Thus, a very high percentage of his output was and still is residing in oblivion—an unexpected situation, considering the stature that he has always had in American popular music and the respect that is now given his work by people across the musical spectrum and around the world. One can hope that his publishers will eventually put out a complete edition of his works or that a record company will present the entirety of his output on disk. But, until then, and maybe even after, there will be a need for a descriptive catalogue—one that can give some guidance as to which among these compositions are the ones most worth pursuing. Such a book might guide not only inquiring non-musicians but performers as well—adventurous singers and instrumentalists who, anxious to bring neglected Gershwin gems to public view, would produce new recordings and inspire new sheet music editions.

And so, all said above, I have written this book—a descriptive inventory of the works of George Gershwin. I would not have been able to get very far into it had I not had permission from the Gershwin family to obtain from publishers photocopies of works that have long been out of print. For that, I am grateful. I am also grateful for the cooperation I received in that regard from Gershwin's publishers at Chappell & Co., T.B. Harms/The Welk Group, and Warner Bros. (special thanks to Henry Cohen and Ethan Neuburg at Warner Bros.). Also, I want to say thank you to the following for their assistance in obtaining other materials: the Canadian Broadcasting Corporation in Toronto, Ontario; Gershwin biographer Edward Jablonski; Jack Nelson of The Record House in San Francisco; Betsy Rosenberg and Annette Farrington of the Goodspeed Opera House in East Haddam, Connecticut; Wayne Shirley of the Library of Congress; Aurora Perez and Barbara Sawka of The Stanford Archive of Recorded Sound. Thanks also to Rob Kerwin for critiquing and to Dana Iapicca and Peg Rimler for proofreading the manuscript.

Included in *A Gershwin Companion* are entries on each of the composer's published compositions. These entries contain information that is divided into the following categories:

Numbering

I have endeavored to number all of Gershwin's published compositions in the order in which they first appeared in print. I say "endeavor" because there were times when some arbitrary choices had to be made. For instance, the half dozen or so songs that would be published from any given Gershwin show would go to press simultaneously and there is no logical way of numbering one ahead of the other. Therefore, in numbering such songs, I have resorted to alphabetical order. For example, "The Babbitt and the Bromide" and "Dance Alone

With You" are both from the 1927 show *Funny Face* and both were published at the same time. But "Babbitt" (number 162), coming alphabetically before "Dance" (number 163), is given numerical preference. On the other hand, where a show's complete piano/vocal score has been published, I have numbered the selections in the order in which they appear in that score. For instance, "Till I Meet Someone Like You" precedes "Isn't It Wonderful" in the *Primrose* score and, thus, it precedes it numerically in this book (they are numbered 99 and 100, respectively). And, in the case of *Porgy and Bess*, I have given a single number (265) to an entire piano/vocal score, using a secondary numbering system for the songs, arias and instrumental compositions that make up that score. This is because *Porgy and Bess* is the only Gershwin show in which all of the selections are truly interrelated (although a case *can* be made in this regard for the political operettas: *Strike Up the Band*, *Of Thee I Sing*, and *Let 'Em Eat Cake*—the latter not yet published in its entirety).

Then there was the question of posthumous publications. Gershwin died in July of 1937 while working on a film called *The Goldwyn Follies*, and the songs that he was able to finish for that project (including "Love Walked In" and "Love is Here to Stay") were published only after his death. Yet, I have decided not to list them as posthumous compositions, but to begin the posthumous numbering with projects conceived after his death. The first of these was "Dawn of a New Day," which was fashioned from several musical fragments in 1938 by Ira Gershwin and Kay Swift and used as the official anthem of the 1939 New York World's Fair. "Dawn" and subsequent posthumous publications are marked by the letter P but they continue the numerical sequence. Thus, "Love is Here to Stay" is 284, while "Dawn" is 285-P. (To further complicate matters: Since "Love is Here to Stay" was Gershwin's last composition, I have given it the final non-posthumous number, even though "Love Walked In" from the same score follows it alphabetically.)

Despite these somewhat arbitrary decisions, I think that this numbering system works well enough to enable one, at a glance, to know when in the course of the composer's career a particular piece was written.

Lyricist, Key, Time, Tempo

This information is included for each of the published pieces. For instrumental works, I have indicated the instrument or combination of instruments for which the work, as written by the composer, was intended.

Introduced by

If a work appeared in a Broadway show, then I have chosen to indicate who first performed it at that venue, rather than the performer, if different, who introduced it in an out-of-town tryout. Otherwise, I have identified the performer or performers who first publicly sang or played the piece. Also included here are the dates and places of the premieres.

Lore

Whenever possible, I have tried to tell how a piece came to be written and pass on remarks or anecdotes about it that have come from those connected with it at or since its creation.

Analysis

I have given a brief musical analysis of each of George Gershwin's published compositions. The intent here has been to point out those features that seem to be of particular interest. Regarding Gershwin works which do not, in my opinion, have much merit, it seemed uncalled for to kick a song like "I Need a Garden," since it has already been down for more than sixty years. One can, thus, take my lack of good things to say about a number as an indication of my inability to find much of interest in it. But we should remember that the music of Gershwin tends to hold delights that are missed by audiences and/or critics the first time around. In the composer's lifetime there were many works that took a while to catch on ("The Man I Love," for instance). Others have become popular only after his death ("How Long Has This Been Going On?," most of *Porgy and Bess*), and there are a number of fine works that still have not gained general acceptance ("Sing of Spring," Hi-Ho!," "Dear Little Girl," "Feeling Sentimental").

Recordings

I have compiled discographies for each of the composer's published works. In doing so, I have tried to be thorough and I think that this is the most complete Gershwin discography available, with well over 2,000 entries—although no claim is being made that this list is complete (a listing of Gershwin on CD will have to wait for another time and place). Whenever possible, I have tried to indicate when these recordings were made. But where no dates are shown, the names of the recording artists have simply been put into alphabetical order. Whenever Gershwin himself recorded a piece, that is the first information given. Second billing has been reserved for versions made by the performer who introduced the song or for other records of historic or special interest.

Unpublished Compositions

In the back of the book is a list of all of Gershwin's as yet unpublished compositions. They are arranged according to the year in which they were written and then by the show, if any, for which they were composed. When several unpublished songs were written for a given show they are presented in alphabetical order.

Some decisions had to be made here as to the definition of the word "published." For instance, one song, "O, Land of Mine, America" was written in 1919 and entered by Gershwin and lyricist Michael O'Rourke in a contest sponsored by the New York *American* to see who could come up with a good national anthem. "O, Land" appeared in the March 2, 1919 edition of that newspaper but has not been in print since then. Because it has never been generally available in a sheet music edition, I have decided to include it in my listing of Gershwin's unpublished works.

Also, there are Gershwin works that have appeared on records but not in sheet music. For example, there is "Comes the Revolution," a song from *Let 'Em Eat Cake* that has been recorded by Bobby Short and also by Michael Tilson Thomas. Although one might define the word "published" as meaning available to the general public—which would mean that "Comes the Revolution" has, indeed, been published— I have chosen to stick with the existence of sheet music as the defining criterion. Therefore, this and the handful of other songs that have been recorded but never made available in sheet music editions are placed in the chapter on unpublished works. Recordings of those songs are noted in that chapter.

Finally, the reader should know that this book is not a biography of

George Gershwin. Of the several currently available full-length biographies, the most recent and complete is *Gershwin* by Edward Jablonski (Doubleday, 1987). It and the others contain selective bibliographies, while a more detailed bibliography can be found in the *New Grove Dictionary of American Music* (Macmillan, 1986).

Indexes

Three indexes conclude this volume: Index to Recording Artists; Index to Compositions; General Index. Index citations refer to page numbers, not to entry numbers.

A Gershwin Companion
Part One
Published Works

1. **WHEN YOU WANT 'EM, YOU CAN'T GET 'EM
WHEN YOU'VE GOT 'EM, YOU DON'T WANT 'EM**

Lyricist: Murray Roth
Key: C
Time: Common
Tempo: Moderato
Introduced by: George Gershwin in a 1916 piano roll (see below).

Lore: This song was turned down by Jerome H. Remick & Co., for whom Gershwin was working as a song plugger. Harry Von Tilzer Music Publishing Company then accepted it on the recommendation of Sophie Tucker. It was Gershwin's first published song and for it he signed his first contract as a composer. The contract was dated March 1, 1916 and, in signing it, Gershwin decided to waive a $15 advance so that he could receive his first royalty check whole. Unfortunately, that check amounted to only $5. Lyricist Roth, a Tin Pan Alley denizen who later became a motion picture executive, was more prescient, having taken his $15 upon publication. Gershwin's partnership with Roth ended after a friendly wrestling match took a sudden serious turn. One other collaboration, "My Runaway Girl," remains unpublished.

Analysis: The sixteen-bar verse ("A little loving now and then") combines a lilting tune with a strict ragtime accompaniment—one whose bass line alternates pounding octaves with softer thirds and fourths. The twenty-bar refrain ("When you want 'em") is based on a nervous and chromatic four-note motive, one that is presented in various registers and atop harmony that shifts constantly from major to minor modes. The chromaticism and the major/minor juxtaposition are elements that would always be part of the Gershwin style. Also worth mentioning is a surprising modulation into E-minor that results in a moment of genuine mournfulness (at "When you lose 'em") and the fact that, for the first sixteen bars, the accompanist is given a more complete melody line than the singer. It is only in a brief recapitulation that the singer gets a chance at all the notes.

Recordings: In September of 1916, the Aeolian Company issued Gershwin's piano roll of "When You Want 'Em" on two of their subsidiary labels: Metro-Art 202864 and Universal Uni-Record 202865. It was not until some forty years later that a second recording of the song appeared, this time on an album entitled *The Gershwin Years* (Decca DXSZ-7160), featuring singers Paula Stewart, Lynn Roberts and Richard Hayes, and conductor George Bassman.

2.   MAKING OF A GIRL

Lyricist: Harold Atteridge
Key: E-flat
Time: 2/4
Tempo: Allegro moderato
Introduced by: Jack Boyle in *The Passing Show of 1916* at Winter Garden Theatre in New York City on June 22, 1916.

Lore: This was the first of Gershwin's songs to be used in a musical production. It was presented in Sigmund Romberg's *The Passing Show of 1916* with Romberg and Gershwin listed as co-composers (although Romberg had nothing to do with the composition). Gershwin had shown Romberg five tunes and the older composer chose this one. Harold Atteridge, who was Romberg's main lyricist at the time, then wrote the words.

"Making of a Girl" was the only Gershwin song to be published by G. Schirmer.

Analysis: This song, which is about how to dress fashionably, consists of a thirty-two-bar verse and a thirty-two-bar refrain. Both are in an extroverted chorus line style and it is easier to imagine them done by an ensemble than by a solo singer. The verse ("Ev'ry girl more or less by her knowledge of how to dress") is in the format of Gershwin's first published song, "When You Want "Em," in that it is through-

2

composed but for a midway reprise of the opening bars. It is notable for its consistent use of minor thirds in the melody against major thirds in the accompaniment—resulting in dissonances that are harsh and bluesy. Those moments occur at "ledge" in "knowledge of how to dress," at "to" in "the way to fix a girlie's looks," and at "in" in "for when in fashion." The refrain ("You take a pretty show") is a syncopated melody that spirals up, rising more than an octave. It too is through-composed but for a fleeting reprise of the opening notes.

Recordings: None.

3.   RIALTO RIPPLES (RAG)

For solo piano

Key: A-minor
Time: Alla breve
Tempo: Marcato
Introduced by: George Gershwin in a piano roll recording made in 1916 (see below).

Lore: By 1916 Gershwin was a well-known and well-respected ragtime pianist. Eubie Blake heard about him that year, after moving to New York from Baltimore. "James P. Johnson and Lucky Roberts told me of this very ofay piano player at Remick's," Blake later recalled. "They said he was good enough to learn some of those terribly difficult tricks that only a few of us could master." As for "Rialto Ripples," Gershwin biographer David Ewen has said that it was inspired by the ragtime piano playing of Felix Arndt, composer of "Nola" (seventeen years later, in the song "Union Square" from *Let 'Em Eat Cake*, George and Ira would make, respectively, a musical and lyrical reference to "Nola"). Gershwin often went to Arndt's studio in the Aeolian Building on 42nd Street to listen to Arndt play.

"Rialto Ripples" was published by Jerome H. Remick & Co. in 1917. They had not published him before, although he had been song plugging for them for nearly three years.

Gershwin's collaborator on this piece, Will Donaldson, is not to be confused with songwriter Walter Donaldson. The latter was the composer of such hits as "Carolina in the Morning" and "My Blue

Heaven." Will Donaldson was a Tin Pan Alley pianist and song-plugger who would later write such numbers as "Doo Wacka Doo" (lyrics) and "I Can't Resist You" (music).

Analysis: This is Gershwin's first published instrumental work. It can be divided into four sections:

1. A zestful A-minor melody, sixteen bars long, that begins with an opening triplet and is accompanied by a chromatic figure in the bass.
2. A bravura, highly syncopated tune in the relative major, F. It is sixteen bars long.
3. Section one returns, this time with a conclusive ending in A-minor.
4. A sunny twenty-four bar trio in F.

Recordings: Gershwin's 1916 piano roll was made for the Aeolian Company and released on two of their subsidiary labels (Metro-Art 202934 and Universal Uni-Record 202935). It has been reissued on Mark 56 Records 667. Recent recordings have been by Richard Rodney Bennett (EMI EMD 5538), William Bolcom (Nonesuch H-71284), John Holmquist and Daniel Estrer (duo guitarists—Pro Arte PAD 226), Katia and Marielle Labeque (duo pianists—Angel 37980), Leonard Pennario (Angel DS-37359), Ken Werner (Finnadar 9019). A Luther Henderson Brass arrangement is on RCA Red Seal 6490-1.

4. **YOU-OO JUST YOU**

> *Lyricist:* Irving Caesar
> *Key:* E-flat
> *Time:* Common
> *Tempo:* Moderato
> *Introduced by:* Vivienne Segal in a concert hall setting (see below) on November 25, 1917. Adele Rowland did it in *Hitchy-Koo of 1918* at the Globe Theatre in New York City on June 6, 1918.

Lore: Gershwin was hired as rehearsal pianist for a Broadway show called *Miss 1917*, whose score was by Victor Herbert and Jerome

Kern. *Miss 1917* opened on November 5, 1917 and, during its brief run, the cast gave Sunday concerts at the Century Theatre with Gershwin serving as accompanist. It was at the November 25, 1917 concert that the star of *Miss 1917*, Vivienne Segal, sang two Gershwin/Caesar songs, "You-oo Just You" and "There's More to the Kiss than the X-X-X." These songs caught the attention of the manager of *Miss 1917*, Harry Askins, who recommended Gershwin to Max Dreyfus, head of Tin Pan Alley's most notable publishing firm, T.B. Harms. In early 1918 Dreyfus offered the composer $35 a week to do nothing but write songs. Gershwin was also to receive three cents for each copy sold. "You-oo Just You" was the second (after "Rialto Ripples") and final Gershwin composition published by Jerome H. Remick & Co., and it was the first published collaboration between Gershwin and Caesar.

Analysis: The verse ("Hon' I'm goin' to sing about you-oo"), which is only eight bars long, employs, in the accompaniment, a descending alto line against a simple, tranquil melody. There is an E-natural in the sixth bar (on "it's" in "it's all goin' to be about you-oo") that sounds somehow wrong, no matter how one tries to slip into or out of it. The refrain ("Who's the most wonderful gal in Dixie") has a striving tune atop rolling E-flat and D-minor chords, in the manner of a spiritual. It is unusual for its twenty-one-bar length and for the fact that it repeats after six, rather than eight, bars.

Recordings: None

5. **SOME WONDERFUL SORT OF SOMEONE**

> *Lyricist:* Schuyler Greene
> *Key:* A-flat
> *Time:* Common
> *Tempo:* Moderato
> *Introduced by:* Nora Bayes in *Ladies First* at the Broadhurst Theatre in New York City on October 24, 1918. The song was revised by Gershwin and Greene a year later and the second version was premiered by Adele Rowland in *The Lady in Red* at the Lyric Theatre in New York City on May 12, 1919.

> *Lore:* This was the first Gershwin song brought out by the firm

of T.B. Harms. They published it in September, 1918. Nora Bayes liked the number well enough to interpolate it into her new Broadway vehicle, *Ladies First*—a show which satirized women in politics—and she introduced it to Gershwin's piano accompaniment during a six-week pre-Broadway road tour. When the show hit Pittsburg, twelve-year old Oscar Levant was in the audience and he was smitten with what he later described as the "fresh, brisk, unstudied, completely free and inventive playing" of his future friend. Gershwin later told Levant that Miss Bayes had considered this virtuosity distracting and had almost fired him.

Analysis: Greene's lyric is about repairing with that special someone to the proverbial little cottage. The opening line of the verse ("In me girls you see one who works ever patiently upon the heart of man") seems to be in the voice of Cupid although later on Cupid is referred to in the third person. The refrain ("Some Wonderful Sort of Someone") contains a couple of musical surprises. When the initial eight bars are repeated they are in a new key, B-flat. This was considered daring twenty-six years later when Jerome Kern did it in "Long Ago and Far Away." Then, in the release ("And when for you life takes on a new charm"), we get a statement of what would in six years become the chief musical phrase in "Fascinating Rhythm."

Recordings: A rendition can be found on an album entitled *The Gershwin Years* that features singers Paula Stewart, Lynn Roberts, and Richard Hayes and Conductor George Bassman (Decca DXSB-7160).

6.   **I WAS SO YOUNG (YOU WERE SO BEAUTIFUL)**

> *Lyricist:* Irving Caesar and Al Bryan
> *Key:* G
> *Time:* Common
> *Tempo:* Moderato
> *Introduced by:* Charles and Mollie King (a brother and sister team) in *Good Morning, Judge* at the Shubert Theatre in New York City on February 6, 1919.

Lore: This was the first Gershwin song to become popular. According to songwriter and music critic Alec Wilder, it was still in print many years after 1919 in a series called "Hits of Bygone Days." It was interpolated into *Good Morning, Judge* because its theme of very young love fit into the play.

Analysis: Lyricist Caesar called this song "quite off the beaten path for the period." He was probably referring to the structure of its twenty-two-bar refrain ("I was so young"), for no section exactly repeats another. The closest that Gershwin comes to a repetition is in the ninth and tenth bars when, during a reprise of the title phrase, bars one and two are nearly repeated—although the harmony is different, having been changed for increased dramatic effect. Toward the end Gershwin suddenly takes us in a new direction with an eight-bar motive ("Each time I looked at you") that is itself unexpectedly extended for a two-bar barbershop-style resolution. This lovely melody, which shows much more restraint than the lyric ("'Twas then I realized why men go mad"), is preceded by a tranquil twenty-bar verse ("I was a boy with a boyish heart").

Recordings: Gershwin made a piano roll of this in 1919 (Universal Song Roll 3357, reissued on Klavier Records KS-122). Another early version was by Joseph C. Smith's Orchestra (Victor 35690). The song is also performed on an album entitled *George Gershwin: His Story and His Music* (written by Alfred Simon and narrated by Arthur Hannes—Vox Music Masters MM3700). Another version is on an album entitled *The Gershwin Years* with singers Paula Stewart, Lynn Roberts and Richard Hayes and with an orchestra and chorus conducted by George Bassman (Decca DXS2-8160). Bobby Short's version was recorded in 1973 (Atlantic SD 2-608).

7.   **THERE'S MORE TO THE KISS THAN THE X-X-X**

Lyricist: Irving Caesar
Key: D
Time: 2/4
Tempo: Moderato
Introduced by: Vivienne Segal in a concert hall setting (see "You-oo Just You"). Mollie King sang it in *Good Morning, Judge* at the Shubert Theatre in New York City on February 6, 1919. Helen Clark did it (it was now called "There's More to

7

the Kiss Than the Sound") in *La La Lucille* at the Henry Miller Theatre in New York City on May 26, 1919.

Lore: See "You-oo Just You."

Analysis: This is a ragtime number with a gimmick: during the forty-bar refrain ("There's More to the Kiss") the singer is asked to pucker up and make the sound of a kiss whenever a capital X appears in the lyric. These kisses are quick, staccato affairs (eighth notes) through the first thirty bars. But then, in bars thirty-one and thirty-two, there is a two-bar long smacker. Preceding the refrain is a twenty-four-bar verse ("I've often tried to realize") that takes an eight-note phrase through six melodic and harmonic permutations.

Recordings: Barbara Cook, Anthony Perkins, Elaine Stritch, and Bobby Short (Painted Smiles PS 1357).

8.   SOMETHING ABOUT LOVE

Lyricist: Lou Paley
Key: E-flat
Time: 2/4
Tempo: Moderato
Introduced by: Adele Rowland and Donald MacDonald in *The Lady in Red* at the Lyric Theatre in New City on May 12, 1919. The song was used again in the 1926 English version of *Lady Be Good*, featuring Fred and Adele Astaire.

Lore and Analysis: The twenty-four-bar verse ("Adam and Eve were once a loving pair") has a sentimental, sighing sound that is broken on occasion by a piano riff first heard in the introduction. The melody of the refrain ("There's something about love that I Love") rises up to a point of harmonic tension (a D7^9), then quickly subsides.

It is ABA^{1}C in form. The C portion is a long coda that begins at the twenty-fifth bar and then suddenly, at bar thirty-one, blossoms into an unrelated new idea. Gershwin biographer Isaac Goldberg called this idea a "trouvaille" and Gershwin must have agreed because eight years later he slowed the tempo of this section and turned it, with Ira's help and Paley's permission, into a new song called "He Loves and

She Loves." Paley's permission was needed because it was not just the music but the words of this section that became the germ of the new song.

Recordings: Ronny Whyte and Travis Hudson (Monmouth-Evergreen MES 7061).

9. **THE BEST OF EVERYTHING**

Lyricist: Arthur J. Jackson and B.G. DeSylva
Key: D
Time: 2/4
Tempo: Marcia Allegro
Introduced by: John E. Hazzard in *La La Lucille* at the Henry Miller Theatre in New York City on May 26, 1919.

Analysis: In the verse of this comic duet the man sings of having been born with a silver spoon in his mouth while the woman complains of having been deprived of life's advantages. Then, in the refrain, each lists his or her every material desire from Stetson hats to Quelques Fleurs perfume. There is a twist at the end. When he says that, having always had the best, he must have her she replies that she needn't have the best if she can have him.

Verse and refrain are both jaunty, self-contained thirty-two-bar ABA songs. The former ("I was born") is most interesting in its release, which begins with a series of minor seventh chords (beginning at "My proud and loving") and then continues with a contrasting series of major seventh chords (at "My milk"). The melody of the refrain ("I get my rings and things from Tiffany") begins by ambling pleasantly down the notes of a D^{9+6} chord.

Recordings: None

9

10. **FROM NOW ON**

Lyricist: Arthur J. Jackson and B.G. DeSylva
Key: G
Time: Common
Tempo: Moderato
Introduced by: Janet Velie and John E. Hazzard in *La La Lucille* at the Henry Miller Theatre in New York City on May 26, 1919.

Analysis: This is a straightforward, if somewhat stilted, profession of love. Its sixteen-bar verse ("Don't you recall the day I was wed to you?") consists of five permutations of a brief, five-bar phrase. The refrain ("From now on") is based on a dotted note motive—one that becomes part of the accompaniment when the melody is at rest. In the second bar (at "My love will belong to you") it sounds very much like the central idea of Jerome Kern's "Whip-Poor-Will," written the same year (the Kern song had its debut in a show entitled *Zip Goes a Million*, whose premiere was some six months later than the premiere of this song).

Recordings: Gershwin's piano roll of this song was released in October of 1919 on Universal Song Roll 3543 (reissued on Klavier KS-122).

11. **THE LOVE OF A WIFE**

Lyricist: Arthur J. Jackson and B.G. Desylva
Key: E-flat
Time: 6/8
Tempo: Marcia moderato
Introduced by: This song was dropped from *La La Lucille*, a show which opened at the Henry Miller Theatre in New York City on May 26, 1919.

Analysis: In this comedy number the bachelors in the audience are addressed by a group of singing married men who praise the state of matrimony in both the verse ("We're of the big majority") and refrain ("Oh, the love of a wife")—until, that is, they deliver a surprise ending ("Oh, the love of a wife is a wonderful thing/But it's something that a husband never gets"). In both verse and refrain Gershwin provides unambitious but good-natured 6/8 tunes. The main idea of the refrain moves up and down the notes of an E-flat triad, making for a bugle call effect. It is thirty-two bars long and ABCA in form.

Recordings: None

12. NOBODY BUT YOU

Lyricist: Arthur J. Jackson and B.G. DeSylva
Key: E-flat
Time: 2/4
Tempo: Allegretto Moderato
Introduced by: Helen Clark and Lorin Raker in *La La Lucille* at the Henry Miller Theatre in New York City. This song was added to the show at some point after the May 26, 1919 opening.

Lore: "Nobody But You" was actually written sometime between May of 1914 and March of 1917, while Gershwin was still a songplugger at Remick's.

Gershwin included a piano transcription of this song in *George Gershwin's Songbook*, published in September of 1932.

Analysis: In the twenty-four-bar verse ("Many queens I have seen/ On the stage and the screen") the singer tells his intended that he would happily choose her over Billie Burke (an actress who was the wife of Florenz Ziegfeld and who, in 1939, played the good witch in *The Wizard of Oz*) and Alice Joyce (a silent screen star). He does so to a repeated note motive sung in various registers. The refrain ("Nobody but you") is an early example of the thirty-two-bar ABAC song, a form that would later become standard. The last note of its initial phrase—the "you" in the title phrase—is carried over the bar line, and the resulting syncopation gives the tune an easy swinging quality. The first note of the B section (on "I" in "I have seen them all"), a high D-natural, is distinctive and ear-catching, being a major seventh above the previous note, an E-flat.

Recordings: Of late, this song has become well known through performances and recordings of the piano transcription of it that appears in *George Gershwin's Songbook.* Otherwise, its recording history has been sparse. The composer's piano roll was released in October of 1919 on Universal Song Roll 3549 (reissued on Klavier KS-122). Then came a 1920 version by the Palace Trio (Victor 35696) and a 1923 record by The Columbians (Columbia A-3977). Another contemporary version was by the Van Eps Banta Trio (Emerson 503). Nearly forty years would pass before "Nobody But You" appeared again, this time on an album entitled *The Gershwin Years* (Decca DXSZ-7160) that featured conductor George Bassman and singers Paula Stewart, Lynn Roberts, and Richard Hayes.

13. SOMEHOW IT SELDOM COMES TRUE

Lyricist: Arthur J. Jackson and B.G. DeSylva
Key: G
Time: Alla breve
Tempo: Allegretto
Introduced by: Janet Velie in *La La Lucille* at the Henry Miller Theatre in New York City on May 26, 1919.

Analysis: The accompaniment to all sixteen bars of the verse ("Don't be downcast, poor little boy") is filled with slightly discordant passing tones which resolve into amen cadences. This effectively underscores the jeremiad quality of the lyric, which tells us to expect things to go wrong—a philosophy that is succinctly stated in the first line of the refrain ("But sometimes our dreaming is all in vain").

Isaac Goldberg was probably referring to the fifteenth bar of the refrain (on "mice and of men") when he remarked on the jazzy nature of this song. The chord progression in this bar (A9 to C7 to D-flat major ninth to D9) must have been an exotic experience for musical theatre patrons in 1919.

Recordings: None

14. TEE-OODLE-UM-BUM-BO

Lyricist: B.G. DeSylva and Arthur J. Jackson
Key: F (verse)
      B-flat (refrain)
Time: 2/4
Tempo: Allegro moderato
Introduced by: Janet Velie and J. Clarence Harvey in *La La Lucille* at the Henry Miller Theatre in New York City on May 26, 1919.

Lore: This was the big crowd-pleaser from Gershwin's first complete Broadway score. For some reason, however—maybe it was the title or the lyric—its popularity ended when the show closed.

Early in 1919, prior to *La La Lucille*, Irving Berlin had come into the Harms office with a new song, "The Revolutionary Rag" (inspired by the Russian Revolution) and publisher Max Dreyfus had, Berlin later recalled, "sent this kid in" to play it through. The kid was the twenty-year-old George Gershwin who, after reharmonizing "The Revolutionary Rag" on the spot (and making it all but unrecognizable to Berlin), proceeded to play a couple of his own tunes, including "Tee-Oodle-Um-Bum-Bo." This was the occasion of the first meeting between Gershwin and Berlin.

Analysis: The lyric predicts that this song will soon be everyone's favorite hum—not a completely idle boast as it turned out, given its real if somewhat limited success and given the ebullience of the music. A bluesy D-flat ninth to C9 cadence in the piano introduction leads to a brisk sixteen-bar verse ("Soon you will meet/Folks on the street") whose melody rests on alternating F6 and D-flat chords—an invigorating combination. The refrain ("Tee-oodle-um-bum-bo/That's how it goes") is a happy-go-lucky thirty-six-bar tune whose best moment comes in bars fifteen and sixteen when, instead of a rest, the singer is given an exclamatory fill ("Man and miss'll/Learn to whistle"). On his piano roll recording (see below) Gershwin used this spot to demonstrate some fine pyrotechnics.

Recordings: The composer's piano roll version was issued in September of 1919 on Universal Song Roll 3517 (reissued on Klavier Records KS-122). Another recording was made by the Van Eps Banta Trio (Emerson 503).

13

15. WE'RE PALS

Lyricist: Irving Caesar
Key: E-flat
Time: Alla breve
Tempo: Moderato (verse)
   Slow with great expression (refrain)
Introduced by: Louis Bennison in *Dere Mable*, a show that closed out of town in 1919.

Lore and Analysis: When the composer of *Dere Mable* was unable to come up with a piece of special material for the leading man to sing to his dog, Gershwin pinch-hit and the result was "We're Pals." The only hint in the lyric that this song is addressed to a canine comes when the singer refers to his pal's aphasic condition ("I have known there's lots of things that you would say to me if you could only speak").

The main idea of the somewhat mundane twenty-bar verse ("Every place we went") is presented first in E-flat and then in the relative minor, G-minor. The refrain ("We're pals") is a heartfelt, surging, Kern-like tune. Gershwin may have been particularly influenced by Kern in bar twenty-two (at "with you along"), which resembles the "banish sadness and strife" section of "Look For the Silver Lining," written the same year. The form here is ABA^1CA^2 and the length is forty bars.

Recordings: In July of 1920, the Van Eps quartet recorded this song as an introduction to a non-Gershwin song entitled "Will You Remember Or Will You Forget?" (Vocalion 14099).

16. COME TO THE MOON

Lyricist: Ned Wayburn and Lou Paley
Key: C
Time: 2/4
Tempo: Allegro moderato
Introduced by: Paul Frawley and Lucille Chalfant in *Capitol Review* at the Capitol Theatre in New York City on October 24, 1919.

Lore: This song and "Swanee" were Gershwin's two contributions to a stage show which, paradoxically, marked the opening of a new movie house. The melody of "Come to the Moon" later was used in the song "All Over Town" in a British production, *The Rainbow*, in 1923.

"Come To The Moon" was performed by Larry Kert in March of 1987 at the Brooklyn Academy of Music, during a commemoration of the fiftieth anniversary of the composer's death.

Analysis: The lyric is an invitation to escape from the earth to the moon where, we are promised, our troubles will vanish and where "Each twinkling star/Has her own solar motor car." It is not clear what stars the writers are referring to but their discussion of solar-powered vehicles in a 1919 song lyric was certainly a coup of sorts. Although the music is in C and marked allegro, it has a lugubrious East-European quality, especially in the refrain ("Come to the moon'), where mournful, yearning piano fills continually imply A-minor. This refrain is thirty-two bars long and ABAC in form. The verse ("Hello ev'rybody, I have come to take you back with me") is sixteen bars long and characterized by a repeated note motive played in various registers.

Recordings: The composer's piano roll of this song was released in February of 1920 on Mel-O-Dee 3701. It is uncertain when Gershwin actually made the recording but he may have been preceded by Gene Rodemich and His Orchestra, whose version was recorded in October of 1919 and released on Brunswick 2026. On January 27, 1920, Prince's Band introduced "Come to the Moon" in their version of "Swanee" (Columbia A-2905).

17. SWANEE

Lyricist: Irving Caesar
Key: F-minor (verse)
　　　 F (refrain)
Time: Alla breve
Tempo: Moderato
Introduced by: Muriel DeForrest in *Capitol Revue* at the Capitol Theatre in New York City on October 24, 1919.

15

Lore: No one these days remembers a tune called "Hindustan" but its popularity in 1919 was directly responsible for the creation of Gershwin's first and biggest hit song. It was Irving Caesar who, aware of the success of "Hindustan," suggested to Gershwin that they write an American version of that song. The composer immediately thought of Stephen Foster's "Swanee River" and they were off. In their book *The Gershwin Years* (Doubleday & Co., 1958) Edward Jablonski and Lawrence D. Stewart quote Caesar as follows:

> That evening we had dinner at Dinty Moore's, discussed the song, boarded a Riverside Drive bus, got up to his home on Washington Heights, and immediately went to the piano alcove, separated by the inevitable beaded curtain of the period from the dining room. There was a poker game in progress at the time.
>
> In about fifteen minutes we had turned out "Swanee," verse and chorus. But we thought the song should have a trio and for a few minutes were deciding about this addition. The losers in the game kept saying, "Boys, finish it some other time" and the lucky ones urged us to complete the song right there and then. This we did, and old man Gershwin lost not a moment in fetching a comb, over which he superimposed some tissue, and [he accompanied] George while I sang it over and over again at the insistence of the winning poker players.

Gershwin contributed "Swanee" and another new song ("Come to the Moon") to *Capitol Revue*. This was a live show performed on the stage of a newly opened movie house called The Capitol Theatre. The revue shared the bill with the theatre's first silent movie showings. As performed by Muriel DeForrest at that venue, "Swanee" was a dud. It did not take off until Al Jolson, having heard Gershwin play it at a party, interpolated it into his revue, *Sinbad*. Jolson was phenomenally successful with it, selling over two million recordings and more than a million pieces of sheet music. In its first year the song earned its authors about $10,000 each—substantial money in 1919 and substantial money even today for a half hour's work.

The song's real, if tenuous, Asian origins came full circle in 1920 when a young composer named Vladimir Dukelsky bought a copy of the music in Constantinople. Immediately, it severed that

16

Russian's musical personality, turning half of him into Vernon Duke (a name later given to him by Gershwin himself), author of such pop standards as "April in Paris" and "I Can't Get Started," while the Dukelsky half continued along separately and independently, writing symphonies and concertos.

On November 1, 1923 Eva Gauthier included "Swanee" in her celebrated Aeolian Hall recital (see "Do It Again!"), with the composer accompanying her at the piano.

Gershwin's piano transcription of this song appears in *George Gershwin's Songbook*, a work published in September of 1932.

Analysis: There may have been a degree of calculation in Gershwin's desire to write a big hit like "Hindustan" but this is not the song of a cautious musician. The thirty-two-bar verse ("I've been away from you a long time")—which is every bit as catchy as the refrain—starts the song off in the key of F-minor even through the refrain is to be in F-major. A sudden and arresting use of a D-natural occurs in the ninth bar of the verse (on "somehow" in "somehow I feel"), which begins a modal cadence. Equally unusual is the sixteen-bar trio section in the refrain ("Swanee, Swanee, I am coming back"). All in all there are eighty bars of exciting music in this song and, luckily, the lyric has the saving grace of not taking itself seriously. Its silliness ("D-I-X-I-E-ven know") has helped keep the song alive.

Recordings: Gershwin's piano roll, released in February of 1920 (Mel-O-Dee 3707), came out a month after Al Jolson made his landmark recording (Columbia A-2884). But Jolson's version was not the first. Gene Rodemich and His Orchestra recorded the piece in October of 1919 (Brunswick 2026), Nicholas Orlando's Dance Orchestra did it in the November-December 1919 period (Pathe 22266), and the Peerless Quartette also did it in late 1919 (Victor 18688). In the year 1920 there were, besides the Jolson and Gershwin versions, recordings by the All Star Trio (Victor 18651), the Arto Dance Orchestra (Arto 9022), the Bostonian Syncopaters (Grey Gull H-1008), the Grey Gull Dance Band (Gray Gull L-1021), Julius Lenzburg (Edison Blue Amberol 4034), Prince's Band (Columbia A-2905), Sanford's Famous Dance Orchestra (Emerson 10185), and Yerkes Novelty Five (Vocalion 14024).

"Swanee" then went unrecorded until the thirties, when versions were released by Stanley Black and His Oriole Modernists (Oriole P-101), Al Bowlly (His Master's Voice B-3944), Eddie Condon (Decca

17

23433), Teddy Foster & His Kings of Swing (His Master's Voice BD-5301), Judy Garland (Decca 2881), the Louisiana Rhythm Kings (Brunswick 4845), Georgie Stoll and His Orchestra (Decca 976), and Elisabeth Welch and Robert Ashley (His Master's Voice C-2992). At a September 8, 1937 George Gershwin memorial concert, Al Jolson sang "Swanee" with an orchestra conducted by Victor Young (Citadel CT 7025). Judy Garland recorded "Swanee" again at her 1961 Carnegie Hall concert (Capitol SWBO-1569) and then again with her daughter, Liza Minnelli (Capitol ST-11191). Other latter-day versions have been by Carlos Barbosa-Lima (Concord Jazz 2005), Al Cajola (Bainbridge 1012), Eddy Howard (HNS 405), and Jimmy Roselli (MRR-1018).

18. LIMEHOUSE NIGHTS

Lyricist: B.G. DeSylva and John Henry Mears
Key: D-minor (verse)
  F (refrain)
Time: 2/4
Tempo: Allegretto
Introduced by: Bessie McCoy Davis, Mae Leslie, Margaret Morris, Peggy Fears, and Helen Lovett in *Morris Gest Midnight Whirl* at the Century Grove in New York City on December 27, 1919.

Analysis: The subject here is the Limehouse district of London where one can spend "charming days and dark mysterious nights" amongst faded women and worthless men. In the thirty-two-bar verse ("London town is full of wonderful sights") an insistent and repetitive thumping in the bass, together with a succession of fourths in the treble accompaniment, suggest not the British but the music of ersatz American Indians. In the refrain ("Limehouse Nights"), a leisurely sustained note eventually leaps up a fourth. Then another leap, this time a fifth, completes an octave jump. It is a graceful tune, even an eloquent one—and the ninth chords in the accompaniment give it a modern sound.

Recordings: Gershwin's piano roll was released in March of 1920 (Mel-O-Dee 3739). Prior to that, in January of 1920, the Columbia Saxophone Sextette recorded a version (Columbia A-2876). A

18

recording by Tom Coakley and His Palace Hotel Orchestra was made in September of 1934 (Victor 24741). Another version is by Fred Douglas (English Regal G7539).

19. POPPYLAND

Lyricist: B.G. DeSylva and John Henry Mears
Key: E-flat
Time: Alla breve
Tempo: Moderato
Introduced by: Bernard Granville and Helen Shipman in *Morris Gest Midnight Whirl* at the Century Grove in New York City on December 27, 1919.

Analysis: The lyric, in speaking of a dreamy paradise called Poppyland, seems well-aware of the narcotic potential of the poppy plant ("lurking deep in the heart of each seductive flow'r that gaily blooms you will find a sweet compelling pow'r"). The music is interesting for its Debussyian piano introduction and for the pick-up chord (Fm7^{-5}—a favorite Gershwin sound) that introduces the refrain. Also, "Poppyland" is unique among Gershwin songs for its alternate, more harmonically adventurous, piano ending. Marked "ossia," it appears in small musical print at the bottom of the final page.

Recordings: Gershwin's piano roll was released in March of 1920 (Mel-O-Dee 3741). In January of 1920, the Columbia Saxophone Sextette recorded "Poppyland" (as an introduction to "Limehouse Nights"—Columbia A-2876).

20. YAN-KEE

Lyricist: Irving Caesar
Key: E-minor (verse)
      C (refrain)
Time: Alla breve (verse)
      Common (refrain)
Tempo: Moderato (verse)
      Slow with unaffected simplicity (refrain)

19

Introduced by: This freelance song, written in 1920, was not associated with any production.

Analysis: "Yan-Kee," one of a number of Gershwin songs with an oriental theme (the list includes "Idle Dreams" and "Mah-Jongg"), is, in its story line, a pop song analog to *Madam Butterfly*. It contains locutions in both the lyric ("'Will you mally me' said Nankee Soo") and the music (the refrain is based on a succession of chopstick fourths) that would probably embarrass a present-day audience. The refrain ("Yankee since you go away") has been said to contain the composer's first published blue note (it can be heard in the penultimate bar on "my" in "fly to my Yankee"). However, that distinction really belongs to a 1916 Gershwin song, "Making of a Girl."

Recordings: The Green Brothers Novelty Band recorded this in March of 1921 (Brunswick 2090). There was also a version by Marion Harris (Columbia A3353).

21. OO, HOW I LOVE TO BE LOVED BY YOU

Lyricist: Lou Paley
Key: A-flat
Time: Alla breve
Tempo: Moderato
Introduced by: Helen Clark and Lorin Raker in *La La Lucille* (where it was replaced by "Nobody But You") at the Henry Miller Theatre in New York City on May 26, 1919. Publication came in 1920, when it was scheduled for but not used in *Ed Wynn's Carnival.*

Analysis: This brief (sixteen-bar verse, sixteen-bar refrain) song has some enjoyable old-fashioned harmony. A barbershop style dissonance occurs in the first bar of the refrain (on "how" in the title phrase) where the singer must hold a C-natural above an E-diminished chord that includes a discordant C-sharp (written as D-flat). Later, as the "you" in the title phrase is being held, there is a pleasing progression in the piano accompaniment—a D-major chord with an added sixth and ninth leading to an A-flat resolution. Paley's lyric is an awkward one ("And when you wave goodnight to me, It's past eleven, I keep

20

wishing it were only seven"). He would soon retire from lyric writing to become a schoolteacher and, eventually, Ira Gershwin's brother-in-law.

Recordings: None

22. IDLE DREAMS

Lyricist: Arthur Jackson
Key: F
Time: Alla breve
Tempo: Moderato mysterioso
Introduced by: Lloyd Garrett and Ann Pennington in *George White's Scandals of 1920* at the Globe Theatre in New York City on June 7, 1920.

Analysis: This song is about a "China boy" who wants the statue of a China maid to rise and join him in life. There is a remarkable moment in the twenty-bar verse ("Beside an idol carved of stone") when, in bars thirteen through sixteen (at "With all the rev'rence of a pray'r"), the initial idea is suddenly restated in the key of A and with bold new harmony. The verse then concludes with a powerful chord sequence that takes us into D-flat and B-flat minor. The melody of the refrain ("Come my China maid") is based on an upward arpeggio along the notes of an F6 chord, beginning with a C and climbing more than an octave up to D. It has the feel of operetta music, becoming particularly melodramatic just before the coda (at "I know").

Recordings: Gershwin's piano roll of this song was incorrectly but understandably mislabeled as "Idol Dreams." It was released in August of 1920 on Mel-O-Dee 203579. Gershwin may be the pianist on a recording made by the Van Eps Specialty Quartet in June of 1920 (Emerson 10211). Isham Jones and His Rainbo Orchestra recorded it the same month (Brunswick 5014) and, a month later, the Palace Trio played "Idle Dreams" during its recording of "Scandal Walk"—a song from the same show (Okeh 4164).

23. MY LADY

Lyricist: Arthur Jackson
Key: G
Time: Alla breve
Tempo: Moderato
Introduced by: Lester O'Keefe in *George White's Scandals of 1920* at the Globe Theatre in New York City on June 7, 1920. This song was also used in *Mayfaire and Montmartre* in London in 1922.

Analysis: Silkworms, wild cotton, lambs, seals, and sables all are hard at work, the lyric tells us, providing suitably fine raiment for the singer's beloved. The sixteen-bar verse ("I never tire of raving/About my sweetie's looks") is most interesting musically for its modulation from G to B-flat and back. The refrain ("The little Silkworm just spins for my lady"), although it uses the key signature of G, begins in A-minor. Its main melodic idea bears a kinship to that of Kern's "They Didn't Believe Me"—a song that greatly influenced Gershwin when it came out in 1914. Although usual in its thirty-two-bar length, this refrain is less ordinary in its structure. It is AA^{1}AA^2.

Recordings: None

24. ON MY MIND THE WHOLE NIGHT LONG

Lyricist: Arthur Jackson
Key: F
Time: Alla breve
Tempo: Moderato
Introduced by: Lloyd Garrett in *George White's Scandals of 1920* at the Globe Theatre in New York City on June 7, 1920.

Analysis: This very brief song (an eight-bar verse and a sixteen-bar refrain) is Gershwin's first thorough excursion into the use of blue notes. In the verse ("We have said 'Goodbye'") it is the piano that sounds them but in the refrain ("'cause you are on my mind the whole night long") the singer joins in. Both sections move syncopated melodies against steady march rhythms and both make use of the shifting from major to minor that was fundamental to the composer's style.

Recordings: Gershwin's piano roll was released in August of 1920 (Metro-Art 20356, reissued on Mark 56 Records 667). A more recent version is on the album *Ira Gershwin Revisited* (Painted Smiles PS 1353).

25. SCANDAL WALK

Lyricist: Arthur Jackson
Key: E-flat
Time: Alla breve
Tempo: Moderato
Introduced by: Ann Pennington in *George White's Scandals of 1920* at the Globe Theatre in New York City on June 7, 1920.

Analysis: Gershwin biographer Isaac Goldberg called this a rehearsal for "Stairway to Paradise"—and the truth of that is most obvious in the verse ("Have you heard the latest Scandal?") which, with its march-like arpeggiated chords, anticipates the "All you preachers" opening of the later song. This verse is less dramatic but it has its own rewards. It is a spirited little sixteen-bar honky-tonk tune. The main melodic idea of the refrain ("Everybody do the Scandal Walk") descends and rises chromatically in a way that brings to mind the opening of Debussy's *Prelude to the Afternoon of a Faun*—although this music is not ethereal but sassy. It is a syncopated march. The lyric is in the "Here's a hot new kind of dance" category.

Recordings: Gershwin's piano roll was issued in August of 1920 (Mel-O-Dee 203583). The Van Eps Specialty Quartet recorded the piece in June of 1920 (Emerson 10211 and Pathe 22399)*, as did Isham Jones and His Rainbo Orchestra (Brunswick 5014). The Palace Trio recorded it in July of 1920 (Okeh 4164), Selvin's Novelty Orchestra in August of 1920 (Lyric 4225). The only recent version is one by Anthony Perkins, Barbara Cook, Bobby Short, and Elaine Stritch (Painted Smiles PS-1357).

* Gershwin may be the pianist on this record.

23

26. TUM ON AND TISS ME

Lyricist: Arthur Jackson
Key: C
Time: Alla breve
Tempo: Moderato
Introduced by: Ann Pennington in *George White's Scandals of
 1920* at the Globe Theatre in New York City on June 7, 1920.

Analysis: The sixteen-bar verse ("There's such a lot of things a
tot can't do") begins with an unusual pick-up (Dm7^{-5} to C6) and is
marked by continuous syncopation. The refrain ("Won't someone help
me out—my lips are starting to pout"), also sixteen bars long, is a
sweet and swinging melody that is almost but not quite done in by the
boop-boop-be-doop turn it takes when it reaches the title phrase. The
lyric, as one might suppose from the title, is filled with cloying baby
talk.

Recordings: None

27. THE SONGS OF LONG AGO

Lyricist: Arthur Jackson
Key: C
Time: Common (verse)
 Alla breve (refrain)
Tempo: Moderato (Very broad) (verse)
 Moderato (Alla Fox-Trot) (refrain)
Introduced by: Lester O'Keefe in *George White's Scandals of
 1920* at the Globe Theatre in New York City on June 7, 1920.

Analysis: The lyric protests against modern music—namely ragtime—in a way that brings to mind Irving Berlin's "Play a Simple
Melody" (written in 1914). The brief eight-bar verse ("I miss the
songs of long ago") is a stately and lyrical melody that sounds a bit
like the triumphal theme from the final movement of Sibelius's *Symphony No. 2* (written in 1901). The refrain ("I love the old ones") is
brief too, just sixteen bars, and it has an easygoing soft shoe quality.
This song's most unusual feature is a footnote at the end of the sheet

24

music which reads: "The following melodies may be sung or played simultaneously with the refrain: 'Home Sweet Home,' 'Silver Threads Among the Gold' (refrain)."

Recordings: Lester O'Keefe (Brunswick 2046); Clicquot Club Eskimos (Columbia 544-D).

28. WAITING FOR THE SUN TO COME OUT

Lyricist: Arthur Francis (Ira Gershwin)
Key: F
Time: 2/4
Tempo: Moderato
Introduced by: Helen Ford and Joseph Lertora in *The Sweetheart Shop* at the Knickerbocker Theatre in New York City on August 31, 1920.

Lore: The brothers tailored this one for producer Edgar MacGregor who wanted something Pollyanna-ish for singer Helen Ford. Ira was afraid that MacGregor would turn the number down if he learned that the brother of the composer had written the lyric, and so he assumed a pseudonym, Arthur Francis, based on the names of his two other siblings. When MacGregor asked George who Arthur Francis was, the composer was ready with an answer: "Oh, he's a clever college boy with lots of talent."

"Waiting For the Sun to Come Out" was Ira Gershwin's first published song. Within a year it had earned him $1,300.

Analysis: Isaac Goldberg, the first Gershwin biographer, called this lyric "sober and dull...aeons away from Broadway sophistication." It cannot be denied that Ira was fairly turgid here ("Yet while clouds are crying, I smile never sighing/For I know that presently, the sun will come out and smile on me"). Still, his lyric does have the advantages of being concise and coherent. Musically, the verse ("When the clouds the skies are filling") offers a pleasing melody—one given depth by a steady use of passing tones and harmonic suspensions. Some daring is shown in having the singer begin on the seventh note of the scale—an E supported by an F-major chord. The refrain ("Weary are the flowers") has an unaffected earnestness. It is thirty-two bars long but contains no release, only an eight-bar coda. That coda ends with a restatement of the title phrase to music that resembles the 1940 tune "Back in the Saddle Again."

Recordings: Gershwin's piano roll was released in October of 1920 (Mel-O-Dee 203733). Two other versions appeared at about the same time, one by Lambert Murphy (Victor 45199) and the other by the Van Eps Specialty Quartet (Emerson 10285).

29. LU LU

Lyricist: Arthur Jackson
Key: G
Time: Common
Tempo: Moderato (verse)
　　　　Slow in a lilting manner (refrain)
Introduced by: Edith Hallor in *Broadway Brevities of 1920* at the Winter Garden Theatre in New York City on September 29, 1920.

Analysis: The verse ("Always in my heart"), just twelve bars long, is spare of notes, stately, and harmonized as if it were a four-part chorale. The refrain ("Never was another gal like Lu Lu") is, at sixteen bars, almost as brief. Its slow and forlorn dotted note idea has a familial relationship to a later Gershwin work—the lovely, catch-in-the-throat verse to "How Long Has This Been Going On?" This refrain is essentially through-composed, although a portion of the first measure is repeated in bar thirteen (at "Little mountain daisy").

Recordings: None

30. SNOWFLAKES

Lyricist: Arthur Jackson
Key: E-flat
Time: Alla breve
Tempo: Moderato
Introduced by: Edith Hallor in *Broadway Brevities of 1920* at

the Winter Garden in New York City on September 29, 1920.

Analysis: The four-bar piano introduction has some harmonic fun with music that will become the first bar of the verse. The tunes in both the verse and refrain have a tinkling, music-box quality. In the former ("Wild winds are blowing") the twelfth of sixteen bars consists of a single note and supporting harmony (an A over a B-flat diminished chord) that sound strangely harsh and out of place. The thirty-two-bar refrain ("Love me, love me, While the snow flakes fall") is interesting in its construction. Its first sixteen bars are made up of three variations on an initial nine-note phrase. In bars seventeen through twenty-four there is a repetition of both the phrase and its first variation. Then, at bar twenty-five (at "Put your arms around me"), a fifth variation becomes the coda.

Recordings: None

31. SPANISH LOVE

Lyricist: Irving Caesar
Key: C
Time: Alla breve
Tempo: Moderato
Introduced by: Hal van Rensellaer in *Broadway Brevities of 1920* at the Winter Garden Theatre in New York City on September 29, 1920.

Analysis: The lyric, a paean to hot-blooded Iberian courtship, is sung by a woman named Chiquita. It contains phrases such as "my heart's a ball of fire" and "volcano of desire." The sixteen-bar verse ("At last I'm returning") consists of a succession of imitative three-note phrases that hover around the mildly dissonant seventh tone of the scale (B-natural). The refrain ("Spanish Love"), a zesty up-tempo tune, is constructed in an unusual manner. It is forty bars long and ABA^1CA^2 in form. The B section ("If your cares and worries you would banish") is the most fun, being less contrived and bouncier than the others. It heads to the A^1 section with a vigorous series of instrumental triplets.

Recordings: None.

27

32. BOY WANTED

Lyricist: Arthur Francis (Ira Gershwin)
Key: F
Time: Alla breve
Tempo: Moderato
Introduced by: The ensemble in *A Dangerous Maid* at Nixon's
  Apollo Theatre in Atlantic City, New Jersey on March 21,
  1921. In 1924 this song was sung by Heather Thatcher in
  Primrose at the Winter Garden Theatre in London, England.

Lore: "Boy Wanted" was published in two versions: first in
1921 and then with revised lyrics (by Desmond Carter and Ira Gershwin) in 1924 when it was included in the printed score to *Primrose*.
As for its 1921 incarnation, "Boy Wanted" had the honor of being the
first song on the Broadway stage to mention Freud.

Analysis: The bubbly twenty-four-bar verse ("I've just finished
writing an advertisement") begins with a run along an F-major seventh
arpeggio. Midway through there is a modulation from F to A and then
F returns. The refrain ("He must be able to dance") is unusually
long—forty measures—and ABA¹C in form, with the final section ("I
know we'll get acquainted mighty soon") accounting for the final sixteen bars. It is a very catchy up-tempo number with a lyric that carries
through expertly on its interesting and original angle: the song is a
young woman's newspaper advertisement for a beau, listing in great
detail all the qualities that he must and must not have.
  The 1921 and 1924 lyrics are substantially the same in the verse.
In the refrain some words like "woo" were deleted, presumably because they were American colloquialisms. But Ira's central idea and
his phrasing are kept intact and his touch is obvious in rhymes such as
advertisement/flirt is meant.
  The only musical difference between the two versions is the
tempo marking. In 1921 it was simply Moderato but in the *Primrose*
score it became slightly cryptic: almost-one step time.

Recordings: Heather Thatcher of the original *Primrose* cast recorded this (English Columbia 9002, reissued on Monmouth-Evergreen
MES 7071). It was also recorded by the Winter Garden Theatre Orchestra (English Columbia 9006). Ella Fitzgerald recorded the first

28

American version (Verve MG V-4029-5). Twiggy and Jill Cook sing "Boy Wanted" on the original cast album of the 1983 Broadway show *My One and Only* (Atlantic 80110-1-E). Kiri Te Kanawa and the New Princess Theater Orchestra have recorded a version employing the orchestrations that were used in 1924 (Angel DS 47454). Another version is on the LP *Ira Gershwin Revisited* (Painted Smiles PS 1353).

33. DANCING SHOES

> *Lyricist:* Arthur Francis (Ira Gershwin)
> *Key:* E-flat
> *Time:* Alla breve
> *Tempo:* Moderato
> *Introduced by:* Vinton Freedley and Juliette Day in *A Dangerous Maid* at Nixon's Apollo Theatre in Atlantic City, New Jersey on March 21, 1921.

Lore: This dates back to Gershwin's days as a songplugger for Remick and Co. and was probably written in 1916. The show into which it was inserted five years later, *A Dangerous Maid*, never made it to Broadway. It closed in Pittsburgh a couple of months after opening in Atlantic City.

Analysis: This exciting and adventurous song has a sixteen-bar verse that begins emphatically (on "Dancing shoes"), then suddenly turns quiet and reflective (on "makes you treasure ev'ry measure"). Then, as the music continues, there are leaps into such far afield keys as G and G-flat. The refrain ("And you'll start to sway"), also sixteen bars long, has a melody that rises unhurriedly to successive plateaus in a way that makes one think of the 1926 song "Birth of the Blues." In the seventh and eighth measures (at "Oh! boy! then! joy!") there are tricky after-the-beat accents and an exciting chord progression (G-flat[7] to F7 to E9 to E-flat). Throughout the refrain the piano comments with appealing amen-style suspensions.

Recordings: None

29

34. **JUST TO KNOW YOU ARE MINE**

Lyricist: Arthur Francis (Ira Gershwin)
Key: D
Time: 3/4
Tempo: Valse moderato (verse)
Tempo rubato (refrain)
Introduced by: Juliette Day in *A Dangerous Maid* at Nixon's
Apollo Theatre in Atlantic City, New Jersey on March 21,
1921.

Analysis: Although he had made use of 6/8 time in two earlier
songs (in the verse of "The Real American Folk Song" and in "The
Love of a Wife"), this is the first true waltz that Gershwin published.
He was known as a composer who disliked the waltz tempo and, although that was not really the case, it is true that many of his 3/4
efforts were tongue-in-cheek. Here, however, he is serious. The
verse ("All gloom and sorrow ended") is a full thirty-two bars. It
begins with a lovely melody, one based on a two-note bird call idea.
That idea is developed, then interrupted by an attractive and contrasting idea in F-sharp minor, then completed. The refrain ("Just to know
that you are mine") is more of a dance. Here the melody rises quickly
up to a high note, then descends. Played the first time through it is
thirty-two bars long. But a second ending, containing a series of
arpeggiated piano fills, extends the length to forty-two bars.

Recordings: None

35. **THE SIMPLE LIFE**

Lyricist: Arthur Francis (Ira Gershwin)
Key: C
Time: 2/4
Tempo: Allegretto
Introduced by: Juliette Day in *A Dangerous Maid* at Nixon's
Apollo Theatre in Atlantic City, New Jersey on March 21,
1921.

Analysis: In praising country over city living Ira shows his

30

fondness for multiple rhymes ("hectic nights"/"electric lights") but he also produces some awkward imagery ("I will leave the town where subways grow"). The music begins with a through-composed twenty-four-bar verse ("I've been all along the gay white way") whose opening achieves a sense of airiness and tranquility via open-voiced chords—mainly fourths and sixths. The refrain ("I love the simple life") begins with an unusual E7 to F-major seventh cadence (we are in the key of C) but is not otherwise adventurous; it has the same contented and loping frame of mind as the verse. It is thirty-two bars long and ABAC in form.

Recordings: None

36. SOME RAIN MUST FALL

Lyricist: Arthur Francis (Ira Gershwin)
Key: E-flat
Time: 2/4
Tempo: Slowly (with simplicity)
Introduced by: Juliette Day in *A Dangerous Maid* in Atlantic City on March 21, 1921.

Lore: Gershwin wrote this tune during his songplugging days with Jerome H. Remick & Co. (May of 1914 until March 17, 1917). It became his second published collaboration with Ira (the first was "Waiting For the Sun to Come Out").

Analysis: In the verse ("I recited once when I was small"), the singer tells us how, when young, he had idly spoken a line of poetry that went: "Into ev'ry life some rain must fall." Then, in the refrain ("Some rain must fall"), he explains how experience has caused him to conclude that that line was all too true. The music was called daringly chromatic by the composer's first biographer, Isaac Goldberg. But Goldberg could only have been referring to a single moment—the final note in bar fourteen of the verse (on "er" in the phrase "and sorrow never")—in which a sudden E-natural is quite jarring and perhaps unnecessary. Otherwise, this verse is an extremely simple twenty-four-bar tune consisting mainly of a dialogue between two pairs of notes: B-flat and C and, later, E-flat and F. The refrain is a slow thirty-two bar ballad, interesting for a recurring four-note instrumental

31

motive and for the fact that the C section of its ABAC form (at "As the poet stated") is actually an amalgam of ideas A and B.

Recordings: None

37. DRIFTING ALONG WITH THE TIDE

Lyricist: Arthur Jackson
Key: G
Time: Common (verse)
      Alla breve (refrain)
Tempo: Molto moderato (verse)
       Slowly (refrain)
Introduced by: Lloyd Garrett and Victoria Herbert in *George White's Scandals of 1921* at the Liberty Theatre on July 11, 1921. It was also used in 1922 in the London production *Mayfair and Montmartre.*

Lore: Gershwin was still a songplugger at Remick's when he wrote this. It was probably composed in 1916. At first it was called "You're the Witch Who is Bewitching Me" with lyrics by Lou Paley.

Analysis: The verse ("Life is an ocean"), although in the key of G, begins in E. It is through-composed and it contains two melodic ideas—the first tranquil, the second sighing—and several variants thereof. The refrain ("I'm drifting along with the tide") is one of those melodies whose beauty is immediately self-evident. The main idea is very simple: two whole notes (Ds) an octave apart are separated by a run up the G scale. In the release ("My boat so frail") another pair of whole notes (a high G and a B) are separated by a downward run. This release is attractively harmonized by a mingling of E-major and D-minor chords. The lyric, in both verse and refrain, sticks to a single metaphor, as the singer describes him/herself as an aimlessly drifting ship.

Recordings: Gershwin's piano roll was released in 1921 (Duo-Art 17445, reissued on Klavier KS-122). There was also a 1921 version by Paul Whiteman and His Orchestra (Victor 18839). A year later, the song was recorded by Harry "Master of the Laughing Trombones"

Raderman (Mark 56 Records 799). Other versions are by Lambert
Murphy (Victor 45259), Anthony Perkins (Painted Smiles PS-1357)
and Bobby Short (SD 2-608).

38. I LOVE YOU

Lyricist: Arthur Jackson
Key: E-flat (verse)
     A-flat (refrain)
Time: 2/4
Tempo: Allegro moderato
Introduced by: Harry Rose in *George White's Scandals of 1921*
   at the Liberty Theatre in New York City on July 11, 1921.

Analysis: The lyric is about the usefulness of the title phrase
when one is in a foreign country and cannot speak the local language.
The twenty-bar verse ("I'm a lady bug") is a simple tune given some
slight dramatic impetus by regularly spaced diminished chords. The
refrain gives the words "I love you" a "Three Blind Mice" sort of
tune. The only surprise here is a brief dip into the key of E in the
coda. It is thirty-two bars long and ABAC in form.

Recordings: None

39. SHE'S JUST A BABY

Lyricist: Arthur Jackson
Key: G
Time: Alla breve
Tempo: Moderato
Introduced by: Ann Pennington in *George White's Scandals of
   1921* at the Liberty Theatre in New York City on July 11,
   1921.

Analysis: The verse ("In baby days") is a sixteen-bar tune that is
tinkly in character until the eleventh measure (at "sawdust doll"), where
a C9 chord gives it a fleeting bluesy moment. The refrain ("Baby
she's just a baby") contains a series of downward leaps. The most

33

prominent is the first in bar one, involving a fifth. The length is thirty-two bars and the form is AA¹AA².

Recordings: This song received five recordings shortly after it appeared. In all but one of them, however, it was only briefly done during the playing of another Gershwin song from the 1921 *Scandals*, "South Sea Isles." The exception is a recording by The Happy Six (Columbia A-3467). The truncated versions are by Selvin's Dance Orchestra (Cardinal 2057), Paul Whiteman (Victor 18801), Yerkes Jazzarimba Orchestra (Olympic 15125) and Yerkes S.S. Flotilla Orchestra (Vocalion 14231).

40. SOUTH SEA ISLES

Lyricist: Arthur Jackson
Key: G-minor (verse)
G (refrain)
Time: Alla breve
Tempo: Moderato
Introduced by: Charles King and Ann Pennington in *George White's Scandals of 1921* at the Liberty Theatre in New York City on July 11, 1921. This song was also presented in *Mayfair and Montmartre*, a play in London in 1922.

Analysis: The first two bars of the piano introduction imply G-major but, somewhat comically, they are followed by a two-bar um-pah in G-minor. Then, in the sixteen-bar verse ("A mystic land"), the minor key dominates. In the refrain ("Sunny South Sea Islands") Gershwin creates an exotic feel by giving to the melody line the ninths of ninth chords and the sixths of sixth chords. The first note of the refrain, for instance, is an E atop D7 harmony. It is a languorous, operetta sort of tune, one that rises and falls gently with few repeated notes. It is thirty-two bars long and ABAC in form.

Recordings: "South Sea Isles" was recorded seven times in the summer of 1921. These records were by the Broadway Dance Orchestra (Edison 50839), the Casino Dance Orchestra (Pathe Actuelle 020619), the Happy Six (Columbia A-3467), Rudy Wiedoeft's Californians (Brunswick 2139), Selvin's Dance Orchestra (Cardinal 2057),

Paul Whiteman and his Orchestra (Victor 18801), Yerkes Jazzarimba Orchestra (Olympic 15125) and Yerkes S.S. Flotilla Orchestra (Vocalion 14231). In November of 1923, the song was recorded by Russo & Fiorito's Dance Orchestra (Brunswick 2743). On July 10, 1938 there was a recording by the RCA Victor Salon Group conducted by Nathaniel Shilkret (RCA Victor EPBT 3055, Victor Red Seal 12335).

41. WHERE EAST MEETS WEST

> *Lyricist:* Arthur Jackson
> *Key:* G
> *Time:* Alla breve
> *Tempo:* Marcia
> *Introduced by:* Charles King and Victoria Herbert in *George White's Scandals of 1921* at the Liberty Theatre in New York City on July 11, 1921. This song was also used in a 1922 London show, *Mayfair and Montmartre.*

Analysis: In the verse a woman of the east beckons to a "boy of the west" and he, after expressing the "East is East and West is West" dilemma, tells her that they can solve their difficulty by getting together in Panama. A bit of American immodesty ensues in the refrain as Jackson proceeds to describe the isthmus as a place where "Yankee brains and Yankee brawn won victory." There is a through-composed twenty-four-bar verse ("I'm way out here in the Eastern sea") that, in its seventh and fifteenth bars, breaks out into instrumental fanfares. The first of these is in G, the second in B-minor. Next comes a pomp and circumstance-style refrain ("Where East meets West in Panama") that is very spare of notes—there are only fifty-four of them in thirty-two bars—and in an unusual AA' construction (twenty-four bars through-composed and an eight-bar recap/coda).

Recordings: None

42. SWANEE ROSE

Lyricist: Irving Caesar and B.G. DeSylva
Key: C
Time: 2/4
Tempo: Moderato
Introduced by: Al Jolson, who interpolated it into his 1921 production *Sinbad.*

Lore: Originally published as "Dixie Rose," the title was changed to cash in on the fame of "Swanee." Although Jolson tried, the song did not catch on.

Analysis: The easy, catchy melodies of the sixteen-bar verse ("Where the sweet magnolias grow") and the forty-bar refrain ("My pretty Swanee Rose") are both made from arpeggiated C and F chords. The form of the refrain is ABA^1BA^2. That Gershwin and his collaborators of this period were more comfortable with pseudo-Southern songs than with pseudo-Oriental or pseudo-Latin numbers is evident by the breeziness of this material, which contains lines such as "I'm leaving on the six-eleven...I know I'm on my way to Heaven."

Recordings: The Green Brothers recorded this song in April or May of 1921 (Pathe Actuelle 020575). The Van Eps Specialty Quartet recorded it in June of that year (Emerson 10415)*.

* Gershwin may be the pianist on this record.

43. TOMALE (I'M HOT FOR YOU)

Lyricist: B.G. DeSylva
Key: C-minor (verse)
        C (refrain)
Time: Alla breve
Tempo: Moderato
Introduced by: This non-production song was taken up by Al Jolson after its publication in 1921.

Lore: In a letter to Ira from London (where he had gone to work on *The Rainbow*), George referred to this as his "Mexican Dance."

Analysis: Tomale is a Spanish lady who is being courted by the singer of this song and by a bullfighter with the conveniently rhyming name of Cholly. It is a comedy song with jokes such as "he took a nasty spear...I got Tomale's ear."

The chromatic melody of the thirty-two bar verse ("I once loved a Spaniard named Tomale") is supported by portentous C-minor chords and by an insistent tango motive in the bass. In the thirty-two-bar refrain ("You belong to me Tomale") the names Tomale and Cholly are sung to the triplet figures that Gershwin habitually used in his Latinesque settings ("Rose of Madrid," *Cuban Overture*, "Land of the Gay Caballero," "Just Another Rhumba").

Recordings: None

44. MY LOG CABIN HOME

Lyricist: Irving Caesar and B.G. DeSylva
Key: G
Time: 2/4
Tempo: Allegro moderato (verse)
Marcato (refrain)
Introduced by: The performer is uncredited but this was introduced in *The Perfect Fool* at the George M. Cohan Theatre in New York City on November 7, 1921.

Analysis: The twenty-bar verse ("I'm getting weary of the city ways") is distinguished by the same kind of competing rhythms that Gershwin would use with great success in "Fascinating Rhythm" three years down the road. The thirty-two-bar refrain ("I'll build a log cabin home") is very melodic, despite the song's marching band demeanor. In the fifth bar (on "one like I was born in") it is melodically and harmonically identical to the "suddenly I found" portion of the Bernstein/Sondheim song "Maria," written some thirty-five years later.

Recordings: None

45. NO ONE ELSE BUT THAT GIRL OF MINE

Lyricist: Irving Caesar
Key: E-flat minor (verse—key signature is E-flat)
     E-flat (refrain)
Time: Alla breve
Tempo: Moderato
Introduced by: The performer is uncredited but this was intro-
duced in *The Perfect Fool* at the George M. Cohan Theatre in
New York City on November 7, 1921. It was used again in a
1923 show, *The Dancing Girl,* this time with some musical
changes, a revised lyric, and a new title: "That American Boy
of Mine."

Analysis: The up-tempo minor key verse ("One year has passed")
is a precursor to the ones that Gershwin would write for "Fascinating
Rhythm" and "Clap Yo' Hands" in that it has some of the same bluesy
back street fun with a minor mode. Its unusual eighteen-bar length is
due to a two-bar tag which humorously yanks us out of E-flat minor,
preparing the way for E-flat—the key of the refrain. In the refrain
("Who cheers me when I'm blue") the melody is based on rising arpeggios in various keys—each beginning and ending on a whole note.
Some of these arpeggios move in staid quarter notes, some in bumpy
syncopation. Some are in a major mode, others in minor.

Recordings: None

46. SOMEONE

Lyricist: Arthur Francis (Ira Gershwin)
Key: G-minor, G, E-minor (verse)
     G (refrain)
Time: 2/4
Tempo: Allegro moderato (verse)
     Not fast (refrain)
Introduced by: Helen Ford and Vinton Freedley in *For Good-
ness Sake* at the Lyric Theatre in New York City on February
20, 1922.

Lore: "Someone" and "Tra-La-La" were the two Gershwin songs interpolated into *For Goodness Sake* and, as such, marked the beginning of the association between the Gershwins and Fred and Adele Astaire.

Analysis: The main point of interest in the twenty-four-bar verse ("When I take a husband") is the contrast between G-minor and G. In the fifteenth bar the tug-of-war seems to have been won by G, what with a decisive cadence and a change of key signature. But then, suddenly, we are in E-minor (at "I must find a way") and the main concern of the final eight bars is a modulation back into G-major. The melody of the refrain ("If someone like you/Loves someone like me") is based on what amounts to a slow-motion, syncopated trill: G down to F-sharp and back up to G again. Although the length is a standard thirty-two bars, the construction is oddly asymmetrical. The initial A section is fourteen bars long. Then comes a two-bar B section ("We would smile"), followed by an eight-bar A^1, a four-bar B^1 and a two-bar conclusion that quotes the opening of A. As for the lyric, this is a single-melody duet in which the singers profess love for one another obliquely, in the third person.

Recordings: A version of this song appears on an album entitled *The Great British Dance Bands Play George Gershwin 1920-1928* (World Records SH 451).

47. TRA-LA-LA (THIS TIME IT'S REALLY LOVE)

Lyricist: Arthur Francis (Ira Gershwin)
Key: D (verse)
   G (refrain)
Time: Alla breve
Tempo: Moderato
Introduced by: Marjorie Gateson and John E. Hazzard in *For Goodness Sake* at the Lyric Theatre in New York City on February 20, 1922. Gene Kelly and Oscar Levant sang it in the 1951 film *An American in Paris.*

Lore and Analysis: In *An American in Paris,* director Vincente Minnelli sought to rescue three fine Gershwin songs from oblivion.

39

He was successful with "By Strauss" (1936) and "Love is Here to Stay" (1937) but the third, "Tra-La-La," somehow missed beatification—and that is a shame, for it is a masterpiece, one with the happy energy of a fine children's song. The unusual eighteen-bar length of the verse ("Am I happy?") is due to the fact that after each phrase Gershwin provides a quarter note rest where, normally, one would expect rests lasting three quarter notes. Had the longer rests been used, the verse would be twenty bars long. But this tailgaiting effect adds to the tune's childlike breathlessness. The refrain ("This time it's really love") is a very warm, endearing thirty-two-bar ABAC tune. It has a simplicity that seems to have been born of musical depth and experience.

Recordings: The soundtrack of *An American in Paris* is available on MGM S-552 and MGM E-93. A more recent version, by Barbara Cook, is on Painted Smiles PS-1357.

48. DO IT AGAIN!

Lyricist: B.G. DeSylva
Key: F
Time: Common (verse)
Alla breve (refrain)
Tempo: Moderato (verse)
In slow fox-trot time (refrain)
Introduced by: Irene Bordoni in *The French Doll* at the Lyceum Theatre in New York City on February 20, 1922.

Lore: Robert Kimball, in his book *The Gershwins* (Atheneum, 1973), quotes George Gershwin as having said,

> I was in the office of Max Dreyfus, my publisher, one day when Buddy DeSylva walked in. DeSylva said jokingly to me, 'George, let's write a hit!' I matched him by saying 'O.K.! I sat down at the piano and began playing a theme, which I was composing on the spot...Buddy listened for a few minutes and then began chanting this title 'Oh, Do It Again!' which he had just fitted to my theme.

40

It was not long after this that singer Irene Bordoni heard the composer play the song at a party given by Jules Glaenzer, and she immediately asked him if she could perform it in her next Broadway show. "I muss haf dat dam song," was how she put it, according to those within earshot. It was Bordoni who made it a hit.

On November 1, 1923 Eva Gauthier included "Do It Again!" in her "Recital of Ancient and Modern Music for the Voice" concert in Aeolian Hall. It was at this recital that she startled the highbrow world by singing American popular songs in a program that also included works by Bartók, Hindemith, and the American premiere of Schoenberg's "Lied der Waltaube" from *Gurrelieder*. And it was either in this song or in "I'll Build a Stairway to Paradise" (accounts differ) that Gershwin, her accompanist for the pop song portion of the program, slipped in a musical quote from Rimsky-Korsakov's *Scheherazade* which, Gauthier later recalled, made the audience howl.

The composer's piano transcription of this song appeared in *George Gershwin's Songbook*, published in 1932.

Analysis: Repeated notes are used for the insistent "Tell me, tell me" opening of the sixteen-bar verse. Then come moments of urgency, created by short-lived shifts to the minor (B-flat minor at "what did you do to me?" and C-minor at "I wasn't snuggling"). In the thirty-two-bar refrain a slow and sensual beat is at work under the long opening note on "Oh" and under the breathy rush of eighth notes that follows on "do it again." The B section ("My lips just ache") is a gradual, steady crescendo leading to a vulnerable little tag ("won't regret it, come and get it").

Recordings: Frances Gershwin's recording is on Monmouth-Evergreen MES 7060. Oddly, Irene Bordoni did not record this song, although she did, in 1923, record Gershwin's follow-up number, "I Won't Say I Will, But I Won't Say I Won't." Paul Whiteman's was the first recorded version, made on March 15, 1922 (Victor 18882). But the Whiteman recording that was released was the one he made on March 28 and, by that time, on March 16, Ray Miller's Black and White Melody Boys had done the first distributed record (Columbia A-3595). Other 1922 versions were by the Bar Harbor Society Orchestra (Vocalion 14346), Bailey's Lucky Seven (Gennett 4872), Ernest Hussar and His Hotel Claridge Orchestra (Pathe Actuelle 020767), Arthur Lange (Cameo 230), the Markels Orchestra (Okeh 4616), Mitchell's

41

Jazz Kings (Pathe 6577), the Moulin Rouge Orchestra with Ben Selvin, Director (Banner 1076), and Harry Raderman's Orchestra (Edison 50964).

The next recorded versions of this song appeared in the late 1930s, with versions by Cab Calloway and His Orchestra (Okeh 5364), Jimmy Dorsey and His Orchestra (Decca 2925), Mary Martin with the Richard Himber Orchestra (Decca 18184), and Georgia White (Decca 7652). There were recordings in the 1940s by Betty Bradley (Jewel 1002) and Griff Williams (Sonora 3028), in the 1950s by Shorty Rogers with Stan Kenton and June Christy (Pausa 9016), in the 1960s by Judy Garland (at her Carnegie Hall concert—Capitol SWBO-1569) and Julie Andrews (sung with slightly revised lyrics in the film *Thoroughly Modern Millie*—Mercury 21149), and in the 1970s and 1980s by Toni Tenille (Mirage 90162-2), Cybill Shepherd (Inner City 1097), and Sarah Vaughan with the Los Angeles Philharmonic conducted by Michael Tilson Thomas (Columbia FM-37277). Vaughan released an earlier version as well, this one with an orchestra conducted by Hal Mooney (Mercury MGP-2-101).

49. YANKEE DOODLE BLUES

Lyricist: Irving Caesar and B.G. DeSylva
Key: F (verse)
        B-flat (refrain
Time: Common (verse)
        Alla breve (refrain)
Tempo: In march time (not too fast) (verse)
        Slowly with rhythm (refrain)
Introduced by: Georgie Price in *Spice of 1922* at the Winter Garden Theatre in New York City on July 6, 1922.

Lore: Sketches of this tune, dated October 5, 1921 and labeled "American Blues," appear in Gershwin's musical notebook.

In 1925 "Yankee Doodle Blues" was a recurring musical motive in *Processional*, a play by Howard Lawson.

In 1945 this song was used in the Warner Bros. film *Rhapsody in Blue*.

Analysis: "Say, have you ever been away? Have you ever

42

missed the good old U.S.A.?" asks the verse to this simple march. Its most interesting musical features are an aggressive bass ostinato and a brief musical quotation from "Dixie." In the refrain the lyricists seem to have been anticipating Woody Guthrie's "This Land is Your Land" ("There's no land so grand as my land/From California to Manhattan Isle") and the music, slower here than in the verse, attempts to swell with patriotic pride—in fact, the word "fervently" appears over bar thirteen (at "I love ev'ry mile!"). But this music has little of the passion of a true patriotic tune. Instead, its melody, which ascends slowly via dotted half and quarter notes, sounds a bit like the 1926 song "Birth of the Blues" (as did "Dancing Shoes"—another Gershwin tune conceived in 1921). At bar nineteen (on "keeps on ringing in my ear") there is a second quote from "Dixie."

Recordings: The first recording of "Yankee Doodle Blues" was made in May of 1922 by Isham Jones and His orchestra (Brunswick 5144). Ten other versions appeared that year. They were by the Broadway Dance Orchestra (Edison 51004), the Coreyfonic Orchestra (Globe 7173), Don Parker's Western Melody Boys (Pathe Actuelle 020824), Jazzbo's Carolina Serenaders (Cameo 258), Ladd's Black Aces (Gennett 4995), the Majestic Dance Orchestra (Banner 1106), Van and Schenck (Columbia A-3668), Vincent Lopez and His Orchestra (Okeh 4654), The Virginians (Victor 18913), and Yerkes' S.S. Flotilla Orchestra (Vocalion 14432). In 1941, there was a recording by the Sid Phillips Quintet (Decca F-8147).

50. ACROSS THE SEA

Lyricist: B.G. DeSylva and E. Ray Goetz
Key: A-flat
Time: 3/4
Tempo: Valse lente
Introduced by: Richard Bold and Pearl Regay in *George White's Scandals of 1922* at the Globe Theatre in New York City on August 28, 1922.

Analysis: "Across the Sea" is Gershwin's second published waltz (the first was "Just to Know You are Mine," written the year before).

43

Its text is about sailing the seas "in a fragile dream boat" in search of "the girl of my dreams" and the melody of the twenty-four-bar verse ("I am a slave to the lure of the sea") looks and sounds like a rising and subsiding wave—an effect bolstered by the dreamy fourths in the piano accompaniment. In the thirteenth bar there is an abrupt key switch to E and four bars later (on "girl" in "girl of my dreams") a B7 chord with the seventh in the bass brings a sense of surprise and urgency. The melody of the refrain ("My heart will sail across the sea") is delicate and simple, but its emotional effect is heightened by tense and unusual harmonies: a B-flat sung over a B-diminished chord in the tenth bar (at "fragile") and a C sung over a C-sharp-minor chord in the twenty-sixth bar (at "sail" in "sail across"). It is thirty-two bars long and ABA^{1}C in form.

Recordings: None

51. ARGENTINA

Lyricist: B.G. DeSylva
Key: F-Minor (verse)
    F-Major (refrain)
Time: 3/4 (verse)
    2/4 (refrain)
Tempo: Allegretto (tempo di bolero) (verse)
    Allegro (refrain)
Introduced by: Jack McGowan in *George White's Scandals of 1922* at the Globe Theatre in New York City on August 28, 1922.

Analysis: "Argentina" expounds on how difficult it is to court a dance hall girl after midnight in a rough and sleazy Argentinian bar. The singer admits that he has lost out to the lady's "savage sweetheart," but he does not seem much the worse for his adventure. Toward the end of the twenty-two-bar verse ("'Twas midnight in a dance hall"), a bolero, there is a burst of major key sunshine (at "art" in "her bewitching art"). Then, in the refrain ("Argentina"), we get a new key, mode, time and tempo. As with other Gershwin Latin efforts (see "Tomale," "Rose of Madrid," "Land of the Gay Caballero," "Just Another Rhumba"), quick, sixteenth-note triplets figure prominently.

Recordings: In September of 1922 this was recorded by The Atlantic Dance Orchestra (including castanets) with Dave Kaplan on Edison 51074, reissued on Mark 56 Records 799. In October of 1922 there was a version by Selvin's Orchestra (Vocalion 14456).

52. CINDERELATIVES

Lyricist: B.G. DeSylva and E. Ray Goetz
Key: E-flat
Time: Alla breve
Tempo: Moderato
Introduced by: The ensemble in *George White's Scandals of 1922* at the Globe Theatre in New York City on August 28, 1922.

Analysis: The lyric, about Broadway actresses who rise from rags to riches, is awkwardly written ("All the dainty darlings of the plays I love in sweetness exceed but they all owe a kiss to Cinderella, for they follow her lead"). The music consists of an outgoing, sentimental thirty-two bar verse ("My days of childhood glory") and a thirty-two-bar ABAC refrain ("All the dainty darlings") whose two main features are a gentle but insistent beat and a musical phrase (on "Each one finally lives" in measures twenty-two through twenty-three) that resembles the 1921 song "Look For the Silver Lining." Gershwin had already used that phrase once before, in the 1919 song "We're Pals."

Recordings: In their September 1922 recording of "Where is the man of My Dreams?" (another Gershwin song from the 1922 *Scandals*), Joseph C. Smith's Orchestra plays "Cinderelatives" (Brunswick 2328).

45

53. I FOUND A FOUR LEAF CLOVER

Lyricist: B.G. DeSylva
Key: B-flat
Time: Alla breve
Tempo: Moderato
Introduced by: Coletta Ryan and Richard Bold in *George White's Scandals of 1922* at the Globe Theatre in New York City on August 28, 1922.

Lore: It was this song and not "(I'll Build a) Stairway to Paradise" that was supposed to be the hit of the show. According to Ira Gershwin, it was concocted without much thought to quality.

Analysis: This is a single-melody duet in which the he tells the she that, although he is not superstitious, it must have been more than coincidence that made him find a four leaf clover on the very day that he met her. She then presents him with the "alarming" news that she too found a four leaf clover on that day. The twenty-bar verse ("It never could ever/Be said I'm superstitious") begins with a tune that is all trust and innocence. In the fourteenth bar, however, the key of B-flat is lost and there is a succession of transitory, mainly minor key centers and an occasional sharp dissonance. The hook of the refrain ("I found a four leaf clover") is a big seventh leap up between "four" to "leaf." It has a forlorn, baying quality. This refrain is thirty-two bars long and ABA^1C in form.

Recordings: The first recording of this number was made by Joe Gibson in July of 1922 (Cameo 275). Other versions that year were by Carl Fenton and His orchestra (played on their recording of "(I'll Build a) Stairway to Paradise"—Brunswick 2316), the Markels Orchestra (Okeh 4697), Max Terr and His Orchestra (Pathe Actuelle 020828), Selvin's Orchestra (Vocalion 14434), and Paul Whiteman (Victor 18950).

54.   (I'LL BUILD A) STAIRWAY TO PARADISE

Lyricist: B.G. DeSylva and Arthur Francis (Ira Gershwin)
Key: C
Time: Alla breve
Tempo: Animato (verse)
          Con spirito (refrain)
Introduced by: The entire cast—including George White himself—in *George White's Scandals of 1922* at the Globe Theatre
in New York City on August 28, 1922. All were in black,
dancing against the backdrop of a white staircase in a scene
called "The Patent Leather Forest." The accompaniment was
provided by Paul Whiteman's orchestra. Nearly thirty years
later the song was done in a similar vein by Georges Guetary
in the film *An American in Paris.*

Lore: George and Ira had written a ditty called "New Step
Every Day" in which the singer brags about the number of dance steps
he is learning. Although they considered it a weak effort, lyricist
Buddy DeSylva thought that it contained the seed of something special. One night, after dinner at DeSylva's Greenwich Village apartment, the three songwriters got to work and by one a.m. they had "(I'll
Build a) Stairway to Paradise." The original had been entirely revamped; only one phrase remained in common between the two efforts, although in the original it had been "I'll build a staircase to
paradise."
The song was a sensation. As George Gershwin later told it:

> "Stairway" was played in the show by Paul Whiteman's
> orchestra, and I'll never forget the first time I heard
> Whiteman do it. Paul made my song *live* with a vigor
> that almost floored me. Curiously enough, another piece,
> "I found a four leaf clover," was written to be the
> featured song or hit in the show. But there was no
> stopping "Stairway to Paradise" once Whiteman got
> his brasses into it. Two circular staircases surrounded
> the orchestra on the stage, leading high up into theatri-

cal paradise or the flies...Mr. White had draped fifty of his most beautiful girls in a black patent-leather material which brilliantly reflected the spotlights...Incidentally, my association with Whiteman in this show I am sure had something to do with Paul's asking me to write a composition for his first jazz concert. As you may know, I wrote the *Rhapsody in Blue* for the occasion. (Quoted from *The Gershwins*, Atheneum 1973)

As for Ira, he had not expected to earn much from this song (he was happy enough to get to work on the *Scandals*) but it paid him $3,500—enough to support him for a year. His and George's father liked to refer to it as the "war song"—due, no doubt, to its march rhythms.

"(I'll Build a) Stairway to Paradise" was included in Canadian soprano Eva Gauthier's November 1, 1923 Aeolian Hall program. As with the other popular songs on the bill, Gershwin was her accompanist.

The composer's piano transcription of this tune appears in *George Gershwin's Songbook*, published in September of 1932.

Analysis: Although we do not hear the title of this song until the start of the refrain, it is depicted musically in the verse ("All you preachers"), wherein the melody rides to a series of plateaus on a succession of bold harmonic jumps. These jumps are far enough afield from one another (C to E-flat to A-flat to E to A) to create surprise, yet connected enough to create forward motion. And, underneath, there is the relentless march-like pulse that made Gershwin's father call this a war song. The beat of the refrain has more of a hopping or skipping quality; it is more playful than that of the verse. The melody is playful too, rising an octave right away, then bouncing up and down, happily ringing the occasional blue note. In its brief four-bar release ("I've got the blues"), however, it does revert back to the march rhythm of the verse.

Recordings: Paul Whiteman's version was recorded in September of 1922 (Victor 18949, reissued on RCA Victor Vintage LPV 555).

48

Two months earlier—and a month before the opening of the *Scandals*—Joe Gibson recorded it (Cameo 275). Other 1922 recordings were by Carl Fenton and His Orchestra (Brunswick 2316), the Markels Orchestra (Okeh 4715), Max Terr and His Orchestra (Pathe Actuelle 020828), the Savoy Havan Band (English Columbia 3289), and Selvin's Orchestra (Vocalion 14434). In 1937 there was a version by Johnny Williams and His Swing Sextette (Variety 638) and in 1939 there was one by Eddie Condon (Decca 23433). George Guetary's version can be heard on the soundtrack recording of *An American in Paris* (MGM S-552 and MGM E-93). More recent versions have been made by Al Caiola (Bainbridge 1012), Joan Morris and William Bolcom (Nonesuch H-71358), and Sarah Vaughan (Mercury MGP-2-101).

55. SHE HANGS OUT IN OUR ALLEY

Lyricist: B.G. DeSylva and E. Ray Goetz
Key: E-flat
Time: 2/4
Tempo: Allegro
Introduced by: Lester Allen in *George White's Scandals of 1922* at the Globe Theatre in New York City on August 28, 1922.

Analysis: This is a nonsense song about a 303-pound maid who hangs out her wash in an alleyway. The singer proclaims that he likes to watch and serenade her while she does so. Presumably, a double-entendre is intended in the line, "She hangs out in our Alley/But oh, what she hangs out." The music in both the twenty-bar verse ("Ev'ry Monday morn") and the sixteen-bar refrain ("She hangs out"), has a cheerful polka feeling and is a more professional piece of work that the lyric.

Recordings: In 1971 a show called *Do It Again!* played for fourteen performances at the Promenade Theatre in New York. A privately made tape of the show exists and, on it, Susan Long, Robin Benson, and Marion Ramsey perform this song.

56. WHERE IS THE MAN OF MY DREAMS

Lyricist: B.G. DeSylva and E. Ray Goetz
Key: G
Time: Alla breve
Tempo: Moderato
Introduced by : Winnie Lightner in *George White's Scandals of 1922* at the Globe Theatre in New York City on August 18, 1922.

Lore: A portion of this number was a ballet danced by hoboes.

Analysis: "I've been troubled by a question," begins the simple verse—and the music is simple and questioning too. It is twenty bars long, through-composed, and its harmonies are affecting, particularly in bar seventeen (on "Maybe you'll" in "Maybe you'll help me out."), where a D-diminished over an A bass is followed by an A-dominant seventh with a diminished sixth.

The question presaged in the verse is, of course, the title phrase of the refrain. Here the music is engaging and full of chance-taking. The unusual intelligence and power of this song are displayed right away when, on the fourth note (on "man" in "man of my dreams"), the G harmony is interrupted by an E-minor sixth chord. Then, after the first seven notes of the title phrase, the singer, instead of pausing, is given a rhythmically tricky interjection ("Where is he/Where can he be?"). A slow and sensuous rising half-note motive in the B section ("I've looked through Cupids[sic] bill of fare") is reminiscent of the same kind of phrase used in the same spot in "Do it again!," written earlier in the same year. And the admirable coda ("I need a Valentino") quotes the first six bars of the verse.

Recordings: Joseph C. Smith's Orchestra recorded this in September of 1922 (Brunswick 2328) and Ben Selvin recorded it in October of 1922 (Vocalion 14456).

57. BLUE MONDAY

Opera in one act with libretto and lyrics by B.G. DeSylva.

Introduced by: Richard Bold, Lester Allen, Jack McGowan and Coletta Ryan with Paul Whiteman conducting in *George White's Scandals of 1922* at the Globe Theatre in New York City on August 28, 1922.

Lore: Gershwin's lyricist for the 1922 edition of George White's *Scandals*, B.G. DeSylva, thought up an idea for a one-act opera and he talked Gershwin into writing the music. Then they both convinced George White to put it into the revue as the opening for the second act (the first act having ended with the resounding "I'll Build a Stairway to Paradise"). They only had five days to write the piece and Gershwin was forced to go to his musical notebooks to look for suitable ideas. As this was to be a "serious" composition, he may have thought it most appropriate to borrow from his only other highbrow effort to date, the string quartet called *Lullaby*. It was from that source that he took the melody that became "Has Anyone Seen My Joe?" in the opera.

Blue Monday is a depiction of black people in Harlem. Though Gershwin and DeSylva wanted a black cast, producer White opted for Caucasian actors in blackface. Thus, the only black hand in the work was that of orchestrator Will Vodery. The latter, a friend of Gershwin, was the one who had orchestrated Eubie Blake's hit musical *Shuffle Along* the year before.

DeSylva's plot for *Blue Monday* seems silly now—and it was just as silly in 1922. It is a romantic triangle involving a gambler named Joe, an entertainer named Tom, and a woman named Vi. The opera's two scenes both take place in Mike's Tavern—a basement cafe at 135th Street and Lennox Avenue in New York City. In the first, a tavern employee named Sam sings "Blue Monday Blues." Then Vi sings "Has Anyone Seen My Joe?" Then Tom convinces Vi that Joe has been seeing another woman, although Joe has simply been trying to arrange to visit his mother in Georgia. But Vi does not find this out until she has shot Joe to death. This she does in Scene Two, after she,

51

Joe and the other barroom patrons have danced to an orchestral interlude. Joe, despite his mortal wounds, manages to finish the opera with
a spiritual, "I'm Going to See My Mother." The opera is about half
and hour long.

Blue Monday opened and closed the same day—August 28,
1922. It was withdrawn by White after a single performance, the
audience and critics having quickly come to the same conclusion. This
is not to say that no one liked the work. The conductor, Paul Whiteman,
was impressed enough to remember Gershwin when he began handing
out commissions for his February 12, 1924, concert at Aeolian Hall.
But the more typical reaction was that of *New York World* critic Charles Darnton, who called *Blue Monday* "the most dismal, stupid, and
incredible blackface sketch that has probably ever been perpetrated. In
it a dusky soprano finally killed her gambling man. She should have
shot all her associates the moment they appeared and then turned the
pistol on herself."

Actually, Gershwin's trouble over *Blue Monday* began even before the critics got hold of it—and they lasted until long after the opera
was forgotten. It was during the New Haven tryout of the piece that he
first developed the digestive problems that he would later dub his
"composer's stomach." This was a condition that would plague him
until the end of his life.

Three and a half years after its premiere, *Blue Monday* was revived by Paul Whiteman. (Whiteman told Gershwin that he liked the
themes of this piece better than those of the *Rhapsody in Blue*.) This
was on October 29, 1925, when he performed it in a concert setting in
Carnegie Hall. He had given it a new name, *135th Street*, and it was
newly orchestrated by Ferde Grofe. Despite the long line of ticket
buyers and some good reviews (particularly the one by Olin Downes in
the New York *Times*) and despite the fact that Whiteman revived it
again in 1936 at Carnegie Hall, Gershwin's little opera failed to catch
on and it remains one of his least-known compositions.

Though never formally published, *Blue Monday* exists in a pi-
ano/vocal adaptation by George Bassman and it can be ordered from
Warner Bros. Music (265 Secaucus Road, Secaucus, New Jersey 07094).

Excepts from *Blue Monday* were performed in the 1945 Warner
Bros. Gershwin film biography *Rhapsody in Blue*.

On May 20, 1968, this work was performed at Lincoln Center, Skitch Henderson conducting.

Analysis: The music of *Blue Monday* can be divided into the following seventeen sections:

1. An instrumental prelude that begins in C with low rumbles from the timpani. This is followed by moody music that makes liberal use of bluesy grace notes. The music concludes with an insistent, march-like idea.
2. A recitativo-style prologue, sung by Joe before the curtain rises. This is a synopsis of the show, accompanied by stark, dramatic chords, many precipitous key changes, and an almost atonal melody line that seems to be trying to steer as far from the pop song style as possible. Toward the end there is a brief instrumental quote from "Has Anyone Seen My Joe?"
3. Spoken dialogue between Mike (the cafe proprietor), and Sam (called a "boy of all work"), with instrumental underscoring. The music here has a comic jumpiness, with much traveling on the blues scale.
4. "Blue Monday Blues" (sung by Sam): an inventive and enjoyable tune in D-flat—one that achieves an easygoing gait without any strain. There is, however, a self-conscious jazziness in the "they just refuse" line, which uses the notes to "Good evening, Friends!"
5. Piano music in G that alternates between jiveyness and mournfulness. There is a maestoso marking at Tom's entrance and then the music becomes nervous as Tom makes a couple of irascible remarks to the cafe pianist (Sweet-Pea).
6. Vi enters to a jazzy seven-bar instrumental idea in E, then sings the main aria of the opera, "Has Anyone Seen My Joe?" in the same key. This is a forerunner of the composer's expansive E-major slow themes in the *Rhapsody in Blue* and in the first and second movements of the *Concerto in F.* Of these, it is most closely related to the moderato cantabile from the first movement to the concerto.
7. Mike goes to ask the boys in the back room if they have seen Joe. Tom approaches Vi and they have a recitativo conversation in which he woos her and she expresses her preference for Joe. As Tom

53

reaches for her, there is a menacing and powerful cadence that suddenly yanks us out of F major and into A-flat (an augmented G chord over an A bass to a A-flat chord).

8.   Static, lethargic instrumental music accompanies mostly spoken dialogue between Mike and Sam. After the former calls the latter lazy and good for nothing, Sam reprises "Blue Monday Blues," this time in C and to a different, more placid and arpeggiated accompaniment.

9.   Recitative between Mike and Joe in which they discuss the fact that Joe "cleaned up" in a crap game the night before.

10.   Joe sings "I'm Goin' South in the Mornin'"—a lyrical thirty-bar statement in G-flat, harmonized like a chorale.

11.   "I Want to See My Mother" is sung by Joe. This aria is a spiritual in A-flat with big rolling congregational chords. After the word "dreamer" in "maybe I'm a sentimental dreamer," there is a brief appearance of a rhythmic figure that will be prominent in the *Rhapsody in Blue* and in the *Concerto in F*.

12.   A soft instrumental afterglow from Joe's hymn leads to the march music of section one. The guests have arrived at the tavern and this is the most determinedly jazzy music of the piece. Vi and Joe enter to the strain of "Has Anyone Seen My Joe?," played with shimmering tremulos. Then that music is given a burlesque hall bump and grind treatment, in the style of the march.

13.   Vi reprises "Has Anyone Seen My Joe?," this time singing it directly to her lover ("I love but you"). In the accompaniment there is a countermelody that is taken from the dance music of section twelve.

14.   Recitative in which Joe says that he is expecting a telegram. He exits and Vi remains on stage, and the music becomes threatening as Tom tells her that the telegram Joe is waiting for is from "a woman."

15.   The tavern crowd hums "Blue Monday Blues."

16.   Vi intercepts Joe's telegram but does not read it. Rising chromatic octaves accompany her jealous rage and she shoots Joe. Then, as she reads the telegram and discovers the truth ("No need to come now, Joe, mother has been dead three years. Sis"), Vi sinks to the floor, accompanied by the weeping sounds that have already begun in the orchestra. Those sounds, in G-minor, are not unlike those of the "Gone, Gone, Gone" music in *Porgy and Bess*. This is especially so

when Vi cries out, "Oh, forgive me."
17. The dying Joe, having forgiven Vi, again sings "I'm going to see my mother."

Recordings: There is a recording of the May 20, 1968 Philharmonic Hall performance conducted by Skitch Henderson (Penzance 43). A full-length recording of *Blue Monday*, using orchestration adapted from Grofe's 1925 setting, was issued in 1976 on Turnabout TV-S 34638. It features Joyce Andrews as Vi, Patrick Mason as Mike, Walter Richardson as Sam, Thomas Bodgan as Joe, and Jeffrey Meyer as Tom. The orchestra is conducted by Gregg Smith.

58. **BY AND BY**

Lyricist: Brian Hooker
Key: E-flat
Time: Alla breve
Tempo: Moderato (verse)
Tenderly (refrain)
Introduced by: Thomas Conkey and Eva Clark in *Our Nell* at the Bayes Theatre in New York City on December 4, 1922.

Analysis: In the twenty-bar verse ("What's the good of dreams that never come true?") the lyric tells us to live life before it has passed us by. The music here is slow and contemplative, and it is carefully harmonized in the manner of a chorale. The lyric of the refrain ("By and by/Clouds will be gone") takes a somewhat different tack, telling us to look to the future, where "Fears will have passed" and where "a white house dozes among red roses." This music is earnest and very slow—mainly whole, half and quarter notes. It is harmonized in a sentimental style, making frequent use of suspensions. The length is thirty-two bars and the form is ABABC.

Recordings: None

59. INNOCENT INGENUE BABY

Lyricist: Brian Hooker
Key: B-flat (verse)
   E-flat (refrain)
Time: Common
Tempo: Moderato (verse)
    Delicately (refrain)
Introduced by: John Merkyl in *Our Nell* at the Bayes Theatre in
New York City on December 4, 1922.

Lore: It was in *Our Nell* that Gershwin began his association
with a musician named William Daly. In this show Daly wrote some
of the songs, Gershwin wrote others and they collaborated on the music of this one. Daly eventually gave up composition to concentrate on
conducting and he wielded the baton at many of Gershwin's shows.
He was also Gershwin's main musical confidant. After a 1932 concert
a viola player, Allan Langley, wrote an article entitled "The Gershwin
Myth" in which he said that Daly knew more about the score of *An
American In Paris* than Gershwin did. Langley concluded that Gershwin used Daly as a ghostwriter. Daly's reply came in the January 15,
1933 edition of the New York *Times*: "I have never written one note
of any of his compositions, or so much as orchestrated one whole bar
of his symphonic works...I suppose I should really resent the fact that
Langley attributes Gershwin's work to me, since Langley finds all of it
so bad. But fortunately for my amour propre, I have heard some of
Langley's compositions. He really should stay away from ink and
stick to his viola."
 If George Gershwin ever had a "best friend" it was probably
Daly. They died within a few months of one another—Daly at the end
of 1936 and Gershwin in the summer of 1937.

Analysis: The sixteen-bar verse ("Dear little maid of sixteen")
has a tender, fragile quality that is due, at least in part, to the fact that
its initial repeated notes are harmonized in sixths. This creates a
feeling of separation and loneliness. After a brief release ("I don't
wish to trouble you") this idea returns. But the last of the repeated

notes (at "see" in "if you see") is now harmonized with a more urgent sound—a major seventh. In the refrain ("Innocent Ingenue Baby") the beat is established by the bass, which descends chromatically in half notes, the harmony changing with each descent. Most of the tune is made up of three notes, played in a doodling, syncopated manner. The hook comes when the final two notes of a phrase (on the second "baby") are suddenly played an octave lower. This, plus the rhythmically changing harmony, makes the song irresistible. The structure is AABA and the length is thirty-two bars. At the end, the instrumental tag is derived from the melody of the verse.

Recordings: For the 1923 British show *The Rainbow*, this song was slightly revised and retitled "Innocent Lonesome Blue Baby." A recording of that song appears on an album entitled *The Great British Dance Bands Play George Gershwin 1920-1928* (World Records SH 451). Bobby Short's version is on Atlantic SD 2-608.

60. WALKING HOME WITH ANGELINE

Lyricist: Brian Hooker
Key: C
Time: Alla breve
Tempo: Allegretto (verse)
        Allegretto grazioso (refrain)
Introduced by: Olin Howland and Emma Haig in *Our Nell* at the Bayes Theatre in New York City on December 4, 1922.

Lore: This music first entered Gershwin's notebook in the spring of 1922.

Analysis: Hooker's lines are evocative ("When I'm walking home with Angeline/And the old Town Clock is striking nine") and his use of a single recurring rhyme is as effective as it is unusual ("Angeline," "striking nine," "heart of mine"). Gershwin's twenty-bar verse ("Down by the schoolhouse gate") brims with contentment and good will and its four-bar coda ("Seems to me I'd rather be") slows the

57

pace down in anticipation of a very gentle refrain. It also provides the material from which the release of the refrain will be built. In the refrain ("When I'm walking home with Angeline"), five repeated notes are followed by a leap up of a sixth and then a fall of a third. This makes for a bird call effect that helps this music achieve its pleasing pastoral quality. The format is thirty-two bars and ABAB^{1}A.

Recordings: None

61. THE SUNSHINE TRAIL

Lyricist: Arthur Francis (Ira Gershwin)
Key: G
Time: Alla breve
Tempo: Moderato (verse)
       Molto expressivo (refrain)
Introduced by: It is unclear who first sang this song. It was written to promote a 1923 silent film of the same name by Thomas H. Ince.

Lore: This was the first writing that either of the Gershwin brothers did for the movies.

Analysis: The sunshine trail is the road to happiness, and Ira advises us that we can embark on it by summoning up a cheerful smile and by lending others a helping hand.

A brief, recitativo-style verse ("When you lend a helping hand to others"), made up mainly of repeated notes, leads into a sentimental thirty-two-bar refrain ("You'll find true happiness lies along The Sunshine Trail"). Of interest is the fact that, although in G, it begins on a C-major seventh chord. Also, the release ("I cannot guide you there") is in A-minor—an unusual choice for a refrain in G. The melody of this release rises ever higher in successive three-note waves, then makes the transition back to the main idea with a musical phrase that recalls a similar point in Jerome Kern's "They Didn't Believe Me." The form here is ABABA.

58

Recordings: None

62. THAT AMERICAN BOY OF MINE

Lyricist: Irving Caesar
Key: C-minor (verse)
      C (refrain)
Time: Alla breve
Tempo: Moderato con moto (verse)
        Slowly and well-marked (refrain)
Introduced by: Sally Fields in *The Dancing Girl* at the Winter
Garden in New York City on January 24, 1923.

Analysis: This is a revision of "No One Else But That Girl of
Mine" from the 1921 show, *The Perfect Fool*. "No One Else" had
been the happy song of a newly betrothed man. "That American Boy"
is sung by a woman who, having traveled abroad, is eagerly returning
to her beloved homeland and to a loving countryman. There are musical differences as well. The new version has a new key, a new accompaniment, and some new harmonies. For instance, the second bar of
the verse of "No One Else" (at "has passed" in "One year has passed")
has a progression from the tonic to a major chord built on the augmented fourth interval of the scale. At the same point in "That American Boy" (at "I must say" in "U-S-A, I must say") we go from the
tonic to a diminished chord based on the first note. The earlier version's
harmony is generally tangier and more interesting.
    The other principal musical change occurs in the second bar of
the refrain. In "No One Else" (on "cheers me when I'm" in "Who
cheers me when I'm blue?") the melody rises up the pentatonic scale
as the harmony stays with the tonic. In "That American Boy" (to the
same words) the melody dips down and then turns up while the harmony moves from the tonic to the subdominant minor. It is a good
song either way but the earlier version is more assured, especially in
its melodic structure and in the aptness of its accompaniment.

Recordings: Paul Whiteman's version (Victor 19024) was recorded on February 2, 1923, a few days after the premiere. Eleven days later the Columbians recorded their version (Columbia A-3838).

63. BENEATH THE EASTERN MOON

Lyricist: Clifford Grey
Key: C
Time: Alla breve
Tempo: Moderato
Introduced by: Lola Raine in *The Rainbow* at the Empire Theatre in London on April 3, 1923.

Analysis: Grey's lyric is determinedly poetic ("Twilight falls as the night spirit calls," "Not a note from a bird's feathered throat"). In the sixteen-bar verse ("All around is a silence profound") an ostinato bass thumps like a jungle drum below a succession of unrelated, mostly major, triads. The refrain ("Beneath the Eastern Moon") is slow and melodramatic. Many of its notes are high ones and some of these are held for more than a bar. Every so often a quick five-note instrumental interlude is heard tinkling in the upper register. The form is ABAB and the length is thirty-two bars.

Recordings: None

64. GOOD-NIGHT, MY DEAR

Lyricist: Clifford Grey
Key: A-flat
Time: Common (verse)
       Alla breve (refrain)
Tempo: Moderato
Introduced by: Grace Hayes in *The Rainbow* at the Empire Theatre in London on April 3, 1923.

60

Analysis: The verse of this unusual song ("When the busy day is through") begins very simply, as if someone had lifted the lid to a music box. Later, however, we come to several measures of polytonality: a C-major melody against A-flat and E-flat chords on "You seem ev'erwhere" in bars twelve and thirteen, and an E-major tune played against an E-flat bass on "though you're away" in bar eighteen.

Throughout the refrain ("Good-night, my dear"), Gershwin's harmonic cadences keep us pleasantly off guard. In the first twenty-four bars the initial idea is stated three times, each time in a different key, each time with an ambiguous first chord, and each time it is developed in a slightly different melodic direction. The fourth restatement, accounting for the final eight bars, begins on an E-flat seventh as did the first, but it quickly moves off to end the song in its own way. Noteworthy too is the Chopinesque piano figure that is different in each of its six appearances.

Recordings: None

65. IN THE RAIN

Lyricist: Clifford Grey
Key: E-flat
Time: Alla breve
Tempo: Not too fast (introduction)
　　　　　Moderato (verse and refrain)
Introduced by: Fred A. Leslie and Stephanie Stephens in *The Rainbow* at the Empire Theatre in London on April 3, 1923.

Analysis: The verse of "In The Rain" ("Little girl, don't be feeling blue") is interesting in two respects. It begins with five-bar rather than the usual four-bar phrasing—which accounts for its odd eighteen-bar length. For this reason, composer Vernon Duke was a fan of the number, noting that five-bar phrases would have still been daring as late as the 1950s. The other point of interest here is that the accompaniment in this verse makes use of a chromatic figure that is the same as the one that, a year later, would serve as the nervous countermelody to the slow theme of the *Rhapsody in Blue*. The refrain ("In the rain I'll try to shelter you") is sad but sweet. It is thirty-two bars long and ABAB^{1}A^1 in form.

Recordings: None

66. **INNOCENT LONESOME BLUE BABY**

Lyricist: Brain Hooker and Clifford Grey
Key: B-flat (verse)
    E-flat (refrain)
Time: Common
Tempo: Moderato (verse)
    Delicately (refrain)
Introduced by: Stephanie Stephens and Alec Kellaway in *The Rainbow* at the Empire Theatre in London on April 3, 1923.

Analysis: The music, by Gershwin and William Daly, is the same as in "Innocent Ingenue Baby" but the lyrics have been revised. The most obvious substitution is that of "lonesome blue" for "ingenue," made, presumably, because the word "ingenue" was unfamiliar to British ears. British sensibilities were also spared in that the "dear little maid" to whom the song is addressed is no longer identified as a sixteen-year old. And there is one more change: Grey's revision gives the lonesome blue baby a stanza of the verse to sing, making this British version a duet.

Recordings: A version is played on an album entitled *The Great British Dance Bands Play George Gershwin 1920-1928* (World Records SH 451).

67. MOONLIGHT IN VERSAILLES

Lyricist: Clifford Grey
Key: C
Time: Common (verse)
    Alla breve (refrain)
Tempo: Moderato
Introduced by: Grace Hayes in *The Rainbow* at the Empire
Theatre in London on April 3, 1923.

Analysis: In florid phrases the words attempt to evoke the poetic
atmosphere of Versailles. The composer provides a somewhat ram-
bling verse ("Follow down the path of mem'ry"), through-composed
but for the repetition, mid-way, of a single minor key phrase. The
refrain ("There in the moonlight") takes an opposite tack. It is a slow,
broad melody, built entirely of repetitive and, eventually, monotonous
phrases. The most interesting moment in this piece is the series of four
bold, resonant and ungermane seventh chords that concludes the verse
and ushers in the refrain.

Recordings: None

68. OH! NINA

Lyricist: Clifford Grey
Key: E-flat
Time: Alla breve
Tempo: Brightly
Introduced by: Earl Rickard and the Fayre Four in *The Rainbow*
at the Empire Theatre in London on April 3, 1923.

Analysis: In the first twelve bars of the verse ("Nina was a little
girl") we are told with a quiet, simple E-flat melody how there once
was a girl who loved to play her concertina. In the next twelve bars,
the music moves into dark C-minor as we learn about the neighbors'
unsympathetic reaction to her music-making. Then, in the first stanza

63

of the refrain ("Nina won't you play some music"), the neighborhood boys come to Nina's aid, encouraging her to play on. In the second stanza, she is grown up and it is her husband who says, "Play some music for me." This refrain is thirty-two bars long, ABAC in form, and its melody features repeated notes (they come in sets of eight) followed by enthusiastic upward leaps.

Recordings: None

69. STRUT LADY WITH ME

Lyricist: Clifford Grey
Key: C
Time: 2/4
Tempo: Allegretto
Introduced by: Grace Hayes in *The Rainbow* at the Empire Theatre in London on April 3, 1923.

Analysis: This lyric, an invitation to the dance, sought to entertain London audiences with such American colloquialisms as "Ready Kid?," "Step on the gas," and "shake up some mean feat" [sic]. The music of the verse ("There's a Dixie Ball down at the/Dance Hall") bears a family resemblance to the slow theme (sosteno e con moto) of the composer's *Second Rhapsody*, and it is an affecting piece of work even in this early up-tempo incarnation. It leads into a second idea or release ("All the belles, all the beaux") and then returns to complete a full thirty-two bars. An unusually bold and effective cadence (C-diminished to E-flat) ushers in the first sound of the refrain: C-major seventh (at the title phrase). This is followed by a syncopated dance tune whose most distinctive moment is an unexpectedly bluesy second piano ending.

Recordings: None

70.   SUNDAY IN LONDON TOWN

Lyricist: Clifford Grey
Key: C
Time: 3/4
Tempo: Tempo di Valse
Introduced by: This song was written for but not used in *The Rainbow*, a show that had its premiere at the Empire Theatre in London on April 3, 1923.

Analysis: The witty lyric makes fun of the drab ways that Londoners choose to enjoy their Sabbaths ("If we take the dog for a run in the fog, it's excitement enough for the day"). Musically, the verse and refrain are a couple of lively waltzes. The former ("Those Sundays in France") has a descending bass line which continuously adds character to the melody above. The refrain ("On Sunday in London") is a fairground sort of waltz—it conjures up a spinning merry-go-round. It is thirty-two bars long, ABAC in form, and boasts an interesting second ending cadence: C to E+ to C.

Recordings: None

71.   SWEETHEART (I'M SO GLAD THAT I MET YOU)

Lyricist: Clifford Grey
Key: E-flat
Time: Alla breve
Tempo: Allegretto
Introduced by: Lola Raine and Elsie Mayfair in *The Rainbow* at the Empire Theatre in London on April 3, 1923.

Lore and Analysis: Gershwin told Vernon Duke that he considered *The Rainbow* his poorest score. He blamed this on the fact that it had to be written very quickly. As he put it in a letter to Ira from London, "Writing the *Scandals* in a month will seem an eternity compared to the time allotted us to write what will probably be called

65

"Silver Linings." It is not known how long it took to write this song but an educated guess can be made on the basis of the lyric ("I'm so spooney/Kind of looney honey-moon-ey")—and the music. The sixteen-bar verse ("Listen honey") is based on a two-note yodel motive. The sing-songy tune of the refrain ("I'm so glad that I met you") begins emphatically, with seven straight accented notes, making for a sense of exertion. It is thirty-two bars long and ABACA in form.

Recordings: A version appears on an album entitled *The Great British Dance Bands Play George Gershwin 1920-1928* (World Records SH 451).

72. LET'S BE LONESOME TOGETHER

Lyricist: B.G. DeSylva and E. Ray Goetz
Key: F
Time: Alla breve
Tempo: Moderato (verse)
          Slow and liltingly (refrain)
Introduced by: Richard Bold and Delyle Alda in *George White's Scandals of 1923* at the Globe Theatre in New York City on June 18, 1923.

Analysis: The twenty-bar verse, which tells the story of a caged canary and a goldfish trapped in a crystal bowl, contains a modern and dramatic jazz progression (at "Canary, so very"), a sudden and heart-lightening modulation up into the key of A (at "swimming" in "Was swimming in a crystal bowl"), and a final four-bar recitative (at "The goldfish said"). In the refrain the penultimate syllable of the title phrase is syncopated, held well into the next bar, and then resolved with a lilting melismatic embellishment. Then we get a restatement in the somewhat distant key of G-minor (at "two together"), a simple release in D-minor (at "We'll soon realize"), and a coda in F based on the initial idea. In other words, this is a fine piece of music from start to finish, full of surprises and very advanced in its sound. Its natural companions would seem to be Gershwin songs of the late 1920s—

66

songs like "Feeling Sentimental"—and not "The Life of a Rose" and "Lo-La-Lo."

Recordings: None

73. THE LIFE OF A ROSE

Lyricist: B.G. DeSylva
Key: G-minor (verse)
  G-major (refrain)
Time: Common
Tempo: Moderato (verse)
  Tenderly (refrain)
Introduced by: Richard Bold and Marga Waldron in *George White's Scandals of 1923* at the Globe Theatre on June 18, 1923.

Analysis: The verse asks, "Tell me, who could help envying the life of a rose?" The refrain then informs us that a rose's petals droop in dismay after the flower's single day in the sun. The music takes an opposite tack. In the verse, when the words are hopeful, it is in mournful G-minor. Then in the refrain, when the tragic fate of the rose is revealed, there is a sweet old-fashioned tune in G-major. Gershwin's musical signature occurs in the eighth bar of the verse (on "rose" in "all except the rose"), when a piano fill makes use of a dominant seventh chord that has both a major and a minor third—this would become a characteristic sound in the slow movement of the *Concerto in F.*

Recordings: In the summer of 1923 this song was recorded by The Columbians (Columbia A-3592), Charles Dorenberger and His Orchestra (Victor 19151), the Emerson Dance Orchestra (Emerson 10665), Carl Fenton and His Orchestra (Brunswick 2518), Lewis James (Mark 56 Records 799), The Markels Orchestra (Okeh 4961), Russell's Dance Orchestra (Cameo 394), and Joseph Samuels and His Orchestra (Banner 1231). More recently, Elaine Stritch sang it in a medley with

67

Bobby Short's rendition of "Rose of Madrid" on *Ben Bagley's George Gershwin Revisited* (Painted Smiles PS 1357).

74. LO-LA-LO

Lyricist: B.G. DeSylva
Key: C
Time: 2/4
Tempo: In the manner of a Hawaiian song
Introduced by: Richard Bold, Olive Vaughn and Tom Patricola in *George White's Scandals of 1923* at the Globe Theatre in New York City on June 18, 1923.

Analysis: The lyric addresses a Hawaiian maid who lives in a palm tree cottage on an island called Hikipo. Musically, there are three sections. The first is a jaunty twenty-four bar verse ("When the sun is setting on Hikipo") which, despite the tempo markng, seems to owe more to the brisk marching style of George M. Cohan than to the South Seas. Then come a rousing sixteen-bar refrain ("Lo-La-Lo") and, instead of a release, a sixteen-bar trio ("I'm waiting"). This music (minus the trio) was also used in "On The Beach At How've You Been," from the same show.

Recordings: None

75. ON THE BEACH AT HOW'VE-YOU-BEEN

Lyricist: B.G. DeSylva
Key: C
Time: 2/4
Tempo: In the manner of a Hawaiian song
Introduced by: Helen Hudson in *George White's Scandals of 1923* at the Globe Theatre in New York City on June 18, 1923.

Analysis: The music here is the same as that in "Lo-La-Lo,"

68

although this version lacks the latter's trio section. In "Lo-La-Lo" DeSylva invented a Hawaiian island called Hikipo. Here, he gives us one called How've-You-Been. It is an island where the natives dress in Shredded Wheat and operate shimmy factories under every tree.

Recordings: None

76. THERE IS NOTHING TOO GOOD FOR YOU

Lyricist: B.G. DeSylva and E. Ray Goetz
Key: E-flat
Time: Alla breve
Tempo: Slow and sentimentally
Introduced by: Richard Bold and Helen Hudson in *George White's Scandals of 1923* at the Globe Theatre in New York City on June 18, 1923.

Analysis: The sixteen-bar verse ("You are as lovely as lilies at dawn") has a string of agreeable harmonies, including a couple of lush major-seventh chords (on "treasures and to" in "to collect the rarest treasures and to lay them at your feet"). It ends with a C-flat seventh chord that leads somewhat surprisingly into an F-minor kickoff for the refrain ("There is nothing too good for you"). This refrain is thirty-two bars long and ABAC in form and its C section quotes from and extends the above-mentioned four-bar ending of the verse.

Recordings: None

77. THROW HER IN HIGH!

Lyricist: B.G. DeSylva and E. Ray Goetz
Key: G (verse)
      A-minor, C (refrain)
Time: Alla breve
Tempo: Moderato
Introduced by: Winnie Lightner and Lester Allen in *George*

White's Scandals of 1923 at the Global Theatre in New York City on June 18, 1923.

Analysis: In the thirty-two-bar verse ("We have had enough of blue laws") the lyricists protest against Puritan propriety, claiming that, because of it, "Our old Ship of State is lagging/In the race of Nations." These sentiments are sung to march music whose insistent quarter notes in both the melody and bass (where there are fourteen Gs in a row) make for a kind of feigned anger. After sixteen bars the same music is given new energy when it is repeated in the key of B. The refrain ("throw her in high!"), which is just half as long as the verse, is, lyrically, little more than the title phrase. Musically, it is interesting because its playful rhythms clearly anticipate such tricky Gershwin songs of the future as "Fascinating Rhythm" and "Fidgety Feet"—especially the latter. This song differs from those two in that the key rhythmic idea pauses occasionally in the melody while it is taken up in the accompaniment.

Recordings: None

78. **WHERE IS SHE?**

Lyricist: B.G. DeSylva
Key: C (verse)
      F (refrain)
Time: Common
Tempo: Moderato (verse)
       Not Too Fast (refrain)
Introduced by: Tip Top Four in *George White's Scandals of 1923* at the Globe Theatre in New York City on June 18, 1923.

Analysis: The singer is sitting in a Pullman car looking out the window and wondering which passing town holds the girl of his dreams. Will it be "Frisco, Detroit, Chicago, or Albany" or "Squeedunk, Dubuque, Hoboken or Kankakee"? Gershwin's sixteen-bar verse ("Traveling, I'm always traveling") has a lazy dotted note melody that is harmonized in fourths. The refrain ("Where is she") is bluesy in a more troubled, melancholy way than was usually the case on Broadway in this era. It consists of a series of blue cadences, each of them an individual, chromatically descending three-note phrase. The release ("I'm going to look around") proceeds to turn those cadences upside down, presenting them as chromatically ascending three-note phrases. These are supported by adventurous—even unsettling—harmonies. This refrain is thirty-two bars long and AABA[1] in form.

Recordings: None

79. YOU AND I (IN OLD VERSAILLES)

Lyricist: B.G. DeSylva
Key: G
Time: Alla breve
Tempo: Moderato
Introduced by: Beulah Berson in *George White's Scandals of 1923* at the Globe Theatre in New York City on June 18, 1923.

Analysis: The lyric, with lines such as "I heard and answered Cupid's call," is sung by a woman who has returned to Versailles, the scene of an old love affair. The music is co-credited to Jack Green. Its tranquil and somewhat subdued thirteen-bar verse ("Fountains of Versailles") passes in the third bar (on "of" in "the greatest day of") into the minor mode, moving through E-minor, B-minor and A-minor before it returns to G. The refrain ("You and I one day in old Versailles") is an everyday, somewhat earnest, thirty-two-bar ballad that begins with and keeps coming back to a little three-note motive (a B and two As). The form is ABA[1].

Recordings: None

80.   I WON'T SAY I WILL BUT I WON'T SAY I WON'T

Lyricist: B.G. DeSylva and Arthur Francis (Ira Gershwin)
Key: G
Time: Alla breve
Tempo: Moderato
Introduced by: Irene Bordoni in *Little Miss Bluebeard* at the Lyceum Theatre in New York City on August 28, 1923.

Lore and analysis: This sequel to the suggestive "Do It Again" has little of the heat or sensuality of its predecessor. While the meaning of "it " was left to the listener's imagination in "Do It Again," here we know that the singer is deciding whether or not to offer a kiss. Issac Goldberg called this song a lied and said that it had *malice* and archness. Upon inspection, however, those qualities are hard to find. The music in the twenty-bar verse ("You're a very naughty boy") presents a sweet and innocent tune in G and then in B-minor. The refrain ("I won't say I will") is characterized by two eighth note leaps up—the first is an octave, the second a minor seventh. Both are followed by quarter note rests, making for a jumpy, jagged, puppet-on-a-string effect. The form is thirty-two bars and ABACA.

Recordings: Irene Bordoni (Victor 19199), George Bassman & His Orchestra with Richard Hayes and Paula Stewart (Decca DL 78910), Ida James and Ellis Larkins Trio (Decca 11004), Sarah Vaughan (Mercury MGP-2-101).

81.   AT HALF PAST SEVEN

Lyricist: B.G. DeSylva
Key: E-flat
Time: Alla breve
Tempo: Moderato (verse)
              Slow with expression (refrain)

Introduced by: Hazel Dawn and Joe Schenck in *Nifties of 1923* at the Fulton Theatre in New York City on September 25, 1923.

Lore: This melody was used later for "Some Far Away Someone" in *Primrose*, a show written for the London stage in 1924. "Some Far Away Someone's lyrics were by DeSylva and Ira Gershwin.

Analysis: In this lyric, which DeSylva did alone, the singer is complaining because he can see his beloved for only four hours a day: from 7:30 p.m. until 11:30 p.m. Just why those are the only hours that she is available is never made clear, but one presumes that she is not incarcerated. In any event, the real invention in the song is in the music, and Gershwin, in the refrain, has produced a lovely and lyrical theme on the order of the one he wrote in "Drifting Along With The Tide." It is thirty-two bars long and ABA[1]C in form. There is some especially fine writing in the release ("and then the world with kisses burning") where complex chords are used unobtrusively to bolster the essential simplicity of the musical statement. For instance, in the final two notes of this section (on "once more" in the phrase "starts turning once more") Gershwin chooses not a simple A-flat to E-flat cadence but, instead, gives us an A-flat ninth with the ninth in the bass before the E-flat resolution. This adds depth to the moment. Preceding this music is a simple, almost pastoral twenty-bar verse ("There are twenty-four hours in the day").

Recordings: None

82. NASHVILLE NIGHTINGALE

Lyricist: Irving Caesar
Key: F
Time: Alla breve
Tempo: Moderato
Introduced by: The first performer of this song is uncredited but it may have been Jane Greene. This was in a show called

Nifties of 1923 at the Fulton Theatre in New York City on September 25, 1923.

Lore: On December 24, 1926 George Gershwin served as piano accompanist for Marguerite d'Alvarez when she gave a combined pop/highbrow song recital. It was at this concert that he premiered his piano preludes, as well as his two-piano version of the *Rhapsody in Blue* (Isidor Gorn was the second pianist). Ms. d'Alvarez and Gershwin did this song as part of their program.

Analysis: "Nashville Nightingale" is a bluesy up-tempo number about a lady in Tennessee who, because of her ability to sing "Do-Do-Di-Do-Do-Di," is accused unfairly of competing with the town's clergy. The twenty-four-bar verse ("There's a sweet singing lady") begins on a blue note and contains a minor key release (on "All the darktown preachers") that anticipates the gritty minor key sound of the "Come on, you children" verse of "Clap Yo' Hands." The thirty-two-bar refrain ("Nashville Nightingale") has a couple of blue notes (the fifth and tenth notes, on the syllables "gale" and "song") that are not only blue, but syncopated, held and accented. Scat singing occurs in the main idea, in the release, and in a brief coda. The song dares to end on an unresolved F7 chord.

Recordings: Marion Harris recorded this in December of 1923 (Brunswick 2539). In 1924, additional versions were made by the California Ramblers (Pathe Actuelle 036167), the Charleston Seven (Edison 51446), Joseph C. Smith and His Orchestra (His Master's Voice 216472), Waring's Pennsylvanians (Victor 19492), and Chick Winter's Orchestra (Triangle 11423). Bobby Short has made the only latter-day record (Painted Smiles PS-1357).

83. HEY! HEY! LET 'ER GO!

Lyricist: B.G. DeSylva
Key: E-flat
Time: 2/4

Tempo: No tempo marking (verse)
With much Ped (refrain)
Introduced by: William Wayne in *Sweet Little Devil* at the Globe Theatre in New York City on January 21, 1924.

Analysis: The philosophy of this number is that "home's the place for using the brain" while the world at large is where one ought to "let 'er Go! Be the life of the Crowd." The verse ("Gloomy Gusses") and refrain ("When you're out, don't be slow!") are unusual in their similarity to one another. Both are youthful thirty-two-bar rousers and each depends for its kick on the same accented high note—a D-flat (which, this being the key of E-flat, is blue). The lack of a tempo marking in the verse is another oddity, as is the injunction to use the pedal in the refrain.

Recordings: None

84. THE JIJIBO

Lyricist: B.G. DeSylva
Key: F
Time: Alla breve
Tempo: Moderato
Introduced by: Ruth Warren and William Wayne in *Sweet Little Devil* at the Astor Theatre in New York City on January 21, 1924.

Analysis: The lyric tells of a dance, the Jijibo, that is prescribed in a book entitled "How to Get Fat or Thin." It is a dance that must have been something to see, inasmuch as it was guaranteed to work wonders on a double chin. As for the music, the introductory piano run hits every blue note in the key of F, and the verse ("I bought a little book by chance") and refrain ("Ev'rybody ought to know the 'Jijibo'") are equally relentless in their bluesyness. The song's most unusual feature is the fact that the fifth and sixth bars of the verse (at "What do you think I read?") are repeated in the fifth and sixth bars of the refrain (at "Try it when you arise").

Recordings: The Columbians recorded this on February 11, 1924, playing it briefly during their rendition of "Virginia"—another Gershwin song from *Sweet Little Devil* (Columbia 88-D).

85. MAH-JONGG

Lyricist: B.G. DeSylva
Key: E-flat
Time: Common (verse)
       Alla breve (refrain)
Tempo: Moderato
Introduced by: This was written for but unused in *Sweet Little Devil*. Richard Bold did it in *George White's Scandals of 1924* at the Apollo Theatre in New York City on June 30, 1924.

Analysis: This is another Gershwin piece on an oriental theme. Already there had been "Idle Dreams" and "Yan-Kee" and in 1929 there would be an unproduced show called *East Meets West* for which he would write "In the Mandarin's Orchid Garden." Then, in 1934, there would be a Chinese variation in the *I Got Rhythm Variations*.

"Mah-Jongg," written at the height of the 1920s' fascination with that game, is addressed to a "maiden fair" by that name. It is more tongue-in-cheek than atmospheric ("From Tibetan ridges you're as nice as bridge is") and DeSylva's reference to "the sly Chinee" would make the lyric offensive to modern ears. That is unfortunate, for Gershwin gives us a gentle ballad—one with some distinctive harmonic moments. In the third and fourth bars of the refrain (on "Jongg") a G chord with augmented fourth and fifth notes leads unexpectedly and pleasingly into A-flat. In the sixteenth bar, to the words "I go off key," the music hits a sour note (a joke the composer had already used in "Mischa" and one that he would make again, most notably in the verse to "Let's Call the Whole Thing Off" on the words "our romance is growing flat"). The refrain ends with an unusual cadence: E-diminished seventh to E-flat.

Recordings : None

86. PEPITA

Lyricist: B.G. DeSylva
Key: C-minor (verse)
        E-flat (refrain)
Time: Alla breve
Tempo: Moderato
Introduced by: This was written for *Sweet Little Devil*, a show that opened at the Globe Theatre in New York City on January 21, 1924. It is not clear who sang it in that show or if it was sung at all.

Analysis: The lyric has such lines as "Hark to my guitar, Pepita" and "you're my guiding star, Chiquita." The music consists of two tangos, one in the twenty-four bar verse ("Day is done") and the other in the thirty-two bar refrain ("Hark to my guitar"). In the former, the singer, on the third note, reaches an exotic B-natural against the C-minor tango motive in the bass. The effect, aided by accompanying harmony, is polytonal, with the vocalist in G and the accompanist in C-minor. The refrain ("Hark to my guitar") is a more conventional tune, one that, like all of Gershwin's Latin efforts, makes use of ornamental triplets (used here on the word "Pepita").

Recordings: None

87. SOMEONE BELIEVES IN YOU

Lyricist: B.G. DeSylva
Key: F
Time: Common (verse)
        Alla breve (refrain)

Tempo: Slowly (verse)
Slow with sentiment (refrain)
Introduced by: Constance Binney and Irving Beebe in *Sweet Little Devil* at the Astor Theatre in New York City on January 21, 1924.

Analysis: "When you're plodding on your weary way it helps a lot to get a bit of cheer," goes the verse, which then reveals that a nice bit of cheer has come to the singer via a letter in the mail. We never learn who sent the note but we do get to hear it, for it is sung in the refrain and its message is the title of the song. It's an affecting lyric and the music makes it doubly so. In the twenty-four bar verse ("When you're plodding"), an affirmative melody is harmonized simply but powerfully, like a chorale. The refrain ("There is someone who believes in you") is similar, with a thirty-two-bar tune that rises in a slow, stately fashion.

Recordings: None

88. UNDER A ONE-MAN TOP

Lyricist: B.G. DeSylva
Key: F
Time: Alla breve
Tempo: Moderato
Introduced by: Ruth Warren and William Wayne in *Sweet Little Devil* at the Astor Theatre in New York City on January 21, 1924.

Analysis: The one-man top is an automobile. The singer, a self-confessed "back to nature guy," hopes to escape in it to the countryside with the woman he loves, their eventual destination being Niagara Falls. DeSylva gets in a couple of good lines ("Let me watch a road unravel" and "ev'ry time we make a mile/We'll thank our Lord, Henry Ford!"). The music of the sixteen-bar verse ("City life's commotion") has a cantering dotted note pulse and its melodic ideas are presented in a pleasant succession of keys (F, D-flat, A-minor). The refrain ("Under a one-man top with a one-man girl"), a thirty-two-bar ballad, is full of placid sixth chords. It is made up mainly of a series of variations (AA^{1}A^{2}BA^3).

Recordings: Anthony Perkins and Barbara Cook sing this on the album *Ben Bagley's George Gershwin Revisited* (Painted Smiles PS 1357).

89. VIRGINIA

Lyricist: B.G. DeSylva
Key: E-flat
Time: Alla breve
Tempo: Moderato
Introduced by: Constance Binney in *Sweet Little Devil* at the Astor Theatre in New York City on January 21, 1924.

Lore: Pianist Lester Donahue recalled being particularly captivated by this song at a performance of *Sweet Little Devil.* George Gershwin was captivated too; he liked to play it at parties, particularly at those given by Mary Hoyt Wiborg, a New York socialite. It was at one of her parties that Gershwin and Igor Stravinsky were asked to sit at a single piano and improvise together. They were reluctantly about to do so when, to their relief, it was discovered that the piano was locked.

"Virginia" was cited by Olin Downes in his 1937 obituary of the composer.

Analysis: The verse is the plaint of a young girl who has inherited her father's rectitude and her mother's wild streak. Because of this puzzling combination she is, she admits, "a sort of Jekyll and Hyde—like a young volcano inside." In the refrain ("Virginia! Virginia! The devil is in ya") she admonishes herself to control that wild streak and not shock her "Southern stock."

The twenty-four-bar verse of this graceful song ("Why did na-

79

ture have to be provided") is a gentle tune, one whose quality of puzzled innocence is a perfect foil for the singer's dilemma. Its first few notes contain a hint of "Dixie" that, while subtle, is obviously intentional. In the refrain ("Virginia!"), a series of six three-note phrases, each of them preceded and followed by a quarter note rest, makes for both a hesitating quality and a sense of forward propulsion. Happily, these two opposites co-exist very well in the music, even if they are warring within Virginia herself. The release ("You're an awful shock") bears the unusual marking, *molto appassionato*.

Recordings: In 1924 there were versions by The Columbians (Columbia 88-D), Carl Fenton and His Orchestra (Brunswick 2518) and Jack Shilkret (Victor 19394). In late 1928 or early 1929 Jack Hamilton and His Entertainers recorded it (Azurephone 1008). In 1932 came a version by Lil Armstrong (Columbia 14678-D). A recording appears on an album entitled *The Great British Dance Bands Play George Gershwin 1920-1928* (World Records SH 451). The only recent recording of "Virginia" is by Anthony Perkins, Bobby Short and Elaine Stritch in *Ben Bagley's George Gershwin Revisited* (Painted Smiles PS- 1357).

90. RHAPSODY IN BLUE

For Jazz Band and Orchestra

Key: B-flat

Introduced by: George Gershwin, piano, and Paul Whiteman with his Palais Royal Orchestra on February 12, 1924 at Aeolian Hall in New York City.

Lore: Paul Whiteman, who, in 1922, had conducted the lone performance of Gershwin's one-act opera *Blue Monday*, asked the composer to write a jazz piece for orchestra for an upcoming concert. The commission was a haphazard one, offered and accepted very informally and without any specific date or venue in mind. Toward the end of 1923, however, Whiteman hurriedly made plans for his jazz concert

80

so as not to be beaten to the punch by Vincent Lopez, another bandleader who wanted to be the first to present a jazz program in a highbrow setting.

It was while playing pool on Broadway at 52nd Street that Gershwin was shown, by Ira, a report in the January 4, 1924 New York *Tribune* saying that he was at work on a jazz concerto, one that would be presented at a February 12 concert in Aeolian Hall.

Gershwin called Whiteman to protest, saying that there was too little time for him to complete such a project. But Whiteman was persuasive and, while on a train to Boston for the out-of-town tryout of *Sweet Little Devil*, Gershwin began thinking about the piece. "There had been so much chatter about the limitations of jazz," he later wrote. "Jazz, they said, had to be in strict time. It had to cling to dance rhythms. I resolved...to kill that misconception with one sturdy blow."

So, on January 7, he began composing. According to Ira, he started by going to his notebook and choosing an already-written theme (the one that opens the piece). For the next three weeks, he worked in his apartment on Amsterdam Avenue and 110th Street and by January 25, he had a two-piano sketch with some indications as to scoring. Ferde Grofe, who was Whiteman's arranger, quickly orchestrated the piece from the composer's manuscript.

Ira had suggested that a slow melody be included in the piece, indicating to George that there was a theme in one of his notebooks that might be appropriate. That theme then became the heart of the work. Ira was also responsible for giving the new piece its name. He had seen an exhibition of paintings by James McNeill Whistler and had noted the artist's fondess for putting the names of colors in this titles (*Nocturne in Black and Gold*, for example). Thus, Ira called the composition, which George had dubbed *American Rhapsody*, *Rhapsody in Blue*.

It was at a rehearsal and in jest that Ross Gorman, the clarinet player, turned the composer's opening seventeen-note run into the famous opening whoop. Gershwin liked the effect and asked Gorman to continue to play it that way.

The concert, called "An Experiment in Modern Music," was touted as an educational experience. But most of it was not very educational or modern. Featured compositions were Zez Confrey's "Kitten on the

Keys," Edward MacDowell's "To a Wild Rose," and Edward Elgar's *Pomp and Circumstance March No. 1.* For the audience, which included Victor Herbert, Jascha Heifetz, Sergei Rachmaninoff, Leopold Stokowksi, and Fritz Kreisler, it was a long and boring experience until the rhapsody commenced, Gershwin playing it with confidence and élan at the piano. During the playing of the piece, he extemporized some of the piano passages, as there had not been time to get them written down, and Whiteman was directed to wait for the composer's nod before re-striking up the band. Then, when it was over, there was a standing ovation for the rhapsody and for Gershwin, whose career as a world famous composer had just begun.

As published, the *Rhapsody in Blue* contains forty-eight fewer measures than were played at the Whiteman concert, Gershwin having done some after-the-fact editing. All but four of these bars were deleted from piano solos. Years later, when music critic Irving Kolodin asked him if he had ever thought of really revising the piece so as to strengthen some of its weak spots, Gershwin replied, "Yes, but people seemed to like it the way it was, so I left it that way."

Grofe reorchestrated the rhapsody in 1926, this time for full orchestra, and he did so again in 1942 for an even larger orchestra. It is the 1942 version that is now most commonly heard in the concert hall.

The published piano solo arrangement was the work of composer Vernon Duke, who was paid $100 by Gershwin's publisher for the job.

In its first decade, the *Rhapsody in Blue* earned the composer more than $250,000. In 1929 he was paid $50,000 so that it could be used in a movie, *The King of Jazz*, which starred Paul Whiteman. In May of 1930 he was paid $10,000 to play it for two weeks as part of a Roxy Theater stage show. As to the irony that Gershwin, the affluent songwriter, had managed to strike it rich with a highbrow composition, the composer told reporters, "That's more than Beethoven or Schubert ever got for a composition, eh?"

Analysis: The first part of the *Rhapsody in Blue* is dominated by the initial theme. It is introduced by an opening clarinet glissando that sounds like New York City's answer to the rebel yell. Two other themes are constantly at play during this portion of the piece: the first, theme two, is a jumpy idea that hammers at the blues scale in groups

82

of repeated notes (four to a group). It is first heard immediately after the initial playing of theme one. The other, theme three, is a simple variation on the familiar "Good evening, friends!" idea. It is the piano's opening statement.

For more than sixty years, music critics have praised the music of *Rhapsody* while complaining about its meandering structure. Actually, the piece seems architecturally uncertain only during the playing of themes four and five. The former is an exuberant idea played in the upper register and made up of hammered repeated notes. Although in stylistic unity with the rest of the work (as are all of the themes) and although it kicks in at just the right moment, it appears out of nowhere and then disappears, never to be heard from again. The same can be said for theme five, a slow, late night, all-alone-at-the-piano idea, played simply and mainly in the bass. While it does undergo some development, it is suddenly dropped in favor of the piano cadenza that leads to the broad E-major melody (andantino moderato).

With the appearance of this beautiful theme, however, the rhapsody returns to and stays on a sure structural footing. In fact, the metamorphosis of this melody from its initial grandeur to a propulsive and thrilling reincarnation, is an accomplishment in form that very few composers have ever achieved. Also interesting from a compositional point of view is the fact that the rhapsody concludes as it began—with statements of the initial three ideas. But here they appear in reverse order: theme three (as always, in a steady succession of different keys), theme two (played with rhythmic hosannas in the bass), and then theme one (trumpeted one last time before the two-bar coda, which is constructed from the notes of theme three).

In the *Rhapsody in Blue*, the essence of George Gershwin's musical personality finds expression. This essence lies, first of all, in harmonies which are highly personal and emotionally affecting in an unhistrionic, almost subliminal way. In that special Gershwin fashion, major melts into minor and vice versa, and accompanimental chords descend with smoky chromatics, adding depth and color to the melodies above.

The rhapsody is also the repository of a number of rhythmic moments that express something that was fundamental in Gershwin. Such moments are often little fills or interjections—small eruptions of

83

nervous energy. But they can also be extended statements: for instance, the brilliant piano interlude (leggiero) in which the pianist's hands take turns dribbling the same note while the right hand manages to play a succession of syncopated chords that seem to be imitating a locomotive gathering steam.

Also a fundamental expression of the composer's personality is the main slow melody, which takes the listener soaring up with it and which is, at once, noble and ennobling.

Recordings: Paul Whiteman recorded this with Gershwin at the piano on June 10, 1924—a recording featuring many of those who played in the original Aeolian Hall concert (Victor 55225-A, reissued on RCA AVM1-1740-B). Whiteman and Gershwin recorded it again on April 21, 1927, this time with an orchestra that included Jimmy and Tommy Dorsey and Bix Beiderbecke (Victor 35822, reissued in 1951 on RCA LPT-29 and in 1968 on RCA Victor LPV-555). The 1927 recording is slightly truncated, lasting some three minutes less than the usual twelve. In 1925, Gershwin made a solo piano roll recording of the piece (Duo-Art 68787, reissued on Archive of Piano Music X-914, on RCA Victor LSP-2058, and Distinguished Recordings 107). In 1976, this piano roll recording was used by Michael Tilson Thomas and the Columbia Jazz Band as the basis of a recreation of the original orchestration (Columbia M34205). On June 8, 1928, Gershwin recorded the andantino of the *Rhapsody in Blue* while in London (Columbia 50107-D).

Oscar Levant was a good friend of the composer and a notable interpreter of his works. In the spring of 1943 he recorded the rhapsody with Morton Gould conducting a studio orchestra that included Benny Goodman on clarinet (Armed Forces Radio Service 16). A later Levant recording, this time with the Philadelphia Orchestra conducted by Eugene Ormandy, was released on Columbia ML4026 and Columbia CL-700). A November 1, 1942 version by pianist Earl Wild, clarinetist Benny Goodman and conductor Arturo Toscanini is on Penzance 43.

Other versions (listed alphabetically by pianist):

Marden Abadi (piano solo—Orion 77265), Leonard Bernstein (pianist and conductor with the Columbia Symphony Orchestra—Co-

84

lumbia MS-6091), Leonard Bernstein (pianist and conductor with the New York Philharmonic—Columbia M31804), Sondra Bianco with the Pro-Musica Symphony Orchestra of Hamburg conducted by Hans-Jurgen Walther (MGM 3-E1), Misha Dichter and the Philharmonia Orchestra conducted by Neville Marriner (Philips 411123-1), Phillippe Entremont with the Philadelphia Orchestra conducted by Eugene Ormandy (Columbia MG-30073), Morton Gould (pianist and conductor with his own orchestra—RCA Victor LM-6033),

Werner Haas with the Monte Carlo Opera Orchestra conducted by Edo de Waart (Philips 6500118), Joyce Hatto with the Hamburg Pro Musica conducted by George Byrd (Forum F70 008), Byron Janus with Hugo Winterhalter and His Orchestra (RCA Victor LPM 1429), Julius Katchen with the London Symphony Orchestra conducted by Istvan Kertész (London CS 6633), Katia and Marielle Labecque (the two-piano version—Philips 9500917), Liberace with the Warner Bros. Symphony Orchestra conducted by George Liberace (Columbia CL800),

Eugene List with the Berlin Symphony Orchestra conducted by Samuel Adler (the original version for jazz band and piano—Turnabout TV-S 34457), Eugene List with the Eastman-Rochester Orchestra conducted by Howard Hanson (Mercury 90002), Jerome Lowenthal with the Utah Symphony Orchestra conducted by Maurice Abravanel (Vanguard VCS-1007), Teodor Moussov with the TVR Orchestra conducted by Vladigerov (MTR MCS-2153), Peter Nero with the Boston Pops conducted by Arthur Fiedler (RCA Victor LSC-2821),

Leonard Pennario with the Hollywood Bowl Orchestra conducted by Felix Slatkin (Seraphim S-60174), Andre Previn (pianist and conductor with the London Symphony Orchestra—Angel S-36810), Andre Previn with Andre Kostelanetz and His Orchestra (Columbia CL 1495), Reid Nibley with the Utah Symphony conducted by Maurice Abravanel (Westminster XW 18683), Jesús Sanroma with the Pittsburgh Symphony Orchestra conducted by William Steinberg (Everest 3067),

Alec Templeton with Andre Kostelanetz and His Orchestra (Columbia CL 795), Andre Watts (a version for solo piano—Columbia M34221), Alexis Weissenberg with the Berlin Philharmonic conducted by Seiji Ozawa (Angel D-38050), Earl Wild with the Boston Pops conducted by Arthur Fiedler (RCA Victor LSC-2367).

91. I NEED A GARDEN

Lyricist: B.G. DeSylva
Key: G
Time: Alla breve
Tempo: No tempo marking
Introduced by: Helen Hudson and the Elm City Four in *George White's Scandals of 1924* at the Apollo Theatre in New York City on June 30, 1924.

Analysis: In the verse ("I haven't any great objection") a girl tells a group of boys that she will only show affection in the "proper time and place." Hence, the title phrase. This verse has a tranquil thirty-two-bar tune that, in its last seven measures, takes a melancholy turn, having moved into B-minor. It ends with a couple of forlorn three-note bird calls. One oddity is the C-natural in the accompaniment at measure nine (on "where" in "where you go"). Because it arrives in the middle of a G-A-D chord progression, a C-sharp would seem to have been called for instead. In the refrain ("I need a garden") the climactic high note (on "dove" in "coo like a dove") also seems open to some second guessing. It is a high F-natural, arrived at via a sudden leap up out of the home key. And it sits there for a measure and a half, towering over the rest of the song. This note might be what critic Alec Wilder had in mind when he said that he could make sense of this song only if he considered it a joke.

Recordings: None

92. KONGO KATE

Lyricist: B.G. DeSylva
Key: A-minor (verse)
      C (refrain)
Time: 2/4
Tempo: Unmarked (verse)
       Moderato Assai (refrain)

Introduced by: Winnie Lightner and Tom Patricola in *George White's Scandals of 1924* at the Apollo Theatre in New York City on June 30, 1924.

Lore: According to Nanette Kutner, a composer-friend of Gershwin, "Kongo Kate" had just been deleted from the show when a devoted member of the cast rescued it. Kutner described the scene:

Its foolish jingle persistent, running through our brains; its fuel replenished by a little girl, sitting cross-legged on the apron of an empty stage, her Dutch bobbed head leaning above a ukelele, her fingers plucking at its strings...the girl, Hannah Williams...singing a discarded song because she couldn't help it.

For all that, it was Winnie Lightner and not Hannah Williams who introduced the song. Williams eventually left show business to marry Jack Dempsey.

The title is spelled "Kongo Kate" but the lyrics, for some reason, have "Congo Kate."

The piano-vocal arrangement is by Vernon Duke.

Analysis: In the verse of this comedy number ("In the land of Kongo") there is a steady pounding of A-minor chords meant, presumably, to represent ominous, insistent jungle drums. Half way through (on "dancer" in "There is not a dancer that this baby cannot beat") a few blue notes are injected for humor. The refrain ("They call her Congo Kate") presents a series of accented bump-and-grind three-note phrases.

Recordings: None

93. **NIGHT TIME IN ARABY**

Lyricist: B.G. DeSylva
Key: C
Time: Alla breve

Tempo: Moderato (introduction)
Moderato ma non troppo (verse)
Con expressione (refrain)
Introduced by: Richard Bold in *George White's Scandals of 1924* at the Apollo Theatre in New York City on June 30, 1924.

Lore: Vernon Duke wrote the piano-vocal arrangement.

Analysis: The singer pines for his beloved who is "Over the sea...calling to me.. in Araby," but the music attempts no Arabian sounds. In the sixteen-bar verse ("When the weary day is slowly fading") the melody is dependent on a series of fairly complex chords. This progression begins in the key of C, moves to E, and then comes back. The refrain ("Nighttime is falling in Araby") is a standard thirty-two-bar ballad, although it has a couple of unusual moments: the initial four-bar idea is repeated not in C but in distant D, and a harmonically evocative piano fill follows the "I can hear, sweet and clear" release.

Recordings: None

94. ROSE OF MADRID

Lyricist: B.G. DeSylva
Key: G-minor (verse)
E-flat (refrain)
Time: 3/4
Tempo: Tempo di Bolero
Introduced by: Richard Bold in *George White's Scandals of 1924* at the Apollo Theatre in New York City on June 30, 1924.

Analysis: This is an unusually adventurous song. Its introduction is a witty four-bar Latinesque vamp. Then comes a sixteen-bar verse ("Far off is Spain"), whose insistent, staccato bass Gs lie beneath conflicting treble harmonies (A, A-flat), making for a sensual but mocking sound. The refrain ("Rose of Madrid I adore you") is a cousin of sorts to "Lady of Spain" (a song written in 1931). But here there is wit in the earnestness. In the seventh bar (on "implore you"), a D-flat in the bass makes for an Iberian blues effect. Then comes a harmonically adventurous release ("Open your lattice"), a sudden jump to the far off key of B-major during the recapitulation (at "Speak of impassioned romances"), and a satisfying leap back to E-flat for the longish eight-bar coda (at "You know each sentence is true").

Recordings: Bobby Short sings this on *Ben Bagley's George Gershwin Revisited* (Painted Smiles PS-1357).

95. SOMEBODY LOVES ME

Lyricist: B.G. DeSylva and Ballard MacDonald
Key: E-minor (verse)
      G (refrain)
Time: Common (verse)
      Alla breve (refrain)
Tempo: Allegro Moderato
Introduced by: Winnie Lightner and Tom Patricola in *George White's Scandals of 1924* at the Apollo Theatre in New York City on June 30, 1924.

Lore: In his autobiography, *Passport to Paris*, Vernon Duke recalled how, as a young man, he desperately needed to earn enough money for a trip to Europe (pianist Artur Rubenstein had promised to play Duke's piano concerto in Paris that summer). Duke asked Gershwin if there were not some task he could perform to earn the money and Gershwin, rushing to complete the new edition of the *Scandals*, was willing to let him ghostwrite a short ragtime ballet sequence for $100. In addition, he let Duke make the piano-vocal arrangements for several songs from the show, including "Somebody Loves Me." Duke was especially proud of his Gershwinesque fill-ins in the arrangement of this song. For this and the other arrangements for the show he received an additional $120.

In September of 1932, Gershwin published his own arrangement of "Somebody Love Me" It appeared, along with the solo piano settings of seventeen other songs, in *George Gershwin's Songbook*.

In 1952 this song provided the title for and was the featured number in a movie starring Betty Hutton.

Analysis: "Somebody Loves Me" has the first modern Gershwin verse ("When this world began"): gentle, tranquil, making its point through the juxtaposition of major and minor modes. Its initial eight bars in E-minor are answered by a second eight in G—a response that has different pitches and different harmonies but the same metrics—it is the brighter side of the coin. The refrain has a blue note (the "who" in "I wonder who") that is not artificial or heavy-handed. It seems inevitable. In the twelfth bar, on the slightly awkward line "who can she be worries me," the music itself becomes worried, slipping into B-minor. Then it modulates into A-minor for a release ("for every girl who passes me") that, although harmonically dark, has a reassuring beat and the same singability as the beginning of the refrain. Vernon Duke's piano-vocal arrangement takes advantage of the many held notes to insert Gershwinesque piano breaks. These are bits of chromatic counterpoint and they come off especially well in and around the release.

Recordings: Tom Patricola and Isabelle Patricola (she wasn't in the show) recorded this in August of 1924 (Vocalion 14866). Other 1924 recordings were by Ben Bernie (Vocalion 14854), the California Ramblers (Pathe Actuelle 036121), Johnny Campbell's Orchestra (New Flexo 302), The Columbians (Columbia 177-D), Nathan Glantz (Banner 1397 and a second version on Edison 51418), Marion Harris (Brunswick 2539), Arthur Lange (Cameo 587), The Lanin Orchestra (Okeh 40170), Ray Miller and His Orchestra (Brunswick 2669), the Pennsylvania Syncopators/Emerson Dance Orchestra (Emerson 10785), Aileen Stanley (Victor 19454), and Paul Whiteman (Victor 19414).

"Somebody Loves Me" has maintained its popularity with recording artists over the years. For example, there were versions in 1929 by Henry Lange and His Baker Hotel Orchestra (Brunswick 4478); in 1930 by Fletcher Henderson (Columbia 2329-D); in 1934 by Adrian

Rollini and His Orchestra (with Benny Goodman—Decca 359); in 1935 by Chick Bullock (with Joe Venuti—Melotone M-13434); in 1936 by Cliff Edwards (Decca 1166), Benny Goodman and His Orchestra (Victor 25497), and Frankie Trumbauer and His Orchestra (with Jack Teagarden and Artie Shaw—Brunswick 7665); in 1937 by Boots and His Buddies (recorded under the title "The Somebody"—Bluebird 7269), Benny Carter (Decca F-42128), Milt Herth (Decca 1445), Sammy Kaye (Vocalion/Okeh 3681), and Eddie South (Swing 31); in 1939 by Eddie Condon (Decca 23430), Bing Crosby (accompanied by Victor Young and His Orchestra—Decca 2874), and Jan Garber (Vocalion 5319); in 1940 by Dinah Shore (Bluebird B-10978); in 1941 by Tommy Dorsey and His Orchestra (Victor 27690); in 1942 by Henry Levine and Linda Keene (Victor 27831); in 1945 by Erroll Garner (Savoy 571) and George Wettling (Key 1318); in 1947 by Bill Harris (Dial 1009); in 1950 by Bud Powell (Roost 509); in 1951 by the Dave Brubeck Quartet (Fantasy 517); in 1952 by Frances Wayne and Neal Hefti (Coral 60840); in 1954 by Roy Eldridge (with Oscar Peterson—Mercury 89110); in 1963 by the Benny Goodman Quartet (Victor LPM2698).

Other versions have been released by Ruby Braff and the George Barnes Quintet (Concord Jazz 5), Chris Conner (Atlantic 2-601), Bob Cooper (Contemporary Records OJC-161), Dizzy Gillespie (Inner City 7010), Corky Hale (Crescendo 9035), Hampton Hawes (Contemporary Records 3523), Woody Herman (V-Disk 411), Earl Hines (Classic Jazz 31), Wayne King (Ranwood 7036), Enoch Light and the Charleston City All Stars (MCA 2-4175), Guy Lombardo (Ranwood 8216), Julia Migenes-Johnson (Victor ARL1-5323), Red Norvo (Fantasy 24108), Don Shirley (Audio Fidelity 5897), and Art Tatum (Crescendo 9025, Pablo 2310875, and Pablo 2310731).

96. TUNE IN (TO STATION J.O.Y.)

Lyricist: B.G. DeSylva
Key: C (verse)
      F (refrain)
Time: Alla breve

Tempo: Moderato

Introduced by: Winnie Lightner in *George White's Scandals of 1924* at the Apollo Theatre in New York City on June 30, 1924.

Lore: The piano-vocal arrangement is by Vernon Duke.

Analysis: In the piano introduction Duke quotes two bars from the slow theme of *Rhapsody in Blue*. Then comes a twenty-bar verse ("Gloomy Guses I've a word to tell you"), whose tune takes a sinuous and modal journey from C major to F major. The refrain ("Tune in—tune in to J.O.Y.") begins with a series of staccato dit-dits, like a telegraph signal. Then comes a precipitous, syncopated fall from C to D—the seventh leap that, per early Gershwin biographer Isaac Goldberg, was the song's most characteristic feature. Six years later, Gershwin would take the same leap and syncopate it in the same way in "Soon."

The lyric fails to tell us what is so joyful about this particular radio station. It has a dashed-off quality, as if written in a hurry, like an autograph.

Recordings: None

97. YEAR AFTER YEAR

Lyricist: B.G. DeSylva
Key: E-flat
Time: Alla breve
Tempo: Con expressione
Introduced by: Richard Bold and Helen Hudson in *George White's Scandals of 1924* at the Apollo Theatre in New York City on June 30, 1924.

Lore: The piano-vocal arrangement is by Vernon Duke.

Analysis: This is a duet with a single melody line in which a husband and wife, after some years together, reaffirm their love for one another with lines such as "Cares are ever lighter, Love is burning brighter." The twenty-four-bar verse ("Looking backward I confess") and thirty-two bar ABAC refrain ("Year after year") are both sentimental ballads. The former makes its way from E-flat to G-minor and then back again, stopping along the way for a couple of delicate dissonances and a churchy plagal cadence. The melody of the latter is basically a noodling between two pairs of notes: G and F to begin with and C and B-flat a little later on. In Duke's arrangement this tune is offset by a line of Gershwinesque chromatic thirds.

Recordings: None

98. PRIMROSE OPENING CHORUS

Lyricist: Desmond Carter
Key: G
Time: 2/4, 6/8
Tempo: Allegro giocoso
Introduced by: The chorus in *Primrose* at the Winter Garden Theater in London on September 11, 1924.

Lore: *Primrose* was the second musical written by Gershwin expressly for the London stage and it was a much greater success than his first, *The Rainbow*, composed the year before, in 1923. The production was tailor-made for English audiences, employing the services of a popular English comedian, Leslie Henson, and a text that continually made references to British history and current events. For his part, Gershwin, in trying to write in the British style, achieved some of the purposefulness that he had invested in the *Rhapsody in Blue*—a heightened sense of self that would be present in nearly all of his highbrow works. Here, however, the Americanisms and jazzisms are toned down in favor of a more sedate British sensibility.

Because of the show's success, its piano-vocal score was published in all but its entirety (missing, but published separately, was "That New-Fangled Mother of Mine"). It was the first of five such publications for the composer (the others were the 1930 version of *Strike Up the Band*, the 1930 show *Girl Crazy*, the 1931 show *Of Thee I Sing*, and the 1935 opera *Porgy and Bess*). It was in this score that Gershwin for the second time (*Blue Monday* was the first) tried his hand at writing entire musical scenes. *Primrose* also marks his first published choral writing (there were no choral scenes in *Blue Monday*) and his first professional attempt at orchestration. Although we do not know which numbers he orchestrated, and although these orchestrations were not themselves published, we do know from various sources (Ira Gershwin among them) that Gershwin was responsible for the instrumentation of two or three of the show's selections.

Analysis: Act One begins with a fifty-six-bar opening chorus. It can be divided into the following sections:

1. A sixteen-bar instrumental fanfare in 2/4. It begins with tremulos in the treble and a four-note motive in the bass that is repeated seven times. It is a distant cousin to the "Introduction" to *Porgy and Bess*. After the seventh repetition there are some Gershwinian chromatics—triads moving dissonantly against a melody line in contrary motion.
2. An untitled refrain in which the chorus sings about having left city life for the country. The affecting melody ("Leaving town while we may"), harmonized with diminished and augmented chords, has a melancholy feel. It will be repeated in several different spots in the show—always with different lyrics and always without a title.
3. A pastoral eight-bar instrumental coda. It is in a new meter (6/8) and is marked "sempre dim." It creates an anticipatory hush.

Recordings: The original cast recorded some selections from *Primrose* (on English Columbia 9001 to 9007, reissued on Monmouth-Evergreen MES-7071), but the opening chorus was not among them. This music has never been recorded.

99. TILL I MEET SOMEONE LIKE YOU

Lyricist: Desmond Carter
Key: E-flat
Time: 3/4
Tempo: Tempo di Valse
Introduced by: Claude Hulbert and Vera Lennox in *Primrose* at the Winter Garden Theatre in London on September 11, 1924.

Analysis: In the jocular lyric the two romantic leads get in some sly double-entendres as they compliment one another on their prowess at golf and tennis ("I've never met another little girl quite like you, one with your instinct for following through," "I've never met another little boy who would play Sunday, Monday, Tuesday, every day").

The verse and refrain are both in waltz tempo. The former ("I can't stand women who foozle") is thirty-two bars long with a release ("Someone who's got") in the relative minor (G-minor). In it, Gershwin achieves a luftpause effect by bringing the tune to a rest on and off the beat. The refrain ("I've never met another"), also thirty-two bars long, is most notable for its beautiful release, wherein lovely harmonies are created by passing tones in and around F-minor and E-flat minor.

Recordings: An instrumental version was recorded in 1924 by the Winter Garden Theatre Orchestra (English Columbia 9006).

100. ISN'T IT WONDERFUL

Lyricist: Ira Gershwin and Desmond Carter
Key: E-flat
Time: Common
Tempo: Moderato
Introduced by: Margery Hicklin in *Primrose* at the Winter Garden Theatre in London on September 11, 1924.

Lore: This music first appeared in Gershwin's notebook on September 21,1921.

95

Analysis: "Isn't It Wonderful" is a carefully written ballad (a single melody duet for soprano and male chorus) with a tuneful, earnest verse ("Any man would appeal") and a refrain ("Isn't it wonderful!") that is distinguished by a graceful melody, a supporting series of finely jeweled and slightly dissonant suspensions, and an unusual structure. Its twenty-four bars consist of the initial four-bar idea, an eight-bar development section (at "The stormy weather has passed"), a repetition of the first four bars, and then a second and distinct eight-bar development section (at "That's what he'll have to say to me").

Recordings: An instrumental version was recorded by the Winter Garden Theatre Orchestra in 1924 (English Columbia 9006). Sixty years later another instrumental version was recorded, this one by pianist Kevin Cole as part of a *Primrose* medley (Fanfare DFL 7007).

101. THIS IS THE LIFE FOR A MAN

Lyricist: Desmond Carter
Key: E-minor
Time: 6/8
Tempo: Con spirito
Introduced by: Percy Heming in *Primrose* at the Winter Garden
   Theatre in London on September 11, 1924.

Lore: "This is the Life For a Man" was published in the *Primrose* piano-vocal score and separately as well.

Analysis: This is a paean to country living and, perhaps, to celibacy as well ("Hill and meadow and scented hay; better them no one can. Leave the women to go their way, I'll have done with them today, oh, this is the place for a man"). The melody is dark and emphatic; its 6/8 beat and minor key make it sound a bit like a pirate song. There is no verse, only a twenty-bar refrain ("Keep your cities and keep your towns") that is all but through-composed (bars one and two are repeated in the ninth and tenth measures). The piano accompaniment punctuates but does not always duplicate the melody line, making for a recitativo effect. Harmonically, there are several distinctive moments. In bars five through seven (on "The moors") an E pedal point supports a Dm-E-Cm-B-flat diminished-C chord progression to create a highly attractive *mysterioso* sort of sound. In bars eleven and twelve (on "Better them no one can") there is a powerful resolution in the key of C. And five bars later (at "this is the place for a man") there is a distinctive A-major to E-minor cadence. On a second run through, the song ends in E-major.

Recordings: Percy Heming of the original cast recorded this in 1924 under the title "The Countryside" (English Columbia 9007, reissued on Monmouth-Evergreen MES 7071).

102. WHEN TOBY IS OUT OF TOWN

Lyricist: Desmond Carter
Key: E-flat
Time: 6/8
Tempo: Allegro con brio
Introduced by: Leslie Henson in *Primrose* at the Winter Garden Theatre in London on September 11, 1924.

Analysis: In *Primrose*, a character named Toby Mopham is trying to escape the romantic intentions of a beautician called Pinkie Peach. Mopham is obviously a first-rate egomaniac. In this song he claims that when he is away from London that city stops functioning: no one eats, the subways stop running and "Mayfair goes into mourning with the blinds all drawn down."

Gershwin's music here has the same meter as "This is the Life For a Man" but none of its dark hues. The verse ("Though I'm anxious not to go") is a bouncy thirty-two bar tune whose appeal is clinched by a rising inner voice in the accompaniment. In the second bar this voice is given a B-natural which, played against the B-flat in the vocal line on "not" in the above-mentioned phrase creates the hook. The refrain ("London is a sorrowful place") is in the same spirit. It is an ingenuous, happy 6/8 number that, in the release ("Mayfair"), takes a

97

devil-may-care leap up, then comes to a dead halt for four beats.

Recordings: Original cast member Leslie Henson recorded this in 1924 (English Columbia 9001, reissued on Monmouth-Evergreen MES 7071).

103. SOME FAR AWAY SOMEONE

Lyricist: Ira Gershwin and B.G. DeSylva
Key: E-flat
Time: Common
Tempo: Moderato (verse)
       Slow with expression (refrain)
Introduced by: Percy Heming and Margery Hicklin in *Primrose* at the Winter Garden Theatre in London on September 11, 1924.

Lore: "Some Far Away Someone" was published in the *Primrose* score and separately as well.

Analysis: Musically, this is almost exactly the same as "At Half Past Seven" (a song from *Nifties of 1923*). The differences are a longer first note in the twenty-eighth bar of this refrain (on "who" in "who will soon be nearer to me") and a single piano ending rather than two. The lyric for "Some Far Away Someone" is written as a duet and it is probably more appropriate to the sweet, romantic nature of the tune than was the somewhat enigmatic lyric of "At Half Past Seven."

Recordings: Percy Heming and Margery Hicklin of the original cast recorded this in 1924 (English Columbia 9005, reissued on Monmouth-Evergreen MES 7071). The Winter Garden Theatre Orchestra, also from the original production, recorded their version as well (English Columbia 9006).

104. THE MOPHAMS

Lyricist: Desmond Carter
Key: F
Time: 2/4
Tempo: Allegretto
Introduced by: Leslie Henson, Heather Thatcher, and Thomas Webuelin in *Primrose* at the Winter Garden Theatre in London on September 11, 1924.

Lore: For a 1960 revival of the 1926 Gershwin show *Oh, Kay!* P.G. Wodehouse rewrote the lyrics to this song, retitling it "The Pophams."

Analysis: This pleasant up-tempo patter song is about what makes the blue-blooded Mopham family tick ("Look on the roll of heroes, look on the floor at Ciro's, you'll always find a Mopham there"). The introduction, which begins in a false key (D-flat), is followed by a thirty-two-bar verse ("You know that I'm descended") that, despite its staccato patter style, has an engaging tunefulness. In its release ("Even I shall be affected") there is a variation on the main idea, presented in a new key (A). The refrain ("A Mopham is always a Mopham") is also thirty-two bars long. Its hook comes in the sixth bar when the syllable "Mo" in "Mopham" is sung on an E that hovers high above a G9 chord. This piece is through-composed and AA¹BC in form.

Recordings: A recording by Leslie Henson, Heather Thatcher, and Thomas Weguelin was released in 1924 on English Columbia 9003 and reissued on Monmouth-Evergreen MES 7071.

105. PRIMROSE FINALE - ACT I

Lyricist: Ira Gershwin and Desmond Carter
Key: Various
Time: Various

Tempo: Various

Introduced by: Percy Heming, Margery Hicklin, Leslie Henson, and Heather Thatcher in *Primrose* at the Winter Garden Theatre in London on September 11, 1924.

Analysis: Act I of *Primrose* ends with a 141-bar finale. Much of it consists of recapitulated themes, although there is some new material as well. It can be broken down into the following sections:

1.   An eight-bar introduction that is on the wild and dissonant side—it seems to have wandered over from *The Sorcerer's Apprentice*.
2.   A reprise of the lovely but untitled tune ("leaving town while we may") that began Act I's opening chorus. Its lyric here ("can we do anything?") is sung by the chorus as an expression of concern over a character named Joan who has fainted.
3.   A fourteen-measure instrumental transition consisting of an agitated two-bar chord progression that seems to be waiting for the first movement of the *Concerto in F*, two bars of "Isn't it Wonderful" and eight bars of a more tranquil and melodic new idea in 6/8 time.
4.   Eight measures of music marked Allegro in which Toby tells Joan, "I saved your life, I saved your life." After she answers recitativo-style, saying "What does it mean?," we get another instrumental reference to "Isn't it Wonderful"—but now this music is ominous, not lyrical. It is an accompaniment to spoken dialogue but, lacking the libretto, we cannot be certain what this dark rumbling means.
5.   Another instrumental undercurrent to spoken dialogue. It begins in march tempo (the bass pounds out Cs in octaves while insistent discords sound above). Then comes a succession of chords (tritones in the left hand, fourths in the right) that move down the keyboard quickly and in triplets.
6.   An instrumental reprise of "Isn't It Wonderful."
7.   A vocal reprise of "Isn't It Wonderful" ending with an instrumental finish marked Grandioso.

Recordings: None.

106. PRIMROSE ACT II OPENING CHORUS/ROSES OF FRANCE

Lyricist: Desmond Carter
Key: E, E-minor
Time: Various
Tempo: Maestoso, Tempo Di Valse, Pesante
Introduced by: Esme de Vayne and Guy Saunders in *Primrose* at the Winter Garden Theatre in London on September 11, 1924.

Analysis: This scene, which is 153 measures long, contains some of the finest music in the *Primrose* score. Its lyric speaks of fleeting moments of summertime happiness at a French seaside resort. It can be divided into the following musical sections:

1. Act I concluded with an instrumental summation of "Isn't It Wonderful" marked Grandioso. Act II begins with the same thing, although this time it is marked Maestoso and this time it is the beginning of a twenty-one-bar introduction, most of it in waltz time.
2. A verseless and untitled waltz which has been referred to by Gershwin biographers as "Roses of France." It is sung by a flower-seller to the guests at a swank dinner dance. The main melody here, in E, is wistful, full of longing, and lovely ("Look at my roses, sweet roses of France"). When this melody repeats, Gershwin peremptorily puts one of its phrases not in E but in E-flat (at "Take them while you have the chance"). From here he moves enharmonically into a C-sharp minor release ("Sweet scented blossoms to perfume your rooms") that swirls ever higher to complex, Ravelian harmony.
3. An instrumental tune in E-minor. Marked Pesante, it is in alla breve time and it has a crying out, Hebraic quality.
4. Now the chorus sings the Hebraic tune wordlessly (on "ah") in counterpoint to a sinewy melody, made up mostly of half notes, that is sung by a character called Turk. The words here are in an ambiguous lingo that seems to be at least partly in French ("Cafe Bwana Cafe noir m'zuri sana").
5. A forte reprise of the "Roses of France" waltz, sung by the

flower-seller and the chorus.

Recordings: The first recording of "Roses of France" appeared in 1985 on an album entitled *The Unknown George Gershwin.* Pianist Kevin Cole played it therein as part of a *Primrose* medley (Fanfare DFL 7007).

107. FOUR LITTLE SIRENS

> *Lyricist:* Ira Gershwin
> *Key:* A
> *Time:* 2/4
> *Tempo:* Allegretto e giocoso
> *Introduced by:* The ensemble in *Primrose* at the Winter Garden Theatre in London on September 11, 1924.

Lore: This is a revision of "The Sirens," a song used in the 1921 production *A Dangerous Maid* but not published. According to Isaac Goldberg, it pays "frank homage" to "The Three Little Maids" from *The Mikado.* Later Gershwin biographers, Edward Jablonski and Lawrence D. Stewart, assert that in it Ira mixed *The Mikado* with the Rhine maidens.

Analysis: The music is written for a four-part female chorus (Gershwin's first published choral writing), divided into sopranos and contraltos. They are singing, as did the Sirens of Greek mythology, to ensnare menfolk. They are, they say, "grace personified/our forms are bonified." As a production number, this is structurally much more complex than a simple show tune. Of the composer's published works, it is most comparable to "In the Swim," a production number from the 1927 show *Funny Face.* The form here is as follows:

1. A cheerful, somewhat dainty fifteen-bar instrumental introduction.
2. A four-bar choral introduction in which the Sirens hum above alternating major and minor chords: it has a bluesy quasi-spiritual feel.

102

3.　A twenty-two-bar main refrain ("Four little Sirens we"). It is a guileless tune above deft, consonant harmony.
4.　A six-bar choral addendum in E ("It's bad to pun, it isn't being done").
5.　A second instrumental theme, this one characterized by a series of descending, imitative phrases.
6.　A graceful, waltz-like sixteen-bar section in E ("if you should come along the beach").
7.　A lively twenty-eight-bar section in E ("For we are beautiful") which pauses briefly in the key of C-sharp (at "So you who linger on the shore").
8.　A reprise of section three ("Four little Sirens we"). This time the singing is more emphatic, rising to a climactic high note.
9.　A repeat of the instrumental introduction, this time with a more emphatic ending.

Recordings: None.

108. **BERKELEY SQUARE AND KEW**

Lyricist: Desmond Carter
Key: E-flat
Time: 2/4
Tempo: Allegretto
Introduced by: Claude Hulbert and Margery Hicklin in *Primrose* at the Winter Garden Theatre in London on September 11, 1924.

Lore: In a July 8, 1924 letter to his friends the Paleys, George made reference to this song, saying that he had not been "in London more than a week when I wrote a number called 'I'll have a house in Berkeley Square, I'll have a cottage at Kew' which Alex [producer Alex Aarons] says is more English than any tune Paul Reubens ever wrote. Desmond Carter wrote the lyric. He is a promising young lyricist."

Analysis: In this song a man and woman discuss their prospective engagement but she is only flirting with him to make her real inamorato jealous, while he has proposed to her only to please his father. Thus, the houses in Berkeley Square and in Kew are to be separate residences. There is a breezy twenty-four-bar verse ("Life with you would bore me") in which the verbal comedy is underscored by wrongish notes (an E-natural in a B-flat dominant seventh chord at "bore me," for instance). This verse ends with the unsettling sounds of two fairly dissonant chords: an A7-ninth with a diminished fifth followed by an A-flat ninth with a diminished fifth. The bubbly refrain ("I'll have a house in Berkeley Square") is somewhat unusual in form. It is thirty-eight bars long and ABCAD—the final section being a lighthearted instrumental dance.

Recordings: Claude Hulbert and Margery Hicklin recorded this in 1924 (English Columbia 9004, reissued on Monmouth-Evergreen MES 7071). It was also recorded by the Winter Garden Theatre Orchestra (English Columbia 9006).

109. WAIT A BIT, SUSIE

Lyricist: Ira Gershwin and Desmond Carter
Key: E-flat
Time: Alla breve
Tempo: Moderato
Introduced by: Margery Hicklin and Percy Heming in *Primrose*
at the Winter Garden Theatre in London on September 11, 1924.

Lore: In 1928 a new lyric was set to this tune for the stage production *Rosalie* but the resulting song, "Beautiful Gypsy," was, although published, dropped from the show. "Wait a Bit, Susie" saw publication in the *Primrose* piano-vocal score and it was also published separately as a popular song.

Analysis: In this song, Susie is advised by her mother to forswear fretting about the man she cannot have, and to wait instead for the right one who will eventually come along. The verse ("Susie wasn't mad about/A dozen men or so") is a melancholy twenty-bar tune, one constructed with imitative phrases. Motive development also plays a part in the refrain ("Wait a bit, Susie")—a bright and catchy piece in E-flat that, instead of a release, has an eight-bar development section in G ("He doesn't say much"). The writing is artful and very self-aware. For instance, the above-mentioned modulation into G is hinted at beforehand in a two-bar piano fill (on "loves you").

Recordings: Percy Heming recorded this in 1924 (English Columbia 9007, reissued on Monmouth-Evergreen MES 7071), as did the Winter Garden Theatre Orchestra (English Columbia 9006). Another version is by a pianist named Renara (Liberty music Shop B.D. 339).

110. NAUGHTY BABY

Lyricist: Ira Gershwin and Desmond Carter
Key: G
Time: Alla breve
Tempo: Moderato
Introduced by: Margery Hicklin in *Primrose* at the Winter Garden Theatre in London on September 11, 1924.

Analysis: The title phrase is aggressively and somewhat boastfully applied by the female singer to herself. The piano introduction adds jazz sounds to the syncopated idea that will be heard in the refrain, and then it concludes with an almost atonal series of chords. The lyric of the verse ("If you want a girl who's sentimental") mocks sentiment to a sixteen-bar melody that is itself highly sentimental. The refrain ("Naughty baby") is in several ways similar to that of "Fascinating Rhythm"—a number that Gershwin was first jotting down at about this time. Like "Fascinating Rhythm," "Naughty Baby" plays two rhythms against one another. In this case, a three-note melody in 6/8 is pitted against a 4/4 accompaniment. The resemblance to "Fasci-

105

nating Rhythm" continues in the release (at "If you're wanting a beginner"), which is a highly melodic change of pace. It is also interesting to note that the *Primrose* vocal score contains a reprise of this song in which a male chorus, accompanying the singer, is given a chromatic countermelody.

Recordings: Margery Hicklin recorded this in 1924 (English Columbia 9004, reissued on Monmouth-Evergreen MES 7071), as did the Winter Garden Theatre Orchestra (English Columbia 9006).

111. PRIMROSE FINALE-ACT II

Lyricist: Desmond Carter
Key: Various
Time: Various
Tempo: Various
Introduced by: Claude Hulbert, Vera Lennox, Leslie Henson, Percy Heming, and Margery Hicklin in *Primrose* at the Winter Garden Theatre in London on September 11, 1924.

Analysis: The Act II finale can be broken down into the following musical sections:

1. A reprise of "Till I Meet Someone Like You."
2. A reprise of the melody that appeared in the opening chorus of Act I as "Leaving town while we may" and then in the finale to that act as "Can we do anything?" Here, the words are "For a day and a night life is gay, life is bright."
3. A song called "It is the Fourteenth of July." Introduced by an eight-bar instrumental fanfare, this is a thirty-two-bar anthem in A-major, one based on emphatic repeated notes. At this point in the show, the action is taking place in a French hotel on Bastille Day.
4. One of the *Primrose* characters, Toby Mopham, has assumed the guise of a spiritualist named Professor Pschovelesky and here, in a forty-bar number, he sings his own praises. The music begins in F-sharp minor with an oom-pah accompaniment, then proceeds through

a recitative-style section in which the composer passes through the keys of C-sharp minor and A-minor, ending up in A-major for a sunny, affirmative conclusion (at "Oh! There never was a man like me").

5. A reprise of "Boy Wanted." It is mainly instrumental, although the chorus enters for eight bars, singing "Girl wanted!"

6. A twenty-six-bar instrumental interlude in D. It employs a droning beat and a modal, Arabian-style melody to create a "take me to the Casbah" atmosphere.

7. Reprises of "Roses of France," "Naughty Baby," "Some Far Away Someone," and "It is the Fourteenth of July."

Recordings: The "Interlude" (section 6) has been recorded as part of a *Primrose* medley by pianist Kevin Cole (Fanfare DFL 7007).

112. PRIMROSE BALLET

Instrumental

Key: A
Time: 4/4
Tempo: Moderato
Introduced by: The Winter Garden Theatre Orchestra in *Primrose* at the Winter Garden Theatre in London on September 11, 1924.

Analysis: This 110-bar composition—Gershwin's third published instrumental work (after *Rialto Ripples* and *Rhapsody in Blue*)—has an airy, Mendelssohnian feel.

The construction is as follows:

1. An ethereal four-bar idea in A-major, played high in the treble.

2. A succession of ascending and crescendoing chords that foreshadows "Liza"—a song that would come in 1929.

3. A return of section one, this time in C.

4. A skittering idea in A-major. It runs up the pentatonic scale with occasional repeated notes in a way that links it to the opening bassoon

melody of the *Concerto in F.*

5.   A sixteen-bar melody in C-sharp minor that glides gracefully down from high to low treble.   The harmony here is complex and chromatic.

6.   A repetition of section three.

7.   A sixteen-bar section in F.   It contrasts low sustained notes with playful, scampering runs.   Arpeggiated chords up high help maintain the overall ethereality of the piece.

8.   An eight-bar crescendo made from a progression of full, accented chords.   Here too the key is F.

9.   A second repetition of section three.

10.   A repetition of section one.

11.   A repetition of section two.

12.   A four-bar coda made from section three.

Recordings: The first recording of this ballet was made in 1924 by the Winter Garden Theatre Orchestra (English Columbia 9005, reissued on Monmouth-Evergreen MES 7071).   Recently, pianist Kevin Cole recorded a portion of it as part of a *Primrose* medley (Fanfare DFL 7007) and pianist Leonard Pennario released a complete version (Angel DS-37359).

113. I MAKE HAY WHEN THE MOON SHINES

> *Lyricist:* Desmond Carter
> *Key:* F
> *Time:* 2/4
> *Tempo:* Allegro non troppo
> *Introduced by:* Heather Thatcher in *Primrose* at the Winter Garden Theatre in London on September 11, 1924.

Analysis: This cheerful up-tempo song praises night over day with lines such as "I don't want a place in the sun" and "day it's dull and flat time/So I sleep through that time."   In the twenty-four-bar verse, a light-hearted simplicity is interrupted toward the end by minor key and dissonant sounds (at "You will ever see").   The refrain ("I make hay"), which is also up-tempo, has an ingratiating series of musical surprises. One is the use of a D-major scale (with an E-flat thrown in) as pick up notes leading into the opening C7 harmony. Another, in bar two (on "hay"), is the use of a Cm7 chord with a diminished fifth—a pinch of musical spice. The length here is thirty-two bars, the form ABAC.

Recordings: In 1924 Heather Thatcher and a male chorus recorded this—the men whistling one round (English Columbia 9003, reissued on Monmouth-Evergreen MES 7071). There was also, that year, a version by the Winter Garden Theatre Orchestra (English Columbia 9006).

114. BEAU BRUMMEL

Lyricist: Desmond Carter
Key: A-flat
Time: Common
Tempo: Marziale
Introduced by: Percy Heming in *Primrose* at the Winter Garden Theatre in London on September 11, 1924.

Analysis: This is a straightforward processional march with big stately chords. There is no verse. The refrain is sixteen bars long and AABA[1] in form, the B section being music in the same vein, but in C-minor. The writing is for two parts: the main line is for the solo singer, who refers to himself as Brummel (there is no reference to the historical Beau Brummell—and the song, in title and lyric, mispells his name) and the other consists of amen-style fills and interjections by the chorus. A sample from the lyric: "If a man can love and a man can laugh then a man is a man indeed/There are lips to kiss, there are lips to quaff; is there more that a man can need?"

Recordings: None.

115. THAT NEW-FANGLED MOTHER OF MINE

Lyricist: Desmond Carter
Key: E-flat
Time: 2/4
Tempo: Moderato
Introduced by: Leslie Henson in *Primrose* at the Winter Garden Theatre in London on September 11, 1924.

Lore: This song was added to the show for comedian Henson. It was not published in the complete piano-vocal score, but was printed separately.

Analysis: This is a comedy number in which the singer complains that his mother, instead of being a docile, silver-haired stay-at-home, is a henna-made blonde who goes in for exhibition dancing and polo. The twenty-bar verse ("Lots of people's mothers") manages to be both melodic and patter-like. It switches to E-flat minor half way through and at that point (on "knitting") Gershwin injects into the accompaniment a C-flat that is witty in its mournfulness. The thirty-two-bar ABA¹C refrain ("That new-fangled Mother of mine") is a catchy tune with a couple of surprise key changes: into G for the release ("While others sit at home") and then into G-flat during the return of the main idea.

Recordings: In 1924 Leslie Henson recorded this on English Columbia 9001 (reissued on Monmouth-Evergreen MES 7071) and the Winter Garden Theatre Orchestra recorded it at the same time on English Columbia 9006. There is a more recent version by Ronny Whyte and Travis Hudson (Monmouth-Evergreen MES 7061).

116. FASCINATING RHYTHM

Lyricist: Ira Gershwin
Key: E-flat
Time: Common (verse)
   Alla breve (refrain)

Tempo: Moderato

Introduced by: Fred Astaire, Adele Astaire, and Cliff Edwards ("Ukelele Ike") in *Lady, Be Good!* at the Liberty Theatre in New York City on December 1, 1924.

Lore: In May of 1923 Bill Daly and Joe Meyer set an Ira Gershwin lyric, "Little rhythm—go 'way," to music. The next year that line was the source of Ira's "Fascinating Rhythm" idea. George Gershwin had foreshadowed the music for "Fascinating Rhythm" in "Some Wonderful Sort of Someone," written six years earlier—although the composer may not have been consciously drawing on that source when, while working in London on *Primrose*, he wrote the first eight bars. The tune was finished when he got back to New York. Producer Alex Aarons had asked that Gershwin have it done in time for *Lady, Be Good!*

During the writing of this song a dispute over the rhyme scheme developed between the Gershwin brothers. George thought that a two-syllable rhyme was needed on the fourth and eighth lines (at "quiver" and "flivver") with the accent on the first syllable in each instance. Ira wanted a single rhyme on the last syllable. The argument went on for several days before George was able to convince Ira that, because the downbeat of this rhythmically tricky song (its phrases are in two concurrent and conflicting meters, 2/4 and 3/4) came on the *first* syllable, a rhyme had to be there.

Morris Gershwin, father of the songwriting team, liked to call this "Fashion on the River."

George Gershwin, a good dancer himself, gave Fred Astaire a welcome suggestion for a travel step exit for this tune. The step was, as Astaire later recalled in his autobiography *Steps in Time*,

> a complicated precision rhythm thing in which we kicked out simultaneously as we crossed back and forth in front of each other with arm pulls and heads back. There was a lot going on, and when George suggested traveling, we didn't think it was possible. It was the perfect answer to our problem, however, this suggestion by hoofer Gershwin, and it turned out to be a

111

knockout applause puller...George threw me a couple
for my solo routine, too. I liked to watch him dance.
It made me laugh.

In *Lady, Be Good!* Cliff Edwards sang this song at a garden
party for the uppercrust. He later became the voice of Jiminy Cricket
in Walt Disney's *Pinocchio*.

The composer's piano variation on this song was published in
1932 as part of *George Gershwin's Songbook*.

In 1940 "Fascinating Rhythm" and several other Gershwin songs
were used in the ballet *The New Yorkers*, performed by the Ballet
Russe de Monte Carlo.

Analysis: The verse ("Got a little rhythm") is similar melodically and harmonically to the refrain of "The Man I Love." Here
Gershwin uses this language to create momentum and, upon the sudden shift to B-flat minor in the ninth bar (on "comes in the mornings"),
power. In the refrain ("Fascinating Rhythm You've got me on the
Go!") he tailgates his musical phrases—something he had done in
earlier songs (see "Tra-La-La") but never so boldly. Ordinarily, one
would expect "go" in "You've got me on the go!" to last half a bar.
But Gershwin gives it only a quarter bar, bringing in the repeat of the
"Fascinating Rhythm" phrase a beat ahead of schedule. Meanwhile,
the accompaniment keeps time as if nothing has happened. The release ("Each morning I get up with the sun") provides a melodic and
unfrenetic contrast with the main strain. It is later altered to make a
coda ("Oh, how I long to be the man I used to be!").

Recordings: One can hear George Gershwin playing and Fred
and Adele Astaire singing "Fascinating Rhythm" on a record made in
London in 1926 (English Columbia 3970, reissued on Monmouth-Evergreen MES-7036). Two years earlier, when *Lady, Be Good!* was
first on Broadway, "Fascinating Rhythm" was recorded by Cliff Edwards (Pathe Actuelle 025126). Edwards' role in the show was taken
over by Buddy Lee when it was produced in London in 1926 and, in
that year, Lee released his version (Columbia 3981). There is also a
version by Frances Gershwin (Monmouth-Evergreen MES 7060).

112

Other December 1924 recordings were by the Bar Harbor Society Orchestra (Banner 1477), Carl Fenton and His Orchestra (Brunswick 2970), Sam Lanin and His Roseland Orchestra (Columbia 276-D), and Paul Whiteman (Victor 19551). Other 1920s versions were by the Green Brothers Novelty Band (Edison 51497) and the Gilt-Edged Four (Columbia 3891). "Fascinating Rhythm" was recorded in the 1930s by Judy Garland (Decca 18543), Nat Gonella and His Georgians (Parlophone F-192), Elisabeth Welch and Robert Ashley (His Master's Voice C-2992), Scott Wood and His Six Swingers (Columbia FB-1556), and Arthur Young and His Youngsters (Regal Zonophone MR-1568). It was recorded in the 1940s by Johnny Claes and His Clay Pidgeons (Columbia FB-2724) and Hazel Scott (Decca 23429). Benny Goodman and His Orchestra recorded it in 1956 (Chess LP1440).

Other versions have been by Maxene Andrews (Bainbridge 6258), George Barnes (Concord Jazz 43), Al Caiola (Bainbridge 1012), Rosemary Clooney (Concord Jazz 112), Eddie Condon (Deeca DL-5137), Tal Farlow (Concord Jazz 26), Frederick Fennell (Mercury 75127), George Feyer (Vanguard VSD-61-62), Ella Fitzgerald (Verve 2-2525), Jane Froman (Victor 12336), Jimmy Giuffre (Atlantic 90144), Ralph Grierson/Artie Kane (Angel 36083), the Vince Guaraldi Trio (Fantasy OJC-149), Yehudi Menuhin/Stephane Grappelli (Angel 37156), Buddy Merrill (Accent 50100), Joan Morris and William Bolcom (Nonesuch 71358), Sarah Vaughan with the Los Angeles Philharmonic Orchestra conducted by Michael Tilson Thomas (Columbia FM-37277).

117. THE HALF OF IT, DEARIE, BLUES

Lyricist: Ira Gershwin
Key: B-flat (verse)
      E-flat (refrain)
Time: Common
Tempo: Moderato (verse)
       Smoothly (refrain)
Introduced by: Fred Astaire in *Lady, Be Good!* at the Liberty Theatre in New York City on December 1, 1924.

Lore: The refrain of this song entered Gershwin's notebook between June 19 and June 27, 1923.

In his book *Lyrics on Several Occasions*, Ira wrote that in using the word "blues" here, he was not "attempting to plumb the melancholy depths of the real blues."

It was to this song that Fred Astaire did his first solo dance routine (sans sister Adele).

Analysis: The sixteen-bar verse ("Each time you trill a song with Bill") is a dotted note tune that rises ever higher but at a leisurely pace. In bars two (on "Will" in "look at Will") and nine (on "really" in "Of course I cannot really blame them") Gershwin uses the strident altered chords that would be so effective in the emotional climax of the second movement of the *Concerto In F*. In the refrain ("I've got the 'You don't know the half of it, dearie,' blues!") the comedy of the overly long opening verbal phrase is matched by an extended musical phrase, one that acts as a prolonged pick-up. After two bars, the melody stops to make way for Astaire's tap dancing. At this point the printed sheet music presents a somewhat perfunctory piano fill. But Gershwin, when playing this song, preferred to throw in a variant of the second theme of the *Rhapsody in Blue* instead. On the recording in which he accompanies Astaire (see below) we get the taps *and* that fill.

Recordings: In April of 1926 Gershwin and Fred Astaire were in London for a production of *Lady, Be Good!* and they recorded some numbers from the score. In "The Half of it, Dearie, Blues" Fred sings and tap dances to the composer's piano accompaniment. At one point in his dance Astaire calls out, "How's that, George?" and Gershwin replies, "That's great, Freddie, do it again!" This recording was originally released on Columbia 3969 and it has been reissued on Monmouth-Evergreen MES-7036, Heritage 0073 and on World Record Club SH 124. Other versions of the song are by George Byron with piano accompaniment by Dick Hyman (Atlantic ALS 410), Mitzi Gaynor (Verve MGV 2115), the Carroll Gibbons Orchestra with Hildegarde (English Columbia DX 786), Jack Hylton and His Orchestra (His Master's Voice C 1261), Ella Fitzgerald (Verve MGV 4027) and Joan Morris and Max Morath with piano accompaniment by William Bolcom (RCA Victor AGL 1-3073).

118. HANG ON TO ME

Lyricist: Ira Gershwin
Key: G
Time: 4/4 (verse)
      Alla Breve (refrain)
Tempo: Moderato (verse)
      In very slow Fox-trot time (refrain)
Introduced by: Fred and Adele Astaire in *Lady, Be Good!* at the
Liberty Theatre in New York City on December 1, 1924.

Lore: "Hang On To Me" was the opening number in *Lady, Be Good!* In the plot, Fred and Adele are a brother and sister who have been evicted by their landlord. As the show opens, they have gamely arranged their furniture into a homey configuration on the sidewalk and, in this song, they stand there pledging fealty to one another.

Analysis: The sixteen-bar verse ("Trouble may hound us") is one of Gershwin's finest. There is tenderness and goodwill in its lovely melody, while the underlying harmony is a bit less sanguine, employing occasional dissonance, especially in the bass. The refrain ("If you hang on to me") is rhythmic and assertive and, yet, not really aggressive. Its melody is built from the tones of a G triad—it sings like a mildly syncopated bugle call. Especially pleasing are the plagal or amen cadences that have been built into the accompaniment. In his decidedly up-tempo recording of the piece (see below), the composer plays these two-chord cadences as three-chord triplets.

Recordings: In April of 1926 Fred and Adele Astaire recorded this with a piano accompaniment by Gershwin (English Columbia 3970, reissued on Heritage 0073, World Record Club SH124 and Monmouth-Evergreen MES 7036). Other versions are by pianist Kevin Cole (Fanfare DFL 7007), Jack Hylton and His Orchestra (Disque Gramophone K 3317) Joan Morris and Max Morath with piano accompaniment by William Bolcom (RCA AGL 1-3703), Ronny Whyte and Travis Hudson (Monmouth-Evergeen MES 7061).

119. LITTLE JAZZ BIRD

Lyricist: Ira Gershwin
Key: G
Time: Alla breve
Introduced by: Cliff Edwards ("Ukelele Ike") in *Lady, Be Good!*
at the Liberty Theatre in New York City on December 1, 1924.

Lore: This tune, called "Jazz Bird," first appeared in Gershwin's musical notebook for 1921-1922. In 1960 it was used in the revival of the 1926 Gershwin show *Oh, Kay!* In 1983 it was scheduled for but dropped from the Broadway show *My One And Only*, although it was included in that show's original cast recording (see below).

Analysis: The lyric is about a little songbird who, having wandered into a cabaret and heard some jazz, returns to spread the gospel to his avine friends. The verse ("Into a cabaret") is twenty-five bars long and has the contours of a full-fledged song. Its melody warbles and trills to achieve a birdcall effect while, underneath, two distinct descending chromatic lines produce a harmonically rich, singing sound. The effect calls to mind the "Old Man Sunshine listen, you!" verse of "But Not For Me"—a Gershwin song from 1930. The refrain ("I'm a little jazz bird") is a natural and effortless tune, one that would make an excellent children's piece. A chromatic six-note piano fill adds a dash of blue. The form is thirty-two bars, ABAB[1].

Recordings: Chris Connor (Atlantic 2-601), Jack Hylton and His Orchestra (Disque Gramophone K 3317), Tommy Tune and Twiggy (Atlantic 80110-1-E).

120. THE MAN I LOVE

Lyricist: Ira Gershwin
Key: E-flat
Time: 4/4
Tempo: Andantino semplice

116

Introduced by: Adele Astaire at the *Lady, Be Good!* tryout in Philadelphia on November 17, 1924.

Lore: "The Man I Love" began its complicated history in April of 1924 when Gershwin entered the main idea in his musical notebook. At first he and Ira thought that it might serve best as a verse but, though it was temporarily used in that manner, it soon became obvious that it was going to become the heart of an entirely new composition.

Financier Otto Kahn invested $10,000 in *Lady, Be Good!* upon hearing this song and it was ably sung by Adele Astaire at the Philadelphia opening of the show, but producer Vinton Freedley withdrew it from the score before the New York premiere on the grounds that it slowed things down.

Still, it had already been published by that time and Lady Mountbatten, who had heard Gershwin play it at a party, took an autographed copy of the sheet music back with her to London where she gave it to the Berkeley Square Orchestra. It then became popular in London and in Paris, though it still had no vogue in America.

In 1927, Philadelphians had their second chance to vote on "The Man I Love" when it was inserted into the acerbic anti-war musical *Strike Up the Band*. Again, the verdict was "No!" (to it *and* the show).

Next came a temporary interpolation into *Rosalie* in January of 1928. Ira reworked the lyric for Marilyn Miller, the star of that show, but, as had been the case in 1924, it was dropped before the New York opening.

It was at this point that the Gershwins' publisher, Max Dreyfus, told the brothers that if they were willing to take a cut in their sheet music royalties he would use that money to publicize the song. And that was what did the trick. In six months it sold more than 100,000 sheets and, shortly thereafter, it was adopted by the torch-singer Helen Morgan, who made it a standard.

The composer's own analysis of the slow take off was as follows:

> The song is not a production number. That is, it allows little or no action while it is being sung. It lacks a soothing, seducing rhythm; instead it has a certain slow

117

lilt that subtly disturbs the audience instead of lulling it into acceptance. Then, too, there is the melody, which is not easy to catch; it presents too many chromatic pitfalls. Hardly anybody whistles or hums it correctly without the support of a piano or other instrument.

A few other notes on the career of this song:

It was first published under the title "The Man I Loved."

The composer's piano transcription of it appeared in *George Gershwin's Songbook*, published by Simon and Schuster in September of 1932. In 1944, that transcription was reworked by Percy Grainger who, in his forward to the piece, called "The Man I Love" "one of the great songs of all time." Grainger also noted its "obvious indebtedness to a phrase in the slow movement of Grieg's C-minor Sonata for violin and piano."

It became the theme music of Gershwin's 1934 radio program, "Music By Gershwin," on station WJZ in New York City.

It became the title of a 1947 movie musical starring Ida Lupino and Robert Alda.

In the 1950s it was attacked by semanticist (and future U.S. Senator) S.I. Hayakawa who, in an essay on popular music, pointed his finger at this and other songs of romantic yearning. According to Hayakawa, the idealization of romance in "The Man I Love," with its invocation of Prince Charming, invited unrealistic expectations between the sexes, thus undermining the institution of matrimony and leading to a higher divorce rate.

Analysis: The undramatic sixteen-measure verse ("When the mellow moon begins to beam") makes much use of repeated notes, yet is not repetitious in structure. In fact, except for a repeat of bars one and two at bars nine and ten (at "Although I realize"), it is through-composed. The refrain ("Someday he'll come along") presents a series of melodic phrases that are almost but not quite identical. The harmony, as Gershwin observed, changes more than the melody, but these changes are so subtle as to be surreptitious. They bring on a sense of disquiet. In the release ("Maybe I shall meet him") we are no longer in E-flat but in C-minor, and the composer, reversing things, moves the

118

melody more than the harmony. This sinuous melody is played over a bass line that is nearly all one note—C. It thuds unobtrusively but ominously.

Recordings: A piano solo by Gershwin has been preserved from a February 19, 1934 radio broadcast (Smithsonian Collection R008, Mark 56 Records 641). Frances Gershwin's version is on Monmouth-Evergreen MES 7060. The earliest recording was by Sippie Wallace, made on August 22, 1925 (Okeh 8251). In 1927, before the song had really caught on, there were recordings by Marion Harris (Victor 21116), Grace Hayes (His Master's Voice B-2688), Sam Lanin's Famous Players (Okeh 40977), Fred Rich and His Hotel Astor Orchestra (vocal by Vaughn de Leath—Columbia 1241-D), and Willard Robison (vocal by Frank Bessinger—Pathe Actuelle 36744).

Versions in 1928 were made by Ben Bernie (Brunswick 3771), Bessie Brown (Vocalion 15688), Fred Elizalde (Brunswick 182), Annette Hanshaw (Pathe Actuelle 32332), Sam Lanin's Troubadors (Cameo 8135), the Markels Orchestra (Banner 7038), Nat Shilkret and the Victor Orchestra (Recording as the Troubadors—Victor 21233), the Victor Salon Orchestra (Victor 35914), and Paul Whiteman (Columbia 50068-D).

It was not until the late 1930s that regular recordings of "The Man I Love" resumed. In 1936 there was a version by Elisabeth Welch (Vocalion 515); in 1937 by the Benny Goodman Quartet (Victor 25644), Gladys Swarthout with the Los Angeles Philharmonic conducted by Victor Young (from a September 8, 1937 George Gershwin memorial concert —Citadel CT 7025), and Hildegarde (Columbia DX-786); in 1938 by Benny Goodman (at Carnegie Hall—Columbia A-1049), the Morton Gould Orchestra (Decca 18207), Elisabeth Welch and Robert Ashley (His Master's Voice C-2991 and C-2992), and Victor Young and His Orchestra (vocal by Jane Rhodes—Decca 1828); in 1939 by Eddie Condon (Decca 23432), Eddie Heywood (Decca 23534), Billie Holiday (Vocalion 5377), Dorothy Lamour (Bluebird B-10302), Frances Langford (Decca 2882), the Quintet of the Hot Club of France (Decca F-7390), Artie Shaw (Bluebird B-10128), and Teddy Wilson (Brunswick 8438),

New recordings have appeared steadily ever since. There have been versions by:

Elly Ameling and Louis Van Dijk (Philips 14284), Carlos Barbarosa-Lima (Concord Jazz 2005), Sidney Bechet (Inner City 7008), Earl Bostic (Majestic 1055), Arthur Fiedler and the Boston Pops (Victor ARL 1-0041), the Page Cavanaugh Trio (Signature 15195), Ray Charles (Atlantic 5-3700, Atlantic 90464-1-Y), Herman Chittison (Bluebird 11333), Nat King Cole Trio (Capitol 20010), Chris Connor (Atlantic 2-601),

Miles Davis (Prestige 012, 7650, 24012), Arne Domnerus (His Master's Voice 7709), Dorothy Donegan (Continental 6058), Peter Duchin (Fortune 299), Roy Eldridge (Crescendo 9009, Inner City 7002, Verve 2-2531), Frederick Fennell Orchestra (Mercury 75127), George Feyer (Vanguard VSD-61-62), Ella Fitzgerald (Pablo 2308234, 1010711, 2310829, Verve 2-2525, 6-4041), Jane Froman (Victor 12333),

Red Garland (Prestige 7859), Erroll Garner (Columbia PG-33424, Savoy 2207), Dizzy Gillespie (Bulldog 2006, Everest 237), Bob Grant and His Orchestra (Decca 24029), Ralph Grierson/Artie Kane (Angel 36083), Johnny Griffin (Inner City 6042), Connie Haines (Coral 60318), Ed Hall (Commodor Music Shop 550), Coleman Hawkins (Pablo 2310707, Doctor Jazz FW-38446, Signature 90001), Barbara Hendricks/Katia and Marielle Labeque (Phillips 9500987), Woody Herman (MGM 30607), Lena Horne (Victor 27818),

Jazz at the Philharmonic (Pablo 2310713, Verve 2-2518, William Jackson (Prestige 7396), Willis Jackson (Prestige OJC-220), Barney Kessel (Atomic 210), Vera Lynn (Decca 41011), Shelly Manne (Discovery 909), Howard McGhee (Savoy 2219), Yehudi Menuhin/Stephane Grappelli (Angel SQ-37533), Julia Migenes-Johnson (Victor ARL1-5323), Liza Minnelli (A&M 6013), Joan Morris/William Bolcom (Nonesuch 71358), Phineas Newborn (Pablo 2310801), Newport Jazz Festival All-Stars (Concord Jazz 260), Marni Nixon with piano accompaniment by Lincoln Mayorga (Reference RR-19), Red Norvo Sextet (Key 1314),

Anita O'Day (Emily 11279), Charlie Parker (Verve VE2-2508), Charlie Parker/Johnny Hodges (Verve UMV 2530), Joe Pass (Pablo 640102), Oscar Peterson/Harry Edison (Pablo 2310741), Jane Pickens (Columbia 35581), Quadrant (Pablo 2310837), Django Reinhardt (Crescendo 9002), Diana Ross (Motown MCDO-6133), Hazel Scott (Decca

23429), Dinah Shore (Victor 20-1650), Zoot Sims (Pablo 2310744), Derek Smith (Progressive 7035), Paul Smith (Outstanding 023), Dick Stabile (Capitol 2819), Rise Stevens (Columbia 4431-M), Gladys Swarthout (Victor 10-1038),

Art Tatum (Jazzman 5030, Pablo 2310789), Art Van Damme (Capitol 15322), Sarah Vaughan (Roulette RE-103), Sarah Vaughan and the L.A. Philharmonic/Michael Tilson Thomas (Columbia FM-37277), Charlie Ventura (Lamp 107), Mary Lou Williams (Crescendo 9029, Pablo 2308218, 2310856), Lester Young (Verve 2-2516).

Oddly enough, Adele Astaire, Marilyn Miller, and Helen Morgan—the three women who, at various times and with varying success, introduced this song—never recorded it.

121. OH, LADY BE GOOD

Lyricist: Ira Gershwin
Key: G
Time: Alla breve
Tempo: Allegretto grazioso (verse)
  Slow (gracefully) (refrain)
Introduced by: Walter Catlett in *Lady, Be Good!* at the Liberty Theatre in New York City on December 1, 1924.

Lore: Gershwin accompanied Marguerite d'Alvarez when she sang this song at the Roosevelt Hotel on December 4, 1925 (see "Nashville Nightingale").

The composer's piano transcription of "Oh, Lady Be Good" appeared in *George Gershwin's Songbook*, published in September of 1932.

In *Lady, Be Good!*, a lawyer played by Walter Catlett sings this to a woman whose help he needs in a real estate scam.

Analysis: The verse ("Listen to my tale of woe") bears a familial resemblance to that of "Somebody Loves Me" ("When this world began"). Both make good use of the same device: a note-for-note repetition of the melody but with a change of key. In "Somebody

Loves Me" the notes are backed first by E-minor and then by G. Here, the keys are E-minor ("Listen to my tale of woe") and then E-major ("I could blossom out I know"). This verse has subtler harmony than the one to "Somebody Loves Me." Shades of feeling are created by passing tones, suspensions and artfully chosen bass notes. The refrain ("Oh, sweet and lovely lady, be good!") can also be compared to its counterpart in "Somebody Loves Me" in that both quickly catch the ear with a blue note. This time, however, the blue note is in the harmony, not the melody—it is the B-flat in the C9 chord under the word "lovely." Like two later Gershwin songs, "Of Thee I Sing" and "I've Got a Crush On You," this one has succeeded both as a rhythm number and as a slow ballad. Maybe the fact that the verse is marked Allegretto grazioso, while the refrain is marked Slow (gracefully) has led to the schizophrenia. In any event, when sung as a ballad, the release ("Oh, please have some pity") has great urgency.

Recordings: Walter Catlett did not record this song, but two members of the original *Lady, Be Good!* cast did: Cliff Edwards (Perfect 11564—recorded shortly after the Broadway premiere) and Fred Astaire (whose several versions were all latter-day: Mercury MG C-1004, Choreo A/AS-1, Daybreak DR-2009, Kapp KL-1165). During the 1926 London production, Buddy Lee was Cliff Edwards' replacement and, in that year, he released a version (Columbia 3981), as did William Kent and the Empire Theatre Orchestra, also from that production (Columbia 3980). George Gershwin was particularly fond of a 1936 record made by the Benny Goodman Trio (Victor 25333 B).

In the month of its first performance, December 1924, "Oh, Lady Be Good" was recorded by Ben Bernie (Vocalion 14955), Carl Fenton and His Orchestra (Brunswick 2790), and Paul Whiteman (Victor 19551). New versions have appeared consistently since that time. In 1925 there were offerings by the California Ramblers (Columbia 293-D), Nathan Glantz (Banner 1486), the Green Brothers Novelty Band (Edison 51497), D. Onivas and His Orchestra (Pathe Actuelle 036204), The Red Hatters, Harry Raderman Director (Okeh 40361), and Paul Van Loan and His Orchestra (Cameo 652); in 1926 by the Gilt-Edged Four (Columbia 2981) and Buddy Lee (mentioned above); in 1930 by the Louisiana Rhythm Kings (Brunswick 4706); in 1934 by Buck &

Bubbles (Columbia 2873-D), the Quintette of the Hot Club of France (Ultraphon 1 AP-1443), and Arthur Young (Regal Zonophone MR-1568);

in 1936 by Larry Adler (Vocalion 536), the Benny Goodman Trio (mentioned above), Nat Gonella and His Georgians (Parlophone F-639), Jones-Smith Incorporated, with Count Basie (Vocalion 3459), and Red Norvo and His Swing Sextette (Decca 779); in 1937 by Larry Clinton and His Orchestra (Victor 25724), Red Jessup and His Melody Makers (American Record Company 7-07-15), Brian Lawrence (Decca F-6383), Gerry Moore and His Chicago Brethren (Decca F-6347), Frankie Reynolds and His Orchestra (Bluebird B-7241), and Dickie Wells and His Orchestra (Swing 10);

in 1938 by Count Basie and His Orchestra (Collectors' Corner 9, Jazz Panorama LP-2), Slim & Slam (Slim Gaillard—Vocalion 4163), and Elisabeth Welch and Robert Ashley (His Master's Voice C-2992); in 1939 by Count Basie and His Orchestra (Decca 2631), Count Basie and His Orchestra/the Benny Goodman Sextet (Vanguard 8524), Eddie Condon (Decca 23431), Ella Fitzgerald (Decca 23956), Mel Henke (Collector's Item 100), Artie Shaw (Bluebird B-10430), and Orrin Tucker and His Orchestra (Columbia 35576);

in 1940 by Felix Mendelssohn and His Hawaiian Serenaders (Columbia FB-2525), Joe Sullivan and His Cafe Society Orchestra (Vocalion/Okeh 5496), Frankie Trumbauer (Varsity 8269), and Teddy Wilson (Columbia 36084); in 1941 by Sidney Bechet and His New Orleans Feet Warmers (Victor 27707), Joe Bushkin (Commodore Music Shop 594), Willie Lewis (Elite Special 4072), Jimmie Noone Quartet (Swaggie S-1210), and Eddie South (Columbia 36193); in 1942 by Joe Daniels and His Hot Shots in "Drumsticks" (Parlophone F-1909);

in 1945 by Lil Armstrong (Black & White 1211); in 1946 by Billy Butterfield (date approximate—Capitol 10037), the Benny Goodman Quintet (V-Disc 694B), and Jazz at the Philharmonic (Disc 2005).

Other additions to the record bins have been by Svend Asmussen (Odeon 449), Al Caiola (Bainbridge 1012), Judy Carmichael (Progressive 7072), Miles Davis/Jimmy Forrest (Prestige 7860), Herb Ellis/Joe Pass (Pablo 10714), Frederick Fennell (Mercury 75127), Ella Fitzgerald (Verve 2-2525), Jane Froman (Victor 12336), Pete Fountain (Capi-

123

tol SN-16224), the Slim Gaillard Trio (MCA 1508), Jan Garber (Hindsight 403), Dizzy Gillespie (Roulette RE-120, Savoy 2209), Benny Goodman (live at Carnegie Hall —London 2PS-918/919), Ralph Grierson/Artie Kane (Angel 36083),

Lionel Hampton (Verve VE2-2543), Coleman Hawkins (Prestige 7647), Earl Hines (Storyville 4063), Jazz at the Philharmonic (Verve 2-2518, Verve UMV-9070), Eddie Jefferson, (Muse 5127), Lee Konitz with the Gerry Mulligan Quartet (Pacific Jazz 608), Howard McGhee (Savoy 2219), Yehudi Menuhin/Stephane Grappelli (Angel 36968), Fats Navarro (Milestone 47041), the New York Philharmonic Orchestra (Conducted by Zubin Mehta (Columbia JS-36020), 101 Strings (Alshire ALCD-12), Joe Pass (Pablo 12133), Oscar Peterson /Milt Jackson (Pablo 2310881), Prez Conference/Joe Williams (Crescendo 2124), Quadrant (Pablo 2310837),

Django Reinhardt (Everest 306), Zoot Sims (Pablo 2310744), Blaine Sprouse (Rounder 0155), Orrin Star (Flying Fish 267), Star Spangled Washboard Band (Flying Fish 27031), Slam Stewart (Jazzman 5010), Sonny Stitt/Harry "Sweets" Edison/Eddie "Lockjaw" Davis (Who's Who in Jazz 21022), Mel Torme/Buddy Rich (Garu 784), Charlie Ventura (Savoy 2243), Joe Venuti (Flying Fish 035), Joe Venuti/George Barnes (Concord Jazz 14), Snooky Young (Concord Jazz 91), Lester Young (Columbia PC-36807).

122. SO AM I

Lyricist: Ira Gershwin
Key: G-minor (verse)
     G-major (refrain)
Time: 4/4
Tempo: Moderato assai
Introduced by: Alan Edwards and Adele Astaire in *Lady, Be Good!* at the Liberty Theatre in New York City on December 1, 1924.

Analysis: Two singers take turns in the verse ("Just before I go"). The male leads off with a yearning melody in G-minor. It is related to the refrain of "The Man I Love," although it does not have the latter's striking and noble juxtaposition of major and minor modes. Then the female takes over, presenting the tune in E-flat (at "Yes, I think I can"). The refrain ("Leaving you") is an operetta-style ballad, one with a static quality: every couple of bars the melody comes to a halt. Gershwin fills these spaces with a series of cascading chords played up in the treble by the piano. It may be worth noting that the release ("Isn't it just wonderful how we agree!") sounds like a first draft for the release in Irving Berlin's 1928 song, "Puttin' On the Ritz."

Recordings: Gershwin's piano roll of this song was released in September of 1925 on Mel-O-Dee 47056 and reissued on Klavier Records KS-122 and KS-133 and on Mark 56 Records 680. Adele Astaire and George Vollaire recorded "So Am I" in London in 1926, backed by the Empire Theatre Orchestra (Columbia 3979, reissued on World Record Club SH 124 and Monmouth-Evergreen MES 7036). As for the earliest recorded version, it appears in the course of a December 1924 recording of "Fascinating Rhythm" by Carl Fenton and His Orchestra (Brunswick 2790). Three months later, Mike Speciale and His Orchestra did their version (Pathe Actuelle 036221). There were versions by Paul Whiteman (Victor 19551), Jack Hylton and His Orchestra (Disque Gramophone K 3317), and the Victor Salon Group led by Nathaniel Shilkret (Victor Red Seal 12335). In 1953 there was a rendition by Mindy Carson and Guy Mitchell (Columbia 39950)

123. SHORT STORY

For violin and piano

Key: G
Time: Various
Tempo: Various
Introduced by: Samuel Dushkin at the University Club of New York on February 8, 1925.

Lore: Violinist Samuel Dushkin (for whom Igor Stravinsky wrote his violin concerto) dropped by Gershwin's residence in late 1924 to ask if the composer had a piece that he might play in an upcoming concert. Gershwin brought out his notebooks and Dushkin noticed that they contained a series of piano pieces called "Novelettes." With the composer's permission, Dushkin fused two of the "Novelettes" into a single work, which he arranged for violin and piano. One of those two pieces, marked Allegretto scherzando, had been written in 1919 or thereabouts and was recorded by Gershwin in that year as a piano piece called *Novelette in Fourths*. That recording appeared on a piano roll issued by the Welte-Mignon Company. The other, marked Andantino con fantasia, was an August 30, 1923 entry in his notebook.

Dushkin performed his arrangement on February 8, 1925 at the University Club of New York and the piece was put out in that form by B. Schott, his publisher.

On December 4, 1926, Gershwin gave a joint recital with Marguerite d'Alvarez, a contralto of Peruvian background. At the recital, he accompanied her in a group of his popular songs and, in addition, he played five piano preludes. Three of those preludes were published as a suite. There is some doubt about the identity of the other two, but they may well have been the pieces that Dushkin used in fashioning *Short Story.*

Short Story was also published in a two-piano arrangement by Al and Lee Reiser (also by Schott). So far, however, it has not been issued as either a piano solo or as the two piano solos that Gershwin originally intended.

Analysis: This work can be divided into the following five sections:

1. A Chopinesque beginning with grace notes and other ornaments acting upon a whimsical idea that is played high in the treble. This was probably the opening of the Andantino con fantasia, written in 1923.
2. A contrastingly stern idea, which becomes louder and more willful, then passionate.
3. A repeat of the first idea.

4.   A lighthearted ragtime in which a syncopated tune is played high in the treble against a stride um-pah bass. This section is derived from the *Novelette in Fourths* written in 1919.

5.   A brief return to the first idea.

Recordings: Samuel Dushkin recorded his violin/piano arrangement of this piece in the mid-1930s (Gramophone Record Shop GP-794). It was not until 1985 that new versions appeared: these were piano solos by Michael Tilson Thomas (CBS Masterworks IM 39699) and Kevin Cole (Fanfare DFL-7007). Cole's version is true to the piece as originally published. Tilson Thomas has done some "reconstructing."

124. BABY!

Lyricist: B.G. DeSylva and Ira Gershwin
Key: E-flat
Time: Alla breve
Tempo: Allegretto
Introduced by: Emma Haig and Andrew Tombes in *Tell Me More* at the Gaiety Theatre in New York City on April 13, 1925.

Analysis: The sixteen-bar verse ("Baby, heed me") is unusual only in that is starts off with the title of the song. The refrain ("You're as cute as you can be") is in a thirty-two-bar ABAC format. As he did in "My Fair Lady" (a number from the same show), Gershwin here fashions a bugle call-style tune from the notes of an E-flat triad. The hook is supposed to be the E-diminished chord that is played under the seventh note (on "be" in "you can be") but the effect is formulaic. Should a man want to sing this number he would have to skip the verse (in which the singer is identified as female), but then, in the refrain, he would suddenly find himself singing "though you're six feet three you will always be nothing but a baby to me."

Recordings: Paul Whiteman's version is played during a rendition of "Tell Me More!," recorded on May 5, 1925 (Victor 19682).

127

125. KICKIN' THE CLOUDS AWAY

Lyricist: B.G. DeSylva and Ira Gershwin
Key: E-flat
Time: 4/4 (verse)
   Alla breve (refrain)
Tempo: Moderato
Introduced by: Phyllis Cleveland, Esther Howard, and Lou Holtz in *Tell Me More* at the Gaiety Theatre in New York City on April 13, 1925.

Analysis: The verse ("I just heard a spiritual"), a bluesy rouser, is jackhammered home with repeated notes in the melody and big rolling chords in the bass. At twenty bars, it is a song in itself, containing an eight-bar release ("When the sky looks cloudy to you") that builds excitement by landing in four successively higher keys. Twenty-four of the thirty-two bars of the refrain ("Come on along!") are derived from an initial two-note call: a syncopated seesawing between B-flat and a very blue D-flat. The eight-bar exception is the release ("be wise and take it to heart"), in which a series of quarter note triplets makes for a de facto switch to three-quarter time.

Recordings: George Gershwin's piano roll was released in July of 1925 on Mel-O-Dee 47014 and later reissued on Klavier KS-122 and Mark 56 680. In March of 1925 there were versions by the Clover Gardens Orchestra (Columbia 362-D) and Bennie Kreuger and His Orchestra (introduced during a recording of "Tell Me More!"—Brunswick 2910). In April of 1925 Paul Whiteman and His Orchestra did their version (introduced on their recording of "Why Do I Love You?" from the same show—Victor 19682). In 1973 "Kickin'" was recorded by Bobby Short (Atlantic SD2-608) and in 1983 by Roscoe Lee Browne on the *My One and Only* cast album (Atlantic 80110-1-E).

126. MY FAIR LADY

Lyricist: B.G. DeSylva and Ira Gershwin

Key: E-flat

Time: 2/4

Tempo: Rather slow (first six bars of the introduction)
Andantino quasi allegretto (final two bars of the
introduction, verse and refrain)

Introduced by: Phyllis Cleveland and Esther Howard in *Tell Me
More* at the Gaiety Theatre in New York City on April 13,
1925.

Analysis: In the verse ("Listen, fair one") the female singer tells
a chorus of suitors that, although she will listen to their collective case,
she prefers the role of sister to that of lover. The fellows proceed to
make their plea in the refrain ("You're as fair as fair can be"), a thirty-
two-bar ditty made from a downward run along the notes of a E-flat
sixth chord. In the first eight bars, this makes for a bugle call sound.
In the final eight, the harmonies are more widely spaced, giving the
melody a more resounding, carillon-style feel.

Recordings: A version of this song appears on an album entitled
The Great British Dance Bands Play George Gershwin 1920-1928
(World Records SH 451).

127. TELL ME MORE!

Lyricist: B.G. DeSylva and Ira Gershwin

Key: G-minor (verse)
B-flat (refrain)

Time: Alla breve (verse)
Common (refrain)

Tempo: Scherzando (introduction)
Languidly (verse)
Slow with expression (refrain)

Introduced by: Alexander Gray and Phyllis Cleveland in *Tell
Me More* at the Gaiety Theatre in New York City on April 13,
1925.

Analysis: In this single melody line duet the man woos the woman with lines such as "You have eyes like the skies when they're blue." The woman, though she knows that he is laying it on thick ("And believe me, those two eyes can see right through you!"), continually prompts him with the title phrase.

In the twenty-bar verse the male singer begins with a sensuous, heavy-lidded idea in G-minor ("All night long I've waited") and then, after eight bars, the female singer comes in with a light-hearted version of the same tune in B-flat ("I have heard that dangers lurk"). The thirty-two-bar refrain is in B-flat ("I'm afraid you're the maid I adore") and it has thick and occasionally very dissonant harmony—an F-sharp diminished chord over an F bass, for instance, in bar two at "I adore." It is a sighing, downward-floating tune in $ABCA^1CA^2$ form. All but the C sections are variations on the main idea.

Recordings: Alexander Gray recorded this on April 23, 1925 (Columbia 368-D). Other 1925 versions were by Bennie Kreuger and His Orchestra (Brunswick 2910), Polla's Clover Garden Orchestra (Edison 51554), and Paul Whiteman and His Orchestra (Victor 19682). In 1938 there was a recording by Elisabeth Welch and Robert Ashley (His Master's Voice C-2992) and in 1940 came Billie Holiday's version (Vocalion/Okey 5719). A more recent version is by Ronny Whyte and Travis Hudson (Monmouth-Evergreen MES 7061).

128. **THREE TIMES A DAY**

Lyricist: B.G. DeSylva and Ira Gershwin
Key: E-flat
Time: Alla breve
Tempo: Allegretto (verse)
        Slow (refrain)
Introduced by: Alexander Gray and Phyllis Cleveland in *Tell Me More* at the Gaiety Theatre in New York City on April 13, 1925.

Analysis: This is a single melody line duet in which the man promises the woman that, for propriety's sake, he will not come calling on her too frequently. Except for three bars, this music, verse and refrain, is entirely through-composed. The verse ("If I had my way") is a calm and singing tune that does not repeat but, instead, suddenly sets sail under a new key, F-minor (at "But, upon my soul"). The refrain ("I'll call 'round about Three times a day"), a very warm and flowing melody, is particularly memorable for its hymn-like release ("When the sky falls into the ocean"), for the pleasing deceptive cadence (at "your smiling face") that caps the song's only repeated section—a repetition at bars twenty-five through twenty-seven of bars one through three—and for the unusual and peaceful final cadence (an A-flat minor chord with G and D notes added, coming to rest in E-flat).

Recordings: Alexander Gray recorded this on April 23, 1925 (Columbia 368-D). Latter day versions are by George Byron with piano accompaniment by Dick Hyman (Atlantic ALS 410) and Anthony Perkins (Painted Smiles PS-1357).

129. WHY DO I LOVE YOU?

Lyricist: B.G. DeSylva and Ira Gershwin
Key: E-minor (verse)
      G (refrain)
Time: Alla breve
Tempo: Moderato
Introduced by: Esther Howard and Lou Holtz in *Tell Me More* at the Gaiety Theatre in New York City on April 13, 1925.

Analysis: In this collaboration, Buddy DeSylva and Ira Gershwin produce such lines as, "Dear, it is my duty to announce 'twas not your beauty that convinced me you're the cutie to woo." In the thirty-two-bar verse ("Once I was so willing") the composer takes an E-minor phrase made of three quarter notes and plays it seven times in a row. He mitigates the monotony by boxing it into 4/4 time and by playing it against a rising chromatic line in the accompaniment. Later, new harmonies are created when the phrase is played in E-major against the same chromatic line. In the refrain ("Why do I love you") long, long high notes alternate with tumbling, syncopated two-note phrases. The length is thirty-two bars and the form is ABAB[1].

Recordings: This song was recorded in 1925 by the Clover Gardens Orchestra (Columbia 362-D), Bennie Kreuger and His Orchestra (Brunswick 2910) and Paul Whiteman and His Orchestra (Victor 19682). There was also a duo-piano version by Jean Wiener and Clement Doucet (English Columbia D 13020).

130. MURDEROUS MONTY (AND LIGHT-FINGERED JANE)

Lyricist: Desmond Carter
Key: D-minor (verse)
      D-major (refrain)
Time: 3/4
Tempo: Tempo di Valse
Introduced by: This song was written for the 1925 London production of *Tell Me More* but it was dropped before opening night.

Analysis: This is a black humor song, sung in the first person plural by two freelance criminals—the title characters—who state, in felicitious rhyme, that they will happily commit any sort of crime for a "remarkably low" price. If their sales pitch is to be believed, they are quite good at their work—able to choke a policeman "without even a gurgle."

Gershwin's verse ("If you've an aunt that you hate") is low and rumbling. A sense of mystery is created by C and G-minor chords superimposed on a D-minor ostinato in the bass. Above, a sighing melody descends slowly from high D to the D above middle C. The refrain ("Murderous Monty") is a lighthearted, carefree waltz that makes for a comic contrast to the macabre lyric. It is thirty-two bars long and through-composed.

Recordings: None.

131. **CONCERTO IN F**

For piano and orchestra

Introduced by: George Gershwin, piano, and the New York Symphony Society conducted by Walter Damrosch in Carnegie Hall on December 3, 1925.

Lore: Gershwin was commissioned to write this concerto by the New York Symphony Society, a project set into motion by the Society's musical director, Walter Damrosch. On April 17, 1925 a contract was signed by which the composer received $500 to produce the concerto and to play it with the orchestra in seven concerts (only six concerts actually took place). After signing this agreement, Gershwin joked self-consciously that he would have to find some books that would tell him what a concerto was.

He began sketching musical ideas for the piece in May, while he was in London working on the British production of *Tell Me More*. Composing began in earnest on July 22 and the work, which he was tentatively calling *New York Concerto*, came into being in his New York City townhouse, in a rented suite at the Whitehall Hotel (at Broadway and 110th Street), and at a retreat in Chautauqua in upstate New York—where his friend Ernest Hutchenson taught master piano classes. The first movement was written in July, the second in August and September, and the third in September. Gershwin's initial setting was for two pianos and then he began the orchestration, which took all of October and was finished on November 10.

By the terms of the contract, the composition was not to be publicly performed until December 3. But that did not rule out private performances, and Gershwin could not resist playing it for everyone within earshot. On August 27 he gave a solo rendition of the first movement at a party for Noel Coward. In September, he and his friend William Daly played the two-piano version of the first two movements for friends.

Shortly before the official premiere, Gershwin elected to call the piece, simply, *Concerto in F*. This was because of his wish that it be listened to as pure music and that it not be fettered with evocative titles or subtitles. As he later told Isaac Goldberg, his biographer:

> Many persons had thought that the *Rhapsody* was only
> a happy accident. Well, I went out...to show them that
> there was plenty more where that had come from. I
> made up my mind to do a piece of absolute music. The
> *Rhapsody*, as its title implied, was a blues impression.
> The Concerto would be unrelated to any program.

Prior to the start of the formal rehearsals with the New York
Symphony Society, Gershwin hired a sixty-piece orchestra for a run-
through at the Globe Theatre. Daly conducted and Walter Damrosch
was in attendance. As a result of this test, some fifty-eight measures
were cut from the first movement, thirty from the second, and sixteen
from the third. Then came the Carnegie Hall rehearsals with Damrosch conducting and with Gershwin playing with a pipe clenched
between his teeth while fellow songwriter Phillip Charig turned the
pages for him.

At the December 3 concert, the work was preceded by Glazunov's
Fifth Symphony, Rabaud's *Suite Anglais*, and an intermission. Then
came the first public performance of this, his second symphonic work—
and, with it, a split decision by the attending music critics. Among
Gershwin's admirers was Samuel Chotzinoff, who wrote, "He alone of
all those writing the music of today...expresses us." But Lawrence
Gilman, who had written of weeping over the lifelessness of the melody and harmony of the *Rhapsody in Blue*, said that the concerto was
"conventional, trite, and at its worst a little dull." Later, other doubts
would be expressed by impresario Sergei Diaghilev ("good jazz but
bad Liszt"), composer Sergei Prokofiev ("A succession of thirty-two
bar choruses"), and Gershwin himself (who said that the structure was
too sequential and that the first movement was in "sonata form...but").

It took quite some time for the concerto to catch on. Gershwin
always programmed it in concerts devoted to his works and Oscar
Levant championed it throughout his career (playing portions of it in
two films: *You Were Meant For Me* in 1948 and *An American in Paris*
in 1951) but, in Gershwin's lifetime, the only available recording was
one by pianist Roy Bargy and the Paul Whiteman Orchestra—one that

134

used a new orchestration by Ferde Grofe.

The European premiere of the piece came on May 29, 1928 with Dimitri Tiomkin at the piano, accompanied by Vladimir Golschmann and the Theatre National de l'Opera of Paris.

To Gershwin's great pleasure, two movements of the *Concerto in F* were played by Harry Kaufman with Fritz Reiner at the 1932 Venice International Festival of Contemporary Music. Gershwin was very impressed by the fact that, due to popular demand, Kaufman and Reiner repeated the finale—something that had not happened at a premiere (as Gershwin proudly told friends) since the 1875 Boston premiere of Tchaikovsky's first piano concerto.

Analysis:

I. *Allegro*

There are three basic musical ideas at work in the first movement. The first, a Charleston motive that is heard immediately after the attention-getting opening for timpani and cymbals, appears initially as a forte rhythmic statement employing alternating F-minor and C-minor (and then F and C) chords. Later, it is used as an undercurrent to the more carefree second theme and as the basis of the folksong-like accompanimental figure that leads into and supports the beautiful and heartfelt Moderato cantabile.

The second idea, a playful ascent along the pentatonic scale played first by the bassoons in the ninth bar of the piece, is the source of most of the ideas that will follow in the movement. It is not so much developed as it is made the basis for a series of variations—most of them using the first few notes and the frisky mood as a point of departure. One variation, however, is the E-major Moderato cantabile, which aims for and achieves majesty and grandeur.

The third idea is the one that marks the first entrance of the piano, which plays it as a solo. This theme is one of the most remarkable of all of Gershwin's musical statements. Its melody, with its throaty major seventh dip, is atop but not part of a series of accompanying diminished chords—to which other complicating sounds are continually added and taken away. This creates a lonely, nocturnal atmosphere—one that becomes more intense when, upon a repetition, a countermelody is given to the English horn. Unfortunately, Gershwin chooses to bring this idea back only late in the movement—and then as an overstated orchestral tutti (we will, however, hear it again in the third movement in an up-tempo and quite effective transformation).

II. *Adagio/Andante con moto*

The second movement begins with a quiet theme that, played by a solo muted trumpet, creates a lying-awake-in-the-night stillness and restlessness. Its harmonies are a succession of consonant but unrelated major chords, made a shade disquieting because they are played in their second inversions.

The second theme is introduced by the piano and accompanying strummed strings. Bright and full of humor, its opening three notes have come from a three-note portion of theme one (first heard in bar eight). It is developed and extended via some cheerful interplay between the piano and various small groups of instruments.

After the first eight bars of this second theme, we get a foreshadowing, by clarinets, of the third theme—the flowing E-major melody (Espressivo con moto) that is the heart of the movement. When it does materialize, we notice that it, too, begins with the above-mentioned three-note motto (three eighth notes preceded by an eighth note rest). This melody is as sublime as the Moderato cantabile—its counterpart in the first movement—but it is more troubled and intense. In fact, it is the occasion for what is probably the most openly emotional moment in all of Gershwin's symphonic works.

III. *Allegro Agitato*

The third movement is a rondo in which we are visited by reprises of themes from the first two movements. They are wound around appearances of three new ideas. These new ideas are:

1.   An aggressive, pounding motive based on a quick succession of repeated notes (according to Ira Gershwin, this was one of the composer's unpublished piano preludes).
2.   A breezy eight-bar idea, played by the trumpets, that helps itself to blue notes as it goes up and down the major scale. It ends with a two-bar change of pace (Poco meno congrazia) in 3/4 time.
3.   A quick, descending blues run.

The reprises are in the following order:

1. Theme three from the first movement. Here, this lonely, calling-to-the-moon music is transformed into a thumping, syncopated whirl.
2. Theme three of the second movement (Expressivo con moto), played briskly now and this time with no tears.
3. Theme two of the second movement, played faster but with the same happy inflections.
4. An exact reprise of the grandioso full orchestral presentation of theme three from the first movement.

Recordings: Gershwin never formally recorded his piano concerto. However, he can be heard playing a portion of the second movement in a recording made from an April 7, 1935 radio broadcast (Mark 56 641). One should be aware of the fact that, after the composer's death, the orchestrations of many of his works, including the *Concerto in F*, were revised by Frank Campbell-Watson and others. Because record jackets rarely say if the recordings inside bear tampered orchestrations, it is important to obtain a version featuring pianist Oscar Levant, who always recorded the piece with the composer's original instrumentation. Levant's recording with Andre Kostelanetz conducting the New York Philharmonic is on Columbia CL-700. At a September 8, 1937 George Gershwin memorial concert, Levant played the first movement, accompanied by Charles Previn and the Los Angeles Philharmonic Orchestra (Citadel CT 7025).

The Grofe scoring of the concerto is available on the above-mentioned Paul Whiteman recording featuring pianist Roy Bargy, made in September and October of 1928 (issued on Columbia 50139-D, 7172-M and 50141-D and reissued on Columbia C3L-35). Recently, pianist Russell Sherman and conductor Gunther Schuller released the first modern recording of this version (Proarte CDD-244).

Other recordings have been made by the following (arranged alphabetically by pianist):

Sondra Bianca with the Pro-Musica Symphony Orchestra conducted by Hans-Jurgen Walther (MGM 3-E1), Phillippe Entremont with the Philadelphia Orchestra conducted by Eugene Ormandy (Columbia

ML 6413), Werner Haas with the Monte Çarlo Opera Orchestra conducted by Edo de Waart (Philips 6500118), Morton Gould (pianist and conductor with his own orchestra—RCA Victor LM2017), Katia and Marielle Labeque (playing the original two-piano version—Philips 9500917), Raymond Lewenthal with the Metropolitan Symphony Orchestra conducted by Danon (Quintessence QUI 7115), Eugene List with the Berlin Symphony Orchestra conducted by S. Adler (Turnabout 34458) and with the Eastman-Rochester Orchestra conducted by Howard Hanson (Mercury 90002),

Jerome Lowenthal with the Utah Symphony conducted by Maurice Abravanel (Vanguard VCS-10017), Peter Nero with the Boston Pops conducted by Arthur Fiedler (RCA LSC3025), Reid Nibley with the Utah Symphony conducted by Maurice Abravanel (Westminster XWN 18685), Andre Previn with Andre Kostelanetz and His Orchestra (Columbia CL1495), Andre Previn (pianist and conducting the London Symphony Orchestra—Angel SF 36810, and as pianist and conductor with the Pittsburgh Symphony Orchestra—Philips 412611-1), Jeffrey Siegel with the St. Louis Symphony Orchestra conducted by Leonard Slatkin (Turnabout 34703), Roberto Szidon with the London Philharmonic conducted by Edward Downes (Deutsch Grammophon 25030 055), Earl Wild with the Boston Pops conducted by Arthur Fiedler (RCA LSC-2586).

132. IT'S A GREAT LITTLE WORLD!

Lyricist: Ira Gershwin
Key: G-minor (verse)
  E-flat (refrain)
Time: 2/4
Tempo: Allegretto
Introduced by: Allen Kearns, Jeanette MacDonald, Andrew Tombes and Gertrude McDonald in *Tip-Toes* at the Liberty Theatre in New York City on December 28, 1925.

Analysis: The verse begins by quoting Robert Louis Stevenson ("The world is so full of a number of things—I'm sure we should all

138

be as happy as kings") and it is probably the only line of nineteenth century poetry that Gershwin ever set to music. His melody for it is eerie and modal, with harmonic dissonances arising from clashes between dimly related chords (C-minor against a G-major seventh in bar two at "num" in "number," for instance). The refrain ("Give in! For it's a great little world") could not be more different: bright and uncompromisingly bubbly, full of the Broadway spirit. Its tossed off quality is 180-degrees from the studied character of the verse.

Recordings: Laddie Cliff and the chorus of the London cast of *Tip-Toes* recorded this (English Columbia 4080, reissued on Monmouth-Evergreen MES 7052). A version was also put out by the London Winter Garden Theatre Orchestra with Percival Mackey on piano, also from the 1926 British production (English Columbia 9123).

133. LOOKING FOR A BOY

Lyricist: Ira Gershwin
Key: G
Time: Common
Tempo: Moderato
Introduced by: Queenie Smith in *Tip-Toes* at the Liberty Theatre in New York City on December 28, 1925.

Lore: The singer, in the verse, declares that she is looking for a boy "'bout five foot six or seven." In his book *Lyrics on Several Occasions*, Ira Gershwin admitted that the source of this height requirement was the fact that he needed a two-syllable rhyme for "heaven." Luckily, Queenie Smith was short and her leading man, Allen Kearns, was appropriately diminutive.

English musicologist Francis Toye noted the Brahmsian personality of this song.

Analysis: The verse ("If it's true that love affairs are all arranged in heaven") is a quiet and delicate twenty-four-bar piece that modulates into B-minor at bar fourteen (on "till I'm on his knee") and ends with a stately eight-measure coda ("I'll be blue"). The refrain ("I am just a little girl") is a slow tune, one that is hypnotic in its consistent use of a dotted quarter note to eighth note motive and in its slow juggling of three principal chords: G, G-minor, and C9. The latter two are almost identical, but for the note C. When that note appears it brings with it a subtle blues feeling.

Recordings: On July 6, 1926 George Gershwin, in London, recorded a piano solo of this song (Columbia 4065, reissued on Monmouth-Evergreen MES 7037). Dorothy Dickson of the 1926 London cast of *Tip-Toes* released her version (Columbia 4078, reissued on Monmouth-Evergreen MES 7052), as did Phil Ohman and Victor Arden—duo-pianists in the *Tip-Toes* orchestra (Brumswick 3035). Other 1926 recordings were by the Bar Harbor Society Orchestra (Pathe Actuelle 36375), Nathan Glantz (Banner 1698), Roger Wolfe Kahn and His Orchestra (Victor 19939), the Knickerbockers directed by Ben Selvin (Columbia 549-D), the Okeh Syncopaters (Okeh 40570), the Red Hatters/Harry Raderman director (Okeh 40570), the Revelers (Victor 35772), Jack Stillman's Orchestra (Edison 51687), and Austin Wylie and His Golden Pheasant Orchestra (Vocalion 15225).

There was a 1934 recording by Arthur Young and His Youngsters (Regal Zonophone MR-1568), a 1946 version by Benny Carter (DeLuxe 1009), and there have been more recent versions by Chris Connor (Atlantic 2-601), Ella Fitzgerald (Verve 629-5 and Decca 8378), the Vince Guaraldi Trio (Fantasy OJC-235), Marni Nixon with piano accompaniment by Lincoln Mayorga (Reference RR-19), Andre Previn (piano—RCA Victor LPM 1011), and Sarah Vaughan (Mercury MG 20311).

134. NICE BABY! (COME TO PAPA!)

Lyricist: Ira Gershwin
Key: D
Time: 2/4
Tempo: Allegretto
Introduced by: Jeanette MacDonald and Robert Halliday in *Tip-*

Toes at the Liberty Theatre in New York City on December 28, 1925.

Lore: The "Come to Papa!" line in the refrain precedes by five years Ira Gershwin's more famous use of the phrase in 1930's "Embraceable You."

Analysis: The verse ("When I look at you") is a full thirty-two-bar song in itself, complete with an eight-bar release ("Just a sweet and charming little baby"). In it, a husband and wife are witty and affectionate in saying that, while the rest of the world thinks of them as mature adults, they are babies to one another. The music is appropriately cute and gurgly here and it is also babylike in the refrain ("Nice baby!"), which begins with an overexcited, hiccupping main idea. However, the very fine release ("If you like candy") has a contrasting yearning quality and some rhythmically tricky moments for the singer. Like "Nightie-Night" from the same show, this song is through-composed but for a few recapitulated notes at bar twenty-five (at "Nice baby!").

Recordings: This number was recorded in 1926 by Evan Thomas and Vera Bryer of the London cast of the show (Columbia 4080, reissued on Monmouth-Evergreen MES 7052).

135. NIGHTIE-NIGHT

Lyricist: Ira Gershwin
Key: F
Time: Common
Tempo: Moderato commodo
Introduced by: Queenie Smith and Allen Kearns in *Tip-Toes* at the Liberty Theatre in New York City on December 28, 1925.

Analysis: The verse and refrain are a dialogue between the female and male leads of the play. He knows that he should say goodnight but doesn't want to while she doesn't want to but insists that they do.

141

It is a charming lyric: when she sings, "I'm afraid that I'll be acting like a loon, for there's a gorgeous moon above," he replies, "But I'll be glad to show you Jupiter and Mars, And lots of little stars you'll love." The music in both the verse and refrain has a sweet, sleepy docility. The verse ("It's time for little boys like you to be in bed") is especially tranquil: in the accompaniment, while the bass drones on an F, a tenor line rocks gently from A to B-flat and back. The refrain ("Nightie Night!") is thirty-two bars long and through-composed, but for a repetition of the first three bars at measures twenty-five through twenty-seven.

Recordings: In 1926 this song was recorded by Dorothy Dickson and Allen Kearns of the London cast of *Tip-Toes* (Columbia 9129, reissued on Monmouth-Evergreen MES 7052). Virginia Rea and Franklyn Baur did another early version (Brunswick 3053). There was a French version ("Bon Nuit") by Loulou Hegoburu with piano accompaniment by M.G. Van Parys (English Columbia D 19185). A more recent interpretation is by Louise Carlyle and Warren Galjour (Citadel CT 7017).

136. SWEET AND LOW-DOWN

Lyricist: Ira Gershwin
Key: G-minor (verse)
     G-major (refrain)
Time: Alla breve
Tempo: Moderato
Introduced by: Andrew Tombes, Lovey Lee, and Gertrude McDonald (accompanied by several kazoos) in *Tip-Toes* at the Liberty Theatre in New York City on December 28, 1925.

Lore: Ira's title phrase, a play on the old song "Sweet and Low," eventually made it into *The American Thesaurus of Slang.* He had first used it in the unpublished song "Singin' Pete," discarded a year earlier from *Lady Be Good.*
     Of this song's performance, Alexander Woollcott wrote in the

142

New York *World*: "When to the lisping of a hundred tapping feet in "Sweet and Low-Down" a forest of trombones suddenly added their moan, then the Liberty Theatre quietly but firmly went mad."

George's piano transcription of this song appeared in *George Gershwin's Songbook*, published by Simon and Schuster in September of 1932.

Analysis: The music of the verse ("There's a cabaret in this city") is melodically and harmonically very similar to that of the verse for "It's a Great Little World!" from the same show. Here there is more rhythmic push and, in the final three bars (at "If you need a tonic"), a foreshadowing of the relentless rhythm that will characterize the refrain. The latter ("Grab a cab and go down") consists of a dotted note tune that scales successively higher registers until it hits the exclamatory title phrase. The lyric becomes particularly witty in the release ("Philosopher or deacon, You simply have to weaken"), whose music begins by developing the initial dotted note idea of the refrain, but ends up with a series of declamations, one of them spoken ("Professor! Start your beat!").

Recordings: The composer's piano roll was released in April of 1926. It and his piano roll of "That Certain Feeling," both of them stating "arranged and played by George Gershwin," were the last two that he did (Duo-Art 713214, reissued on Klavier KS-122). Another piano rendition by the composer, made in London on July 6, 1926, was issued on Columbia 4065 (reissued on Monmouth-Evergreen MES 7037 and World Record Club SH 144). *Tip-Toes'* duo pianists Phil Ohman and Victor Arden recorded their version in February of 1926 and released it on Brunswick 3035. Laddie Cliff and Peggy Beatty of the 1926 *Tip-Toes* London cast released theirs on Columbia 4079. And, recently, Gershwin's sister Frances recorded this song (World Records SH-208, Monmouth-Evergreen MES 7060).

Other versions include December 1925 recordings by Chick Endor (Vocalion 15270) and Paul Whiteman and His Orchestra (Victor 19920); 1926 versions by Lou Gold and His Orchestra (Harmony 98-H), the Knickerbockers directed by Ben Selvin (Columbia 549-D), the Revelers (Victor 35772), and Austin Wylie and His Golden Pheasant

Orchestra (Columbia 549-D); 1939 versions by Louis Prima and His New Orleans Gang (Decca 2749) and Lee Wiley (Liberty Music Shop L-284, reissued on Monmouth-Evergreen MES 7034); and recent recordings by Charles "Honi" Coles, Tommy Tune, and Twiggy from the *My One and Only* cast recording (Atlantic 80110-1-E), Puttin' on the Ritz (Pausa 7161), and Sarah Vaughan with the L.A. Philharmonic conducted by Michael Tilson Thomas (Columbia FM-37277).

137. THAT CERTAIN FEELING

Lyricist: Ira Gershwin
Key: E-flat
Time: Common
Tempo: Moderato semplice
Introduced by: Queenie Smith and Allen Kearns in *Tip-Toes* at the Liberty Theatre in New York City on December 28, 1925.

Lore: Gershwin's piano transcription of this song appeared in *George Gershwin's Songbook*, published by Simon and Schuster in September of 1932.

"That Certain Feeling" provided the title of and was prominently showcased by Pearl Bailey in a 1956 Bob Hope movie.

Analysis: The winsome and appealing verse ("Knew it from the start") is of an unusual length—fifteen bars. This is because the first eight bars are given a brief development, rather than a repetition. The refrain ("That Certain Feeling"), one of the most fully evolved of the composer's 1920s rousers, is daring in its use of clashing harmony, especially in bar two, where a C-natural is sung against the C-sharp in an E-diminished chord (on "Feeling"). Elsewhere, major continually fights minor while, in each of the thirty-two bars, the melody develops out of the initial five-note phrase.

Recordings: Gershwin made a piano roll of "That Certain Feeling." It and his roll of "Sweet and Low-Down" (stating "Arranged and played by George Gershwin") were released in April of 1926 and they

144

were the last two that he made (Duo-Art 713216, reissued on Mark 56 680 and on Klavier KS 122 and KS 133). The composer recorded this song again in London on July 6, 1926 (Columbia 4066, reissued on Monmouth-Evergreen MES 7037). Also, there are versions by Dorothy Dickson and Allen Kearns from the 1926 London production of *Tip-Toes* (English Columbia 9129), by *Tip-Toes'* duo-pianists Phil Ohman and Victor Arden (recorded in February of 1926 and issued on Brunswick 3035), and by Frances Gershwin (Monmouth-Evergreen MES 7060).

The earliest recordings, made in December of 1925, were by Chick Endor (Vocalion 15270) and Paul Whiteman and His Orchestra (Victor 19920). In 1926 came versions by Alfredo's "New Princess" Orchestra (Edison Bell Winner 4475), Josephine Baker (Parlophone R-3232), Fred Elizalde's Cinderella Roof Orchestra (Hollywood 1012), Nathan Glantz (Banner 1678), the Knickerbockers directed by Ben Selvin (played during a rendition of "Sweet and Low-Down"—Columbia 549-D), Vincent Lopez and His Hotel Pennsylvania Orchestra (Okeh 40574), the Revelers (Victor 35772), the Tennessee Happy Boys (Edison 51736), and Austin Wylie and His Golden Pheasant Orchestra (Vocallion 15225).

In 1934 there were recordings by Victor Young and His Orchestra (Decca 426) and by Arthur Young and His Youngsters (Regal Zonophone MR-1568). Elizabeth Welch and Robert Ashley released their version in 1938 (His Master's Voice C-2992), and Shirley Ross with The Foursome released theirs in 1939 (Decca 2878). In 1959 came Ella Fitzgerald's rendition (Verve 823279-1) and Bobby Short's came along in 1973 (Atlantic SD 2-608).

Others: Pearl Bailey (Roulette 42002), Chris Connor (Atlantic 2-601), Cleo Laine (Jazz Man 5033), and Lincoln Mayorga (Sheffield Lab LAB-1).

138. THESE CHARMING PEOPLE

Lyricist: Ira Gershwin
Key: E-flat
Time: 2/4

145

Tempo: Moderato

Introduced by: Harry Watson, Andrew Tombes, and Queenie Smith in *Tip-Toes* at the Liberty Theatre in New York City on December 28, 1925.

Lore: This was one of Ira Gershwin's favorite lyrics, one that he likened to P.G. Wodehouse's "Bongo on the Congo."

Analysis: The verse ("We must make it our ambition") has the singer and assembled chorus bragging in turn over who can act in the most pedigreed fashion ("the lady isn't born yet who can beat me at a lorgnette"). Then, in the refrain ("We'll be like these charming people"), they proceed to mock the upper crust with some choice gossip. Musically, the verse has a brisk, worried, patter-style feel. The tension is caused by a duel between A-flat sixth harmony in the treble and E-flat in the bass. After eight bars there is a switch to C-minor sixth against G-minor. Bars twelve through thirty-two further develop this material. The refrain is more relaxed and melodic, but in a mocking way—the tune having an edge, like a child's catcall. It is thirty-two bars long and AA[1]BC in form (it is through-composed but for a repetition of bars one and two at nine and ten).

Recordings: Dorothy Dickson, Laddie Cliff, and John Kirby from the 1926 London production of *Tip-Toes* recorded this (Columbia 4079, reissued on Monmouth-Evergreen MES 7052). Another 1926 version was by the Revelers (Victor 35772). More recently, this song was recorded by Joan Morris and Max Morath with piano accompaniment by William Bolcom (Victor AGL1-3703).

139. WHEN DO WE DANCE?

Lyricist: Ira Gershwin
Key: E-flat
Time: Alla breve
Tempo: Moderato
Introduced by: Allen Kearns, Gertrude McDonald, and Lovey

146

Lee in *Tip-Toes* at the Liberty Theatre in New York City on December 28, 1925.

Analysis: The singer complains about intellectuals in the verse ("I'm fed up with discussions about the music of Russians"), setting up the simple and direct question of the title phrase, which begins the refrain. The melody of this twenty-bar verse is similar to that of "The Trolley Song" (written in 1944 by Hugh Martin and Ralph Blaine), although here the tempo is sedate and the chords churchy. In bars seven and eight, while the tune is at rest (after "when you talk about art") there is a bluesy piano fill. Later, in measures sixteen through twenty, the singer and accompanist are given some chromatically adventurous runs. The melody of the thirty-two-bar refrain has a quietly insistent, almost pleading quality and its release ("Just can't help swaying") is especially lyrical. Worth noting too is the fact that it was in this song that the Gershwin brothers first made mention of their songwriting peers, Irving Berlin and Jerome Kern. Eleven years later, in "By Strauss," they would do it again, adding the names of Cole Porter and Gershwin himself.

Recordings: The composer's piano solo was recorded in London on July 6, 1926 (Columbia 4066, reissued on Monmouth-Evergreen MES 7037). Frances Gershwin, sister of the songwriters, also released a version (World Records SH-208 and Monmouth-Evergreen MES 7060). In 1926, Allen Kearns and Peggy Beatty of the London cast of *Tip-Toes* recorded the song (Columbia 4078, reissued on Monmouth-Evergreen 7052), as did *Tip-Toes* duo-pianists Phil Ohman and Victor Arden (who incorporated it into their version of "That Certain Feeling"—Brunswick 3035). Other 1926 recordings were by the Revelers (Victor 35572) and Austin Wylie and His Golden Pheasant Orchestra (who also incorporated it into a rendition of "That Certain Feeling"—Vocalion 15225).

140. COSSACK LOVE SONG (DON'T FORGET ME)

Lyricist: Otto Harbach and Oscar Hammerstein II

147

Key: G (verse)

G-minor (refrain)

Time: Alla breve

Tempo: Moderato (verse)

Ben moderato (refrain)

Introduced by: Tessa Kosta and Guy Robertson in *Song of the Flame* at the Forty-fourth Street Theatre in New York City on December 30, 1925.

Analysis: In this song a Russian soldier asks his lover, to whom he is bidding good-bye, what she wants him to give her. She replies that she wants only his promise that he will never forget her.

Gershwin, who composed this music in collaboration with Herbert Stothart, was in the habit of juxtaposing a minor key verse with a major key refrain ("Swanee," "So Am I," "Sweet and Low-Down") but here that situation is reversed, with a verse in G and a refrain in G-minor. The verse ("When a Russian soldier bids his girl good-bye") is a sixteen-bar tune fashioned on a bugle call pattern. It is played first in G, then in B-minor. The refrain ("Don't forget me") has the heavy feel of a Russian march, its trudging aspect accentuated by the constant use of repeated notes. The length is thirty-two bars, the form AA^1BA^2.

Recordings: In 1926 Tessa Kosta recorded this with the Russian Art Choir (Columbia 618-D). There were also recordings that year by Carl Fenton and His Orchestra (Brunswick 3033), Bob Haring (Cameo 876), the International Novelty Orchestra (Victor 19948), the Ipana Troubadors (Columbia 565-D), the Tuxedo Orchestra (Vocalion 15223), Van Phillips and his Concert Band (Columbia DX-83), and the Victor Light Opera Company (Victor 19954). In 1928 there was a version by the Anglo-Persians (Brunswick 4483) and in 1939 there was one by Tony Martin (labeled "Don't Forget Me, Don't Forget Me"—Decca 2883).

141. MIDNIGHT BELLS

Lyricist: Otto Harbach and Oscar Hammerstein II

Key: F
Time: Alla breve
Tempo: Moderato
Introduced by: Tessa Kosta in *Song of the Flame* at the Forty-fourth Street Theatre in New York City on December 30, 1925.

Analysis: The bells are ringing in a new year and the singer's concern is that this new year bring a halt to the sorrow of the one just ended. The somewhat stilted twenty-bar verse ("Ding Dong Ding Dong") is characterized by whole note octave leaps between the dings and the dongs. The refrain ("Ring on Beautiful midnight Bells") has operetta-style high notes and languid triplets. It does not repeat for sixteen bars. Then bars one through eight are repeated at seventeen through twenty-four and bars twenty-five through thirty-two are a further development of the initial idea.

Recordings: The Victor Novelty Orchestra recorded this song in 1929 (Victor 22280).

142. THE SIGNAL

Lyricist: Otto Harbach and Oscar Hammerstein II
Key: D
Time: 3/4
Tempo: Moderato semplice
Introduced by: Tessa Kosta and Guy Robertson in *Song of the Flame* at the Forty-fourth Street Theatre in New York City on December 30, 1925.

Analysis: This charming little twenty-four-bar waltz has an un-Broadway-like folksong structure (ABABAB). Its abbreviated length and the fact that it has no verse are due to its integral place in the action on stage in *Song of the Flame*. That is obvious from lines like "We had better go, I think we'd better go, we are not wanted here," which refer to a situation that is not explained elsewhere in the song.

Recordings: None.

143. **SONG OF THE FLAME**

Lyricist: Otto Harbach and Oscar Hammerstein II
Key: G-minor
Time: 2/4
Tempo: Molto deciso (introduction)
       Un poco mysterioso (verse)
       Tempo di Marcia molto marcato (refrain)
Introduced by: Tessa Kosta, Greek Evans, and the Russian Art
    Choir in *Song of the Flame* at the Forty-fourth Street Theatre
    in New York City on December 30, 1925.

Analysis: The lyric is about the soul of Russia, described as an
enthralling fire that beckons in the night. The music, which Gershwin
wrote in collaboration with Herbert Stothart, begins with big forte
chords and then a sixteen-bar verse ("Helpless children of the night")
in which the singer is given minor key triplets that sound more Arabic
than Russian. The refrain ("What's that light that is beckoning?"),
however, has the feel of a Russian march, one that has less trudging
and more momentum than "Cossack Love Song," a number from the
same show. In the release ("Come, come") there is a shift to E-flat and
that tonality is then contrasted with G-minor in the very dramatic climax to the song (at "On! On!"). The last note of this soulful, crying
crescendo is a high G and it is held for four bars while the accompaniment takes a two-octave dive along the chromatic scale.

Recordings: In 1926 there were recordings by Tessa Kosta and
the Russian Art Choir (Columbia 618-D), Carl Fenton and His Orchestra (Brunswick 3033), Nathan Glantz (Banner 1698), Bob Haring
(Cameo 876), the International Novelty Orchestra (Victor 19948), the
Ipana Troubadors (Columbia 565-D), Vincent Lopez and His Hotel
Pennsylvania Orchestra (Okeh 40586), Jack Stillman's Orchestra (Edison
51696), the Tuxedo Orchestra (Vocalion 15223), Roger Wolfe Kahn
and His Orchestra (Victor 19935), Van Phillips and His Concert Band

(Columbia DX-83), and the Victor Light Opera Company (Victor 19954). In 1939 came a version by Tony Martin (Decca 2883). A recording by the Robert Trendler Orchestra and Chorus with baritone Jerry Abbott was released on Waldorf Music-Hall MH 55-124.

144. VODKA

Lyricist: Otto Harbach and Oscar Hammerstein II
Key: G-minor
Time: 2/4 (verse)
　　　 Alla breve (refrain)
Tempo: Moderato
Introduced by: Dorothy Mackaye in *Song of the Flame* at the Forty-fourth Street Theatre in New York City on December 30, 1925

Analysis: This is a comedy number in which the singer, a woman, confesses that there is just one sort of liquor that she cannot handle, one that makes her too passionate for her own good. "Vodka," she puts it succinctly, "makes me feel odd-ka." The eighteen-bar verse ("Of all concoctions alcoholical") begins with an octave leap up and continues with a series of spastic up and down jumps. The thirty-two-bar refrain ("Vodka, Don't give me Vodka") is a simple declarative tune sung to a marching beat, first in G-minor, then in C-minor. Gershwin wrote this in collaboration with Herbert Stothart.

Recordings: In 1926 this song was recorded by Bob Haring (played during a rendition of "Cossack Love Song"—Cameo 876), the International Novelty Orchestra (Victor 19965), and the Ipana Troubadors (played during "Song Of The Flame"—Columbia 565-D). Another recording was by the Vanderbilt Orchestra (Vocalion 15233). More recently, a version was released by Ronny Whyte and Travis Hudson (Monmouth-Evergreen MES 7061).

151

145. YOU ARE YOU

Lyricist: Otto Harbach and Oscar Hammerstein II
Key: E-flat
Time: 2/4 and 3/4 (introduction)
       2/4 (verse)
       Alla breve (refrain)
Tempo: Con gentilezza (introduction)
        Allegretto grazioso (verse)
        Gracefully (refrain)
Introduced by: This song was written for but not used in *Song of the Flame*, a show which had its premiere at the Fourty-fourth Street Theatre in New York City on December 30, 1925.

Analysis: Considering the talents of the two lyricists, the words here are oddly enervated ("You are you and that is why I love you/You are you and I am only I"). The music, written by Gershwin in collaboration with Herbert Stothart, contains a tranquil nineteen-bar verse ("When you're in love") that features twelve straight measures of droning E-flat ninth harmony in the accompaniment against a simple, placid tune, one made mostly of the notes of an E-flat ninth chord. At bar thirteen, as if to say, "Enough of this, already!," there is a sudden switch to the key of C. The refrain ("You are you") is based on a chromatic, noodling "Tea For Two"-type of idea. It is thirty-two bars long and ABA^{1}B^{1}A^2 in form.

Recordings: None.

146. I'D RATHER CHARLESTON

Lyricist: Desmond Carter
Key: E-flat
Time: Alla breve
Tempo: No tempo marking
Introduced by: Fred and Adele Astaire in the London production of *Lady, Be Good!*, which had its premiere at the Empire

Theatre on April 14, 1926.

Lore: In his autobiography, *Passport to Paris*, Vernon Duke described lyricist Carter as "Gentle, sloe-eyed...a wonderful lyric writer who died young." Duke was present in London as "Desmond, a model of tact and reticence, sat in an armchair, pencil in hand, while George, a big cigar in his mouth and eyes shining, played 'I'd Rather Charleston' over and over in every existing key."

Analysis: The lyric, in identifying the singers as brother and sister, makes it plain that this song was tailored for the Astaires. In the verse Fred complains that his dancer sister lives only to use her feet, never her mind. This theme is carried into the refrain, where he keeps asking her why she won't make more of herself and she keeps replying, "I'd rather Charleston."

The twenty-bar verse ("I've seen for days") is a swinging, striving tune that, after eight bars, is inventively modified and extended. The thirty-two-bar refrain ("Take a lesson from me") is a Charleston, as one might expect, and that rhythm appears on every mention of the word "Charleston." The highlights are an emotionally expressive, yet syncopated release ("I'm double-jointed") and a highly syncopated eight-bar coda ("leave it behind").

Recordings: On a recording made in London on April 26, 1926, Gershwin accompanied Fred and Adele Astaire (Columbia 3970, reissued on Heritage 0073, the World Record Club SH 124 and Monmouth-Evergreen MES 7036). Other versions are by Jack Hylton and His Orchestra (His Master's Voice C 1261), Arthur Young and the Youngsters (Liberty Music Shop MR 1568).

147. SWISS MISS (THE CAB-HORSE TROT)

Work for solo piano

Key: Various
Time: 2/4

153

Tempo: No tempo marking
Introduced by: Fred and Adele Astaire in *Lady, Be Good!* at the
  Liberty Theatre in New York City on December 1, 1924.

Lore: This was written as a song with lyrics by Arthur Jackson
and Ira Gershwin, but that version remains unpublished. An instrumental version was published in 1926, upon the London production of
Lady, Be Good!

  "Swiss Miss" was the occasion for some spectacular dancing by
the Astaires in what had come to be known as their "run-around"
routine. They first used the run-around, a sure-fire show stopper, in a
musical called *The Love Letter* in 1921. Choreographer Edward "Teddy"
Royce had suggested that Fred and Adele run shoulder to shoulder in
circles holding their arms out as if each was grasping the handlebars of
a bicycle. The accompanying music was always a nonsense song built
around a repetitive series of um-pahs.

Analysis: The humor in this dizzy 155-bar composition is not as
inspired as in such other Gershwin works as "The Babbitt and the
Bromide" and "Wintergreen For President." This piece is nearly
through-composed and consists of the following eleven contiguous sections:

  1. A four-bar introduction consisting of a series of C7 to F cadences.
  2. A seventeen-bar melody in F characterized by the good-natured
leaps of a Swiss-style folk song.
  3. A twenty-bar stretch in D-minor that begins quietly and then,
amidst um-pahs in the bass, makes its way to an emphatic resolution in
F, followed by a modulation into B-flat.
  4. In B-flat now, with E-flat minor chords dabbed in here and there,
this fourteen-bar section has a kind of unfocused jauntiness, like circus
music.
  5. Sixteen bars of music in the same key and vein, ending suddenly
and comically with tremulo A7 chords that bring us peremptorily to
the key of D.
  6. Sixteen bars of skittering broken chords in D above an um-pah

bass.

7. A four-bar G-major introduction to

8. A sixteen-bar section marked "Dance" that is characterized by yodel-style melodic leaps.

9. Eighteen bars of brassy circus music. The key is still G and the melody is played in octaves in the bass while above it come staccato bursts in full fanfarish chords.

10. A yodel tune accompanied by um-pahs. It is in C and is sixteen bars long.

11. A sixteen-bar repetition of section 9.

Recordings: Fred and Adele Astaire (English Columbia 3979, reissued on World Record Club SH 124 and Monmouth-Evergreen MES 7036).

148. THAT LOST BARBERSHOP CHORD

>*Lyricist:* Ira Gershwin
>*Key:* E-flat
>*Time:* 4/4
>*Tempo:* Moderato
>*Introduced by:* Louis Lazarin and the Pan-American Quartet in *Americana* at the Belmont Theatre in New York City on July 26, 1926.

Lore: The title is derived from two songs. One, "The Lost Chord," was Sir Arthur Sullivan's setting of a poem by Adelaide Proctor. It had been one of Gershwin's childhood favorites. The other, "Play that Barber Shop Chord," was written circa 1910 by MacDonald, Tracey, and Louis Muir. The latter, who was also the composer of "Waiting For the Robert E. Lee," had at one time given Gershwin some well-appreciated encouragement.

Analysis: This song was critically acclaimed when first presented and it has since been fondly mentioned by various Gershwin biographers. But it never caught on with the public. Actually, it has been some sixty years since the public has had a chance to hear it, for it has not, since *Americana*, been performed on stage or in films or on records. Verse ("Seated one day") and refrain ("I'm looking for") tell the story of a chord that was sung once but nevermore by a Harlem barbershop quartet. The thirty-two-bar verse has sentimental but not atavistic or unusual harmonies. At bars six (at "certainly" in "certainly could harmonize") and fourteen (at "certainly could vocalize") it presages the music that will appear at the title phrase in the refrain—an unusual touch. The unusual forty-bar length of the refrain is due to two false endings. In this piece, as in the verse, we are not given as many harmonic points of interest as might have been expected, given the title and the care and relish that went into the writing. Two interesting moments are the D-natural sung against an A-flat chord on "lost" in bar one, and the final cadence where (on "can" in "can it be?") a B-dominant seventh with an augmented fifth is used as part of the resolution into E-flat. Also of interest is the release ("I'm growing gray"), which seems to be anticipating by more than thirty years Maurice Jarre's big tune from *Lawrence of Arabia*. The form is ABA^{1}CA^2.

Recordings: None.

149. **CLAP YO' HANDS**

> *Lyricist:* Ira Gershwin
> *Key:* D-minor (verse)
>   F (refrain)
> *Time:* Alla breve
> *Tempo:* Moderato
> *Introduced by:* Betty Cooper and Harlan Dixon in *Oh, Kay!* at the Imperial Theatre in New York City on November 8, 1926.

Lore: In the summer of 1926, shortly after writing this song, George and Ira played it for some friends in Belmar, New Jersey. One of them was Arthur Caesar (lyricist Irving Caesar's brother), who took issue with the lyric, insisting that there can be no pebbles on the sands of time because he had never seen any pebbles at the beach. Everyone

156

present immediately walked over to the seashore to go pebble-hunting and, to Ira's satisfaction, pebbles were found.

When it came time to wedge this song into the plot of *Oh, Kay!*, the librettists, Guy Bolton and P.G. Wodehouse, came up with a novel idea. They had Harlan Dixon ask an assemblage of young ladies if they were interested in hearing a mammy song. When the chorines responded "No!" they had Dixon simply go ahead and sing "Clap Yo' Hands" anyway.

Shortly after the premiere of *Oh, Kay!* George Gershwin served as piano accompanist to Peruvian singer Marguerite d'Alvarez at the latter's December 4, 1926 concert at the Roosevelt Hotel in New York City and this was one of the songs they performed.

Six years later, in September of 1932, his piano transcription of it appeared in *George Gershwin's Songbook*, published by Simon and Schuster.

In 1959, Ira Gershwin admitted in his book *Lyrics on Several Occasions* that he had no idea why he made "Clap Yo' Hands" the title of this piece when the lyric, as printed and sung, went "clap-a yo' hand." As for the verse, lyricist Howard Dietz, in his autobiography *Dancing in the Dark*, claimed that it was he and not Ira who wrote it.

Analysis: "Clap Yo' Hands" follows "Swanee" and "Fascinating Rhythm" as a rhythm song in which Gershwin precedes a major key refrain with a powerful minor key verse. This verse ("Come on, you children") has a devilish, furrowed-brow zest. There is a spirited instrumental run in the bass at bars seven and eight on "Voo-doo" (played by Gershwin and others in early recordings of the piece) and there is a sinuous four-bar release ("Let me lead this way") in A-minor. The refrain ("Clap-a yo' hand!") is much more cheerful. Its initial and principal idea features a sunny pentatonic opening and a good-natured bluesy conclusion (on "jubilee"). Then, during the release ("On the sands of time"), the minor mode returns. But here the gleam in the eye is missing and the effect is lyrical and melodic.

Recordings: Gershwin's piano solo was recorded in New York on November 12, 1926 and released on English Columbia 4538 and American Columbia 809-D. It has been reissued on Monmouth-Evergreen MES 7071 and on The Smithsonian Collection R011-RCA. Phil Ohman and Victor Arden, duo-pianists from the *Oh, Kay!* orchestra, also recorded this song in November of 1926 (Brunswick 3377). Claude Hulbert, who was in the cast of the 1927 London production of the show, released his version on Columbia 4617.

Other 1926 recordings were by Willie Craeger's Rhythm Aces (Gennett 6007), Lou Gold and His Orchestra (Harmony 314-H), Roger Wolfe Kahn (Victor 20327), Sam Lanin and His Orchestra (Pathe Actuelle 36570), the Pennsylvania Syncopaters (Emerson 3094), Fred Rich and His Hotel Astor Orchestra (Columbia 802-D), Vincent Rizzo and His Hotel Sylvania Orchestra of Philadelphia (Okeh 40725), Willard Robison (Perfect 12311), Adrian Schubert and His Salon Orchestra (Banner 1888), Jack Smith (Victor 20372), and the Swinging Sophomores (Columbia 838-D).

The Revelers recorded "Clap Yo' Hands" in 1927 (Victor 35811), Elisabeth Welch and Robert Ashley in 1938 (His Master's Voice C-2991), the Merry Macs in 1939 (Decca 2877), and it was done in the 1950s by Ella Fitzgerald (Verve 2-2525) and the Hi-Lo's (DRG SL-5184). Also, there was a version by duo-pianists Edgar Fairchild and Ralph Rainger (Victor 20435) and one by Allen Case in a studio recording of *Oh, Kay!* (Columbia OS 2550).

150. DO-DO-DO

Lyricist: Ira Gershwin
Key: E-flat
Time: Common
Tempo: Moderato grazioso
Introduced by: Oscar Shaw and Gertrude Lawrence in *Oh, Kay!* at the Imperial Theatre in New York City on November 8, 1926.

Lore: The brothers wrote this one in half an hour. They knew it took half an hour because just as they started it Ira's fiancée called to say that she was coming over and just as they finished it her taxi arrived, having completed the thirty-minute drive to their 316 West 103rd Street residence.

158

The composer's piano transcription of this song appeared in *George Gershwin's Songbook*, published by Simon and Schuster in September of 1932.

Analysis: This song begins with the kind of melodic and winsome verse ("I remember the bliss") that usually presages a ballad. The refrain ("Oh, do, do, do"), however, has a jaunty, almost silly feel—at least in the beginning, for in the release ("Let's try again") it has the lilt of a ballad and in the coda ("My heart begins to hum"), even a hint of heartbreak.

Recordings: Gershwin recorded a piano solo in New York on November 8, 1926 (Columbia 809-D, reissued on Monmouth-Evergreen MES 7071 and on The Smithsonian Collection R011-RCA). Gertrude Lawrence did three versions. In the first, made in Camden, New Jersey on November 15, 1926 and sung as a ballad, she was accompanied by pianist Milt Rettenberg (Victor 20331, reissued on The Smithsonian Collection R011-RCA). The second, recorded in London on October 25, 1927 and done up-tempo, is a duet with Harold French (Columbia 4617, reissued on Monmouth-Evergreen MES 7043 and on The Smithsonian Collection R011-RCA). In the third, recorded in London in 1936, she is accompanied by Carroll Gibbons (His Master's Voice C-2835). *Oh, Kay!* duo pianists Phil Ohman and Victor Arden recorded the piece in November of 1926 (Brunswick 3377).

Other 1926 recordings were by Willie Craeger and His Orchestra (Pathe Actuelle 36561), Lou Gold and His Orchestra (Harmony 314-H), Annette Hanshaw (Pathe Actuelle 32226), Bob Haring (Cameo 1082), Roger Wolfe Kahn (Victor 20327), Bert Kaplan and His Collegians (Emerson 3103), George Olsen (Victor 20327), Harry Pollock and His Diamonds (Gennett 6016), Fred Rich and His Hotel Astor Orchestra (Columbia 802-D), Vincent Rizzo and His Hotel Sylvania Orchestra of Philadelphia (Okeh 40725), and Adrian Schubert and His Salon Orchestra (Banner 1888).

There were 1927 recordings by Helen Morgan with Chick Endor and Paul Reese, accompanied by Leslie A. Hutchinson, piano (Brunswick 129), and by the Revelers (Victor 35811). There was a 1934 version by Arthur Young and His Youngsters (Regal Zonophone MR-

1568), a 1938 version by Elisabeth Welch and Robert Ashley (His Master's Vice C-2992), and a 1949 record by Benny Goodman (vocal by Buddy Greco—Armed Forces Radio Service 1931). There was also a duo-piano version by Edgar Fairchild and Ralph Rainger (Victor 20435). In a studio recreation of *Oh, Kay!*, Barbara Ruick and Jack Cassidy do the song up-tempo as well as ballad-style (Columbia OS 2550).

151. FIDGETY FEET

Lyricist: Ira Gershwin

Key: E-flat

Time: Alla breve

Tempo: Moderato

Introduced by: Harland Dixon and Marion Fairbanks in *Oh, Kay!* at the Imperial Theatre in New York City on November 8, 1926.

Lore: Nanette Kutner, writing of Gershwin after his death (in Merle Armitage's book *George Gershwin*), recalled encountering the composer one morning and hearing him say: "I woke up at 3 with a tune, even the title! I got right up and wrote it, like you read about! But now...it's not so hot." The tune in question, "Fidgety Feet," was sung in Act II, Scene 1 of *Oh, Kay!* by Harland Dixon, whose specialty was eccentric dancing. Dixon played a bootlegger who is trying to convince a lady (one of the Fairbanks twins) that, yes, he will still go dancing with her after they are married.

Analysis: The twenty-bar verse ("Something is the matter with me") has the simple lilt of a nursery tune—perhaps because the melody vaguely resembles the prayer theme from *Hansel and Gretel*. The refrain plays 3/4 against 4/4 but in a less tuneful way than was the case in "Fascinating Rhythm." Interesting is the unusual harmony of the lead in (a B7 chord with the seventh in the bass followed by F7 and then the B-flat ninth chord that begins the song) and the fact that the release ("Say, Mate") begins in a contrasting lyrical vein (as had been

160

the case in "Fascinating Rhythm") but then turns into a variation on the main idea. The eight-bar coda ("All I need's a partner") is another variation. The length is thirty-two bars, the form ABAC.

Recordings: Victor Arden and Phil Ohman, Gershwin's favorite duo-pianists, recorded this with their orchestra in 1926 (it is introduced during their version of "Clap Yo' Hands"—Brunswick 3377, reissued on The Smithsonian Collection R011-RCA). Another duo piano version was by Edgar Fairchild and Ralph Rainger (Victor 20435). Ronny Whyte's recording is on Monmouth-Evergreen MES 7061. Allen Case and Roger White sing it in a studio version of *Oh, Kay!* (Columbia OS-2550). Nelson Riddle included an instrumental rendition in the deluxe set of *Ella Fitzgerald Sings the George and Ira Gershwin Song Book,* recorded in 1959 (Verve MG V-4029-5).

152. HEAVEN ON EARTH

Lyricist: Ira Gershwin and Howard Dietz
Key: E-flat
Time: Alla breve
Tempo: Moderato
Introduced by: Oscar Shaw, Betty Compton and Constance Carpenter in *Oh, Kay!* at the Imperial Theatre in New York City on November 8, 1926.

Analysis: The philosophy of this song—that worry doesn't get you anywhere—is sung quite simply and calmly in the declarative verse ("At a very early age"). Then all restraint is abandoned in the refrain with the imaginative line, "Reach up high, pull down the sky/ Make this a heaven on earth." This refrain is a joyous thirty-two-bar AABA rouser, one that is recharged a couple of times en route by Gershwin's use of sevenths in the bass (on "pull" in "pull down the sky" and, in the release, at "This" in "This is the advice I'm giving").

Recordings: Barbara Ruick and Jack Cassidy perform this in a studio version of *Oh, Kay!* (Columbia OS-2550)

153. MAYBE

Lyricist: Ira Gershwin
Key: F
Time: 4/4 (verse)
       Common (refrain)
Tempo: Moderato
Introduced by: Gertrude Lawrence and Oscar Shaw in *Oh, Kay!* at the Imperial Theatre in New York City on November 8, 1926.

Analysis: A sweet and unaggressive verse ("Though today is a blue sky") leads to an even less aggressive refrain ("Soon or late, maybe"). There are just fifty-one notes in its thirty-two bars, most of them on the pentatonic scale. Many of these notes are held for a bar or more and the accompaniment takes advantage of this with canonic interjections. In fact, the piano accompaniment in the published sheet music is unusually accomplished and well-thought out—so much so that, as written, it could stand as a piano piece. There is no release as such, but a minor key development of the main idea (at "Will help you discover"). At the end of the eight-bar coda ("Paradise will open its gate") the accompaniment fleetingly recalls the main idea of the verse.

Recordings: Gershwin's piano solo, recorded in New York on November 11, 1926, was issued on English Columbia 4539 and American Columbia 812-D. It has been reissued on Monmouth-Evergreen MES 7043 and on the Smithsonian Collection R011-RCA. A version by Gertrude Lawrence and Harold French was recorded in London on October 25, 1927. It was released on Columbia 4618 and reissued on Monmouth-Evergreen MES 7043 and on the Smithsonian Collection R011-RCA. Phil Ohman and Victor Arden, duo-pianists from the *Oh, Kay!* orchestra, recorded this song in 1926 (vocal by Virginia Rea and Franklyn Baur—Brunswick 3381).

Other 1926 recordings were by Franklyn Baur (Victor 20417), Jesse Crawford (Victor 20392), and Nat Shilkret (Victor 20392). There were recordings in 1927 by the Revelers (Victor 35811); in 1936 by the Swing Rhythm Boys (Crown 227); in 1939 by Bing Crosby (ac-

companied by Victor Young and His Orchestra—Decca 2874) and Dick
Robertson and His Orchestra (Decca 2541); in 1940 by Chick Bullock (Okeh 5764), Harry James and His Orchestra (Varsity 8353), and
Gene Krupa and His Orchestra (Okeh 5643); in 1948 by Skitch Henderson (Capitol 15234).

Other versions are by Ella Fitzgerald (Decca 8378 and DL 74451),
Mary Martin (Columbia ML-2061 and CBS Encore P-14282), Andre
Previn (piano—RCA Victor LPM 1011), duo pianists Edgar Fairchild
and Ralph Rainger (Victor 20435), Bobby Short (Atlantic 2-608).

154. OH, KAY

Lyricist: Ira Gershwin and Howard Dietz
Key: E-flat
Time: Alla breve
Tempo: Moderato
Introduced by: Gertrude Lawrence and the ensemble in *Oh,
Kay!* at the Imperial Theatre in New York City on November
8, 1926.

Lore: Lyricist Dietz, though given credit for this song, did not
actually write any of it—or so he claimed in his autobiography. According to Dietz, "Ira made me a present of the credit for it. It was the
opposite of plagiarism. We'll call it donorism." Dietz had been brought
in to work on *Oh, Kay!* when Ira had appendicitis.

Analysis: The verse ("You've got a charm that is all your own")
skips happily for twenty bars. Its main distinction is the wrongish G-
flat sung on "there" in "Lady, you are there!" in bar eight. The music
of the thirty-two bar refrain ("Oh, Kay! You're O.K. with me!"), besides being catchy, is harmonically very bold. Like "That Certain
Feeling" from the year before, it begins with a quarter rest and then
three emphatic repeated quarter notes. Here they are the sixth in an
$F7^6$ chord—a sound that was prominent in the opening bars of the
Concerto in F. The harmonic pungency continues in the release ("Venus couldn't compare"), where a G7+ chord suddenly leads us into C-

minor. Then, in the recapitulation and without any forewarning, the main idea is presented in a new key, G. One should also notice the brief and charming little asides sung at the end of the principal four-bar phrases ("You're a dear!," "Listen here," "it is clear") and the funny lyric (comparing Kay with Venus, the chorus sings, "you've her charms and two good arms").

Recordings: An excerpt from this song is played in a 1926 recording by duo pianists Constance Mering and Frank Banta with the Columbia Light Orchestra (Columbia 50031-D, reissued on Smithsonian R-011 and RCA DPL1-0310). Barbara Ruick and Jack Cassidy perform it in a studio version of *Oh, Kay!* (Columbia OS-2550, OL-7050).

155. SHOW ME THE TOWN

Lyricist: Ira Gershwin
Key: C
Time: Alla breve
Tempo: Allegretto moderato
Introduced by: This song was written for but dropped from *Oh, Kay!* Bobbe Arnst introduced it in *Rosalie* at the New Amsterdam Theatre in New York City on January 10, 1928.

Analysis: The twenty-four-bar verse ("Boy! It's simply grand to have the gang around") is made up of a winning and artfully harmonized melody that rises an octave in two bars and then takes five to subside, falling halfway down. As it is being repeated (on "don't you leave") it moves into new melodic territory and new harmonic terrain as well, having shifted to the key of E. The main musical idea of the refrain ("Hey! How about a dance?") is a tune with an inborn, infectious beat and a soft-spoken charm. Its opening, an easy, swinging shift between C and F-major seventh chords, has a warm and modern sound. In the release there is a leap into the key of E (on "Woof! Want to raise the roof!"). It is sudden and invigorating.

Recordings: None

164

156. SOMEONE TO WATCH OVER ME

Lyricist: Ira Gershwin
Key: E-flat (also published in C)
Time: Alla breve
Tempo: Scherzando (introduction)
Moderato (verse and refrain)
Introduced by: Gertrude Lawrence in Oh, Kay! at the Imperial
Theatre in New York City on November 8, 1926.

Lore: Gershwin originally planned this as an up-tempo number
but he chanced to play it slowly one day and realized that it was a
ballad.

The title was suggested by lyricist Howard Dietz, who was giving Ira a hand while the latter recovered from an appendectomy.

In *Oh, Kay!*, Gertrude Lawrence sang "Someone to Watch Over
Me" to a rag doll that the composer had found in a Philadelphia toy
store. It was his idea that she do this and it proved very effective. The
song was introduced at that point in the play when the man she loved
was preparing to marry another woman. Later, Lawrence reprised the
tune in a duet with him after he had left the other woman for her.

The plot of *Oh, Kay!* must also be referred to to explain an in-
consistency in the lyric. In the verse the singer refers to a man she
hasn't yet met but who, at the same time, she cannot forget. This
makes sense only when we know that she had saved him from drown-
ing without learning his identity.

After the premiere of *Oh, Kay!* critic Percy Hammond wrote in
the New York *Tribune*: "'Someone to Watch Over Me' wrung the
withers of even the most hardhearted of those present." Gershwin,
aware of the emotional impact of the song, told a friend that he wanted
it "to be a sort of 'Long, Long, Trail.'"

Analysis: In the verse ("There's a saying old"), the composer, as
he did in "Fascinating Rhythm," takes a melody that should have been
in triple time and fits it into a 4/4 pattern. But here the effect is not the
brittle tension of "Fascinating Rhythm" but an insistent, sighing sound.
After sixteen bars, with a shift into G-minor (at "I'd like to add his

165

initials to my monogram"), the music becomes even more heartfelt. In the refrain ("There's a somebody I'm longing to see"), Gershwin demonstrates his ability to write a catch-in-the-throat ballad without resorting to grand or melodramatic gestures. Like a musical lapidary, he gets emotional effects from harmonic minutiae, strategically placing diminished chords so that they pull the bottom out from under the melody whenever it attempts to rest (on "see" in "longing to see," on "he" in "I hope that he," and on "be" in "turns out to be"). Later, in the release ("Although he may not be the man some girls think of as handsome"), the melody returns again and again to a D-natural—a note that creates a poignant tension because it is well outside the supporting A-flat harmony.

Recordings: On November 11, 1926 Gershwin, in New York, made a solo piano recording of this song (English Columbia 4539 and American Columbia 812-D, reissued on Monmouth-Evergreen MES 7071 and The Smithsonian Collection R011-RCA). Gertrude Lawrence released several versions. On the first, recorded in Camden, New Jersey on October 29, 1926, she is accompanied by pianist Tom Wargin (Victor 20331). On another, recorded in London on October 25, 1927, she sings a duet with Harold French (Columbia 4618). For a third, recorded in London in 1932, she was accompanied by pianist Claude Ivy (Decca K-689). Then, in 1936, she recorded it in London again, this time accompanied by Carroll Gibbons (His Master's Voice C-2835). Oh, Kay! duo-pianists Phil Ohman and Victor Arden introduce "Someone to Watch Over Me" in the course of their recording of "Do-Do-Do" (Brunswick 3377). They also recorded it with a vocal by Virginia Rea and Franklyn Baur (Brunswick 3381). Frances Gershwin's recording is on Monmouth-Evergreen MES 7060.

Other 1926 recordings were by Joe Candullo and His Everglades Orchestra (Pathe Actuelle 36571), George Olsen (Victor 20392), and Nat Shilkret (Victor 20392). In 1927 there were versions by Bert Kaplan and His Collegians (Emerson 3115) and the Revelers (Victor 35811); in 1938 by Elisabeth Welch and Robert Ashley (His Master's Voice C-2992); in 1939 by Eddie Condon with Lee Wiley (Decca 23432) and Frances Langford (Decca 2882); in 1942 by Linda Keene and Henry Levine (Victor 27832); in 1946 by Frank Sinatra (Columbia 36921); in 1951 by Kay Winding (Roost 531); in 1952 by Arnett Cobb (Okeh 6912).

For other versions, one can choose from Elly Ameling and Louis Van Dijk (Phillips 6514284), Gene Ammons (Prestige 2514 and 24079), Claire Austin (Contemporary OJC-1711), Jerry Butler (Vee Jay 1046), the Charlie Byrd Trio (Concord Jazz 252), Donald Byrd (Savoy 1101), Little Jimmy Dempsey (Plantation 520), Peter Duchin (Fortune 299), Roy Eldridge (Crescendo 9009), Michael Feinstein (Parnassus PR 0100), Ella Fitzgerald (Verve 2615-063), Jane Froman (Victor 12335), Benny Goodman (live at Carnegie Hall—London 820349-1), the Great Jazz Trio (Inner City 6003), Art Hodes (Muse 5252), Lena Horne (Victor AYL1-4389), Eiji Kitamura (Concord Jazz 217), Liberace (AVI 8304), Melissa Manchester (Arista ALB6-8350), Helen Merrill (Inner City 1080), Julia Johnson-Migenes (Victor ARL1-5323), Joan Morris with piano accompaniment by William Bolcom (Nonesuch H-71358), Willie Nelson (Columbia FC-35305), the 101 Strings Orchestra (Alshire ALCD-12), Norrie Paramor (Angel 38119), Oscar Peterson and Joe Pass (Pablo 2308232), Bud Powell (Verve 2-2526), Jimmy Raney (Prestige OJC-1706), Linda Ronstadt (Asylum 7-69725), Barbara Ruick (Columbia OS 2550), Little Jimmy Scott (Savoy 1145), Artie Shaw (Victor AXM2-5580), Dinah Shore (Victor 2-1651), Zoot Sims (Pablo 2319744), Paul Smith (Outstanding 007), Barbra Streisand (Columbia PC-9136), Art Tatum (Pablo 2310870), Robert Trendler and Orchestra (Pilotone 5113/20), the Louis Van Dyke Trio (Jazzman 5047), Sarah Vaughan (Mercury MGP-2-101), Lawrence Welk (Ranwood 8195), Lee Wiley with Fats Waller (Monmouth-Evergreen 7034).

157. PRELUDES FOR PIANO

For solo piano

Introduced by: George Gershwin at the Hotel Roosevelt in New York City on December 4, 1926.

Lore: In a March 1925 article in *Vanity Fair*, music critic Carl Van Vechten said that Gershwin was working on a suite of twenty-four

167

piano preludes, to be called *The Melting Pot*. As it turned out, Gershwin, in his lifetime, published only three piano preludes—and, then, he did not do so under any collective title. But there were others. As early as 1919 he was sketching what he called "novelettes" for piano and he recorded one of them, marked Allegretto scherzando and called "Novelette in Fourths," on a piano roll that year. A second, marked Andantino con fantasia, was dated August 30, 1923 in Gershwin's notebooks and it, along with the "Novelette in Fourths," were joined together by violinist Samuel Dushkin to make *Short Story*, a piece for violin and piano that was published in 1925.

On December 4, 1926, Gershwin gave a joint recital at the Hotel Roosevelt with an English/Peruvian contralto named Marguerite d'Alvarez. This concert was conceived as an experimental juxtaposition of highbrow and popular music. d'Alvarez sang art songs and then Broadway numbers (Gershwin accompanied her in the latter); Gershwin premiered his two-piano version of *Rhapsody in Blue* (Isidore Gorin was the other pianist) and five preludes for solo piano. Three of these he published. As for the others, conjecture has it that they were the "Novelette in Fourths" and the Andantino con fantasia—the pieces that had been used by Dushkin in the creation of *Short Story*. Then, in Boston on January 16, 1927, Gershwin and d'Alverez repeated their concert and this time the composer played not five but six preludes. This sixth prelude, sometimes called "the lost prelude," may have been based on a 1924 sketch—one that Gershwin did not get around to finishing on paper until 1936 (Ira Gershwin later gave it the title "Sleepless Night" but, so far, it has not been published). On the other hand, it may have been another piece entirely.

Analysis:
I. *Prelude in B-flat* (Allegro ben ritmato e deciso).

This aggressive piece in 2/4 time starts with a little blues riff in the right hand. It is followed by a jerky, syncopated accompanimental figure in the left. The latter then becomes the accompaniment for the former. Throughout the piece, each hand sticks to the material that it introduced in these first four bars.

II. *Prelude in C-sharp minor* (Andante con moto e poco rubato).

Gershwin referred to this piece as a "blue lullaby"—and its opening bars, a slow and dreamy chordal pattern for the left hand, move up and down in a cradle-rocking fashion. After three measures, the right hand enters playing a melody that, in its insistent use of the minor third interval, resembles "The Man I Love. "The middle section, in F-sharp, gives the left hand a ruminative, jazzy recitative, for which the right hand plays accompanimental chords. Then the initial idea returns, this time in octaves and with a chromatic countermelody.

III. *Prelude in E-flat minor* (Allegro ben ritmato e deciso).

Gershwin referred to this 2/4 piece as the Spanish prelude— possibly because it begins with a succession of minor sixth and major sixth chords that are stomped out flamenco-style low in the bass, as if on the floor. The main idea is a downward blues run played in E-flat minor, then E-flat major. Some of the composer's most brilliant piano writing occurs in this piece, particularly in the polyrhythmic idea that comes after the initial exposition.

Recordings: Gershwin recorded his preludes in London on June 8, 1928 (Columbia 50107-D, reissued on Victoria AVM1-1740 and Monmouth-Evergreen MES 7071). Other versions are by Jeanne Behrend (Victor Red Seal 17910), Richard Rodney Bennett (EMI EMD 5538), Sondra Bianca (MGM 3-E1, 33237), William Bolcom (Nonesuch 71284), Frank Glazer (Concert Disc 217), Morton Gould (RCA Victor LM 2017, LM 6033), Michael Jamanis (Book of the Month Club Records 61-5426), Grant Johannesen (Golden Crest S-4065), Oscar Levant (Columbia ML2073, MS-7518, reissued on CBS MLK-39454), Eugene List (Turnabout TV-S 34457), Lincoln Mayorga (TownHall M-4), Perry O'Neill (Kapp KCI 9029), Eric Parkin (Preamble PRCD-1776), Leonard Pennario (RCA Victor LSC-2731, LSC-5001, Angel DS-37359), Andre Ratusinsky (Trax Classique TR&CD-111), Pavel Stepan (Sonic 10), Michael Tilson Thomas (CBS FM-42516), Ralph Votapek (London 411835-1 LJ), Andre Watts (Columbia M 34211), Ken Werner (Finnadar 9019).

At a September 8, 1937 George Gershwin memorial concert, Otto Klemperer conducted the Los Angeles Philharmonic in his arrangement of the *Prelude #2* (Citadel CT 7017). Jascha Heifetz transcribed these pieces for violin and piano and his recording of them was released on Decca DL-7003). Violinist Elmar Oliveira and pianist Robert McDonald recorded that arrangement and released it on Vox Cum Laude 9057.

158. MILITARY DANCING DRILL

Lyricist: Ira Gershwin
Key: F
Time: Alla breve
Tempo: Moderato (verse)
   Tempo di marcia molto deciso e marziale (refrain)
Introduced by: Maz Hoffman, Jr. and Dorothea James in *Strike Up the Band* at the Schubert Theatre in New York City on September 5, 1927.

Analysis: The title refers to a soldier's drill step that is actually a dance step, learned for the art of wooing, not war. The twenty-four-bar verse ("The military man") is a straightforward march, one without the bite of the verse to "Strike Up the Band." The refrain ("Soldier, advance!") is clipped and staccato; it does not have the forward propulsion of the "Strike Up the Band" refrain. The length is thirty-two bars and the form AABA, the main musical effect in the A sections being the harmonic contrast between F and B-flat ninth chords. The B section ("Throw out your chest"), in A-minor, is a lyrical eight-bar melody—it sounds like "I Have A Love" from the 1956 Broadway show *West Side Story*.
   When a revised version of *Strike Up the Band* appeared on Broadway in 1930, "Military Dancing Drill" was provided with a new verse.

Recordings: None

159. SEVENTEEN AND TWENTY-ONE

Lyricist: Ira Gershwin

Key: A-flat
Time: Alla breve
Tempo: Moderato
Introduced by: Dorothea James and Max Hoffman, Jr. In *Strike Up the Band* at the Shubert Theatre in New York City on September 5, 1927.

Analysis: In this duet, a seventeen-year old girl and a twenty-one year old boy regret that they have had to wait until such advanced ages to find one another. The thirty-three-bar verse ("Age was creeping on me")—the extra bar due to a vamp figure at the end—has a whimsical, jocular melody, one consisting of imitative phrases in a succession of keys. It is not an easy piece to sing. The refrain ("I had to wait till I was seventeen") is unusual for its extended second ending ("Heigh ho!"), one that presents new material and brings the length to forty-four bars. This ending is similar in music and words to that of the expansive "Hi-Ho," which the brothers would write in 1936. For that matter, the sighing opening of this refrain foreshadows the "Oh, my Porgy" section of "Bess, You is My Woman." Also interesting is the playful four-bar instrumental ending marked grazioso.

Recordings: Betty Gillett and David Craig do this on an album entitled *Gershwin Rarities* (Citadel CT 7017).

160. STRIKE UP THE BAND

Lyricist: Ira Gershwin
Key: B-flat minor (verse)
      B-flat (refrain)
Time: Alla breve
Tempo: In slow march time (verse)
       Very marked (refrain)
Introduced by: Max Hoffman, Jr. in *Strike Up the Band* at the Shubert Theatre in New York City on September 5, 1927. Jerry Goff sang it in the 1930 revival of the show.

Lore: Gershwin had written and rejected four march tunes before coming up with this one. According to Ira, it was thought up while the composer lay in the dark in his Atlantic City hotel room late one spring evening in 1927. Pajama-clad, he played it for his brother a few minutes later.

In a series of revisions over the years, the original intent of the lyric was totally changed. "Strike Up the Band" began as a sarcastic anti-war song ("We're in a bigger, better war for your patriotic pastime. We don't know what we're fighting for but we didn't know the last time!"). But in 1940, with war in Europe spreading, Ira changed it "(We hope there'll be no other war but if we're forced into one the flag that we'll be fighting for is the red and white and blue one!"). Then, after America's entry into World War II, he altered the lyric again and this time he was in a fighting mood, putting in a line about turning the Hun away from the gate. And there was still another version. In 1936 the Gershwins allowed U.C.L.A. to use the piece as a football song, retitled "Strike Up the Band for U.C.L.A." In payment they received lifetime passes to all Bruins games.

Upon the 1930 revival of *Strike Up the Band*, William Bolitho, in an essay about this song, wrote, "Here is a bitter, rather satirical attack on war, genuine propaganda at times, sung and danced on Broadway to standing room only."

The composer's piano transcription appeared in *George Gershwin's Songbook*, published by Simon and Schuster in September of 1932.

"Strike Up the Band" and other Gershwin songs were used in the 1940 ballet *The New Yorkers*, performed by the Ballet Russe de Monte Carlo.

Analysis: Points of interest in the marvelous verse ("We fought in nineteen seventeen") are the tramping, trudging minor chords, recurring drum motive ("Rum-ta-ta-tum-tum-tum!"), the way a musical phrase is presented somberly at first in F-minor at "We're in a bigger better war" and then giddily in F major at "We don't know what we're fighting for"), and the powerful, sometimes dissonant chords at the conclusion. The famous anthem-like refrain ("Let the drums roll out!") features a surging melody accompanied by drum rolls in the bass. It is thirty-two bars long and, but for a repetition of bar one at bar twenty-four, is through-composed.

Recordings: Recordings of this song did not begin until 1930, when a second, and this time successful, version of *Strike Up the Band* came to Broadway. A rehearsal for that show was captured on film and there is a soundtrack recording that has Gershwin playing this song (20th Century Fox 03013). Loring "Red" Nichols and his orchestra played in the 1930 edition and their recording, made in January of 1930, features Tommy Dorsey (Brunswick 4695).

Other 1930 recordings were by Victor Arden-Phil Ohman and their Orchestra (Victor 22308), Bert Lown and his Loungers (Banner 0659), the Revelers (Victor 22401), Fred Rich and his Orchestra (Columbia 21320D), and Bob Tams and His Orchestra (Broadway 1373).

In 1938 there was a recording by Elisabeth Welch and Robert Ashley (His Master's Voice C-2991). In 1940 this song was featured in the film *Strike Up the Band*, which starred Judy Garland and Mickey Rooney (Curtain Calls 100-9/10). Stan Getz recorded the tune in 1950 (Roost 520) and Sonny Stitt recorded it in 1952 (Prestige 758).

Other versions are by Sidney Bechet (Crescendo 9012), Tony Bennett and Count Basie (Roulette RS-107 and 59021), The Boston Pops Orchestra conducted by Arthur Fiedler (Victor CRL1-2064), Al Caiola (Bainbridge 1012), Rosemary Clooney (Concord Jazz 112), Chris Connor (Atlantic 2-601), Rolf Ericson (Discovery 1731), Ella Fitzgerald (Verve 2615063), Ralph Grierson/Artie Kane (Angel 36083), Bobby Jaspar (Inner City 7013), Duke Jordan (Prestige 7849), Bobby Knight and the Great American Trombone Company (Seabreeze 2009), the Elliott Lawrence Band (Fantasy OJC-117), Ann Leaf (New World 227), Andre Previn (RCA Victor LPM 1011), Tommy Tune (Atlantic 80110-1-E), Joe Venuti (Flying Fish 077), Lawrence Welk (Ranwood 8194), and Bob Wilber/Kenny Davern (Concord Jazz 52).

161. YANKEE DOODLE RHYTHM

Lyricist: Ira Gershwin
Key: G

Time: Alla breve
Tempo: Allegretto (verse)
        Lively (refrain)
Introduced by: Jimmy Savo, Ruth Wilcox, Max Hoffman, Jr. and Dorothea James in *Strike Up the Band* at the Shubert Theatre in New York City on September 5, 1927. In 1928 this song was inserted into and then dropped from *Rosalie*.

Analysis: American music—"the piping of the Jazzbo!" as Ira Gershwin puts it here—is winning the world, sweeping aside the music of the Sirens and Pan and the minstrels. As musical evidence, however, this song is not quite a smoking gun. There is a sixteen-bar verse ("Talk about the music of the Sirens") that features prominent blue notes and, at bar thirteen, a pastoral restatement in B of the initial G-major idea. The main idea of the thirty-two-bar refrain ("Yankee Doodle rhythm is in demand") is a stuttering, syncopated phrase. The form is AABA^{1}CA^2—with A^2 being a climactic extention of the stuttering idea.

Recordings: None

162. THE BABBITT AND THE BROMIDE

Lyricist: Ira Gershwin
Key: E-minor (introduction)
       Ambiguous (verse)
       G (refrain)
Time: 2/4
Tempo: Allegretto humoroso
Introduced by: Fred and Adele Astaire in *Funny Face* at the Alvin Theatre in New York City on November 22, 1927.

Lore: *Funny Face* was having a hard time of it during its Philadelphia tryout and this song was written to add life to the show. The idea for it came to Ira when he heard comedian Billy Kent say, "Heigh ho, that's life!"—a true bromide if ever there was one.

After George and Ira demonstrated the song for Fred Astaire and producer Vinton Freedley, Astaire took Ira aside to say, "I know what a babbitt is but what's a bromide?" And, not long after that, Freedley buttonholed the lyricist and said, "I know what a bromide is—but what's a babbitt?"

Ira had a special reason for being particularly proud of "The Babbitt and the Bromide," as it was the only song lyric included in Louis Kronenberger's *Anthology of Light Verse*, published in 1934.

In 1946 the number was revived for a film, *The Ziegfeld Follies*, in which it was sung by Fred Astaire and Gene Kelly.

Analysis: The introduction is an um-pah vamp in E-minor—not unlike the um-pahing in "Wintergreen For President," which, though used in 1931 for *Of Thee I Sing*, was conceived at about this time. But when the verse begins E-minor is nowhere to be found. Instead, C7 chords alternate with A7 chords, followed by F#7 chords which alternate with E-flat7 chords. The juxtaposition of these unrelated chords makes for a strange and otherworldy effect. Given the mundaneness of the title characters, this is humorously ironic. Yet, it is appropriate, too, as both of them will expire during the course of the song. In the refrain ("Hello! How are you?") the music shifts to G, becoming light-hearted. And, when Gershwin concludes with an ebullient ten-bar instrumental polka, it becomes light-headed.

Recordings: Fred and Adele Astaire's version was recorded in London in November of 1928 (English Columbia 5174, reissued on Monmouth-Evergreen MES 7037). In 1940 there was a recording by Danny Kaye (Columbia 36584). The 1946 Fred Astaire/Gene Kelly version from *Ziegfeld Follies* is available on Curtain Calls 100/15-16. Recent renditions by Joan Morris and Max Morath with piano accompaniment by William Bolcom (RCA ARL1-2491) and by Marni Nixon with piano accompaniment by Lincoln Mayorga (Reference RR-19).

163. DANCE ALONE WITH YOU

Lyricist: Ira Gershwin

175

Key: E-flat
Time: Alla breve
Tempo: Moderato
Introduced by: This song was dropped from *Funny Face* before its November 22, 1927 premiere.

Lore: A new lyric was attached to this tune and the resulting song, "Ev'rybody Knows I Love Somebody," was used in *Rosalie* in 1928.

Analysis: The twenty-four-bar verse is made of two fine but very different melodies. The first ("There are lots of fellows at ev'ry dance") has an insistent beat and a bluish cadence (on "chance"). The second ("He's just a gag-line") has a yearning, almost noble bearing. In the refrain ("Why does ev'rybody have to cut in") the composer plays a rhythmic game, getting a series of five-note phrases to fit into 4/4 time. But this does not play as a trick—it comes off as an ingratiating melody backed by a swinging beat. Worth noting too is the fact that Gershwin, in the accompaniment, quotes from two other songs in the *Funny Face* score. At bars seven and eight (on "you" in the title phrase) we get the main idea from "The World Is Mine," and at bars fifteen and sixteen (on "me" in "love me?") there is a quote from "Let's Kiss and Make Up." Also of interest is the highly dramatic and musically powerful G-minor release. Here the singer threatens to kill those who are cutting in on him on the dance floor.

Recordings: "Dance Alone With You" was used in the 1978 revival of *Funny Face* in Buffalo, New York and in the 1981 revival in East Haddam, Connecticut. Privately made tapes of these shows exist.

164. FUNNY FACE

Lyricist: Ira Gershwin
Key: E-flat
Time: Alla breve
Tempo: Moderato

176

Introduced by: Fred and Adele Astaire in *Funny Face* at the Alvin Theatre in New York City on November 22, 1927.

Analysis: Here Ira tackles the fairly unusual theme of how someone can be loved despite his or her plainness of face. But he does not do so with any high purpose in mind, as the lines are all light-hearted and witty. The music is cheerful too, at least on the surface. But in both the twenty-four-bar verse ("Frankie, dear") and the thirty-two-bar refrain ("I love your Funny Face") there is a woebegone layer. In the verse it can be heard in the sighing melodic descents and in the anxious augmented harmony. In the refrain, the rosy sixty-four-note tune is offset by a chromatic figure in the accompaniment that is much like the one that is joined to the slow theme of the *Rhapsody in Blue*. The form is ABA plus a coda ("Though you're no handsome Harry") made from both A and B. Also worth noting is the harmonic progression toward the end of the B section (at "You've got a lot of")—a tour de force—and its variant in the coda ("Though you're no").

Recordings: Gershwin recorded a solo version of "Funny Face" as part of a medley with "'S Wonderful" (Columbia 5109, reissued on Monmouth-Evergreen MES 7037). Fred and Adele Astaire recorded it in London in 1928 (Columbia 5174, reissued on Monmouth-Evergreen MES 7037). Fred Astaire performed it again in the 1957 Paramount film *Funny Face* (Verve MGV-15001). *Funny Face* duo-pianists Victor Arden and Phil Ohman recorded this song twice: the first time was in 1927 with a vocal by Johnny Marvin (Victor 21114) and the second was in 1928 as part of a *Funny Face* medley (Victor 35918). Other early recordings were a 1927 version by Bernie Cummings and His Orchestra (Brunswick 3750), and 1928 renditions by Jack Smith (His Master's Voice B-2864) and the Revelers (Victor 35918). More recent recordings have been by Ella Fitzgerald (Verve MGV-4028), Denny Dillon and Bruce McGill (from the cast of *My One and Only*—Atlantic 80110-1-E) and Yehudi Menuhin/Stephane Grappelli (Angel DS-37860).

165. HE LOVES AND SHE LOVES

Lyricist: Ira Gershwin

Key: A-minor (verse)
F (refrain)
Time: Alla breve
Tempo: Moderato (verse)
Slowly (with sentiment) (refrain)
Introduced by: Adele Astaire and Allen Kearns in *Funny Face* at the Alvin Theatre in New York City on November 22, 1927.

Lore: The music and lyrics of this song grew out of the thirty-first through thirty-fourth bars of a 1919 George Gershwin/Lou Paley song entitled "Something About Love."
"He Loves and She Loves" replaced "How Long Has This Been Going On?" during the out-of-town tryouts of *Funny Face*.

Analysis: The sixteen-bar verse ("Now that I have found you") consists of a series of forlorn, imitative phrases, first in A-minor, then in A-flat (at "If the human race"). The thirty-two-bar refrain ("He Loves and She Loves") employs an unusual harmonic procedure: the simple chords of the accompaniment are modified by the notes that are sung. For instance, the singer's second note ("Loves" in "He Loves"), a D, turns the supporting F-chord into an F6. The fourth note ("Loves" in "She Loves"), also a D, turns the supporting C-chord into a C9. The seventh note ("they" in "they love"), an E-flat, turns the supporting A-minor seventh into an Am7^{-5}. These harmonies and the numerous melodic leaps, give the song its sorrowful, lonesome quality. The release ("Oh, I always knew") is an extension of rather than a contrast to the main portion of the refrain.

Recordings: Adele Astaire and Bernard Clifton recorded this in London on November 29, 1928 (Columbia 5175, reissued on Monmouth-Evergreen MES 7037). It was sung in the 1957 Paramount film *Funny Face* by Fred Astaire (Verve MGV-15001). *Funny Face* duo pianists Victor Arden and Phil Ohman recorded the tune in April of 1928 as part of a medley from the show (Victor 35918). In addition, there was a 1927 recording by the B.F. Goodrich Silvertone Cord Orchestra (Victor 21167), 1928 recordings by Al Friedman and His Orchestra (Edison 52190) and the Revelers (Victor 35918), a 1959 version by Ella Fitzgerald (Verve MGV 4027), and more recent renditions by the Barbara Carroll Trio (Verve MGV 2063), Michael Feinstein (Parnassus PR 0100), George Feyer (Vanguard VSD 62), Zubin Mehta and the New York Philharmonic (from the soundtrack of Woody Allen's *Manhattan*—Columbia JS36020), Yehudi Menuhin/Stephane Grappelli (Angel DS-37860), Tommy Tune and Twiggy (from the cast of *My One and Only*—Atlantic 80110-1-E), Ronny Whyte and Travis Hudson (Monmouth-Evergreen MES 7061).

166. HIGH HAT

Lyricist: Ira Gershwin
Key: F
Time: 2/4
Tempo: Allegro moderato
Introduced by: Fred Astaire in *Funny Face* at the Alvin Theatre in New York City on November 22, 1927.

Lore: "High Hat" was Fred Astaire's first top hat and tails routine.

Analysis: The verse ("When a fellow feels he's got to win a girlie's handie") is a dialogue between the singer and a male chorus. The singer tells the chorus that he has a solution to the high financial cost of wooing a young lady. He then divulges that solution in the refrain, saying that one must treat her "High hat!" Musically, this twenty-eight-bar verse consists of a series of delicately made imitative phrases that ascend at first, then descend. The first note of the refrain ("hat" in "High hat!") is held for two full bars while, in the accompaniment, inner voicings move against one another, creating playful suspensions. These long notes, which provided Astaire with dancing breaks, are separated by bursts of repeated notes ("You've got to treat them"). There is no release, only a repetition of the main idea in B-flat.

Recordings: Fred Astaire recorded this on November 29, 1928 during the London run of *Funny Face* (Columbia 5173, reissued on

179

Monmouth-Evergreen MES 7037). In May of 1928, Duke Yellman and His Orchestra recorded it (Edison 52328), as did Jesse Crawford (Victor 21666). Bobby Short's version appeared in 1973 (Atlantic SD 2-608).

167. LET'S KISS AND MAKE UP

Lyricist: Ira Gershwin
Key: E-flat
Time: Alla breve
Tempo: Moderato (verse)
  Gracefully (refrain)
Introduced by: Fred and Adele Astaire in *Funny Face* at the Alvin Theatre in New York City on November 22, 1927.

Lore: This was originally called "Come! Come! Come Closer!" The present title was taken from the first line of the original verse, which made a new opening line necessary.

Analysis: The refrain of "Let's Kiss and Make Up," like that of "Fascinating Rhythm," is an experiment in metrics that aims to disorient the listener. On the title phrase Gershwin takes a 7/4 melody and holds one note (on "make") for an extra beat, bringing it into a very wobbly 4/4 meter. In the meantime, the accompanist is playing 4/4 in a very roundabout way: 3/4, 3/4 and 2/4. In other words, singer and accompanist both end up in 4/4, but each gets there by a different, circuitous route.

After an eight-bar release ("I'll give you your way") there is, rather than a verbatim repetition of the opening material, a twelve-bar development of it ("If we'd be happy"), bringing this refrain in at thirty-six rather than thirty-two bars. As for the verse ("I didn't mean to start any scene"), it is a complete thirty-two bar song in itself and its beautiful and oddly modal release ("Don't you know Ben Franklin wrote") is as daring as anything that happens in the refrain.

Recordings: Frances Gershwin's recording is on Monmouth-

Evergreen MES 7060. This song was sung in the 1957 Paramount film *Funny Face* (Verve MGV-15001). It has also been recorded by Louise Carlyle and Warren Galjour (Citadel CT 7017), the Barbara Carroll Trio (Verve MGV 2063), Ella Fitzgerald (Verve MGV-4028), duo-pianists Jacques Fray and Mario Braggiotti (His Master's Voice B 2910), the New Mayfair Orchestra (His Master's Voice C 1588), Bobby Short (Atlantic SD 2-608).

168. MY ONE AND ONLY

Lyricist: Ira Gershwin
Key: F (verse)
    B-flat (refrain)
Time: Alla breve
Tempo: Moderato
Introduced by: Fred Astaire, Gertrude MacDonald and Betty Compton in *Funny Face* at the Alvin Theatre in New York City on November 22, 1927.

Lore: In its review of *Funny Face*, the *New Republic* called this tune "the sensational event of the evening," describing it as "An odd dark melody in despairing Polish minors which Fred Astaire taps out opposite Gertrude MacDonald." In 1931, Isaac Goldberg, Gershwin's first biographer, said that in this song "the Khassid and the Negro join hands melodically." And a later Gerswhin biographer, Charles Schwartz, claimed that this refrain "closely resembles Jewish cantillation...and seems to have emerged almost intact from the Old Testament and the synagogal tradition."

Analysis: The verse consists of a sneering, chromatic tune ("To show affection"), followed by a series of syncopated arpeggios ("There must be lots of other men you hypnotize") that sounds like a vocalist's exercise. In the refrain ("My One And Only"), harmonies usually reserved for dramatic slow tempo songs are made to propel a rhythm number. These harmonies—the "despairing Polish minors" talked about by the *New Republic*—are minor seventh chords with diminished fifths,

181

and here they make for an angry, charging sound. The release ("I tell you I'm not asking any miracle") juxtaposes major and minor harmonies and it continues the mood of the opening with abrupt and tricky rhythms and a highly evolved blue sound (on the final "and make us one"), wherein the minor third is harmonized not by the usual IV chord but, instead, by a #V^9.

Recordings: Gershwin's solo piano version was recorded in London on June 8, 1928 (Columbia 5109, reissued on Monmouth-Evergreen MES 7037). A recording by Fred Astaire was made on November 29, 1928 (Columbia 5173, reissued on Monmouth-Evergreen MES 7037). Victor Arden and Phil Ohman, duo-pianists from *Funny Face*, did their version on April 5, 1928 (in a *Funny Face* medley—Victor 35918). Frances Gershwin's recording is on Monmouth Evergreen MES 7060.

In 1927 there were versions by the Clicquot Eskimos (Columbia 1213-D), Jane Green (Victor 21114), the Ipana Troubadors (Columbia 1213-D), Johnny Johnson and His Statler Pennsylvanians (Victor 21113), and Sam Lanin and His Orchestra (vocal by Scrappy Lambert—Pathe Actuelle 36734). In 1928 there were releases by the Revelers (Victor 35918) and Jack Smith (His Master's Voice B-2863). Henry King and His Orchestra recorded the tune in 1936 (Decca 1890), Elisabeth Welch and Robert Ashley in 1938 (His Master's Voice C-2991), and, in 1939, came records by Eddie Condon (Decca 23421) and Lee Wiley (Liberty Music Shop 281). More recent versions have been by Louise Carlyle (Citadel CT 7017), Charles "Honi" Coles and Tommy Tune (from the *My One and Only* cast recording—Atlantic 80110-1-E), Ella Fitzgerald (Verve MGV-4024), and Sarah Vaughan (Mercury MGP-2-101).

169. 'S WONDERFUL

Lyricist: Ira Gershwin
Key: E-flat
Time: Alla breve
Tempo: Moderato
Introduced by: Adele Astaire and Allen Kearns in *Funny Face*

at the Alvin Theatre in New York City on November 22, 1927.

Lore: Ira Gershwin's use of "fash" for "fashion" and "pash" for "passion" in the verse of "'S Wonderful" was a mannerism borrowed from a comedian named Walter Catlett (he had introduced the title song in *Lady, Be Good*). Slicing off the *beginnings* of words, however (as it is done in the refrain), was the lyricist's own invention.

George Gershwin's piano transcription of this song appeared in *George Gershwin's Songbook*, published by Simon and Schuster in September of 1932.

In the film *An American in Paris* "'S Wonderful" is sung by Georges Guetary and Gene Kelly and, for them, Ira came up with some new rhymes using French words ("'S exceptionel/'S why I fell"). He also provided some new rhymes for Ella Fitzgerald when she included this song in *Ella Fitzgerald Sings the George and Ira Gershwin Songbook*.

Gershwin biographer Charles Schwartz was advised by noted Yiddish composer Sholom Secunda that there is a similarity between the refrain of "'S Wonderful" and four bars of "Noach's Teive" ("Noah's Ark")—a melody from *Akeidas Izchok* (*The Sacrifice of Isaac*) by another Yiddish composer, Abraham Goldfadden. Gershwin was familiar with the works of Goldfadden and with the Yiddish musical theater in general.

Analysis: The twenty-four-bar verse ("Life has just begun") is a first cousin to the refrain of "That Certain Feeling" in that both take a five-note phrase and try it out in various registers. In this song the idea is less agressive than the one in "That Certain Feeling"; it has a sighing quality. The thirty-two-bar refrain ("'S wonderful! 'S marvelous!"), one of the most famous in American song literature, boasts Ira's apocopic truncations and a natural and effortless melody. Under the tune, the harmony sways back and forth between E-flat chords and E-flat sixth chords (on "'S wonderful") and between C7 and C-sharp diminished chords (on "'S marvelous")—the melody is the baby on a swing and the harmony is the parent doing the pushing. For the release ("You've made my life so glamorous") there is a refreshing key change, from E-flat to G.

183

Recordings: In London on June 12, 1928, Gershwin recorded a piano solo of this song as part of a medley with "Funny Face" (Columbia 5109, reissued on Monmouth-Evergreen MES 7037). At the same time, Adele Astaire and Bernard Clifton recorded a version (Columbia 5175, reissued on Monmouth-Evergreen MES 7037). Latter-day versions by Fred Astaire are on Mercury MG C-1001 and Daybreak OR 2009. *Funny Face* duo-pianists Victor Arden and Phil Ohman released two versions: the first was recorded on December 8, 1927 (Victor 2114) and the second on April 5, 1928 (as part of a *Funny Face* medley—Victor 35918).

There were recordings in 1927 by Frank Crumit (Victor 21091), Bernie Cummins and His Orchestra (Brunswick 3750), The Ipana Troubadors (Columbia 1213-D), Sam Lanin and His Orchestra (vocal by Scrappy Lambert—Pathe Actuelle 36734), and by Tom Stacks and His Orchestra (Okeh 40954); in 1928 by Ernie Golden and His Hotel McAlpin Orchestra (Edison 52275), Victor Irwin and His Orchestra (Harmony 571-H), Sam Lanin's Troubadors (Cameo 8131), the Rounders (directed by Harry Reser—Banner 7049), the Revelers (Victor 35918), and Jack Smith (His Master's Voice B-2863);

in 1934 by Arthur Young and His Youngsters (Regal Zonophone MR-1568); in 1936 by Hildegarde (Columbia FB-1541), Henri King and His Orchestra (Decca 1890), and Frankie Trumbauer and His Orchestra (with Jack Teagarden and Artie Shaw—Brunswick 7663); in 1938 by the Benny Goodman Quartet (Victor 2609A) and Elisabeth Welch and Robert Ashley (His Master's Voice C-2991); in 1939 by Larry Clinton and His Orchestra (Victor 26341), Eddie Condon (Decca 23430), Jack Marshard and His Orchestra (Brunswick 8417), and Lee Wiley (Liberty Music Shop 283);

in 1942 by Bob Grant and His Orchestra (Decca 24041); in 1944 by Coleman Hawkins (Key 609); in 1945 by Artie Shaw (Victor 20-1638) and Charlie Ventura (Black & White 1220); in 1947 by Tex Beneff (MGM 10079); in 1950 by Paul Smith (Discovery 137); in 1951 by Gene Kelly and Georges Guetary (From the *An American In Paris* film soundtrack—MGM 30401); in 1955 by Julie London (Liberty 55006).

Other versions are by Carlos Lima-Barbosa (Concord Jazz 2005),

184

Count Basie/Joe Williams (Verve UMV-2650), Ruby Braff/George Barnes Quintet (Concord Jazz 5), the Dave Brubeck Trio (Fantasy 24726), Al Caiola (Bainbridge 1030), Buck Clayton (Vanguard VSD-103-04), Ray Conniff (Columbia 13-33033), Chris Connor (Atlantic 2-601), "Wild" Bill Davison (Savoy 2229), Harry Edison (Pablo 2308237), Michael Feinstein (Parnassus PR 0100), the Frederick Fennell Orchestra (Mercury 75127), Ella Fitzgerald (Verve 2-2525 and Verve 15063), Jan Garber (Hindsight 403), Dizzy Gillespie (Crescendo 9028), Ralph Grierson/Artie Kane (Angel 36083), the Bobby Hackett Sextet (Storyville 4059), Al Haig (Prestige 7841), Lionel Hampton (MCA 1351), Earl Hines (Quicksilver 9000), Guy Lombardo (Ranwood 8216),

Yehudi Menuhin/Stephane Grappelli (Angel 37156), Helen Merrill/Clifford Brown (Emarcy 1038), Herbie Nichols (Savoy 2247), Anita O'Day (Glendale 6000), Joe Pass (Pablo 2312133), Bobby Short (Atlantic SD-2-608), Zoot Sims (Pablo 2310744), Paul Smith/Bellson & Brown (Outstanding 009), Sonny Stitt (Prestige 7585 and Prestige 24044), Art Tatum (Pablo 2310732), the Lennie Tristano Quartet (Atlantic 2-7006), Tommy Tune/Twiggy (from the *My One and Only* cast recording—Atlantic 80110-1-E), Warren Vache (Concord Jazz 87), Joe Venuti (Flying Fish 035), Lawrence Welk (Ranwood 8194), and the Teddy Wilson Trio (Storyville 4046).

170. THE WORLD IS MINE

Lyricist: Ira Gershwin
Key: E-flat
Time: Alla breve
Tempo: Moderato
Introduced by: This song was written for but dropped from the 1927 show *Funny Face*. It was later retitled "Toddlin' Along" and became a George and Ira Gershwin contribution to the 1930 show *Nine-Fifteen Review*. Nan Blackstone introduced it in that show on February 11, 1930.

Analysis: The lyric here is an unusual specimen of the "I'm poor but happy genre" in that the source of the singer's happiness is not his beloved but, rather, the fact that he has true friends. Ira Gershwin does not use this angle sentimentally, but only in passing. Most of the lines are made of carefree colloquialisms such as "toddling along" and "making hay."

The music begins with an almost atonal piano introduction, made from the conclusion of the twenty-four-bar verse ("I'm not as rich as Henry Ford is"). The verse itself is happy and simple, its melody being made mostly of repeated notes. The thirty-two-bar refrain ("Toddling along") is a variation on or a sister to "Fascinating Rhythm." Its left hand accompaniment duplicates that of the earlier song and its release, like that of "Fascinating Rhythm," presents a lyrical contrast to the rhythmic doings at the beginning and end. The melody of this release ("It's a grand and glorious feeling") is stated brightly at first in E-flat, then mournfully in B-flat minor. Also interesting are the lead-ins to each repetition of the refrain. For each of these lead-ins, Gershwin uses a different chord, and every one of these chords is unexpected (for instance, the B7 in bar eight, just before "How can I complain?").

Recordings: Jacques Fray and Mario Braggiotti of the original London cast of *Funny Face* recorded this (His Master's Voice K-5310). More recent versions are by Kevin Cole (piano solo—Fanfare DFL 7007) and Michael Feinstein (Parnassus PR-0100).

171. BEAUTIFUL GYPSY

Lyricist: Ira Gershwin
Key: E-flat
Time: Alla breve
Tempo: Moderato (verse)
  Languorously (refrain)
Introduced by: This song was dropped from *Rosalie* before that show's January 10, 1928 opening.

Analysis: The music is the same as that in "Wait a Bit, Susie" from *Primrose* in 1924. Ira Gershwin's new lyric (he had collaborated with Desmond Carter on "Wait a Bit, Susie") has lines such as "Couldn't

186

forget you once I had met you; sought you ev'rywhere; hither, thither, yonder, here and there."

Recordings: None

172. EV'RYBODY KNOWS I LOVE SOMEBODY

Lyricist: Ira Gershwin
Key: E-flat
Time: Alla breve
Tempo: Moderato
Introduced by: Marilyn Miller and Jack Donahue in *Rosalie* at the New Amsterdam Theatre in New York City. This song was added after the show's opening date of January 10, 1928.

Analysis: This is the same tune as "Dance Alone With You" from *Funny Face*. Ira may have rewritten the lyric due to the exigencies of *Rosalie*'s plot. On the other hand, he may have had second thoughts about the threat to commit murder that is contained in the earlier version ("Hear me! I'm sure the judge and jury will clear me, if any one of them I kill"). Here, the threat is only suicide ("Save me! This little feller needs a friend. Crave me! Or in the river I will end!").

Recordings: None

173. HOW LONG HAS THIS BEEN GOING ON?

Lyricist: Ira Gerswhin
Key: G
Time: Alla breve
Tempo: Moderato
Introduced by: Bobbe Arnst premiered this song in *Rosalie* at the New Amsterdam Theatre in New York City on January 10, 1926. It had been written for Adele Astaire and Jack Buchanan in *Funny Face* but was dropped from that show.

187

Lore: During the Philadelphia tryout of *Funny Face*, a music publisher called Ira and asked if he would remove "How Long Has This Been Going On?" from the show. His concern was that the public would confuse it with a song of the same title that he had recently purchased. The Gershwins, he figured, would be willing to do him the favor since their "How Long" was getting a lukewarm reception. Shortly thereafter, the brothers did drop this song, but only after it was decided that "He Loves and She Loves" would do better in its spot. The next year, they put it into *Rosalie* but it did not become popular for another ten years.

Analysis: The first four bars of the verse ("'Neath the stars at bazaars") create a sense of vulnerablility. They are answered by a four-bar phrase ("five or ten dollars I'd collect") which, because of its higher register and altered chords, creates a sense of urgency. Vulnerability and urgency continue to vie until the ambiguous sound of a diminished chord—an extraordinary touch—leads us into the refrain.

In the refrain the melody rises ("I could cry") and then it falls ("salty tears") and then it rises again ("Where have I") and then it falls again ("been all these years") and the listener is left with the impression of a complaint followed by resignation followed by complaint and then more resignation. All this is to ambiguous harmony which, though in G, rarely visits that tonal center. When, in the release ("Oh, I feel that I could melt"), the singer begins with a B-natural over a C-chord, there is a sense of peace and stillness—a blissful contrast to the sadness and restlessness of the refrain's beginning and end. Among the wonderful lines in the lyric are "That divine rendezvous" and "I know how Columbus felt finding another world!"

Recordings: Frances Gershwin, sister of the writers, released her version of this song and it is available on World Records SH-208 and on Monmouth-Evergreen MES 7034). Lee Wiley's recording, made on November 15, 1939, was released on Liberty Music Shop L-281 and has been reissued on Monmouth-Evergreen MES 7034. Peggy Lee's November 13, 1941 recording with Benny Goodman and His Orchestra is on Columbia CL6100. The 1941 recording by the Benny

188

Goodman Sextet was issued on Okeh 6544.

Others:

Mose Allison (Prestige 7446, 24055), Louis Armstrong and Oscar Peterson (Verve UMV-2656), George Brown (London LL 3331), Barbara Carroll Trio (Verve MGV 2063), Rosemary Clooney (Concord Jazz 112), Al Cohn (Savoy 1126), Buddy Collette/Chico Hamilton/Jimmy Hall (V.S.O.P. 20), Cal Collins (Concord Jazz 71), John Coltrane and Kenny Burrell (Prestige 24059), Chris Connor (Atlantic 2-601), Buddy DeFranco (Progressive 7014), Ella Fitzgerald (Decca 8378), Ella Fitzgerald and Oscar Peterson (Pablo 2310759), Ella Fitzgerald and Duke Ellington (Verve 6-4072),

Judy Garland (Capitol SWBO-1569), Jane Harvey with the Ray Ellis Orchestra (Discovery 888), Lena Horne and the Phil Moore Four (Victor 45-0001), Joni James (MGM E4225), J.J. Johnson/ K. Winding/B. Green (Prestige 24067), Barney Kessel (Contemporary OJC-238), Teddi King (Inner City 1044), Shelly Manne (Discovery 909), Phil Matson (Doctor Jazz FW-40349), Julia Migenes-Johnson (Victor ARL1-5323), Joan Morris and William Bolcom (Nonesuch 1358), Joe Pass (Pablo 2310752, 2312133), Oscar Peterson/Joe Pass/Niels Pedersen (Pablo 2520112), Pete Peterson/Collection Jazz Orchestra (Pausa 7191),

Andre Previn (RCA Victor LPM 1011), Don Ralke and His Orchestra (Warner Bros. W1360), Bernie Privin Orchestra (Savoy 2236), Frank Rosolino Quartet (V.S.O.P. 16), Zoot Sims (Pablo 2310744), Tonight Show Band with Doc Severinsen (Amherst AMH-3311), Mel Torme (Glendale 6007), Twiggy and Tommy Tune (Atlantic 80110-1-E), Sarah Vaughan (Mercury MGP-2-101, Pablo 2310821), Ronnie Whyte and Travis Hudson (Monmouth-Evergreen MES 7061).

174. OH GEE!-OH JOY!

Lyricist: Ira Gershwin and P.G. Wodehouse
Key: C (verse)
F (refrain)
Time: Alla breve
Tempo: Moderato con spirito

189

Introduced by: Marilyn Miller and Jack Donahue in *Rosalie* at the New Amsterdam Theatre in New York City on January 10, 1928.

Analysis: The verse ("Yea bo") is a happy sixteen-bar tune, one whose main melodic idea sounds like a squeal of pleasure. The refrain ("Oh gee! Oh joy!") is a joyful little rouser. Eleven of its first twelve notes are Cs and the one non-C (a D on "sing" in "the birds are singing") is the hook. In the sixth bar (on "am" in "I am in love") there is a blatant and, by 1928, old-fashioned blue note. Ira Gershwin and P.G. Wodehouse wrote the lyric but it could have been a babbitt and bromide, what with lines such as "Yea bo, but isn't love great! Gee whiz! Heigh-ho! I'm willing to state, it is!"

Recordings: Frances Gershwin's recording is on Monmouth-Evergreen MES 7052. In January of 1928 there were recordings by Sam Lanin's Famous Players and Singers (Okeh 40978) and by Ben Selvin and His Orchestra (Columbia 1285-D). In February of that year a version was released by Johnny Johnson (Victor 21224) and the following month saw a rendition by Lou Raderman and His Pelham Inn Orchestra (Harmony 611-H). Other versions are by the RCA Victor Salon Group conducted by Nathaniel Shilkret (RCA Victor EPBT 3055), Bobby Short (Painted Smiles PS-1357).

175. ROSALIE

Lyricist: Ira Gershwin
Key: E-flat
Time: Alla breve
Tempo: Moderato con sentimento (verse)
        Moderato (liltingly) (refrain)
Introduced by: This song was dropped from *Rosalie* before that show's January 10, 1928 opening.

Analysis: In the twenty-four-bar verse ("In my dreams you've always played the leading part") the melody rises and falls in a gentle

190

arc, then hits a sudden blue note (on "part"). The final eight bars (at "I must tell you") are a dynamic, even passionate second idea, stated first in G-minor, then B-flat. In the refrain ("Rosalie, Loveliest of names to me"), the name Rosalie is called out in a gently taunting manner, with an octave leap up, then a fall of a fourth. Ira, searching for rhymes for this name, came up with a meagre catch: "Prosily" and "won the key." The length is thirty-two bars, the form AABA[1].

Recordings: Marilyn Miller recorded this on June 12, 1928 but that recording was never released (Victor Test Recording). A version by the Rhythmic Eight was recorded on June 6, 1928 (Zonophone 5149).

176. SAY SO!

Lyricist: Ira Gershwin and P.G. Wodehouse
Key: A-flat
Time: Alla breve
Tempo: Moderato con molto sentimento
Introduced by: Marilyn Miller and Oliver McLennan in *Rosalie* at the New Amsterdam Theatre in New York City, January 10, 1928.

Analysis: The sixteen-bar verse ("When your eyes look into mine"), which is in the earnest style of operetta, consists of numerous repeated notes. In fact, if one removed the repetitions, the resultant melody would retain its character and, yet, would be only eight bars long. The refrain ("Say so! Say you love me") is in the thirty-two-bar AABA format. It is a simple, pleasing tune, one whose beat comes from a series of little syncopated kicks—the first appearing just after the title phrase. An F-minor release ("There are just three little words") leads into the recapitulation with a most unusual sound—an F chord with an F-sharp in the bass.

Recordings: There were January 1928 recordings by Johnny Johnson (Victor 21224), Sam Lanin's Famous Players and Singers

(Okeh 40978), Ben Selvin and His Orchestra (Columbia 1285-D), and Winegar's Pennsylvania Boys (Edison 52255). Recently, there was a version by Joan Morris and Max Morath with piano accompaniment by William Bolcom (RCA ARL1-2491).

177. FEELING I'M FALLING

Lyricist: Ira Gershwin
Key: G (verse)
      C (refrain)
Time: Alla breve
Tempo: Moderato
Introduced by: Gertrude Lawrence and Paul Frawley in *Treasure Girl* at the Alvin Theatre in New York City on November 8, 1928.

Lore: This song was a favorite of Frances Gershwin, sister of the songwriters.

Analysis: In the twenty-bar verse an initial slightly syncopated idea in G ("Just a little while ago") gives way to a second and more sedate theme ("When Love Gets You") that is presented first in B and then in B-minor. Then the first idea returns. In the refrain ("No fooling") Gershwin creates a lush and romantic sound via a series of suspensions. For example, on the first beat the chord is C but in it are three alien notes—F, D, and A. On beat two these notes are resolved into those of another C chord—E, C and G respectively. In the second bar (on "feeling") the same thing happens but to a D-minor chord. Such suspensions and resolutions continue until the end of the song. In the lyric, Ira Gershwin has some fun with fricatives in what otherwise would be a straightforward love song. The two Fs in the title phrase are joined by those in "fooling," "felt it," "found you," "fatal," "flame," "flutter" and so on.

Recordings: Duo-pianists Victor Arden and Phil Ohman from the *Treasure Girl* pit orchestra recorded this song on November 22,

192

1928 (vocal by Lewis James—Victor 21795). The next day, Lou Gold and His Orchestra recorded their version (Harmony 789-H). More recent efforts have been by Betty Comden with piano accompaniment by Richard Lewine (That's Entertainment Records TER 1039), Joan Morris and Max Morath with piano accompaniment by William Bolcom (RCA ARL1-2491) and Bobby Short (Atlantic SD2-608).

178. GOT A RAINBOW

Lyricist: Ira Gershwin
Key: E-flat
Time: Alla breve
Tempo: Moderato
Introduced by: Walter Catlett, Peggy O'Neil and Virginia Frank in *Treasure Girl* at the Alvin Theatre in New York City on November 8, 1928.

Analysis: The singer is protected against bad luck by a rainbow that watches out for him like a guardian angel. The verse ("Born on the thirteenth, on a Friday") is twenty-four bars long and sprinkled with blue notes, mostly in the accompaniment. The refrain ("What makes my misery fly") is an effective rouser, one with a hearty, optimistic tune and big churchy chords. In the release ("Oh, it may rain and thunder") it becomes a pounding G-minor march. At bar four the lyric mentions "There's A Rainbow 'Round My Shoulder"—a song by Dave Dreyer, Billy Rose and Al Jolson, written in 1928.

Recordings: Duo-pianists Victor Arden and Phil Ohman recorded this on November 22, 1928 (with a vocal by the Revelers—Victor 21795).

179. I DON'T THINK I'LL FALL IN LOVE TODAY

Lyricist: Ira Gershwin
Key: E-flat

Time: Alla breve
Tempo: Moderato
Introduced by: Gertrude Lawrence and Paul Frawley in *Treasure Girl* at the Alvin Theatre in New York City on November 8, 1928.

Lore: Ira Gershwin got the idea for this song from a line in G.K. Chesterton's "A Ballad of Suicide" that goes: "I think I will not hang myself today."

Analysis: In this precursor to 1937's "Let's Call the Whole Thing Off" a man and a woman wonder if they can be lovers despite one another's idiosyncrasies. They sing lines such as "Imagine signing up for life/Then finding peas roll off his knife." "Wrong" chords in the piano introduction are a tipoff to the comic intent. Yet, the memorable melody of the verse ("Just think of what love leads to") has a flowing rather than a joking quality. Bars eight through twelve (beginning with "But we mustn't be/Like the other sheep") are an attractive and unusually long extension of the main idea. The melody of the refrain ("Who knows if we'd agree") is, for the first five bars, made entirely from the three notes of an E-flat triad. It is defiant, but in a cute, childlike way. The release ("But it would be fun to bring your carpet slippers") has a more substantial, lyrical melody, one that ends in an odd stream of chords containing diminished fourths as well as augmented fifths. The form is thirty-two bars, AABA.

Recordings: There are recordings by Betty Comden (ava AS-26), Nancy Walker and David Craig (Citadel CT 7017), Joan Morris and Max Morath (RCA ARL1-2491), Blossom Dearie and Charles Rydell (Painted Smiles PS 1353), Ronny Whyte and Travis Hudson (Monmouth-Evergreen MES 7061).

180. K-RA-ZY FOR YOU

Lyricist: Ira Gershwin
Key: E-flat
Time: 2/4
Tempo: Allegretto
Introduced by: Clifton Webb and Mary Hay in *Treasure Girl* at the Alvin Theatre in New York City on November 8, 1928.

Analysis: A song that begins with "When a guy like Byron would meet up with a siren" has to have something going for it and this one has Ira's wordplay, which includes other double rhymes, such as "Skin burn"/"Swinburn" and "toney"/"bologney." In the verse a fellow tells a lady that he must express his love for her in his own down-to-earth style and not in the highfalutin language of the poets. Then, in the refrain, he lets out with "I'm k-ra-zy for you."

Musically, the verse ("When a guy like Byron") moves along pleasantly in E-flat for sixteen bars and then, for the final eight (at "though I'm not the slightest bit poetic"), becomes more ruminative. The refrain ("Let me give you the low down: I'm k-ra-zy for you") is a lean and vigorous rhythm piece, one whose main idea is a quick harmonic sequence in bar two (on "you the"), where Cm7^{-5} and B-diminished chords make a bridge between the E-flat opening and a pause on C7. The m7^{-5} chord is one that Gershwin had been using effectively for a long time, first in ballads such as "The Man I Love" (at "And when he comes my way") and later in up-tempo numbers like "My One and Only" (at the beginning of the refrain). It is a dark sound, one that can give a jolt, as it does here. The remainder of this thirty-two-bar AABA song is full of ideas, including a carefully considered piano accompaniment that includes modern jazzy harmony and sleight of hand fills.

Recordings: This was recorded in March of 1929 by Horace Heidt (Victor 21957) and Vaughn de Leath (Edison 52543) and in April of that year by Zelma O'Neal (Brunswick 4322). In 1973, Bobby Short recorded his version (Atlantic SD 2-608).

181. OH, SO NICE

Lyricist: Ira Gershwin
Key: E-minor (verse)
     G (refrain)
Time: Alla breve
Tempo: Moderato e semplice
Introduced by: Gertrude Lawrence and Paul Frawley in *Treasure Girl* at the Alvin Theatre in New York City on November 8, 1929.

Lore: In 1928 George Gershwin told an interviewer: "The waltz

195

will always be in vogue. By that I mean the three-four time. I find it interesting to experiment. My number 'Oh, So Nice' is an effort to get the effect of a Viennese waltz in fox-trot time." And Ira Gershwin told Isaac Goldberg: "Sometimes I work days and days on a lyric. An example is 'Oh, So Nice' from *Treasure Girl*. Here there is a waltz effect in a fox-trot, but the musical phrases were so short and definite they called for plenty of internal rhymes."

Analysis: The twenty-bar verse ("Never thought I'd ever meet a man like you") is an evocative and beautiful E-minor piece—a natural waltz that becomes a foxtrot when Gershwin lengthens the half note pauses to dotted halfs (on "meet" and "man" and "you"). The refrain is a soaring, lyrical ballad, one that is just as rhythmically disconcerting as was the up-tempo 1927 song "Let's Kiss and Make Up." What we get here is not so much a waltz made into a foxtrot as a combination of waltz and foxtrot meters. The first nine bars could have been notated as 3/4 ("I was a"), 4/4 ("bove love be"), 3/4 ("fore"), 3/4 ("But now I"), 4/4 ("love love be"), 2/4 ("cause"), 4/4 ("you're"), 4/4 ("Oh, oh, so"), 4/4 ("nice!"). The release ("When you are near me") is a development of this idea in A-minor. The length is thirty-two bars, the form AABA.

Recordings: Frances Gershwin (World Records SH-208, Monmouth-Evergreen MES 7060), Louise Carlyle (Citadel CT 7017), Ella Fitzgerald (Verve MGV-4028), Betty Comden with piano accompaniment by Richard Lewine ("That's Entertainment Records TER 1039).

182. WHAT ARE WE HERE FOR?

Lyricist: Ira Gershwin
Key: C
Time: Alla breve
Tempo: Moderato
Introduced by: Gertrude Lawrence and Clifton Webb in *Treasure Girl* at the Alvin Theatre in New York City on November 8, 1928.

Analysis: Despite its title, this song does not care to linger over any of the eternal questions. We're here, writes the lyricist, "to dance

196

and to play." The twenty-four-bar verse ("The sea is bright blue") consists of a tranquil first half in C that ends on a prominent blue note (on "darn" in "This is a pretty darn good world"), followed by another easygoing idea, this one in E ("Never can understand"). The refrain ("What are we here for") is a straightforward tune made mostly of the notes of C and G triads. The release ("We are all actors") takes a jazzier approach. The length is thirty-two bars, the form AABA.

Recordings: Betty Comden with piano accompaniment by Richard Lewine (That's Entertainment Records TER 1039).

183. WHERE'S THE BOY? HERE'S THE GIRL!

Lyricist: Ira Gershwin
Key: E-flat
Time: 4/4
Tempo: Moderato (introduction)
             Calm and gracefully (verse and refrain)
Introduced by: Gertrude Lawrence in *Treasure Girl* at the Alvin Theatre in New York City on November 8, 1928.

Lore: In her autobiography, *A Star Danced*, Gertrude Lawrence pointed to this as the one song that she sang in *Treasure Girl* that went over big.

Analysis: The sixteen-bar verse ("There is no doubt About The fact, that life without A lord and master Is a disaster") consists of a slow, reflective, dotted-note tune. In bar fifteen, just before the end, there is a delicate deceptive cadence (at "met him" in "Though I've not met him"). The refrain ("Where's the boy?") is thirty-two bars long and ABA in form. Those A sections are sighing and resigned, while the B section, or release, couples a deflating, humorous lyric ("Maybe we shall meet on some romantic mountain; Probably I'll meet him at a soda fountain") with an unreservedly emotional and quite beautiful melody in C-minor. The piano accompaniment is very carefully written throughout, with stately arpeggios in the A sections and alto voicing of the melody line in the release.

Recordings: Frances Gershwin (World Records SH-208, Mon-

197

mouth-Evergreen MES 7060), Louise Carlyle (Citadel CT 7017), Betty Comden with piano accompaniment by Richard Lewine (That's Entertainment Records TER 1039).

184. AN AMERICAN IN PARIS

Tone poem for orchestra

Key: F
Introduced by: The New York Symphony Orchestra, Walter Damrosch conducting, at Carnegie Hall on December 13, 1928.

Lore: When Gershwin first visited Paris in 1923 he was given a tour of the city by two friends: lyric writer Buddy DeSylva and Cartier's executive Jules Glaezner. As the trio was passing through the Arc de Triomphe and heading down the Champs-Elysées, Gershwin suddenly exclaimed, "Why, this is a city you can write about!"

"Don't look now, George," came DeSylva's quick rejoinder, "but it's been done."

Gershwin was not daunted. Three years later he was in Paris again, spending a week with his friends Robert and Mabel Schirmer. The former was of the Schirmer music publishing family and the latter had, like Gershwin, studied music with Charles Hambitzer. Thus, they were sensitive to the composer's musical doings and they looked on with interest as he began to consider his next orchestral composition.

"He only had....that first theme, the way *An American in Paris* starts," Mabel Schirmer recalled some years later. "And I know that after that first theme he was a little stuck. He said, 'This is so complete in itself. I don't know where to go next.'" Never entirely at a loss, however, Gershwin asked the Schirmers to take him to Avenue de la Grande Armée, where automobile parts were sold. There he looked for and found a set of French taxi horns. Presumably, he had already decided to include them in the orchestration of the piece.

Another two years would pass, however, before he began giving the new composition his undivided attention. It was on March 25, of 1928 that he returned to Paris for a third visit, taking up quarters at the Majestic Hotel, and there he worked from two separate drafts—one for solo piano and the other for two pianos. It was also during this stay in France that he met with many of Europe's most prominent composers,

198

including Ravel, Stravinsky, Milhaud, Prokofiev, Poulenc, Walton and Dukelsky. As was customary with Gershwin, everyone within earshot heard the work in progress and everyone offered his or her opinion. Dukelsky (shortly to become pop songwriter Vernon Duke—a name devised by Gershwin), thought it somewhat saccharine. Prokofiev, who had called Gershwin's previous orchestral work, the *Concerto in F*, a series of thirty-two-bar choruses, saw some hope in this one. As for Ravel, he was already an avowed Gershwin fan, having gone out of his way to meet the young American during a visit to New York. From Paris, Gershwin made an excursion to Vienna, where work on *An American in Paris* continued and where he met Franz Lehár and Alban Berg.

On June 6, 1928, the New York *Times* heralded the premiere of *An American in Paris*, saying that the work was scheduled for the upcoming season of the New York Philharmonic Symphony Orchestra. Walter Damrosch would conduct this premiere, as he had conducted the debut of the *Concerto in F*. On June 20 the Gershwin party (including Ira and the latter's wife, Leonore) returned to New York and the brothers began work on *Treasure Girl*. Simultaneously, George worked on the new piece. It was finished on August 1 and the orchestration (including four French taxi horns) was complete as of November 18. The first performance took place on December 13, 1928.

It was customary by now for any new Gershwin highbrow effort to be greeted by competing hoots and cheers. The primary hooters were, as usual, the established music critics, this time led by Herbert Peyser of the New York *Telegram*. According to Peyser, *An American in Paris* was "so dull, patchy, thin, vulgar, long-winded and inane that the average movie audience would be bored by it into the open remonstrance."

On the other hand, there was the *Musical Courier*, which said that *An American in Paris* was "in a class, atmospherically, with Berlioz's *Roman Carnival*, Svendsen's *Carnival de Venise* and Chabrier's *España*." And there was also the testimony of Francis Poulenc, who declared that *An American in Paris* was his favorite twentieth century musical composition. In any event, audiences immediately loved the piece because it was pure Gershwin and they loved Gershwin all the more for having written it. It was because of them that *An American in Paris* became an instant classic (the *Rhapsody in Blue* was Gershwin's only other highbrow work to catch on so quickly).

The published piano solo of this piece is by William Daly, a

199

close Gershwin friend.

Analysis: Although *An American in Paris* depicts the experiences of a grown man in a city renowned for its sophistication, musically it has the feel of a return to childhood. This point of view is adopted right away in the initial walking theme, which does not walk so much as it skips, and in its melodic tag, which consists of a schoolyard style "nyanny-nyah." The same spirit is present in the nose-thumbing of the taxi horns and, later, in the brief staccato calls that make up the two other walking themes. It is even present in the blues, which has a comic edge: this homesick melody co-exists with continuing jocular asides by the flutes.

The childlike spirit of the work and its irrepressible delight with life were best caught in its first recording, made on February 4, 1929 by Nat Shilkret and the Victor Symphony Orchestra (see below). On that record, the music is lean and without bombast, the tempo is brisk, the humor never flags, and all of the asides and comments by small, gleeful instrumental groups are unfailingly revealed. Also revealed in this and other good performances are the rich polytonal chord sequences (one of the first is a slow variation on the initial walking theme; another, wonderfully orchestrated for pizzicato strings and celesta, appears during the violin solo that introduces the blues), zesty rhythms and cross-rhythms (alternating eighth and quarter note triplets; triplets pitted against twos and fours), and the well-planned and satisfying overall structure.

There are six principal musical themes:

1.   The opening insouciant walking theme, characterized by a flip grace note and a sudden minor seventh fall.
2.   The taxi horn theme.
3.   A second walking theme. Introduced by the clarinet, it is seven notes long and uses the four quick sixteenth notes that first appeared at the conclusion of the theme one.
4.   A third walking theme, introduced by the brass section. It, too, is very brief—just six notes.
5.   Tempo Blues. This slow melody does not have the grandeur of the Andantino moderato of the *Rhapsody in Blue* or the haunted mysterioso quality of the first piano solo in the *Concerto in F*. It is slow and sensuous, but full of fun underneath.
6.   A sassy, syncopated dance idea introduced by the trumpet and

200

interrupted by another dance, this one exotic and pulsating.

Recordings: The first (and probably the best) recording of *An American in Paris* was made on February 4, 1929 by Nathaniel Shilkret conducting the RCA Victor Symphony Orchestra, George Gershwin appearing briefly at the celeste (Victor 35963 and 35964, reissued on RCA Victor LPT 29).

Other choices are (listed alphabetically by conductor):   Maurice Abravanal and the Utah Symphony Orchestra (Vanguard C-10017, Westminster 8122), Leonard Bernstein and the RCA Victor Symphony Orchestra (recorded in 1950—RCA Victor LM1031), Leonard Bernstein and the New York Philharmonic (recorded in 1973—Columbia M31804, MG 31155, MS6091), Stanley Black and the London Festival Orchestra (London 417 098-4), George Byrd and the Hamburg Pro Musica (Forum F70 008), Salvador Camarata and the Kinsway Symphony Orchestra (Decca DL 8519), Antal Dorati and the Minneapolis Symphony Orchestra (Mercury 90290),

Arthur Fiedler and the Boston Pops (RCA Red Seal LSC 3319, RCA Victrola VICS 1423), Morton Gould and His Orchestra (RCA Victor LM 2002, LM 6033), Andre Kostelanetz (Columbia CL795, ML 4455), Erich Kunzel and the Cincinnati Symphony (Telarc DG-10058), Lorin Maazel and the Cleveland Orchestra (London 414067, 41776-2), Eduardo Mata and the Dallas Symphony (RCA ARCL-4551), Zubin Mehta and the Los Angeles Philharmonic (London CSA 2246), Alfred Newman and the Hollywood Symphony Orchestra (Mercury MG 20037), Eugene Ormandy and the Philadelphia Orchestra (Columbia MS 7258, MS-7518), Seiji Ozawa and the San Francisco Symphony Orchestra (Deutsche Grammophon 2530-788), Andre Previn and the London Symphony Orcestra (Angel SFO 36810), Andre Previn and the Pittsburgh Symphony (Philips 412611-1),

Artur Rodzinski and the New York Philharmonic (Columbia 4026), Leonard Slatkin and the St. Louis Symphony (Vox CBS-5132, CT-2101), Felix Slatkin and the Hollywood Bowl Symphony Orchestra (Capitol SP 8343, Seraphim S-60174), Michael Tilson Thomas and the New York Philharmonic (Columbia 34205), Arturo Toscanini and the NBC Symphony Orchestra (recorded May 18, 1945—Victor LM-9020, RCA Victrola AVM1-1737), Edo de Waart and the National l'Opera de Monte Carlo (Philips 6500-290), Hans Jurgen Walther and the Pro Musica, Hamburg (MGM 3-E1), Paul Whiteman (recorded October 21, 1938—Decca 29054 and 29055, Capitol P-303).

201

The composer's version for two pianos has been recorded by Katia and Marielle Labeque (Angel DS-38130) and by Anognoson and Klinton (Pro Arte CDD-367).

185. DO WHAT YOU DO!

Lyricist: Ira Gershwin and Gus Kahn
Key: F
Time: Alla breve
Tempo: Moderato
Introduced by: Ruby Keeler and Frank McHugh in *Show Girl* at the Ziegfeld Theatre in New York City on July 2, 1929.

Lore: Lyricist Gus Kahn was brought into the *Show Girl* collaboration by producer Florenz Ziegfeld because Ziegfeld owed him a musical comedy assignment. For some reason, this song and "Feeling Sentimental" are the only ones from the score that put Ira Gershwin's name before Kahn's, instead of vice-versa. The Gershwins' sister Frankie liked to sing this song at parties.

Analysis: The sixteen-bar verse ("I never knew love was so nice") presents a sighing chromatic idea in F, then in A (on "You came along"). The refrain is a ballad with some of the slow sensuality of "Do it Again!" The fact that the title phrase is harmonized in fourths helps give it an appealing languor, as does the constant, almost hypnotic use of the word "do"—it is sung seventeen times in the thirty-two-bar refrain.

Recordings: In July of 1929 there were versions by Roger Wolfe Kahn and His Orchestra (Brunswick 4479), Leo Reisman and His Orchestra (Victor 22069) and B.A. Rolfe and His Lucky Strike Dance Orchestra (vocal by J. Donald Parker—Edison 52640, reissued on Mark 56 Records 800). Zelma O'Neal recorded this song in August of 1929 (Brunswick 4476). Other releases are by Travis Hudson (Monmouth-Evergreen MES 7061), the Ipana Troubadors (Columbia 1903), and Bobby Short (Atlantic SD-608).

186. FEELING SENTIMENTAL

Lyricist: Gus Kahn and Ira Gershwin
Key: F
Time: Alla breve
Tempo: Allegretto
Introduced by: This song was dropped from *Show Girl*, a production that opened in New York City at the Ziegfeld Theatre on July 2, 1929.

Analysis: "Feeling Sentimental," whose obscurity is now well into its second half century, contains one of Gershwin's greatest verses ("One time I was as gay as a king"): a sixteen-bar piece that begins in quiet intensity, achieved in part by use, in the key of F, of a Bm7^{-5} sound (on "was as gay"). Urgent minor key episodes then lead to a fragile C major conclusion. The refrain ("Feeling sentimental"), also one of the composer's finest efforts, begins with a held note, followed by a brief chromatic descent—and then it becomes a slow and soaring tune, one carried by an easy, sensual beat. The release ("When the sun goes down"), has a simple, vulnerable quality that is equally fine and also romantic. But for a repetition of bars one and two at bars twenty-five and twenty-six, this refrain is through-composed.

Recordings: Elaine Stritch (Painted Smiles PS-1357), Bobby Short (Atlantic SD 2-608).

187. HARLEM SERENADE

Lyricist: Ira Gershwin and Gus Kahn
Key: E-flat
Time: Alla breve
Tempo: Allegretto moderato
Introduced by: Ruby Keeler in *Show Girl* at the Ziegfeld Theatre in New York City on July 2, 1929.

Analysis: The lyric promises a "New kind o' music and a new kind o' time, New kind o' rhythm and new kind o' rhyme." However, the song is not nearly so innovative as all that. In fact, the refrain, in its use of the crescendo and in its opening line ("Take a taxi and go

203

there"), is reminiscent of "Sweet and Low-Down," a Gershwin song from 1925 whose refrain began "Grab a cab and go down." Here, an eighteen-bar verse contrasts a menacing idea in dark E-flat minor ("From the Congo jungle it came") with a light-hearted arpeggiated idea in B-flat ("I'm referring to that Harlem Serenade"). The above-mentioned refrain is a forceful but good-natured rouser whose main idea is a syncopated tune, full of repeated notes, that rises in pitch and volume. For the release ("Oh, stop! Look! Listen to the uptown jungle wail!"), there is a thudding jungle drum effect. The length is thirty-two bars, the form AA^{1}BA^2.

Recordings: None

188. I MUST BE HOME BY TWELVE O'CLOCK

Lyricist: Gus Kahn and Ira Gershwin
Key: G-minor (verse)
      E-flat (refrain)
Time: Alla breve
Tempo: Moderato
Introduced by: Ruby Keeler in *Show Girl* at the Ziegfeld Theatre in New York City on July 2, 1929.

Analysis: In the verse the singer complains about young ladies who continually vent their guilt about dancing until dawn by saying again and again that they ought to be getting home. In the refrain he suddenly begins an impersonation of one of them, using the title phrase in doing so.

The principal musical idea in the twenty-four-bar verse ("There is one at ev'ry party") is an octave fall. It is presented in G-minor, B-flat, and G-major. The refrain, in E-flat, is full of fun. Thee is no other Gershwin song quite like it. It begins with a two-bar phrase ("I'll say I'm having a hot time") whose main attraction is the huskiness of voice created on the word "hot" by means of a B-flat minor seventh chord with a diminished fifth. After this phrase is repeated, the melody suddenly embarks on a giddy ascent, beginning on an E-natural and moving up by half steps until, with a leap, it arrives at high-E-flat and a tonic resolution. Accompanying this tune is a bizarre chord progression, one that lurches forward until it too makes it to E-flat. In the release ("Bup-a-rup-a-rup-pup!") there is a modulation into A-flat for a toe-tapping phrase that is presented in three rhythmic guises. The first time, it arrives on the downbeat. The second, it starts on the second beat. And the third time, it starts on the third beat. Then it is repeated in E-major before a peremptory leap back into E-flat (on "Oh, good grief!").

Somehow, despite its lunacy, this ends up as a hummable and very charming piece of music.

Recordings: Ronny Whyte and Travis Hudson (Monmouth-Evergreen MES 7061), Bobby Short (Atlantic SD 2-608).

189. LIZA

Lyricist: Gus Kahn and Ira Gershwin
Key: E-flat
Time: Alla breve
Tempo: Moderato
Introduced by: Ruby Keeler and Nick Lucas in *Show Girl* at the Ziegfeld Theatre in New York City on July 2, 1929.

Lore: When asked about the genesis of "Liza," George Gershwin recalled:

> Mr. Ziegfeld said, "I would like to have a minstrel number in the second act with one hundred beautiful girls seated on steps that cover the entire stage."
> This minstrel number was to be sung and danced by Ruby Keeler. So we went to work on a minstrel number and wrote "Liza."

Shortly before *Show Girl*'s premiere Al Jolson married Ruby Keeler. It was during the out-of-town tryouts and then on opening night in New York that he stood in the audience and joined her in this song.

In July of 1931, Gershwin played "Liza" in an early television broadcast that also included appearances by New York City Mayor Jimmy Walker, Kate Smith and the Boswell Sisters.

The composer's piano transcription of "Liza" appeared in *George*

Gershwin's Songbook, published in September of 1932.

Analysis: The main idea of "Liza" was foreshadowed in the 1924 ballet music for *Primrose*. But there is no indication that Gershwin was consciously drawing on that source when he wrote this song. As he did in many of his other great major-key rhythm songs ("Swanee," "Fascinating Rhythm," "Clap Yo' Hands," "I Got Rhythm," "Love is Sweeping the Country"), Gershwin begins here with a minor key verse. This one ("Moon shinin' on the river") has an unhurried spaciousness and an inherent, easy swinging beat. The refrain ("Liza, Liza, skies are gray") has a slow and stately build-up in the first four bars, followed by a fall in the second four—restrained at first, then a tumble—back to the starting point. In the first four bars it is the chord progression that creates the excitement, defying expectations, yet creating a feeling of inevitability. In the second four bars, the principal interest is melodic. Then, in the release ("See the honeymoon a shinin' down"), there is another great chord progression along with a stately and highly lyrical tune. The length is thirty-two bars, the form AABA.

Recordings: There is a recording of Gershwin playing this on "The Rudy Vallee Hour" radio broadcast of November 10, 1932 (Mark 56 Records 667). Gershwin loved Art Tatum's 1934 recording (Decca 1373). Al Jolson's first recording of this song was made in July of 1929 (Decca 4402).

Other 1929 versions were by the Bar Harbor Society Orchestra (Harmony 966-H), Sammy Fain (accompanied by Benny Goodman—Harmony 993-H), Lou Gold and His Orchestra (Gennett 6950), the Ipana Troubadors (Columbia 1903-D), Roger Wolfe Kahn and His Orchestra (Brunswick 4479), the McKenzie-Condon Chicagoans (Okeh 40971), Leo Reisman and His Orchestra (Victor 22069), and B.A. Rolfe and His Lucky Strike Dance Orchestra (vocal by J. Donald Parke—Edison 52640).

There were versions in 1934 by Fletcher Henderson (Decca 555), Jimmy Noone (Vocalion 2862) and Art Tatum (mentioned above); in 1935 by Willie Bryant and His Orchestra (Victor 25160) and Teddy Wilson (Brunswick 7563); in 1936 by Don Albert and His Orchestra (Vocalion 3491), Blanche Calloway (Vocalion 3112), and Joe Turner (Ultraphon AP-1573); in 1937 by the Benny Goodman Quartet (Victor 25660), Benny Goodman and His Orchestra (Columbia 12609), James P. Johnson (recorded at Fats Waller's home in New York—Ristic 22), and Red Norvo and His Orchestra (Brunswick 7868); in 1938 by Chick Webb (Decca 1840) and the Clarence Williams Trio (Vocalion 4169); in 1939 by Jimmie Lunceford (Vocalion/Okeh 5207), Chick Webb (Polydor 423248), and Teddy Wilson (Columbia 35711); in 1942 by Stephane Grappelli and His Quartet (Decca F-8204); in 1945 by the Benny Goodman Quintet/Sextet (Columbia DB2287) and Gene Schroeder (Black and White 33); in 1950 by Al Haig (New Jazz 822).

Other versions are by the Laurindo Almeida Trio (Concord Jazz 238), Ruby Braff/George Barnes Quintet (Concord Jazz 5), Earl Bostic (Gotham 172), Chris Connor (Atlantic 2-601), Michael Feinstein (Parnassus PR 0100), the Frederick Fennell Orchestra (Mercury 75127), Herbie Hancock/Chick Corea (Columbia PC2-35663), Yehudi Menuhin/Stephane Grappelli (Angel 37156), Thelonious Monk (Pausa 2014), Benny Morton's Trumpet Choir (Key 1309), Django Reinhardt (Crescendo 9001), Jimmy Roselli (M&R 1018), Sonny Stitt (Prestige 060), Ross Tompkins (Concord Jazz 46).

190. SO ARE YOU! (The Rose is Red - Violets Are Blue)

Lyricist: Gus Kahn and Ira Gershwin
Key: C
Time: Alla breve
Tempo: Moderato
Introduced by: Eddie Foy, Jr. and Kathryn Hereford in *Show Girl* at the Ziegfeld Theatre in New York City on July 2, 1929.

Analysis: In "K-ra-zy For You," written a year earlier, the singer admits his inability to write highfalutin poetry and settles instead for slang. In this song, the singer boasts of his poetic ability and then, when he tries to come up with some poetry, ends up delivering a greeting card-style message (hence, the subtitle).

Musically, the main interest here is the key structure. The instrumental introduction begins in E-flat and then modulates into the key of the song, C-major. The verse ("When a fella tries to tell a girl what's in his heart") is mainly in C but it spends a fair amount of time in E-minor. The refrain ("The rose is red") continues the C key signature but it is mainly in melancholy D-minor. And its release ("This may be a silly way") begins in far-off D-flat and repeats in G. The piece does end in C.

207

Recordings: None

191. IN THE MANDARIN'S ORCHID GARDEN

Lyricist: Ira Gershwin
Key: B-flat
Time: 4/4
Tempo: Allegro moderato
Introduced by: Eleanor Marum in a song recital at the Blackstone Theatre in Chicago on November 10, 1929. Her piano accompanist was Carroll Hollister.

Lore: Originally written in 1928 for the unproduced operetta *East is West*, this was published in 1930 as the Gershwins' only concert aria or art song. Performances have been very rare but Ira Gershwin had the satisfaction of learning that a Los Angeles speech specialist was using the words in his elocution lessons.

Analysis: The singer, a soprano, tells the story of a buttercup that, having found itself growing in a mandarin's orchid garden, politely begs the pardon of the surrounding orchids and then shrivels up and dies. The singer then compares herself to that misplaced flower. It is a lyrical, even poetic piece of writing, perfectly understated. In the music, the composer creates an ethereality that had been absent in his writing since the ballet music from *Primrose* in 1924. The piece is fifty-two bars long and can be divided into the following sections:

1. An eight-note piano motive, both hands playing in unison.
2. A gentle twelve-bar melody ("Somehow by fate misguided") that rises slowly after a long series of repeated notes. It is accompanied by a succession of simple triads. Most are in B-flat, although B, F-sharp and E triads come and go—Gershwin may have meant them as musical representations of outsiders.
3. A three-bar section ("Poor little buttercup") that is the heart of the piece and, melodically, its most memeorable moment.
4. A repetition of the unison motive, except that this time it ends not on F but on F-sharp, leading the way into section five.
5. Marked Poco più mosso, this part ("The bees came buzzing daily")

is more agitated, with a busier and more complex piano accompaniment. It is in G-minor.

6.   The melody of section three, sung forte this time and with a more emphatic piano backing.

7.   Another repetition of the unison theme.

8.   A repetition of section two ("I too, have been misguided") but with more elaborate piano writing.

9.   Another repetition of section three ("A lonely buttercup") with another reworking of the accompaniment.

10.   A restatement of the opening piano motive.

Recordings: Rosalind Rees with piano accompaniment by Oresta Cybriwsky (Turnabout TV-S 34638).

192. STRIKE UP THE BAND OVERTURE

Instrumental

Key: Various
Time: Various
Tempo: Various
Introduced by: George Gershwin conducting the *Strike Up the Band* pit orchestra at the Times Square Theatre in New York CIty on January 14, 1930.

Lore: Kay Swift, the composer's good friend, has recalled the first performance of this piece:

> Halfway through the overture, George Gershwin turned around and said to me, as I sat in the first row directly behind him, "April and Andy." He referred to two of my little girls, who had worked up a routine, singing and dancing to the music being played in the overture. It seemed remarkable to me then—and it still does— that any composer, on the first night of one of his shows, as well as during his initial stint of conducting in the pit, could feel easy enough in his mind to remember the children and their routine.

Analysis: This overture, a medley, contains some material written expressly for the 1930, as opposed to the 1927, production of *Strike Up the Band*. The sequence is as follows:

1. Fanfare from the Act I opening
2. "Soldier's March" from Act II
3. A development of the first five notes of "Strike Up the Band"
4. "I Mean to Say"
5. "How About a Boy Like Me?"
6. "Dream Music"
7. "Soon"
8. A jazz style clarinet cadenza
9. A two-bar passage from the "He Knows Milk" finale to Act I
10. "Hangin' Around With You"
11. "Strike Up the Band"

Recordings: The Buffalo Philharmonic with Michael Tilson Thomas conducting has recorded this piece (Columbia M34542) but their version, arranged by Don Rose, is not true to the overture that is published in the piano/vocal score.

193. STRIKE UP THE BAND OPENING ACT I

Lyricist: Ira Gershwin
Key: A-flat
Time: 6/8
Tempo: Allegro moderato
Introduced by: Dudley Clements, Robert Bentley and Gordon Smith in *Strike Up the Band* at the Times Square Theatre in New York City on January 14, 1930.

Analysis: Act I opens with a musical scene that is 258 measures long. It is called, simply, "Opening Act I" in the printed score, although it has been dubbed "Fletcher's American Chocolate Choral Society Workers" by various Gershwin biographers. It can be divided into the following nine musical sections:

1. An instrumental prelude consisting of the overture's opening fanfare and then a succession of brittle, staccato chords in 6/8, interrupted

midway by a more lyrical counterstatement. This is followed by a third, somewhat nervous tune.

2. The chocolate workers, divided into sopranos, altos, tenors and basses, sing a cheerful ditty, In it, they tell us who and where they are and note the fact that their boss likes to have them harmonize at eight o'clock in the morning.

3. The females in the chorus sing in unison a 6/8 tune that is even more cheerful—it is as sing-songy as a nursery rhyme. In it they affirm their happiness on the job. However, when they come to the line "if we're happy—oh, Tra la la la la la work is snappy," there is a restatement of the melancholy notes that appeared halfway through the instrumental prelude. Then comes the agitated music that closed the prelude.

4. The foreman is greeted by the workers. Then he, maintaining the 6/8 beat, tells us how well things are going in the factory. He does so with music that is full of simple well-being.

5. The chorus congratulates the foreman and then greets the manager (using the same greeting theme as per Section 4).

6. The manager delivers a Spartan message of "work, work, work" to music that, although in 6/8, has shifted to a melancholy minor key. Meanwhile, the agitated music from the opening prelude makes another appearance.

7. The chorus, singing in unison, agrees wholeheartedly with the manager and then, reprising the greeting melody, it introduces the boss, Mr. Fletcher.

8. Fletcher is full of self-congratulatory optimism and his workers chime in to agree with him. At one point, to low-lying, portentous chords, he has them recite a pledge of confidence in his company.

9. The scene ends with a forty-bar dance. For thirty-two bars it is an instrumental made from the music in the prelude. In the last eight bars the chorus sings its greeting theme once more, this time to the line "Tra-la-la-la we're off to work, tra-la-la-la we're off to work."

Recordings: None

194. I MEAN TO SAY

Lyricist: Ira Gershwin
Key: F

Time: Alla breve
Tempo: Moderato
Introduced by: Doris Carson and Gordon Smith in *Strike Up the Band* at the Times Square Theatre in New York City on January 14, 1930.

Analysis: In this ballad, a tongue-tied man is coaxed by his lady friend into expressing his love for her. She does not quite get him to say "I love you" but does hear a "That's it" after she says, "You mean you love me?" The twenty-four-bar verse ("Haven't you a lot of things to say to me?") is a gentle and legato tune, one that uses simple harmony and sticks to the home key. In the refrain ("I mean to say") the halting manner of the male singer is brought out by a series of two-note phrases, each one punctuated by a quarter note pause. These pauses might have made for a stuttering, comic effect—yet, the music manages to build smoothly. The release ("Why, oh why") presents a dramatic contrast to this somewhat easygoing opening. It is an urgent G-minor melody with exotic, modal voicing in the accompaniment.

Recordings: Ronny Whyte and Travis Hudson (Monmouth-Evergreen MES 7061).

195. A TYPICAL SELF-MADE AMERICAN

Lyricist: Ira Gershwin
Key: Various
Time: Common
Tempo: Various
Introduced by: Herbert Corthell and Roger Pryor in *Strike Up the Band* at the Shubert Theatre in New York City on September 5, 1927. Dudley Clements and Jerry Goff introduced it in the second version of *Strike Up the Band* at the Times Square Theatre in New York City on January 14, 1930.

Lore: Isaac Goldberg considered this a take-off on "He is an Englishman" from Gilbert and Sullivan's *H.M.S. Pinafore*.

Analysis: This piece can be divided into the following sections:

212

1.   A twenty-bar introduction in which business magnate Horace J. Fletcher, singing solo, tells how, even as a poor boy, he had a sense of his own remarkable destiny. This section is in A-major, marked Moderato con moto, and is sung recitative-style to simple churchy chords.
2.   A twenty-six-bar verse in E-major with an Allegretto tempo marking. Here Fletcher continues his story with the assistance of a subordinate, Jim Townsend, and a male chorus. The melody they sing is bright, although the accompaniment contains sighing chromatics.
3.   A refrain in G-major with an Allegretto pomposo tempo marking. Sung by Fletcher and the chorus, it has the kind of zany simplicity that had marked "The Babbitt and the Bromide" (the two songs were actually written in the same year). It is brief, just sixteen bars, and is capped with a series of majestic chords.

Recordings: In 1979 the Smithsonian Institute produced a show called *The Gershwins, 1930 and Girl Crazy*. A privately made tape of the production is in existence and it includes a performance of "A Typical Self-Made American."

196. SOON

Lyricist: Ira Gershwin
Key: B-flat (verse)
        E-flat (refrain)
Time: Common (verse)
         Alla breve (refrain)
Tempo: Moderato (verse)
          Not fast (with tender expression) (refrain)
Introduced by: Jerry Goff and Helen Gilligan in *Strike Up the Band* at the Times Square Theatre in New York City on January 14, 1930.

Lore: The refrain of "Soon" was based on a four-bar recitative from the Act One Finale of the original 1927 version of *Strike Up the Band*.

Analysis: The sixteen-bar verse ("I'm making up for all the years that I waited") is one of the composer's loveliest. It is mainly shy and unemphatic, although in bars six through eight (at "shirking") a succession of ninth and major seventh chords over an F pedal point leads to a dramatic $Cm7^{-5}$ chord (on "fast"). The drama continues in the refrain ("Soon the lonely nights will be ended") where, after an opening in simple, diurnal E-flat, another $Cm7^{-5}$ chord (on "ly" in "lonely") and a B-flat minor sixth chord (on "nights") make for a dark and pleading quality. When, after four bars, this idea is repeated, there is no comfortable E-flat, but a presentation in F-minor. Also contributing to this song's status as a standard are an eloquent release ("I've found the happiness") and a tranquil four-bar coda ("Let's make that day come Soon").

One should note that in the finale to Act I of *Strike Up the Band*, "Soon" is given an alternative, second release—one that, although worthy, is never used when the song is recorded or performed.

Recordings: Red Nichols, who played in the *Strike Up the Band* pit orchestra, recorded this song in 1930 (with Tommy Dorsey—Brunswick 4695). Other 1930 versions were by Victor Arden-Phil Ohman and their Orchestra (Victor 22308) and Lou Gold and His Orchestra (Gennett 7133). Additional recordings were made in 1939 by Connie Boswell (Decca 2879), in 1943 by Bobby Hackett (Brunswick 80009), in 1958 by Benny Goodman (Westinghouse 2), and in 1959 by Ella Fitzgerald (Verve 2-2525). In March of 1987, Bob Dylan sang "Soon" at a "Gershwin Gala" at the Brooklyn Academy of Music. PBS taped that performance.

Other versions are by Cannonball Adderly (Landmard 1301), Kaye Ballard (Walden 302), Al Caiola (Bainbridge 1012), Cal Collins (Concord Jazz 59), Chris Connor (Atlantic 2-601), Paul Desmond (Fantasy 8082), Eddie Duran (Fantasy OJC-120), Red Garland (Prestige 7276), Corky Hale (Crescendo 9035), Mitzi Gaynor (Verve MGV 2115), the Ernie Henry Quartet (Riverside OJC-1722), Alberta Hunter (DRG 5195), Kiri Te Kanawa (Angel DS 74754), Dorothy Kirsten with Percy Faith and Orchestra (Columbia 52-G), Teddi King (Inner City 1044), Yehudi Menuhin/Stephane Grappelli (Angel 37156), Marni Nixon with piano accompaniment by Lincoln Mayorga (Reference RR-19), Joe Pass (Pablo 2312133), Artie Shaw (Victor AXM2-5580), the Paul Smith Trio (Outstanding 012), Sonny Stitt (Muse 5067), Ross Tompkins (Concord Jazz 28), and Tommy Tune (Atlantic 80110-1-E).

197. STRIKE UP THE BAND INCIDENTAL MUSIC

Instrumental

Key: G
Time: 4/8
Tempo: Allegretto
Introduced by: George Gershwin conducting the *Strike Up the Band* pit orchestra at the Times Square Theatre in New York City on January 14, 1930.

Analysis: This is a straightforward instrumental reading of the refrain from "A Typical Self-Made American." It was published as numbers 4A and 16A in the piano/vocal score of *Strike Up the Band.*

Recordings: None.

198. DREAM MUSIC

Instrumental

Key: Ambiguous
Time: Various
Tempo: Con moto
Introduced by: George Gershwin conducting the *Strike Up the Band* pit orchestra at the Times Square Theatre in New York City on January 14, 1930.

Lore: In the post-mortem on the unsuccessful 1927 production of *Strike Up the Band* it was concluded that George S. Kaufman's anti-war libretto had been too sour and that the show, if it was to be successfully revived, would have to be watered down. Morris Ryskind—a venomous writer himself on occasion—was brought in to do the diluting and his idea was to have the war between the United States and Switzerland relieved of any vestiges of reality. For the 1930 production, therefore, it was presented as a dream in the head of Horace J. Fletcher. And, to further sweeten things, the war was no longer over cheese but, instead, chocolate. Fletcher's dream is introduced by this instrumental music.

Analysis: This twenty-six-bar piece is filled with eerie tremulos and rising/falling chromatic lines such as those that would later punctuate *Porgy and Bess.* There is no clear resolution into any particular key. In fact, the piece does not have a real finish; after a trumpet call it concludes with a series of pick-up notes marked with the instruction to "repeat until cue."

Recordings: The "Dream Music" is included in the *Strike Up the Band Overture*, recorded by Michael Tilson Thomas and the Buffalo Philharmonic (Columbia M34542).

199. THE UNOFFICIAL SPOKESMAN

Lyricist: Ira Gershwin
Key: Various
Time: Various
Tempo: Various
Introduced by: Lew Hearn and Herbert Corthell in *Strike Up the Band* at the Shubert Theatre in New York City on September 5, 1927. Bobby Clark, Paul McCullough, and Dudley Clements introduced it in the second version of the show at the Times Square Theatre in New York City on January 14, 1930.

Lore: This is one of the few instances wherein Ira's words preceded George's music. It was George's idea, however, to have the singer stutter on the word "unofficial." According to Isaac Goldberg, the stuttering Americanized a number that might otherwise have sounded too much like Gilbert and Sullivan.

Analysis: "The Unofficial Spokesman" is ninety-three bars long and it can be separated into the following six sections:

216

1.　　An instrumental introduction first heard as the third theme of the prelude to the Act I Opening. It is in G major and in 6/8 time.

2.　　A reprise of the greeting theme, also from the Act I Opening. Here, the ensemble is greeting Colonel Holmes, one of the characters in Fletcher's dream. Holmes is modeled after Colonel Edward House, an influential figure in the administration of President Woodrow Wilson.

3.　　Fletcher's recitativo introduction of Holmes remains in the key of G but leaves 6/8 for 4/8 time. The tempo is allegretto moderato.

4.　　A presentation by the ensemble of Holmes' impressive resume. This music is sometimes referred to by one of its lines, "a man of very high degree." It is characterized by simple harmony and by a melody that, like Holmes, rises to great heights. It moves slowly and persistently from the E above middle C up a tenth to high G.

5.　　A verse in which Holmes sings about his childhood, indicating that he was born into the world by "a process which I do not care to mention" and that he never bothered to say goo-goo to his nurse. This music is in recitativo-style and is colored darkly in F- minor.

6.　　A refrain in which Holmes indicates that he has risen to political heights by keeping his mouth shut. Here the key is F major and the tune is a mindless ditty, such as the one given to Fletcher in "A Typical Self-Made American." To make things as difficult as possible for the stuttering politician, the repeated words are set to music in the type of disorienting, tailgating phrasing that Gershwin used in "Fascinating Rhythm" and other songs.

Recordings: None.

200. STRIKE UP THE BAND OPENING SCENE III, ACT I / PATRIOTIC RALLY

Lyricist: Ira Gershwin
Key: Various
Time: Various
Tempo: Various
Introduced by: The ensemble in *Strike Up the Band* at the

Times Square Theatre in New York City on January 14, 1930.

Analysis: This piece continues the simple children's tune style of Gershwin's choral numbers in *Strike Up the Band*, although he peppers the music with odd bass notes and a quote from "Rally 'Round the Flag." There are three sections:

1. A twenty-four-bar instrumental introduction in G marked Allegro vigoroso, followed by a choral presentation of the same material. The target here is war fever and there are lines such as, "Oh, isn't it exciting? There may be lots of fighting."
2. A contrasting Andantino section sung in unison by the females of the chorus. They remark that the U.S.A. is "the land of Washington and Lincoln, Henry Ford and Morris Gest" (the latter, a Broadway producer, presented several of Gershwin's songs in 1919). After fourteen bars of name dropping (other Americans mentioned are Big Chief Muddy Waters and Babe Ruth), the tempo picks up for the final six bars as the ladies chant "We could go on naming great men, but we have our fears. This could go on for years."
3. A thirty-two-bar instrumental dance in C-major and 2/4 time.

Recordings: None.

201. IF I BECAME THE PRESIDENT

Lyricist: Ira Gershwin
Key: G
Time: 2/4
Tempo: Allegro moderato
Introduced by: Blanche Ring and Bobby Clark in *Strike Up the Band* at the Times Square Theatre in New York City on January 14, 1930.

Lore: After writing this comic number, Ira was approached by the actor Bobby Clark, who had written an additional set of lyrics.

218

Clark was a big star in his day and Ira was advised to humor him and let him use a few of his own lines. As it turned out, they got as many laughs as did those of the professional lyricist.

Analysis: In this duet a character named Mrs. Draper promises to make Colonel Holmes President. He then promises to make her First Lady. That settled, they embark on a joint daydream to see what it will be like when they are in office.

Some of Ira's choicest rhymes are to be found in this song ("We could receive ambassadors, the kind the upper class adores," "The joys of domesticity will bring us great publicity"). The music's appeal lies mainly in its pungent harmonies. There is a four-bar instrumental introduction in G which quotes from "Dixie," a twenty-four-bar verse in G-minor ("If I made you ruler of this great democracy"), and a thirty-two-bar through-composed refrain in G ("If I became the President"). The song ends with a repeat of the "Dixie" quote.

Recordings: A privately made tape of the 1979 Smithsonian Institute production *The Gershwins, 1930 and Girl Crazy* includes a performance of "If I Became the President."

202. HANGIN' AROUND WITH YOU

Lyricist: Ira Gershwin
Key: F
Time: Alla breve
Tempo: Moderato
Introduced by: Doris Carson and Gordon Smith in *Strike Up the Band* at the Times Square Theatre in New York City on January 14, 1930.

Analysis: In this duet, the lovers do not sing at the same time. Instead, she complains that he is two-timing her and he then pleads his innocence, getting off the best line: "I simply must deny it, I swear it isn't true. My heart is on a diet, Darling, except for you." The twenty-bar verse ("Once you would hang around me") is tuneful despite its many repeated notes and it has an easy, swinging gait. The melody of the refrain ("What's the use of hanging around with you") is peppered with blue notes and the tenths in the left hand of its accompaniment make for a jazzy, stride piano feel. The phrases tailgate or, to use Isaac Goldberg's word, telescope one another. Goldberg correctly observed that there is barely enough breathing space in this song for the singer to get in all the words. Another critic, Alec Wilder, wondered why Ira Gershwin let "hangin'" in the title become "hanging" in the text. "Hanging," he concluded, "has nothin' to do with this song."

Recordings: The composer can be heard playing this song at a *Strike Up the Band* rehearsal (20th Century Fox FOX-3013 and JJA 19777). A more recent version is by Ronny Whyte and Travis Hudson (Monmouth-Evergreen MES-7061).

203. STRIKE UP THE BAND FINALE ACT I/HE KNOWS MILK

Lyricist: Ira Gershwin
Key: Various
Time: Various
Tempo: Various
Introduced by: Jerry Goff, Helen Gilligan, Robert Bentley, and Dudley Clements

Analysis: This, the longest musical setting in *Strike Up the Band* (it is 262 bars long and takes up twenty-three pages in the piano/vocal score), is made up of the following eight parts:

1. A sixteen-bar instrumental introduction marked Allegro that is in 2/4 and A-major. It is mainly a series of eighth notes rising inexorably and nervously toward the emphatic A chord that begins section two. A secondary and syncopated countermelody rises alongside it.
2. This section, marked Vigoroso, is in A-major and 4/4 time. In it Jim Townsend, singing to the assembled chorus, inveighs against the war between America and Switzerland. Messrs. Fletcher and

220

Sloane reply in unison, "Be careful of a trick! He's just a Bolshevik!" Their very simple vocal lines are not reproduced in the accompaniment, as is customary, but, instead, are accompanied by what looks and sounds like the subject of a fugue.

3. In a two-bar F-major passage marked Recitativo Jim asks the chorus for their attention. Then, after a one-bar vamp (marked Vivo), he goes into the "He Knows Milk" refrain. Here he tells the assembled that he knows all about milk, having been born on a farm (every time he says "I know milk" the chorus comes back with "He knows milk"—hence, the title). Knowing milk, he knows that Fletcher has been using Grade B and not Grade A in his chocolate. That is what has led him to conclude that the war against Switzerland is being fought under false pretenses.

    The music here is a march in Allegretto moderato tempo. It is, like so much of Gershwin's writing for this show, a ditty. (By now it is clear that the composer was consciously fashioning melodies with a nursery rhyme feel so as to poke fun at the childishness of the play's characters and situations and, by extension, at war itself.) "He Knows Milk" is similar in form to the AABA of a standard song refrain, although the first two A sections are lengthened slightly (to allow the chorus to shout the title phrase), while the release is shortened and the final A extended. There is a tag ("Grade B. Not A? No, B!") in a new key, G-major, leading into section four.

4. Here, to very jumpy music—a highly chromatic melody atop a succession of unresolved chords—Fletcher, Sloane (the manager of Fletcher's factory) and Colonel Holmes refute and Jim restates the Grade B charge.

5. Moving from the key of G to that of A-flat, the chorus, singing quietly and in unison, mulls over these conflicting assertions and gradually comes to the conclusion that Jim might be telling the truth. As this realization sinks in, the pitch of their notes becomes higher and their voices louder. Finally, as they sing "maybe he is telling us the truth," they break into four-part harmony.

6. To the melody of "Soon," Fletcher's daughter, Joan, asks Jim (whom she loves) why he is making accusations against her father. Jim replies that it is something that he just has to do. This

section is musically interesting for the new release given to "Soon" ("Look at my father and see")—one that is almost as appealing as the original one—and for the nicely wrought choral passage that accompanies the two lovers.

7.   Here Joan voices her dilemma. Not only is her beloved (Jim) in fundamental conflict with her father (Fletcher) but, to top it off, she has become engaged to Sloane. The music, marked Moderato (with expression) is in D-major and it is very brief—just seven bars. It is a fleeting fragrance but a charming one.

8.   To the music of section four the chorus suddenly turns against Jim. They assert that he is a fake, that he has been feeding them propaganda, and they slip back into their war fever.

Recordings: None.

204. ENTRANCE OF THE SOLDIERS

Instrumental

Key: B-flat
Time: Alla breve
Tempo: Tempo di Marcia
Introduced by: George Gershwin conducting the *Strike Up the Band* pit orchestra at the Times Square Theatre in New York City on January 14, 1930.

Lore and Analysis: A few days before the premiere of the 1930 version of *Strike Up the Band* Isaac Goldberg visited George Gershwin at the Ritz-Carlton in Boston. There he found the composer in bed orchestrating what Goldberg has referred to as "The Entrance of the Soldiers." Actually, Goldberg may have been confusing "Entrance of the Soldiers" with "Soldiers March." Gershwin's intention, according to Goldberg, was to sabotage a trumpet flourish with a series of descending chords in the piano/vocal score. The "Soldier's March," an autonomous instrumental composition, displays the heavy satire that would call for such a treatment. "The Entrance of the Soldiers," on the other hand, is just an instrumental version of the title song.

Recordings: None.

205. STRIKE UP THE BAND OPENING ACT II

Lyricist: Ira Gershwin
Key: Various
Time: 4/4
Tempo: Various
Introduced by: The ensemble in *Strike Up the Band* at the Times Square Theatre in New York City on January 14, 1930.

Analysis: The Act II opening of *Strike Up the Band* is in four sections:

1. A thirty-two-bar instrumental introduction in A-major, marked Allegro moderato. This is a reworking of the title song. In the first few bars it is juxtaposed with "Soon."
2. "In the Rattle of the Battle" is a twenty-bar march in which a truculent male chorus, singing in unison, pledges itself to military victory over "those foreign traitors," as it calls the enemy.
3. A two-bar instrumental introduction in the key of C leads to "Military Dancing Drill." The verse here ("Soldier, soldier, listen, do!") is not the one used in the version of this song that was published in 1927 but, like the earlier verse, it is agreeably melodic. The refrain, in F-major, is the same in both versions.
4. The final portion of the Act II opening, marked "Dance," is a straightforward instrumental rendition of "Strike Up the Band."

Recordings: None.

206. MADEMOISELLE IN NEW ROCHELLE

Lyricist: Ira Gershwin
Key: C (verse)
     F (refrain)
Time: 4/4, 6/8 (verse)
      6/8 (refrain)

Tempo: Moderato (verse)
       Allegretto (refrain)
Introduced by: Bobby Clark and Paul McCullough in *Strike Up the Band* at the Times Square Theatre in New York City on January 14, 1930.

Analysis: The lyric is a spoof on the "Mademoiselle From Armentiéres" theme. Here the American expeditionary soldier mentions not the exotic French city of his new found love but the mundane New York suburb of the girl he has all too willingly left behind. The twenty-bar verse ("Little lady, as you stand before me") is a quiet, melancholy piece—one that, mainly through deft use of harmonic suspensions, has a heartbreak quality. Worth noting are the unusual five-bar phrases with which it begins and the change of meter from 4/4 to 6/8 at the seventeenth bar (at "forget about the gal back home"). In contrast, the forty-four-bar refrain ("I left my mademoiselle in New Rochelle") has a raucous nature—and an adventurous one too. In the first bar the singer must negotiate a disorienting line that feigns toward one key (G), then another (C), before it heads toward the actual key (F). An extended sixteen-bar release ("I love your lips") continues this idea, presenting a crescendo in which there are resolutions in a long succession of keys, beginning in C and going farther and farther afield. Also interesting is the pattern of commentary in the accompaniment, also written in the form of cadences. They have a congratulatory, amen quality.

Recordings: Gershwin was recorded rehearsing the refrain with Clark and McCullough (20th Century Fox 3013).

224

207. I'VE GOT A CRUSH ON YOU

Lyricist: Ira Gershwin
Key: B-flat
Time: 2/4
Tempo: Allegretto giocoso (gaily)
Introduced by: Clifton Webb and Mary Hay in *Treasure Girl* at the Alvin Theatre in New York City on November 8, 1928. The song was performed by Gordon Smith and Doris Carson in the second edition of *Strike Up the Band* in 1930. It was first published in 1930.

Lore: Like "Someone to Watch Over Me," this was an up-tempo number at first. However, Lee Wiley's recording in 1939, the first recording (see below), turned it into a ballad, and that has been the preference ever since. Wiley was also the first to add two measures to the song's finish by singing "I have got a crush" instead of "I've got a crush."

Analysis: The verse is distinctive and substantial—being thirty-two bars long and AA¹BA² in form. Its initial idea ("How glad the many millions of Annabelles and Lillians would be") is unusual in that, for the first four measures, vocal line and accompaniment are in unison. Midway, there is a brief move into the distant key of D (at "I fell"). As for the refrain, the composer may have thought it a rhythm number because of its clashing harmony. In fact, much of it is polytonal. For instance, the first two bars have D-minor and A chords in the treble against B-flat harmony in the bass. Bars three and four have E-flat harmony above C and F tonalities. The harsh chords that are created when these sounds combine add propulsion to an up-tempo reading. But they also add emotional depth to a balladic interpretation. This polytonality continues throughout the refrain—note the simultaneous F and B-flat chords in the accompaniment during the vocalist's rest after the final "must" in bar twenty-seven.

Recordings: Lee Wiley's premiere recording was made on November 15, 1939 (Liberty Music Shop L-282, reissued on Monmouth-Evergreen MES 7034). Elliott Lawrence also recorded this song in

1939 (Decca 27124). The next year, there was a version by Joe Sullivan and His Cafe Society Orchestra (Okeh 56470), and in 1947 came a rendition by Sarah Vaughan (Musicraft 505). Frances Gershwin, sister of the composer and lyricist, can be heard singing this song as well (World Records SH-208, Monmouth-Evergreen MES 7060).

Other choices: Nat Adderly (Milestone 47047), Teresa Brewer (Doctor Jazz W2X-3952 and Project 3 5108), Rosemary Clooney (Concord Jazz 47 and 278), Chris Connor (Atlantic 2-601), Ella Fitzgerald (Verve 2-2525), Buddy Greco (Bainbridge BT-8004), Helen Humes (Muse 5217), Cleo Laine (Columbia FM-37936), Gertrude Lawrence (Decca 28266), Marian McPartland (Concord Jazz 272), Marni Nixon with piano accompaniment by Lincoln Mayorga (Reference RR-19), the Oscar Peterson Trio (Pausa 7059), Andre Previn (RCA Victor LPM 1011), the Riviera Orchestra (Wing SRW 11012), Linda Ronstadt and Nelson Riddle (Asylum 7-69752), David Rose (MGM E3123), Zoot Sims (Pablo 2310744), Frank Sinatra (Columbia 13-33306, Capital SABB-11357, Capital SN-16204, Columbia PG-31358), Bobby Short (Atlantic SD 2-608), Ross Tompkins (Concord Jazz 46), and Mike Wofford (Discovery 784).

208. STRIKE UP THE BAND INCIDENTAL MUSIC (2)

Instrumental

Key: E-flat
Time: Common
Tempo: Più moderato
Introduced by: George Gershwin conducting the *Strike Up the Band* pit orchestra at the Times Square Theatre in New York City on January 14, 1930.

Analysis: This is a straightforward instrumental abbreviation of the refrain from "Soon." It was published as number 13A in the *Strike Up the Band* piano/vocal score.

Recordings: None.

209. HOW ABOUT A BOY LIKE ME?

Lyricist: Ira Gershwin
Key: F
Time: 2/4
Tempo: Allegro moderato
Introduced by: Bobby Clark, Paul McCullough, Dudley Clements, and Blanche Ring in *Strike Up the Band* at the Times Square Theatre in New York City on January 14, 1930.

Analysis: A song entitled "How About A Man Like Me" was an unpublished portion of the 1927 version of *Strike Up the Band.* If "Man" was changed to "Boy" as part of the deliberate weakening of the plot (see "Dream Music"), then the authors can justly be accused of overzealousness.

This song's unusually long verse is a duet between a woman and three importuning men who sing in unison. In measures seventeen through twenty-two (beginning with "I've seen foreign beauties") it contains an interesting run through the cycle of fifths via a succession of $m7^{-5}$ chords. The thirty-two-bar refrain is a rouser that brings two earlier Gershwin songs to mind. Like "Sweet and Low-Down," it consists of a joyous crescendo leading to a bluesy, syncopated climax. Like "Liza," it rises slowly and with force up the pentatonic scale. It also contains a most unusual rhyme: "You'll make no faux-pas if you let me be your Sonny Bwah!"

Recordings: An instrumental version can be heard in the *Strike Up the Band* Overture as played by the Buffalo Philharmonic (Columbia M34542). A vocal version exists on a privately made tape of the 1979 Smithsonian institution production *The Gershwins, 1930 and Girl Crazy.*

210. SOLDIER'S MARCH

Instrumental

Key: B-flat
Time: 2/4
Tempo: Tempo di Marcia
Introduced by: George Gershwin conducting the *Strike Up the Band* pit orchestra at the Times Square Theatre in New York.

Analysis: This and the "Dream Music" are Gershwin's two instrumental compositions for *Strike Up the Band.* "Soldier's March" consists of a four-bar introduction and a thirty-two-bar chorus. In keeping with the nursery rhyme quality of much of his music for this show, the main idea sounds like the nyanny-nyah mocking of children.

Recordings: In 1959 this piece was recorded by Nelson Riddle as a bonus record that was included in the deluxe edition of *Ella Fitzgerald Sings the George and Ira Gershwin Songbooks* (Verve MG V-4029-5).

211. ENTRANCE OF GIDEON AND SWISS GIRLS

Instrumental

Key: G
Time: 6/8
Tempo: Allegretto
Introduced by: George Gershwin conducting the *Strike Up the Band* pit orchestra at the Times Square Theatre in New York City on January 14, 1930.

Analysis: This is an instrumental reading of the refrain from "Mademoiselle in New Rochelle." The only change is the key, which is G-major here.

Recordings: None.

228

212. OFFICIAL RESUME

Lyricist: Ira Gershwin
Key: Various
Time: 2/4
Tempo: Various
Introduced by: The ensemble in *Strike Up the Band* at the
Times Square Theatre in New York City on January 14, 1930.

Analysis: Here the chorus summarizes the plot of the play. This
is done in four sections:

1. A ten-bar instrumental introduction that begins with the trumpet
call that was heard at the beginning of the overture and at the
beginning of the Opening Act I. It is marked Allegro moderato
and is in the key of C.
2. The story proceeds via the "He Knows Milk" music that made up
the third section of the Finale to Act I. It is in A-major and then
F and is marked Moderato.
3. The resume continues with the agitated G-major music that was
first encountered in the fourth section of the Act I finale. The
tempo marking here is Allegretto.
4. The words in the next eight bars are spoken while occasional
chords in the key of A-flat serve as punctuation. This is an
introduction to the wedding music ("Ding Dong") that follows.

Recordings: None.

213. DING DONG

Lyricist: Ira Gershwin
Key: C
Time: 2/4
Tempo: Moderato
Introduced by: The ensemble in *Strike Up the Band* at the
Times Square Theatre in New York City on January 14, 1930.

Analysis: This wedding song has on occasion been referred to by one of its lines: "Oh, ring-a-ding-a-ding-dong bell." It consists of a verseless thirty-two-bar refrain ("Hear the bells in the belfry go ding dong") and a long twenty-four-bar release ("Keep the trumpeter blowing"). The melody of the refrain, like that of "How About a Boy Like Me?," is marked by a constant rising in pitch. In contrast, the release stays put—although it does make its way to a cadence in A-major (on "shoes" in "tons of rice and old shoes").

Recordings: None.

214. STRIKE UP THE BAND FINALE ULTIMO

Instrumental

Key: B-flat
Time: Alla breve
Tempo: Tempo di Marcia
Introduced by: George Gershwin conducting the *Strike Up the Band* pit orchestra at the Times Square Theatre in New York City on January 14, 1930.

Analysis: This is a straightforward thirty-two-bar instrumental reading of "Strike Up the Band."

Recordings: None

215. I WANT TO BE A WAR BRIDE

Lyricist: Ira Gershwin
Key: E-flat
Time: 3/4
Tempo: Tempo di Valse Moderato
Introduced by: Kathryn Hamill in *Strike Up the Band* at the Times Square Theatre in New York City on January 14, 1930.

Lore: Isaac Goldberg, who called this song one of George and Ira's brightest compositions, complained when it was not included in the printed score of *Strike Up the Band*. He felt that it had been discriminated against because it was a waltz. A less petulant reason for excluding it may have been the fact that it was dropped from the show shortly after the New York opening. In any case, it was published independently.

Analysis: It is hard to imagine just who the publishers thought might buy or sing this number, what with lines such as "Oh, to be rapt in love with a captain," "if he's a colonel I'll promise love eternal," and "even a private could still contrive it to make me a war bride too." The long forty-four-bar verse ("I grow all excited") is a contented and simple tune, one made of imitative phrases. In it, the singer expresses her admiration for and desire to emulate Joan of Arc and other female warriors. Then, in the refrain ("I've an idea"), she indicates that she will be pleased to do her suffering on the home front. Attached to this sarcastic lyric is an incongruously uncynical waltz. It is thirty-two bars long and AA^1A^2 in form and, aside from some chromatics in the accompaniment, is sunny and uncomplicated.

Recordings: Louise Carlyle (Citadel Records CT 7017).

216. BIDIN' MY TIME

Lyricist: Ira Gershwin
Key: In 1930, "Bidin' My Time" was published in E-flat. In the
    Girl Crazy piano vocal score, published in 1954, it is in C.
Time: 4/4
Tempo: Moderato
Introduced by: The Foursome in *Girl Crazy* at the Alvin Theatre in New York City on October 14, 1930.

Lore: Ira Gershwin took the title of this song from the last line ("I'm going to bide my time") of a poem that he had written in 1916 for New York City College's monthly *Cap and Bells*. It occurred to him, while writing *Girl Crazy*, that the "Bide my time" phrase would work well in parodying the western-style ballad. Toward that end, the Foursome, portraying a group of sleepy-eyed cowboys, accompanied themselves on tin flute, jew's harp, ocarina and harmonica.

Ira had some additional fun in the verse, referring in rhyme to several popular songs of the day: "Tiptoe Through the Tulips With Me" (1929), "Singin' in the Rain" (1929), "Painting the Clouds With Sunshine" (1929—actually, Ira calls this "Painting Skies With Sunshine"), and "Swingin' Down the Lane" (1923). For a reprise, he added other titles: "Tell it to the Daisies," "Stroll Beneath the Honeysuckle Vines," "Climbed the Highest Mountain," and "A Crying For the Carolines."

Analysis: The cheerful and contented verse ("Some fellows love to 'Tip-toe Through the Tulips'") quotes, in its sixth and seventh bars, not just the title but the melody of "Singin' in the Rain." It was Ira's suggestion that the refrain ("I'm Bidin' My Time") not repeat after the first eight bars and the resulting twenty-four-bar ABA format gives it a more folklike, less Broadwayish quality. On the syllable "diz" in the phrase "while other folks grow dizzy," the melody suddenly moves up a half step and out of the home key. This is an effective hook and a foretaste of the release ("Next year"), which will be in that other key. The release is notable for the way that it gently interrupts the studied lethargy of the refrain with some subdued, Charleston-style syncopation.

Recordings: The Foursome recorded this in 1930 (Brunswick 4996), as did the Blue Jeans (the only recording they ever made— Victor 23036). Succeeding renditions were in 1932 by Edgar Jackson's Gargoyle Five (Oriole P-110) in 1938 by Elisabeth Welch and Robert Ashley (His Master's Voice C-2992), in 1946 by Phil Moore (Black and White 803), and in 1959 by Ella Fitzgerald (Verve 2-2525).

"Bidin' My Time" was also featured in all three film versions of *Girl Crazy*. The 1932 version is on JJA-19773. The 1943 version (sung by Judy Garland) is on Decca DL-5412. The 1965 version (this movie is entitled *Where the Boys Meet the Girls* and, in it, "Bidin' My Time" is sung by Herman's Hermits) is on MGM 4334 and MCA

25013.

Other recordings are by Ruby Braff and Dick Hyman (Inner City 1153), Jackie Cain and Roy Kral (Concord Jazz 186), Frederick Fennell (Mercury 75127), Jane Froman (Victor 12332), Mary Martin (Columbia OS 2560), Joe Pass (Pablo 2312133), and Sarah Vaughn (Mercury MG-20310).

217. BOY! WHAT LOVE HAS DONE TO ME!

Lyricist: Ira Gershwin

Key: In 1930, "Boy! What Love Has Done To Me!" was published in G. In the *Girl Crazy* piano/vocal score, published in 1954, it is in F.

Time: 4/4 (verse)

Alla breve (refrain)

Tempo: Moderately fast (verse)

Rather slow (sorrowfully) (refrain)

Introduced by: Ethel Merman in *Girl Crazy* at the Alvin Theatre in New York City on October 14, 1930.

Analysis: The verse ("It happened down at the Golden Gate") has a light and innocent quality and is easily tuneful enough to have become a memorable song in itself. The refrain ("I fetch his slippers") is kin to that of "The Man I Love" in that much of the time the melody takes its cue from a fresh chord sounded at the beginning of a new bar. Here this technique is used to create a crescendo, as each succeeding musical phrase is attached to another of the singer's complaints about her man. The very adventurous release ("When a guy looks my way") also uses the crescendo, doing so via a rising melody and increasingly complicated E-chords: an $E9^{+6}$ on "Does he get," an $E7^{+9}$ on "Say! he gets," and an $E7^{+9+6}$ on "dramatic." It is worth noting that on the word "emphatic" in this section the version in the *Girl Crazy* score uses a ninth chord with an added fourth while the separately issued sheet uses a dominant-seventh chord with an added fourth. The latter is probably more appealing. Also worth mentioning are the notes given to the final "done to me!" These notes (in the G-major version they are D-

233

flat, B-flat and G) make for a highly unusual sequence, one that is not easy to sing.

There are three piano arrangements of this song in the *Girl Crazy* score. They can be found on pages 123-124, 127 and 129-130. Additional lyrics are to be found in a reprise on pages 124-127.

Recordings: Ruby Braff and the Shubert Alley Cats (Warner Bros. WS 1273), Jane Froman (Epic SN-6059), Nancy Walker (RCA Camden CAL/CAS-561), Mary Martin (Columbia OS 2560, OL 7060), Ella Fitzgerald (Verve MGV-4028).

218. BUT NOT FOR ME

Lyricist: Ira Gershwin

Key: In 1930, "But Not For Me" was published in E-flat. In the *Girl Crazy* piano/vocal score, published in 1954, it is in B-flat.

Time: Alla breve

Tempo: Moderato (verse)
Rather slow (refrain)

Introduced by: Ginger Rogers and Willie Howard in *Girl Crazy* at the Alvin Theatre in New York City on October 14, 1930.

Lore: Originally, this song was called "Not For Me."

Analysis: The very fine twenty-four-bar verse ("Old Man Sunshine listen, you!") begins with a string of repeated notes played against descending major thirds. These thirds are like a succession of costumes for that lone melodic note. Being major thirds, they make every second chord an augmented one—creating a stress-filled sound. This tension continues until bar sixteen, when it is relieved by a new idea ("I never want to hear/From any cheerful Pollyannas")—one that is waltz-like and less intense.

The refrain ("They're writing songs of love, But Not For Me") begins with a quarter note rest (in this way it is like three other prominent songs from the *Girl Crazy* score: "I Got Rhythm," "Embraceable

234

You," and "Sam and Delilah"). Then come the three pick-up notes ("They're writing") that are the basis for all thirty-two bars of this beautiful melody. One should also be aware of the greatness of this song's lyric. In the verse, Ira Gershwin manages to convey real frustration and anguish without forsaking humor ("Old Man Sunshine listen, you! Never tell me, 'Dreams come true!' Just try it And I'll start a riot"). And the refrain is also full of extraordinary moments ("I found more clouds of gray Than any Russian play Could guarantee," "I know that love's a game; I'm puzzled just the same, Was I the moth or flame? I'm all at sea"). Beatrice Fairfax, by the way, was the writer of an advice column—a predecessor of Ann Landers and Abigail Van Buren.

Recordings: It took almost ten years for recording artists to discover this song. Then, after Lee Wiley recorded it in 1939 (Liberty Music Shop L-284, reissued on Monmouth-Evergreen MES 7034), there were versions in 1940 by Teddy Wilson (Columbia 36084), in 1941 by Harry James and His Orchestra (Columbia 36599), in 1942 by Bing Crosby (Columbia DB-30175), and in 1944 by Judy Garland (Decca 23309). Recordings in the 1950s were by the Jackie Gleason Orchestra (Capitol 2439) and Ella Fitzgerald (Verve 2-2525). Bobby Short's rendition came along in 1973 (Atlantic SD 2-608).

Ginger Rogers, who sang "But Not For Me" first, did not record it until the 1960s (Citel CLP-201). Ethel Merman, who was also in the *Girl Crazy* original cast, can be heard in another latter-day version (Reprise R 6032).

In addition, this song has been featured in the three movie versions of *Girl Crazy*. The 1932 production is on JJA-19773. Judy Garland sang it in the 1943 production (Decca DL-5412). The 1965 version (this movie is entitled *Where the Boys Meet the Girls*) is on MGM 4334 and MCA 25013. A more recent version is by Marni Nixon with piano accompaniment by Lincoln Mayorga (Reference RR 19).

219. COULD YOU USE ME?

Lyricist: Ira Gershwin
Key: In 1930, "Could You Use Me?" was published in G. In the *Girl Crazy* piano/vocal score, published in 1954, it is in A-flat.
Time: Alla breve
Tempo: Moderato
Introduced by: Allen Kearns and Ginger Rogers in *Girl Crazy* at the Alvin Theatre in New York City on October 14, 1930.
Analysis: In the verse ("Have some pity on an Easterner") a man courts a woman as if he is applying for employment. He does so to music that, by setting its blue notes within minor chords, creates what sounds like a fusion of blues and Hebraic elements. The lively refrain ("I'm the chappie to make you happy") contains bumpy syncopations, funny rhymes ("I'd shake the mat out And put the cat out"), and a dramatic and powerful release ("Do you realize"). There is a second chorus, in which the lady is given a chance to respond to her suitor, and she firmly expresses her preference for a more outdoorsy, less effete man.

In the *Girl Crazy* piano/vocal score there is a solo piano version of the refrain (pages 27-28).

Recordings: This song was included in the 1932 film version of *Girl Crazy* (JJA-19773) and in the 1943 remake (where it is sung by Judy Garland and Mickey Rooney—Decca DL-5412). Eddie Chappell and Louise Carlyle do it in a studio recreation of the score (Columbia ML-4475, reissued on Columbia CL-822). Other versions are by the George Bassman Orchestra (Decca DX/DXSZ-7160), Ruby Braff and the Shubert Alley Cats (Warner Bros. WS 1273), Jackie Cain and Roy Kral (Roulette R-25278).

220. EMBRACEABLE YOU

Lyricist: Ira Gershwin
Key: In 1930, "Embraceable You" was published in G. In the

236

Girl Crazy piano/vocal score, published in 1954, it is in A-flat.

Time: Alla breve
Tempo: Whimsically (verse)
Rhythmically (refrain)
Introduced by: Allen Kearns and Ginger Rogers in *Girl Crazy* at the Alvin Theatre in New York City on October 14, 1930.

Lore: "Embraceable You" was originally written in 1928 for the aborted Ziegfeld operetta *East is West* (which was also called *Ming-Toy*). After its inclusion in *Girl Crazy* it found favor not only with the public but with Morris Gershwin, father of the songwriting team. He took personal pride in the line "Come to Papa, come to Papa do!" and at parties he would ask George to "play that song about me."

Analysis: It is a source of wonder that, without resorting to the sentimental or the grandiose, a ballad could have been written with so much feeling. In particular, it is Gershwin's mastery of harmony that is at work here. With reference to the G-major edition: the C-sharp diminished chord in bar two (on "my sweet") unsettles the listener, the A-minor chord in bar five (at the second "Embrace me") brings a sense of urgency, and the F-dominant seventh chord—well outside the G-major tonality—in bar six (prior to "you" in "you irreplaceable") gives a sensation of power and significance. In this way the composer affects his listener's feelings without breast-beating or arm-waving. And, harmony aside, there are many other remarkable moments in the song: its sweet, lilting verse ("Dozens of girls would storm up"), its "Come to papa" tag, and the beautiful high E-flat in the penultimate bar (on "brace" in the final "Embraceable you").

The *Girl Crazy* piano/vocal score has three reprises, each containing lyrics not included in the usual sheet music. They can be found on pages 57, 69 and 97. The score also contains four separate arrangements for solo piano on pages 59-61 and 68. All are brief and simple renditions of the refrain.

Recordings: Loring "Red" Nichols and His Orchestra (the pit band for *Girl Crazy*) recorded this song on October 23, 1930 (with

237

Benny Goodman, Charlie Teagarden, Glenn Miller, Gene Krupa, Scrappy Lambert, and a vocal by Dick Robertson—Brunswick 4957). Ginger Rogers, who introduced "Embraceable You," did not record it until the 1960s (Citel CLP-201). Ethel Merman, another member of the original cast of *Girl Crazy*, also recorded it at a later date (Decca DX-153). Frances Gershwin, sister of the composer and lyricist, has released her version (World Records SH-208, Monmouth-Evergreen MES 7060).

Other 1930 renditions were by Victor Arden-Phil Ohman and Their Orchestra (Victor 22558), Lou Gold and His Orchestra (Perfect 15384) and Fred Rich and His Orchestra (Columbia 2328-D). Then came versions in 1938 by Eddie Condon and His Windy City Seven (Commodore Music Shop 1501), in 1939 by Bobby Hackett and His Orchestra (Vocalion/Okeh 4877) and by Judy Garland (Decca 2881), in 1940 by Teddy Wilson and His Orchestra (Columbia 35905) and Bob Crosby (Decca 3271), in 1941 by Jimmy Dorsey and His Orchestra (Decca 3928) and Tommy Dorsey and His Orchestra (Victor 27638), in 1942 by Henry Levine and Linda Keene (Victor 27829) and Ted Straeter and His Orchestra (Decca 24053), in 1946 by Don Byas (Super Disc 1011), The Pied Pipers (year approximate—Capitol 10065), and Hazel Scott (Decca 18341), in 1948 by Marion Morgan (Columbia 38349), in 1952 by Benny Goodman (Columbia GL102), in 1953 by Benny Green (Prestige 847), and in 1959 by Ella Fitzgerald (Verve 2-2525).

Others: Joe Albany (Seabreeze 1004), Elly Ameling and Louis Van Dijk (Philips 6514284), Anthony and the Sophomores (Collectable 1067), Sidney Bechet (Inner City 7008), the Boston Pops conducted by Arthur Fiedler (Victor AGL1-4363), Earl Bostic (Gusto 2052), Ruby Braeff/the George Barnes Quintet (Concord Jazz 5), Clifford Brown (Emarcy 1011), Carol Bruce (V-Disc 87), the Billy Butterfield Orchestra (Ranwood 8221), Ron Carter/Jim Hall (Concord Jazz 245), Kenny Clark (Prestige 7065), Al Cohn (Concord Jazz 241), Nat King Cole (Capitol N-16260), Ornette Coleman (Atlantic 1353),

Chris Connor (Atlantic 2-601), Bing Crosby (Decca DL-5081), Bing Crosby and Judy Garland (Star Tone ST-201), Wild Bill Davison (Dixieland Jubilee 508), Peter Duchin (Fortune 299), Michael Feinstein (Parnassus PR 0100), Frederick Fennell (Mercury 7512), Ferrante and Teicher (Liberty N-10242), Connie Francis (MCA 25013), Erroll Garner (Mercury 1001), Ralph Grierson/Artie Kane (Angel 36083), Barbara Hendricks and Katia and Marielle Lebeque (Philips 5900987), Earl Hines (Classic Jazz 21), Johnny Hodges/Charlie Shavers (Storyville 4073), Billie Holiday (Verve UMV–2597), Jazz at the Philharmonic (Verve UMV–9070), Duke Jordan (Inner City 2024), Dorothy Kirsten (Glendale 9003), Eric Kloss (Prestige 7442), Cleo Laine (Columbia FM 39736), Billy Mays and Red Mitchell (ITI 004), Marian McPartland (Savoy 2248),

Yehudi Menuhin and Stephane Grappelli (Angel 37156), Helen Merrill (Inner City 10807), Julia Migenes–Johnson (Victor ARL1-5323), Glenn Miller (V–Disc 183), Charlie Mingus (Prestige 24092), Frank Morgan (Contemporary 14013), Peter Nero and the Boston Pops (Victor LSC–3223), Marni Nixon with piano accompaniment by Lincoln Mayorga (Reference RR-19), Helen O'Connell (Victor UPM–6076), Norrie Paramor (Angel 38119), Charlie Parker (Columbia JG–34808), Joe Pass (Pablo 2312133), Bud Powell (Fantasy 86006, Prestige 24024), Harve Presnell (MCA 25013), Zoot Sims (Pablo 2310744), Frank Sinatra (Capitol SN–16204), Soundtrack/Irene Cara (Warner Bros. 1–25219), Supersax (Pausa 9028), Tania Maria (Concord Jazz 200), Art Tatum (Pablo 2310835), Sarah Vaughan (Emarcy 1009), Madeline Vergari (Outstanding 033), Ben Webster/"Sweets" Edison (Columbia PC–37036), Jimmy Witherspoon (Prestige 7425), Pia Zadora/the London Philharmonic Orchestra (CBS Associated FZ–40259).

221. I GOT RHYTHM

Lyricist: Ira Gershwin
Key: In 1930, "I Got Rhythm" was published with a G-minor verse and a B-flat refrain. In the *Girl Crazy* piano/vocal score, published in 1954, it has an E-minor verse and an F-major refrain.
Time: Alla breve
Tempo: Lively (verse)
  With abandon (refrain)
Introduced by: Ethel Merman and The Foursome in *Girl Crazy*

239

at the Alvin Theatre in New York City on October 14, 1930.

Lore: Ethel Merman, then a 21-year old unknown, had been brought for an audition to George Gershwin's Riverside Drive Apartment. After she sang a few numbers for him, he played her the three songs in the show that would be hers: "I Got Rhythm," "Sam and Delilah," and "Boy! What Love Has Done to Me." A quarter of a century later, she recalled the occasion in her autobiography *Who Could Ask For Anything More* (Doubleday & Co., 1955):

> It was the first time I'd met George Gershwin and if I may say so without seeming sacrilegious, to me it was like meeting God. Imagine the great Gershwin sitting down and playing his songs for me...When he played "I Got Rhythm," he told me, "If there's anything about this you don't like, I'll be happy to change it." There was nothing about that song I didn't like. But that's the kind of guy he was. That I'll never forget. I smiled and nodded, but I didn't say anything. I was thinking how to phrase the music. Gershwin seemed puzzled at my silence. Finally he said again, "If there's anything about these songs you don't like, Miss Merman, I'll be happy to make changes." It wasn't that; it was only that I was so flabbergasted. Through the fog that had wrapped itself around me, I heard myself say, "They'll do very nicely, Mr. Gershwin."

According to Isaac Goldberg, Gershwin's first biographer, this song was originally slated for *Treasure Girl*, which would have put its composition in 1928. Goldberg also notes that it was originally in a slower tempo.

It took Ira Gershwin two weeks to come up with the lyric to this music. That he later felt that it was worth the effort is proven by three subsequent Gershwin songs—"I'm About to Be A Mother," "Slap That Bass," and "Nice Work If You Can Get It"—which all quote lines from "I Got Rhythm." That George Gershwin loved the song is proven by the fact that it was the only one he ever used as the basis of a symphonic composition—the *I Got Rhythm Variations.*

In *Girl Crazy* Ethel Merman held the final "more!" in "I Got Rhythm" for a full sixteen bars.

The composer's piano transcription of this song appeared in *George Gershwin's Songbook*, published by Simon and Shuster in September of 1932.

Verna Arvey, wife of American composer William Grant Still, wrote an article in the November 1969 issue of *Music Journal* in which she said that Gershwin may have derived a portion of "I Got Rhythm" (she does not identify which portion) from a motive that had been played nightly by her husband when he was oboist in the pit orchestra of Eubie Blake's 1921 Broadway show *Shuffle Along*. In 1930, when Still used that motive in the scherzo of his *Afro-American Symphony*, the public thought that he had gotten it from Gershwin.

Analysis: Gershwin was no physicist but in writing this song he seems to have discovered a force of nature. The verse ("Days can be sunny"), as is true in so many of his rousers ("Swanee," "Fascinating Rhythm," "Clap Yo' Hands"), is in a minor key. In the *Girl Crazy* vocal score this is E-minor with a refrain in F while, in the separately issued sheet music, it is in G-minor with a refrain in B-flat. E-minor and F are less closely related than G-minor and B-flat.

The refrain, an artfully harmonized and vigorously syncopated excursion up and down the pentatonic scale, can be broken down into sixteen two-bar phrases. The odd-numbered ones are rising melody lines. The even-numbered ones are answering, descending melody lines. This is the pattern throughout the song from the first statement ("I got rhythm") and its answer ("I got music") to the release ("Old Man Trouble") and its answer ("I don't mind him") to the tag (where "I got my man" is answered by two "Who could ask for anything more"s).

In some Gershwin rhythm songs, such as "Fascinating Rhythm" and "Liza," the release provides an unfrenetic contrast to the main idea. Here, however, the release really steps on the gas. It does so by maintaining the foregoing rhythmic and melodic patterns while peremptorily leaving the home key. In the B-flat edition this is a move from B-flat to G via a wonderfully upstart D7 chord.

241

The *Girl Crazy* score has several arrangements of "I Got Rhythm" apart from the song itself. There are two straightforward piano readings (pages 81-82 and pages 87-90), two variations for piano (pages 85-87 and pages 93-94) and a full choral treatment (pages 83-85).

Recordings: On one occasion, Gershwin was filmed and recorded playing "I Got Rhythm" (20th Fox 3013). Other versions by the composer are on Mark 56 Records 641 (there are two Gershwin renditions on this record: one from a November 9, 1933 "Rudy Vallee Hour" radio broadcast and the other from the February 19, 1934 edition of the composer's own radio show, "Music By Gershwin") and on Mark 56 Records 667 (from a November 10, 1932 "Rudy Vallee Hour" broadcast).

Ethel Merman released a number of versions, all of them recorded well after the premiere. On Decca 24453 she is accompanied by an orchestra conducted by Jay Blackton. On Decca DV 999 she sings "I Got Rhythm" with Mary Martin, as part of a medley. On Decca DX 153 she is accompanied by the Buddy Cole Quartet. On Reprise R 6062 she is accompanied by the Billy May Orchestra. On London XPS-901 the accompaniment is by Stanley Black and the London Festival Orchestra.

Lorin "Red" Nichols, who was in the *Girl Crazy* orchestra, recorded this on October 23, 1930 (with Benny Goodman, Charlie Teagarden, Glenn Miller, Gene Krupa, Scrappy Lambert, and a vocal by Dick Robertson—Brunswick 4957).

Other 1930 recordings were by Victor Arden-Phil Ohman and Their Orchestra (Victor 22558), Sam Lanin and His Orchestra (Perfect 15396), Lloyd Newton and His Varsity Eleven (Crown 3012), Paul's Novelty Orchestra (Champion 16151), Fred Rich and His Orchestra (Columbia 2328-D and Harmony 1234-H), Louis Russell and His Orchestra (Melotone M-12000), Kate Smith (Harmony 1235-H), and Ethel Waters (Columbia 2346-D).

In 1931 there were versions by Louis Armstrong (Okeh 41534), Paul Ash (Harmony 1234) and Adelaide Hall (Oriole P-109).

In 1932: The Blue Mountaineers (Broadcast 3213), Al Bowlly (Decca F-3014), Roy Fox and His Band (Decca F-3014), Bobby Howes (Columbia DB-824), Don Redman and His Orchestra (Brunswick 6354), and Ray Starita and His Ambassadors (Sterno 1023).

In 1933: Arthur Briggs and His Boys (Brunswick A-500263), Glen Gray and the Casa Loma Orchestra (Brunswick 6800), Freddie Johnson and His Harlemites (Brunswick A-500341), and the Spirits of Rhythm (Brunswick 01715).

In 1934: Joe Venuti and His Orchestra (London HMG-5023).

In 1935: Carnet Clark (His Master's Voice K-7645), Stephane Grappelli (Decca F-5780), and Fats Waller (His Master's Voice HE-2092).

In 1936: the Ballyhooligans (His Master's Voice BD-5056), Joe Daniels and His Hot Shots in "Drumsticks" (Parlophone F-629), Hildegarde (Columbia FB-1541), and Red Norvo and His Swing Sextette (Decca 779).

In 1937: Count Basie and His Orchestra (Collectors' Corner 8), the Emilio Caceros Trio (Victor 25710), Jimmy Dorsey and His Orchestra (Perfect 15396), the Benny Goodman Quartet (MGM Series 102), Glenn Miller (Brunswick 7915), Valaida (Parlophone F-1048), Chick Webb and His Little Chicks (Decca 1759), Dicky Wells and His Orchestra (Swing 27), and Scott Wood and His Six Swingers (Columbia FB-1832).

In 1938: Larry Adler (Columbia DF-2427), Louis Armstrong and Fats Waller (Palm Club 10, Swaggie S-1210), the Benny Goodman Quartet (at the Benny Goodman Carnegie Hall Jazz Concert—Columbia A-1817), and Elisabeth Welch and Robert Ashley (His Master's Voice C-2991).

In 1939: the Benny Goodman Sextet (Vanguard VRS 8523), the Merry Macs (Decca 2877), and the Clarence Profit Trio (Epic LN-24028).

In 1940: the Max Geldray Quartet (Decca F-7736), Fletcher Henderson conducting Horace Henderson and His Orchestra (Vocalion/Okeh 5518), the Sid Phillips Trio (Parlophone F-1803), and Casper Reardon (Schirmer 512).

There were recordings in 1942 by Ted Straeter and His Orchestra (Decca 24053) and the Metronome All-Star Leaders (including Benny Goodman, Count Basie, and Gene Krupa—Columbia C-601 and Columbia 36499); in 1944 by the Kansas City Six (Commodore Music Shop 555); in 1945 by Bud Freeman (Majestic 1018); in 1951 by Gene

Kelly (MGM 30399); in 1959 by Ella Fitzgerald (Verve 2-2525).

Others: Elly Ameling/Lovis Van Dijk (Philips 6514284), Sidney Bechet/Lionel Hampton (Everest 228), Ruby Braff/George Barnes Quintet (Concord Jazz 5), Jackie Cain/Roy Kral (Concord Jazz 186), Joe Carroll/Grant Green (Olympic 7135), Arnett Cobb (Progressive 7054),

Johnny Dankworth (Pathe Actuelle 3871), the Frederick Fennell Orchestra (Mercury 75127), Jane Froman (Victor 12332), Judy Garland (MCA 2-4046), Coleman Hawkins/Lester Young (Doctor Jazz FW-38446), Barbara Hendricks/Katie and Marielle Labeque (Philips 9500987), Jazz at the Philharmonic (Verve UMV-9070), Bobby Knight (Seabreeze 2009), Andre Kostelanetz (Columbia 4268-M), Rob McConnell/Boss Brass (Palo Alto 8074), Yehudi Menuhin/Stephane Grappelli (Angel 37156),

Marni Nixon with piano accompaniment by Lincoln Mayorga (Reference RR-19), Harry Parry (Pathe Actualle 3110), Django Reinhardt (Crescendo 9019) Zoot Sims (Pablo 2310744), Singers Unlimited (Pausa 7039), Paul Smith/Belsson and Brown (Outstanding 009), Barbra Streisand (Columbia PC-32655), Art Tatum (MCA 4019), Ben Webster (Inner City 2008), Roger Williams (MCA 2-4106), Teddy Wilson (Crescendo 9014), and the Yellowjackets (Warner Bros. 1-23813).

222. SAM AND DELILAH

Lyricist: Ira Gershwin

Key: In the 1954 piano/vocal score of *Girl Crazy* "Sam and Delilah" was published in B-flat (with modulations into E-flat and C). In the 1930 sheet music, the key is C (with a single modulation into E-flat).

Time: 4/4

Tempo: The piano/vocal score version states Molto lento ("Blues tempo"). The separate sheet music has a Tempo di Blues marking.

Introduced by: Ethel Merman in *Girl Crazy* at the Alvin Theatre in New York City on October 14, 1930.

Lore: Ira Gershwin admired Ethel Merman's ability to hold the

244

ungainly word "kootch" in this song for five beats, singing a "koo" for four and then somehow retaining the stamina to give a good "tch" on the fifth. She sang the song dressed in a black satin skirt, a red low-cut blouse, and with bangles on her arms.

Analysis: This is a seventy-two-bar long ballad about a hard-drinking, hard-loving, vindictive woman named Delilah who casts her spell over and ensnares a "swell buckaroo" named Sam. They live together happily until he gets homesick and returns to his wife—whence Delilah hunts him down and hacks him to death.

The music aims for a gritty low-down blues style and, toward that end, it has a bump and grind bass and an uninhibited, call-of-the-wild sort of melody replete with old-fashioned blue notes. There is no verse. The refrain ("Delilah Was a floozy") is built on an AABC pattern with the first three sections telling the story and the final one commenting on the lessons to be learned.

It is interesting to note the substantial differences between the two published versions of this song. In the *Girl Crazy* score there is a fourteen-bar instrumental introduction that is missing from the sheet. The version in the vocal score also has a different piano accompaniment and a different ending. It concludes with a sudden modulation from D-flat to G (on the final "Delilah, Oh! Delilah"). In the sheet this modulation is not so bold—it is from E-flat to G. Thus, in the sheet, the final cry of "Delilah" is sung a fifth higher than it had been on its first appearance while, in the score, it is placed a sixth higher. Both modulations are exciting, although the one in the score delivers a bigger jolt.

Recordings: Ethel Merman's recording was made many years after she introduced the song (accompanied by the Billy May Orchestra—Reprise R 6032, Stanyon SR-10070). In 1931 there was a version by Duke Ellington and His Cotton Club Orchestra (vocal by Chick Bullock—Victor 23036, reissued on JJA-19777). In 1939 came Lee Wiley's rendition (Liberty Music Shop L-283, reissued on Monmouth-Evergreen MES 7034). Other performances have been by Louise Carlyle (Columbia OS-2560) and Ella Fitzgerald (Verve MGV-4024).

223. BLAH-BLAH-BLAH

Lyricist: Ira Gershwin
Key: F (verse)
  B-flat (refrain)
Time: Alla breve
Tempo: Moderato
Introduced by: El Brendel and Janet Gaynor in *Delicious*, released by Fox Film Corporation on December 3, 1931.

Lore: Originally called "Lady of the Moon" and written in 1928 for a Ziegfeld operetta entitled *East is West*, both the song and the show were scuttled. In its second incarnation the tune, now called "I Just Looked At You" (with lyrics by Ira Gershwin and Gus Kahn), was intended for but not used in the 1929 production *Show Girl*. It finally ended up in *Delicious* with a lyric purporting to demonstrate how a song rhymester goes about his trade.

Analysis: In "Blah-Blah-Blah" Ira Gershwin makes fun of the Moon/June efforts of conventional songwriters. The refrain consists of three quatrains and for each we are given only the endings. The rest of the lyric consists of "blah"s and "tra la la"s. The listener is to use his or her imagination to fill in these blanks. Thus, Ira manages to be at his vaguest and, at the same time, most explicit in the final line: "Blah, blah, blah, blah, blah, darling with you!"

Musically, the verse contrasts a lyrical, yearning idea ("I've written you a song") with one that is more chipper and staccato ("I studied all the rhymes"). The refrain does the same thing, following a lyrical idea ("Blah, Blah, Blah, Blah moon") with a rhythmic dance figure ("Tra la la la"). It is interesting to note that when the romantic "Blah, Blah" melody returns it concludes with a phrase that was used as the climax of the homesick blues theme in *An American in Paris*, also written in 1928.

Recordings: To indicate the tempi and phrasings that were to be used in the songs for *Delicious*, the composer and Bing Crosby made a demonstration disc. It was subsequently lost, though it may turn up someday. Other versions are by Georgia Brown (London LL 3331), George Byron with piano accompaniment by Dick Hyman (Atlantic ALS 410), Chris Connor (Atlantic 2-601), David Craig (Citadel CT 7071), Marni Nixon, with piano accompaniment by Lincoln Mayorga (Reference RR-19), John Miller (Rounder 3034), Tommy Tune (Atlantic 80110-1-E).

224. DELISHIOUS

Lyricist: Ira Gershwin
Key: E-flat
Time: 4/4 (verse)
Alla breve (refrain)
Tempo: Moderato (verse)
Gracefully (refrain)
Introduced by: Paul Roulien in *Delicious*, released by Fox Film Corporation on December 3, 1931. It was also included in the 1945 Warner Bros. Gershwin film biography, *Rhapsody in Blue*.

Lore: George and Ira signed a $100,000 contract with Fox in April of 1930 (the composer received $70,000) and they wrote this song around that time, while still in New York. As to why Ira misspelled the title of the song (while the studio used the correct spelling in the title of the film), it is his spelling of the way his father, Morris Gershwin, pronounced the word.

Singer/pianist Bobby Short visited Ira Gershwin in the early 1940s and heard the lyricist sing this number and call it one of his favorites.

Analysis: "Delishious" has one of the composer's loveliest verses ("What can I say"). Its main idea is anticipated but not revealed by a piano introduction that, like the one to "Somebody From Somewhere," is classical in style and made of restrained, imitative phrases. When the melody of the verse does appear it is different by just one note (a G has become an A-flat) but that change makes the tune compelling. The verse lasts twenty bars and it too is made up of a series of imitative

247

phrases, all of them with artful embellishments and many with attractive but unobtrusive piano fills. The more conventional refrain ("You're so delicious") is sassy in sound. It moves to D-major for its release ("Oh, I've had one, two")—a melody that consists mainly of repeated notes. For variety, each note is backed by a different variant of the basic D7 (D7$^{\text{flat}9}$, D7^9, etc.).

Recordings: On December 31, 1931 this song was recorded by Nat Shilkret and the Victor Orchestra (Victor 22902). In January of 1932 there were versions by Ralph Bennett and His Seven Aces (Melotone M-12316), Lou Gold and His Orchestra (Crown 3252), and Ben Selvin and His Orchestra (Columbia 2604-D). In February of 1932 there was a recording by Bob Causer and His Cornellians (Perfect 15556). Bobby Short's version was released in 1973 (Atlantic SD 2-608).

225. KATINKITSCHKA

Lyricist: Ira Gershwin
Key: D
Time: 2/4
Tempo: Allegretto giocoso
Introduced by: Mischa Auer and Manya Roberti in *Delicious*, released by Fox Film Corporation on December 3, 1931.

Analysis: The sheet music for this comedy number includes script directions from the *Delicious* screenplay. "Popitschka and Momitschka sing: Katinka performs" is the direction above the verse ("Katinkitschka, Katinkitschka, Out all night long!") The parents are scolding their daughter for going "on a spree With a soldier boy!" Just before the refrain ("Popitschka, Momitschka") another cue states, "Kat. Shows wedding ring parents are ecstatic." The verse and refrain are both unaffected peasant-style polkas. The verse is twenty bars, while the refrain is only twelve (it is followed by a four-bar instrumental section marked "Dance" that duplicates the piano introduction).

248

Recordings: None

226. SOMEBODY FROM SOMEWHERE

Lyricist: Ira Gershwin
Key: E-flat
Time: Common
Tempo: Moderato (verse)
   Gracefully (refrain)
Introduced by: Janet Gaynor in *Delicious*, released by Fox Film Corporation on December 3, 1931.

Lore: George and Ira wrote this in Hollywood in October of 1930, more than a year in advance of the release of the film *Delicious*. In the movie Janet Gaynor has illegally entered the United States and is hiding on the Long Island estate of a wealthy young man (Charles Farrell). She sings this song after one of Farrell's household objects— a musical whiskey bottle—provides her with the instrumental introduction.

Analysis: In the piano introduction the melody that will become the verse is given a Bach-like canonic treatment, Then, in the sixteen-bar verse ("When a body knows nobody"), both hands continue to play in the treble as the melody, which is as simple as a children's tune, is sung. The refrain ("Somebody from somewhere") is also just sixteen bars. It is a gentle and affecting ballad, through-composed and very lyrical.

Recordings: This was recorded on December 31, 1931 by Nat Shilkret and the Victor Orchestra (vocal by Sylvia Froos—Victor 22902) and on January 2, 1932 by Bob Causer and His Cornellians (with, among others, Red Nichols and Artie Shaw and with a vocal by Kenny Sargant—Perfect 15556). Ella Fitzgerald's recording was made in 1959 (Verve MG V-4029-5).

227. **OF THEE I SING OVERTURE**

Instrumental

Key: C-minor
Time: Various
Tempo: Various
Introduced by: George Gershwin conducting the *Of Thee I Sing* pit orchestra at the Music Box Theatre in New York City on December 26, 1931.

Lore: In conducting the orchestra on the first night, Gershwin admonished them to "Play it hot—not Harlem hot, Park Avenue hot."

Analysis: Until this one, all of the overtures to Gershwin's Broadway shows had been medleys. The *Of Thee I Sing* overture is a medley too, but with a difference: instead of a smorgasbord from the show, it offers just a small sampling of themes and, for most of its four and a half minutes, develops them to create a piece of music with an identity of its own. The overture can be broken down into nine sections:

1. The opening bars of "Wintergreen For President," played in C-minor and with a 3/4 + 2/4 meter (the song itself is in 2/4). This fifteen-bar passage concludes with an arresting vamp that is in the spirit of the song, although not in the song itself.
2. A frenetic dotted-note motive based on opening notes common to two *Of Thee I Sing* themes: "Because, Because" and "The Senator From Minnesota." Here the idea is played faster than in those songs and Gershwin develops it at length, mainly via harmonic transmutation.
3. "Who Cares?" played with the dotted-note motive as counterpoint. The development of that motive continues here unabated, although now the transmutations are primarily melodic.
4. A straightforward rendition of "Who Cares?"
5. A slow reading of the first seven notes of "Wintergreen For President" played against shifting harmonic colors, in C-minor.
6. "I Was the Most Beautiful Blossom" performed as a violin solo.

250

This melody contains a hint of "Summertime."

7.   A return to the dotted-note motive, developed here with increasing frenzy and dissonance.

8.   A four-bar transitional melody which plays insistent minor thirds against chromatically descending harmony.

9.   A straightforward reading of "Of Thee I Sing" in E-flat.

Recordings: In the first broadcast of his radio program "Music By Gershwin," on February 19, 1934, the composer presented a slightly abridged orchestral performance of this piece (Mark 56 Records 641). Robert Russell Bennett was one of the orchestrators of *Of Thee I Sing* (the others were William Daly and George Gershwin) and he recorded this piece on Sonora 1106.   In 1977 the Buffalo Philharmonic with Michael Tilson Thomas conducting recorded this piece (Columbia M34542) and they were faithful to the printed score.   In 1987, Michael Tilson Thomas recorded this overture again (as part of a concert version of *Of Thee I Sing*), this time with the Orchestra of St. Luke's (CBS S2M 42522).

228. WINTERGREEN FOR PRESIDENT

Lyricist: Ira Gershwin
Key: G-Minor
Time: 2/4
Tempo: Tempo di Marcia
Introduced by: The ensemble in *Of Thee I Sing* at the Music Box Theatre in New York City on December 26, 1931.

Lore: This was originally a mock medieval march called "Trumpets of Belgravia" (that lyric went, "Trumpets of Belgravia/Sing ta-ra, ta-ra, ta-ra").   It was written in the mid-1920s for an unproduced show called *The Big Charade*.   Several years later, when Gershwin was stuck for a campaign march while writing *Of Thee I Sing*, Ira recalled "Trumpets" and he and George turned it into "Wintergreen For President."

In *Let 'Em Eat Cake*, the 1933 sequel to *Of Thee I Sing*, "Wintergreen For President" is played in counterpoint to a second (and as yet unpublished) campaign song, entitled "Tweedledee For President."

Oscar Hammerstein II pointed to "Wintergreen" as a perfect example of words wedded to music, saying that it is impossible to think of its words without its music and vice versa.

Analysis: The lyric consists of just fifteen words. But the music, at eighty-five bars, is more than twice the length of the usual popular song. Also, it is through-composed. At its heart is an emphatic, basso seven-note motive ("Wintergreen For President"). This motive is usually followed by an ethereal seven-note idea, one that is sometimes sung to the syllable "Ah" and sometimes relegated to the accompaniment. The accompaniment is a collection of ingenious oom-pah figures. New oom-pahs appear throughout the song, as do Fourth of July-style musical quotations. These come in the following order:

1. "Stars and Stripes Forever" by John Philip Sousa
2. "Tammany" by Gus Edwards
3. "Sidewalks of New York" by Charles B. Lawler
4. "Hail Hail the Gang's All Here" by Sir Arthur Sullivan
5. "Hot Time in the Old Town Tonight" by Theodore Mets

One should note the way in which Gershwin handles these quotations: the way they arise out of the minor key material in sudden major key fanfares and then melt back into the march. The piece ends with a twelve-bar coda made from a final development of the original seven-note motive.

Recordings: In the April 30, 1934 edition of his "Music By Gershwin" radio program (Mark 56 Records 641), the composer led an orchestra in a snippet of "Wintergreen For President," saying that the piece would be played in its entirety on his next show. Unfortunately, that next broadcast was not preserved. Hal Kemp and his Orchestra recorded the song in September of 1932 (Brunswick 6416). Frankie Carle recorded his version on RCA Victor LPM 3083. A rendition by the Victor Salon Group conducted by Nathaniel Shilkret is on Victor Red Seal 12332. Other versions are available on recordings of the

1952 New York City revival of *Of Thee I Sing* (Capitol S-350, reissued on Capitol T-11651), the 1972 television presentation of the show (Columbia S-31763), in an instrumental version by Andre Kostelanetz and His Orchestra (Columbia CL 2133), and by the New York Choral Artists and the Orchestra of St. Luke's conducted by Michael Tilson Thomas (CBS S2M 42522).

229. WHO IS THE LUCKY GIRL TO BE?

Lyricist: Ira Gershwin
Key: Various
Time: Various
Tempo: Various
Introduced by: Grace Brinkley and ensemble in *Of Thee I Sing* at the Music Box Theatre in New York City on December 26, 1931.

Analysis: This piece consists of three tunes, all of them twenty-four bars long. The first ("Who is the lucky girl to be?"), a lovely melody with a hint of pathos, is sung in the key of D and at a jovial tempo—Allegretto giocoso—by a chorus of beauty pageant hopefuls. The second ("We're in Atlantic City") is also in D and it explains the purpose of the beauty contest (the winner will become the President's wife). This tune has the childish ditty-like quality that characterized so many of Gershwin's satirical numbers in *Strike Up the Band*. After these two themes are sung in counterpoint, an F-major melody ("The Dimple on Your Knee")—one with some of the sweetness of "Who is the lucky girl to be?" and some of the childishness of "We're in Atlantic City"—is presented by a group of photographers. "Dimple" is then taken up by the assembled beauty contestants who wonder in unison what will become of those who lose the contest. At this point the music segues into one of the show's few verse-and-chorus songs, "Because, Because." But, before leaving "Who is the Lucky Girl to Be," mention should be made of its inventive twelve-bar instrumental introduction. After briefly foreshadowing the first melodic idea it spins a lovely melody of its own, one that is distinct from the three ideas discussed above.

Recordings: This music was included in the 1952 New York City Revival of *Of Thee I Sing* (Capitol S-350, reissued on Capitol T-11651) and in the 1972 television presentation of the show (Columbia-S–31763). In 1987 it was recorded by Paige O'Hara and the New York Choral Artists with the Orchestra of St. Lukes conducted by Michael Tilson Thomas (CBS S2M 42522).

230. BECAUSE, BECAUSE

Lyricist: Ira Gershwin

Key: In the piano/vocal score of *Of Thee I Sing* "Because, Because" is published in the key of A. In separately issued sheet music it is in B-flat.

Time: 2/4

Tempo: Allegro moderato (verse) Not too fast, in strict rhythm (refrain)

Introduced by: The ensemble in *Of Thee I Sing* at the Music Box Theatre in New York City on December 26, 1931.

Lore: In the piano/vocal score of *Of Thee I Sing* there is no pause between "Who Is The Lucky Girl To Be?" and this song. "Because, Because" was also published independently and the sheet music version has a different introduction, arrangement and key.

Analysis: The twenty-two-bar verse ("Don't worry, little girl") begins with a repeated note idea sung by a group of photographers. They are trying to convince an assemblage of beauty contestants that, even if they lose, they will still be charming and desirable. The repeated note motive alternates with another idea ("if you lose the prize"), one that has a fanfare-like quality, although it is more tender than bold. In the eighth bar the ladies take over the song, commencing with the same repeated note idea ("I'll worry little boy") but then moving into new territory, including a striking moment in the harmonic minor (at "until you tell").

The refrain begins with not two but four consecutive "becauses" and the melody is as repetitious as the lyric. This melody appeared

254

earlier in the score as the jumpy motive that ran through and around the other themes in the overture. Here, its pace is slower and the aim is for a scherzando rather than a frantic effect.

In the piano/vocal score "Because, Because" is followed by a sixteen-bar instrumental coda.

Recordings: This music was included in the 1952 New York City revival of *Of Thee I Sing* (Capitol S-350, reissued on Capitol T-11651) and in the 1972 television presentation of the show (Columbia-31763). In 1987 it was recorded by the New York Choral Artists and the Orchestra of St. Luke's conducted by Michael Tilson Thomas (CBS S2M 42522).

231. OF THEE I SING: OPENING ATLANTIC CITY SCENE

Instrumental

Key: D
Time: 2/4
Tempo: Allegretto
Introduced by: George Gershwin conducting the *Of Thee I Sing*
    pit orchestra at the Music Box Theatre in New York City on
    December 26, 1931.

Analysis: This is a straightforward twenty–four-bar instrumental version of "Who is the Lucky Girl to Be?"

Recordings: None

232. OF THEE I SING: EXIT ATLANTIC CITY SCENE

Lyricist: Ira Gershwin
Key: Various
Time: 2/4
Tempo: Moderato

Introduced by: Grace Brinkley in *Of Thee I Sing* at the Music Box Theatre in New York City on December 26, 1931.

Analysis: The first twenty–four bars here are a mingling of two ideas from "Who is the Lucky Girl to Be?"   The first of these is the initial melody from that number.   The second comes from the "We're in Atlantic City" section.   Some of the lyrics here are new (Diana Devereaux addresses Wintergreen, asking him to select her over the other beauty contestants as his future wife).   Then the beauty contest selection committee steps in and addresses Wintergreen ("We'll present you with a bride") with twenty–three bars from "Wintergreen For President."

Recordings: None

233.   OF THEE I SING: FINALETTO SCENE IV - ACT I

Lyricist: Ira Gershwin
Key: Various
Time: Various
Tempo: Various
Introduced by: Dudley Clements, Grace Brinkley, Harold Moffet, Sam Mann and William Gaxton in *Of Thee I Sing* at the Music Box Theatre in New York City on December 26, 1931.

Analysis: This scene from *Of Thee I Sing* spans twenty pages in the piano/vocal score and, although the music is continuous, it can be broken down into eleven distinct sections:

1.   A twelve-bar instrumental introduction in D marked Andante pomposo.   The music here is from the "How Beautiful" waltz that will be heard in section three.   Here it is a 2/4 fanfare consisting of full, sometimes dissonant chords played over a tremolo bass.
2.   The chairman of the beauty contest selection committee announces that a future first lady has been chosen ("As the chairman of this Committee").   As was the case in *Strike Up the Band*, the composer sets

absurd lyrics to a nursery school style ditty. Underneath, however, he includes sophisticated harmony. The music in this section will appear again and again in the course of the score (for its first reappearance see section five).

3. Now we switch to the key of G and to 3/4 time for one of *Of Thee I Sing's* several fine waltzes. This one ("How Beautiful") begins with an instrumental accompaniment to the spoken announcement that Diana Devereaux is the beauty contest winner (and, thus, the next first lady). It is an animated sixteen-bar dance built on a dotted-note figure, downward leaps, and F-sharp chords that slide home into G-major. After the announcement has been made a four-part chorus picks the theme up and uses it to sing Ms. Devereaux's praises.

4. The selection committee takes over from the chorus and they praise Devereaux with a tune of their own. This one ("Never was there a girl so fair") is in a different key and meter (A-flat and 2/4) but it too has great appeal, wending its way through unexpected and delightful twists and turns. After eight bars we do not get a repetition but, instead, there is a second eight-bar idea ("a voice so lyrical"), one with its own pleasing and intelligent circuities. Then the initial phrase returns (on "ruby lips")—but it is brought to a conclusion after five bars and is followed by an entirely new idea, one sung by a couple of politicians named Gilhooley and Lippman ("Did you ever see such tootsies"). This idea begins with repeated notes and then tacks radically, becoming a succession of octave leaps.

5. In this sixteen-bar section the committee invites a group of newspapermen to step up and interview Diana Devereaux. Musically, this invitation is based on the "As the chairman" melody of section two. Here, however, the tune is in the minor mode (B-flat minor). After eight bars it moves peremptorily back into E.

6. Suddenly, Wintergreen halts the proceedings ("Stop! No!") to deliver the startling news that he will be unable to marry Devereaux. The melody he sings is another one of Gershwin's satiric children's tunes, yet it has an agitated, dissonant quality and the key is a worried E-minor. In a brief recitative, Wintergreen tells the assembled that he is in love with someone else—Mary Turner.

7. Here the committee that has selected Diana Devereaux as the future first lady sings "The man is mad" to the "As the chairman" tune

from section two. They are followed by Diana herself who, sticking with the same tune, sings "This jilting me, it cannot be!" Then the committee chimes in to make a crescendo of the idea ("We must know why"). Wintergreen responds with a brief recitative in which he declares his love for Mary Turner. The principal idea then returns, this time in 3/4 and in a succession of minor keys, as the committee wonders what can be done about the situation.

8.   In this eight-bar section ("He will do nothing of the sort") Diana threatens litigation. This is to the "Never was there a girl so fair" music from section four.

9.   A recitative colloquy ensues between Diana, the ensemble and Wintergreen. The upshot is that Wintergreen's newly announced intended, Mary Turner, can make corn muffins while Diana Devereaux cannot. When Diana admits that this is so, we get one of the rare blue notes in the score.

10.   Wintergreen praises Mary's corn muffins ("Some Girls Can Bake a Pie") with music that is romantic, flowing, and full of simple, wholesome good cheer. It is a miniature song: the first idea, in E-flat, is only eight bars long. It is followed by a quick four-bar release in G-minor ("Some lovely girls") and then a knowing, emphatic coda in B-flat ("But I have found the one"). After a brief recitative in which Diana asks "Who cares about corn muffins?" three different melodies are presented simultaneously: Wintergreen sings "Some Girls Can Bake a Pie," the beauty contestants sing "Don't Surrender!" to Diana, and the committee sings of the ineluctable drive that causes men to marry women who are able to bake corn muffins. At one point they sing "She takes the cake" to the tune of "Good evening friends."

11.   The final musical section is a repeat of the music of section six. But here, instead of Wintergreen's "Stop! No!" we get a four-part chorus singing "Great! Great! It really must be fate." This sixteen-bar section remains in E-minor until, on the last note, there is a sudden, riveting conclusion in A on the word "rejoice."

Recordings: This music can be heard in the cast recording of the *Of Thee I Sing* 1952 New York City revival (Capitol S-350, reissued on Capitol T-11651). Portions of it can be heard on the recording from the 1972 television presentation (Columbia S-31763). In 1987, "Never

Was There a Girl So Fair" and "Some Girls Can Bake a Pie" were recorded by Paige O'Hara, Larry Kert, the New York Choral Artists and the Orchestra of St. Luke's conducted by Michael Tilson Thomas (CBS S2M 42522).

234. LOVE IS SWEEPING THE COUNTRY

Lyricist: Ira Gershwin

Key: In the piano/vocal score of *Of Thee I Sing* this song is published in the key of F. In separately issued sheet music it is in E-flat.

Time: 2/4

Tempo: Moderato

Introduced by: George Murphy and June O'Dea in *Of Thee I Sing* at the Music Box Theatre in New York City on December 26, 1931.

Lore: In the piano/vocal score the verse and refrain are followed by a patter section whose music was originally written in 1928 for the unproduced *East is West* operetta (see "We Are Visitors").

Analysis: The twenty-eight-bar verse has two alternating ideas. The first is a somewhat harshly harmonized four-note descending phrase ("Why are people gay") and the other a more tranquil four-note rising phrase ("What is the thing"). The latter is developed at some length at the end. The refrain ("Love is sweeping the country") is a brilliant rouser with adventure in every one of its thirty-nine bars. It begins with an octave fall followed by a bounding ascent. Then comes an extraordinary maneuver—a melodic, harmonic and rhythmic device that, while singable, is also very pianistic. The words here are almost as interesting as the notes: "All the sexes/From Maine to Texas have never known such love before." Next, Gershwin repeats the beginning of the refrain, but only four bars worth—for suddenly we are presented with a second maneuver ("Each girl and boy alike")—one that is rhythmically related to "All the sexes" but different in both melody and harmony. After eight bars it is followed by an eight-bar variation on the initial idea and this variation serves as the coda.

In its pop song incarnation, "Love is Sweeping the Country" consists of just this verse and refrain. In the *Of Thee I Sing* score, however, there is an additional thirty-nine-bar patter section ("Spring is in the air") whose music was, as is stated above, originally written in 1928. There is a strong resemblance between this additional section and the more well-known verse; they both rely on a central descending four-note phrase.

Recordings: The April 30, 1934 edition of the composer's radio program, "Music By Gershwin," has been preserved and it contains an orchestral version of this song (Mark 56 Records 641). In January of 1932, Abe Lyman recorded his version (in a medley with "Of Thee I Sing" and "Who cares?"—Brunswick 20103). Other renditions are available in the cast recordings of the 1952 New York City revival of *Of Thee I Sing* (Capitol S-350, reissued on Capitol T-11651), the 1972 television production (Columbia S-31763), and by Frankie Carle (RCA Victor LPM 3083), Chris Connor (Atlantic 2-601), the Frederick Fennell Orchestra (Mercury 75127), and Ella Fitzgerald (Verve MGV 4027). In 1987 this music was recorded by George Dvorsky, Louise Edeiken, the New York Choral Artists, and the Orchestra of St. Luke's conducted by Michael Tilson Thomas (CBS S2M 42522).

235. OF THEE I SING

Lyricist: Ira Gershwin
Key: E-flat, G (verse)
    C (refrain)
Time: 4/4 (verse)
    Common (refrain)
Tempo: Assai moderato (verse)
    Slowly (with expression) (refrain)
Introduced by: William Gaxton in *Of Thee I Sing* at the Music Box Theatre in New York City on December 26, 1931.

Lore: George and Ira sketched this song during their stay in

California while writing the score for the film *Delicious*.

George S. Kaufman, co-writer (with Morrie Ryskind) and director of *Of Thee I Sing*, disliked the word "baby" in this song and he pressed the Gershwin brothers for a straightforward non-comic love song. The Gershwins disagreed, knowing full-well that sassy colloquialisms can be both funny and touching in popular songs.

Analysis: The first four bars of the verse ("From the Island of Manhattan") are mainly repeated notes but there is lyricism and warmth in the chorale-like accompaniment. This eloquence is then taken up in the melody ("From North to South"). The refrain, like that of "Love is Sweeping the Country" (the song that precedes it in the show), is ABA¹C in form. Its first idea, on the title phrase, is slow and stately (there are just six notes in the first four bars). The second is another chorale-like passage ("you're my silver lining"). A reprise of the initial idea then leads into yet another chorale ("Shining star and inspiration"). It is harmonized with simple, powerful chords and it builds to a four-bar coda based on the first idea.

Had Kaufman gotten the slangy "baby" removed, "Of Thee I Sing" might have become, like Irving Berlin's "God Bless America," a standard of pop song patriotism—although the lyric stresses romantic over patriotic love.

Recordings: In 1932 this song was recorded by Victor Arden-Phil Ohman and Their Orchestra (Victor 22911), Sleepy Hall and His Collegians (Melotone M-12299), the Knickerbockers (Columbia 2598-D), Abe Lyman (in a medley with "Who Cares?" and "Love is Sweeping the Country"—Brunswick 20103), Ben Selvin and His Orchestra (Columbia 2598-D), Paul Small's Collegians (Crown 3256), and Hal White and His All-Star Collegians (Perfect 15570). Louis Prima and His New Orleans Gang recorded it in 1939 (Decca 2749).

Other versions are on the recording of the 1952 New York City revival of *Of Thee I Sing* (Capitol S-350, reissued on Capitol T-11651), the recording of the 1972 television production (Columbia S-31763), and by Frankie Carle (RCA Victor LPM 3083), Chris Connor (Atlantic 2-601), Eddy Howard (Hindsight 405), Ella Fitzgerald (Verve V/V6-29-5) Jane Froman (Victor 12332), Marni Nixon with piano accompaniment by Lincoln Mayorga (Reference RR-19), and Sarah Vaughan (Mercury MG-20310). In 1987 this music was recorded by Larry Kert, Maureen McGovern, the New York Choral Artists, and the Orchestra of St. Luke's conducted by Michael Tilson Thomas (CBS S2M 42522).

236. DRILL

Instrumental

Key: G-minor
Time: 2/4
Tempo: Tempo di Marcia
Introduced by: George Gershwin conducting the *Of Thee I Sing* pit orchestra at the Music Box Theatre in New York City on December 26, 1931.

Analysis: This is a somewhat abbreviated instrumental version of "Wintergreen For President."

Recordings: None

237. OF THEE I SING: FINALE ACT I

Lyricist: Ira Gershwin
Key: Various
Time: Various
Tempo: Various
Introduced by: William Gaxton, Lois Moran, Ralph Riggs, Grace Brinkley in *Of Thee I Sing* at the Music Box Theatre in New York City on December 26, 1931.

Analysis: Comprising thirty pages of the *Of Thee I Sing* piano/ vocal score, this is the longest musical scene in the show. It can be broken down into the following thirteen sections:

1. A brief four-bar fanfare based on the refrain of "Of Thee I Sing." It is in G and in common time and is marked Allegro moderato.

2. The Supreme Court judges enter to another instrumental quote from "Of Thee I Sing" (this time the "shining star and inspiration" music), marked Pomposo. They then introduce themselves by singing, in unison, a weird tune that has one foot in G-minor and the other in a whole tone scale. As this music proceeds they announce that they will be officiating at the President's wedding celebration. At this point the music becomes sepulchral.

3. The fanfare is played again and then the four-part chorus, in a bright, consonant quasi-bugle call, hails the entrance of John P. Wintergreen, who in a single ceremony, is to be inaugurated and married.

4. At this point a verse and refrain song appears. Though untitled in the piano/vocal score (it was not published separately), Gershwin biographers have referred to it as "Here's a Kiss For Cinderella." In the verse ("I have definite ideas") Wintergreen declares that, while he is a man who thinks about everything—even the herring situation in Bismark—he is on this special day more preoccupied with thoughts about former girl friends. This verse is marked Allegro but it has a mournful quality due to its A-minor tonality and ominous triplets in the bass—they sound like snaredrums in a funeral march. The refrain ("Here's a kiss for Cinderella") is a broad, romantic and somewhat contrived melody in E-flat with a tempo marking of Allegretto grazioso. Its most persistent feature is the F to F-sharp pick-up motive with which it begins. That motive appears nine times in thirty-two bars. When Wintergreen repeats this refrain the on-stage chorus sings a countermelody ("he is toodle-ooing all his lady loves"). The mindlessness of these words is reinforced by the nursery-rhyme quality of the tune.

5. A ceremonial fanfare introduces a full choral rendition of the release from "Here's a Kiss For Cinderella." The lyrics sung here announce the arrival of the bride. Then, to the music from the refrain of "Here's a Kiss," Mary expresses the happiness that she feels on her wedding day.

6. To a seven-bar instrumental rendition of the refrain from "Of Thee I Sing," the Chief Justice administers the presidential oath of office to Wintergreen and nuptial vows to Wintergreen and Mary.

7.   The bride and groom simultaneously express, to the refrain from "Here's a Kiss," their joy at having been made husband and wife.

8.   Suddenly, the jilted Diana calls a halt to these proceedings. To emphasize the abruptness of her appearance and the drastic change of mood, her interjection of "Wait!" launches a new key (we have moved from E-flat to C), a new time signature (from 4/4 to 2/4) and a new tempo (from Allegretto grazioso to Agitato). She sings that word, "Wait!," on a high G held for four bars. Against this shriek the assembled ask "Who is this intruder?" to the "We're in Atlantic City" tune from "Who is the Lucky Girl to Be?"

9.   Diana sings "I Was the Most Beautiful Blossom"—a sensuous recitativo melody punctuated with exotic arpeggiated chords. A recurring fill (it first appears on "southland" in the phrase "in all the southland") seems to be quoting the "Roses of France" music from Gershwin's 1924 show *Primrose.* "I Was the Most Beautiful Blossom" continues for 37 bars, passing through changes of key, tempo and mood as Diana tells about the beauty contest, how she was examined by the committee ("My lily white body fascinated them"), her victory, the summary dismissal and rejection. She ends by declaring her intention to sue the President for breach of promise.

10.   Now, to the music that first appeared in the Finaletto to Scene IV-Act I (the "Stop! No!" music of section 6), the ensemble comments on this new development with lines such as "What! What! The water's getting hot!" This time the music has an ominous, creepy edge due to newly added dissonances, especially in the bass.

11.   A sixty–eight-bar recitative in which a number of brief musical ideas are presented without pause. Wintergreen begins by trying to explain why he jilted Diana but he is quickly interrupted by the Chief Justice who exclaims, "We're having fits!/The man admits!/This little sinner/Was nearly winner!" The music here has been heard before in the "As the chairman" portion (section two) from the Finaletto Scene IV-Act I. It then becomes a canon between the Chief Justice and the ensemble and then between Diana and the ensemble. In the Scene IV-Act I Finaletto the "As the chairman" music was presented a second time ("the man is mad") and on that occasion it was extended ("we must know why you should prefer"). Here, this musical extension appears again, as the assembled men say to President Wintergreen, "and

264

if it's true she has a claim/You should be called a dirty name." This four–bar line is repeated by the female ensemble. Next, Mary, the new First Lady, stands by her husband in a four–bar recitative that, with intended irony, is a musical variant of Diana's "I Was the Most Beautiful Blossom." (Later in the show Mary responds to Diana's plaintive waltz "Jilted" with an answering waltz—"I'm About to Be a Mother.") Diana responds with four bars of her own, singing "I'm a queen who has lost her king!" to music that was last heard in section four of the Finaletto Scene IV-Act I as "never was there a girl so fair." At this point Wintergreen, as before, attempts to explain his actions with "Some Girls Can Bake a Pie." "Who cares about corn muffins?" is Diana's recitative response. And then a question is posed that is immediately considered by the Supreme Court: "Which is more important? Corn muffins or justice?" Two bars of suspenseful rising triplets accompany the judges' huddle and then they announce their decision: corn muffins.

12. Jubilantly, the assembled sing "Great! Great! It's written on the slate/There's none but Mary Turner/ Could ever be your mate." The music here was last heard in section ten of this finale ("What! What!").

13. The finale ends with a reprise of "Of Thee I Sing." It is preceded by a very Gershwinesque four-bar passage heard previously in section eight of the overture. This "Of Thee I Sing" reprise is begun by Wintergreen who, after four bars, is joined by a four-part chorus.

Recordings: "Here's a Kiss For Cinderella" can be heard on the cast recording of the 1952 New York City revival of *Of Thee I Sing* (Capitol S-350, reissued on Capitol T-11651). It has also been recorded by Bobby Short (Atlantic SD-1574). "I Was the Most Beautiful Blossom" can also be heard on the 1952 cast recording, as well as in a recording of the 1972 television production (Columbia S-31763). The "Entrance of the Supreme Court Judges" is another feature of the 1952 revival recording. A 1987 recording by the New York Choral Artists and the Orchestra of St. Luke's conducted by Michael Tilson Thomas features music from this scene (CBS S2M 42522).

238. OF THEE I SING: OPENING ACT II

Lyricist: Ira Gershwin
Key: E
Time: 4/4, Alla breve
Tempo: Various

Introduced by: The ensemble in *Of Thee I Sing* at the Music Box Theatre in New York City on December 26, 1931.

Analysis: The music for the act two opening of *Of Thee I Sing* is in seven contiguous sections:

1.   A nine–bar instrumental opening based on the refrain of "Who Cares?" Marked Vigoroso, it employs loud, full-bodied chords that make unabashed use of the song's dissonances.
2.   To a stage direction noting the entrance of the secretaries (the scene takes place in the White House), the accompaniment presents a listless shuffling theme and then a group of "Boys" alternates with a group of "Girls" in whistling an easygoing tune above it. This section is sixteen bars long.
3.   This is a portion of the *Of Thee I Sing* score that has sometimes been referred to by its opening phrase, "Hello, good morning!" (Gershwin would write another good morning sequence in the sequel to this show, *Let 'Em Eat Cake*, and still another one would begin Act III, Scene III of *Porgy and Bess*). Here we have the same harmonic sequence that appeared in section two but the melody is more songlike. It lasts thirty-two bars and takes a couple of interesting harmonic turns: a sudden switch from E to A–flat in the tenth bar (at "swell" in "I'm feeling swell") and in the final three bars (on "isn't this a lovely day?"), an unusual and highly sophisticated preliminary cadence consisting of an Em6 over a D# bass, then a D#m6 over a G# bass, and then a B9 with a diminished fifth. This is followed by a more conventional cadence as the same words are repeated.
4.   An eight-bar instrumental version and extension of section three.
5.   Here we get a new tune—and it is a memorable one. It is a twenty-bar chorale in A–major that is full of simple good will. It is

also an example of Gershwin's predilection for setting satirical lyrics to childlike music (the White House secretaries sing about how much they like their jobs with lines such as "You get the inside information on Algeria/You know ev'ry move they're making in Liberia").

6.   A repetition of the final six bars of section three.

7.   A repeat of the shuffling and whistling music of section two.

Recordings: The "Hello, good morning!" sequence can be heard in a cast recording of the 1952 New York City revival of *Of Thee I Sing* (Capital S-350, reissued on Capitol T-11651) and on a recording of the 1972 television production of the show (Columbia S-31763). In 1987 this music was recorded by George Dvorsky, Merwin Goldsmith, the New York Choral Artists and the Orchestra of St. Luke's conducted by Michael Tilson Thomas (CBS S2M 42522).

239. WHO CARES?

Lyricist: Ira Gershwin
Key: C
Time: Alla breve
Tempo: Moderato (brightly) (verse)
          In a lilting manner (refrain)
Introduced by: William Gaxton and Lois Moran in *Of Thee I Sing* at the Music Box Theatre in New York City on December 26, 1931.

Lore: Gershwin's piano transcription of this song appeared in *George Gershwin's Songbook*, published by Simon and Schuster in September of 1932.

Ira changed some of its lyrics for the 1952 Broadway revival of *Of Thee I Sing.*

Analysis: In *Of Thee I Sing* the verse and refrain of "Who Cares?" are preceded by fifty bars of music. In the first portion of this music an assemblage of reporters aggressively asks President Wintergreen what he intends to do about Diana Devereaux, whom he has

267

jilted. They sing their queries to the tune of "The Dimple on Your Knee"—heard earlier in the show as part of "Who is the Lucky Girl to Be?" Wintergreen responds briefly in A-minor ("It's a pleasant day/ That's all I can say"), his wife Mary responds too, via the whole tone scale ("Love's the only thing that counts"), the reporters repeat their question in urgent C-minor, and then the President reaffirms his love for Mary with twenty-six consecutive Gs ("When the one you love is near/Nothing can interfere").

Now comes the song's well-known verse—but not with the well-known words. Instead of "Let it rain and thunder/Let a million firms go under," the President sings, "Here's some information I will gladly give the nation." (The information he gives is that he is for true love.) But the music is that of the familiar verse. It is an extraordinary tune, one that weaves easily and gracefully in and out of two keys—C and A-flat. Nearly the length of a full refrain—twenty–eight bars—it contains a release ("I love you and you love me" in the more familiar version) whose melody rises bit by bit in a serpentine fashion to create a crescendo on its own, without any assistance from harmony or syncopation.

The refrain of "Who Cares?" is the same in the vocal score as in the separately issued sheet music. It is an unsettling tune, one based on three dominant seventh chords with augmented fifths—a very restless sound. Gershwin chooses to end this series with a minor seventh chord with a diminished fifth—making for an uneasy, eerie pause. Only with bar nine (and a great line: "Who cares how history rates me/ Long as your kiss intoxicates me!") do we land on solid ground in the key of C. It is the spirit of this section that infuses the optimistic coda ("Life is one long jubilee/So long as I care for you and you care for me").

Recordings: In 1932 this song was recorded by Victor Arden-Phil Ohman and Their Orchestra (Victor 22911), Sleepy Hall and His Collegians (Melotone M-12299), the Knickerbockers (Columbia 2598-D), Abe Lyman (in a medley with "Of Thee I Sing" and "Love is Sweeping the Country"—Brunswick 20103), Ben Selvin and His Orchestra (Columbia 2598-D), and Hal White and His All-Star Collegians (Perfect 15570).

There were versions in 1940 by Fred Astaire/Benny Goodman and His Sextet (Columbia 35517), in the 1952 revival of *Of Thee I Sing* (Capitol S-350, reissued on Capitol T-11651), in 1958 by Benny Goodman (Westinghouse 2), in 1959 by Ella Fitzgerald (Verve 2-2525), in 1961 by Judy Garland (at Carnegie Hall—Capitol WBO 1569), in the 1972 television production of *Of Thee I Sing* (Columbia S-31763), and in a 1987 recording of the show featuring Larry Kert, Maureen McGovern, the New York Choral Artists, and the Orchestra of St. Luke's conducted by Michael Tilson Thomas (CBS S2M 42522).

Others: Cannonball Adderly (Milestone 47053), Cannonball Adderly/Bill Evans (Riverside OJC-105), Ray Brown/Jimmy Rowles (Concord Jazz 66), Frankie Carle (RCA Victor LPM 3083), Sammy Davis, Jr. (MCA 2-4019), the Bill Evans Trio (Milestone 47068), Tal Farlow (Concord Jazz 266 and Prestige 24042), Dick Johnson (Concord Jazz 107), Huey Lewis and the News (Chrysalis PV-41292), Helen O'Connell (Victor VPM-6076), Oscar Peterson (Pablo 2310796), Sonny Rollins (Verve UMV-2655).

240. THE ILLEGITIMATE DAUGHTER

Lyricist: Ira Gershwin
Key: Various
Time: Various
Tempo: Various
Introduced by: Florenz Ames, Lois Moran, Grace Brinkley, Dudley Clements, George E. Mack, Harold Moffet, William Gaxton in *Of Thee I Sing* at the Music Box Theatre in New York City on December 26, 1931.

Lore: After the opening of *Of Thee I Sing* the government of France, through the France-America Society, passed a resolution condemning those portions of the show that it considered offensive. France was miffed at the way the authors mocked its ambassador, its war department, and the ancestry of Diana Devereaux (see sections 1, 2, 3 and 6 below).

"The Illegitimate Daughter," written by the Gershwins during their November 1930 to February 1931 stay in California (to work on the film *Delicious*), was issued in and independently from the *Of Thee I Sing* piano/vocal score (see section 3 below).

In his book, *George S. Kaufman and His Friends* (Doubleday & Co., 1974), Scott Meredith casts some light on Gershwin's intentions in the play (see section 7 below):

> One night, standing inside the theatre with George Gershwin and watching the reactions of a typical audience, he [Kaufman] was amazed to see that some of the people had tears glistening in their eyes during one of the love scenes. "What's the matter with them?" Kaufman whispered. "Don't they know we're kidding love?" "You're doing nothing of the kind," Gershwin whispered back. "You may *think* you're kidding love—but when Wintergreen faces impeachment to stand by the girl he married, that's *championing* love. And the audience realizes it even if you don't."

Analysis: "The Illegitimate Daughter" is a portion of the second act of *Of Thee I Sing* comprising some twenty pages of the piano/vocal score. It can be divided into seven sections:

1. The first eight bars of *An American in Paris* are used to introduce six French soldiers who then enter singing a bugle call-like tune to a pseudo-French lyric. Gershwin biographers have referred to this melody as "Garçon, S'il Vous Plait." The French lines are nonsense lyrics ("Encore Chevrolet coupé Pa-pa pooh, pooh, pooh!"). After singing in this vein for sixteen bars the soldiers offer a "translation" of what they have said: to the music of the "shining star and inspiration" coda section of "Of Thee I Sing," they say "We're six of the fifty million and we can't be wrong!" The sound of "La Marseillaise" punctuates this declaration.
2. The first walking theme of *An American in Paris* introduces the French Ambassador who engages in a recitativo colloquy with the ensemble that serves as a verse to "The Illegitimate Daughter." The ambassador has come to express   his nation's displeasure over the jilting

of Diana Devereaux. His protest is to music that changes meter constantly, moving restlessly from 2/4 to 4/4 to 3/4 and back until it settles into the 6/8 march time of the refrain.

3. "The Illegitimate Daughter" is long (fifty–eight bars) and complex (the form is ABCA¹DC¹A²). Its main idea ("She's the illegitimate daughter of an illegitimate son/Of an illegitimate nephew of Napoleon!") is a dignified, even stately march in 6/8 time. The other sections, although they present new ideas, all maintain the same military bearing as the number makes its way to an emphatic conclusion.

One ought to pay special attention to the way a descending bass line in section C¹ ("You so and so!") underscores a dramatic interjection by the ensemble.

4. "The Illegitimate Daughter" concludes with three emphatic G chords. Then, without pause, Diana Devereaux delivers an off stage G-minor vocalise (on "Ah!"), reprising her "I Was the Most Beautiful Blossom" melody. This very effectively turns the spotlight back on her and away from the ambassador and the ensemble, who have gotten carried away with themselves while singing "The Illegitimate Daughter." A moment later, Diana enters to sing "I was the Most Beautiful Blossom" in E-minor.

5. Recitative between Mary, the ambassador and Wintergreen leads to a reprise of "Because, Because," sung by Diana. The song has different lyrics this time ("I won the competition/But I got no recognition") and it also has changed both meter (now it is in 4/4, not 2/4) and accompaniment. Here it is supported by threatening, accusatory chords.

6. In this section the French ambassador demands that the marriage between John and Mary Wintergreen be annulled. He does this to the "Garçon, S'il Vous Plait" music, which changes key, rising higher and higher—in step with the ambassador's blood pressure. Finally, as the music is presented forte to ominously augmented chords, he says that, should they refuse to separate, they must "be prepared for the consequences."

Now a recitativo section appears in which members of Congress express their concern over the ambassador's threats. They do so in monotonous repetitions of a single note. When a character named Matthew Arnold Fulton sings, the note is E. When Senator Robert E. Lyons takes over, the note becomes F. Wintergreen voices his thoughts

271

on F-sharp. Meanwhile, a more frantic rising in pitch is occurring in the accompaniment. A fellow named Francis X. Gilhooley becomes the first to voice the dreaded word "resignation." That subject is quickly taken up to the tune of "As the Chairman"—first heard in the Finaletto Scene IV Act I. President Wintergreen's succinct response is, "I decline to resign."

This leads Gilhooley and Lyons to bring up the even more dreadful subject of impeachment and this they do in a reprise of the repeated note motive described above. A new musical idea ("You decline to resign") is sung to full, consonant chords by The Committee and it is answered by the presidential secretaries (for comic effect, The Committee sings in the soprano range while the secretaries sing an octave lower). The upshot is The Committee's conclusion that impeachment will proceed. "Humpty Dumpty," they conclude, "has to fall."

7. The end of "The Illegitimate Daughter" scene is a reprise of "Who Cares?" sung by Wintergreen to his wife. Gershwin marks this section Meno mosso con expressione and he provides a plangent violin obligato that continues until the final "So long as I care for you/And you care for me," when it and Wintergreen sing in unison.

Recordings: This scene can be heard in a recording of the 1952 Broadway revival of *Of Thee I Sing* (Capitol S-350, reissued on Capitol T-11651). In 1987, it was done by Jack Dabdoub, Larry Kert, the New York Choral Artists and the Orchestra of St. Luke's conducted by Michael Tilson Thomas (CBS S2M 42522).

241. OF THEE I SING: OPENING SCENE III - ACT II/THE SENATOR FROM MINNESOTA

Lyricist: Ira Gershwin
Key: E-flat
Time: 4/4
Tempo: Grandioso/Calmato
Introduced by: Victor Moore in *Of Thee I Sing* at the Alvin Theatre in New York City on December 26, 1931.

Analysis: This scene, sometimes referred to as "The Senatorial Roll Call," is just that—a roll of the Senate called by the Vice President. The introduction, marked Grandioso, is characterized by chords built from fourths which descend gradually against trumpets that play a repeated note theme that sounds like the hammering of a gavel. Then, after four bars of tranquil humming by the gathered senators, the Vice President calls the roll. The tune he sings, with its insistent dotted notes, is closely related to "Because, Because" but it has little character of its own. At the end, as the legislators boast laughingly of their own incompetence, the composer produces the most melodic and musically pleasing portion of the piece.

Recordings: This portion of *Of Thee I Sing* is included in the recording of the 1952 Broadway revival (Capitol S-350, reissued on Capitol T-11651), and the 1972 television presentation (Columbia S-31763), and it is performed by Jack Gilford, the New York Choral Artists, and the Orchestra of St. Luke's conducted by Michael Tilson Thomas in a 1987 recording (CBS S2M 42522).

242. THE SENATE (SCENE III)

Lyricist: Ira Gershwin
Key: Various
Time: Various
Tempo: Various
Introduced by: Martin Leroy, Victor Moore, George E. Mack, Edward H. Robins, Dudley Clements, Florenz Ames, Grace Brinkley, William Gaxton, Lois Moran and Ralph Riggs in *Of Thee I Sing* at the Music Box Theatre in New York City on December 26, 1931.

Analysis: In this portion of *Of Thee I Sing* the Senate meets to consider the impeachment of President Wintergreen. Musically, it can be divided into nine parts:

1.   "The next business before the Senate," intones the Senate clerk,

"Is the resolution on the impeachment of the President." This is followed by a fanfare made from the title phrase music of "Of Thee I Sing." Then, briefly, the same music serves as a processional march as several solons enter the Senate chambers. Senator Carver Lyons chants the bill of impeachment.

2.   Again, as in "The Illegitimate Daughter," French soldiers enter to the "Garçon S'il Vous Plait" music and they again sing the same quasi-French lyrics. They are received by members of the Senate who sing an obsequious and slangy eight-bar greeting ("We say how de do/ Which means that we welcome you").

3.   Enter the French ambassador who, in a simple seventeen-bar ditty ("You've dealt a lovely maid/A blow that is injurious"), reviews the event that has wounded his nation's pride: the jilting of Diana Devereaux.

4.   Asked to explain "why France is so concerned about the plaintiff," the ambassador sings a reprise of "The Illegitimate Daughter."

5.   Now the Atlantic City bathing beauties enter to a forte five-bar bugle call that is oddly harmonized with pastoral chords (they call to mind the chorale-like harmonization of the first theme of the second movement of the *Concerto in F*). With another fanfare, Diana Devereaux enters and is asked to tell her story.

6.   She proceeds to sing "Jilted," a beautiful and heartfelt thirty–two-bar waltz (it sounds like "Clara, Don't You Be Downhearted" from *Porgy and Bess*) characterized throughout by downward falls. In the beginning they are fourths ("Jilted, jilted") and fifths ("Blighted, blighted"). Then, in the graceful release ("When men are deceivers"), Diana's letdown is embodied in fourth, fifth and octave falls. The return of the first section leads into a dramatic coda. There is not a hint of buffoonery or sarcasm in this piece—or, in fact, in any of the songs sung by Diana in *Of Thee I Sing*. The authors obviously thought it important to show as much sympathy for her predicament as for the love between the president and his wife. "Jilted," after Diana has introduced it, is given a full choral t reatment by the bathing beauties and the gathered senators. In their hands, some fun creeps into the song: they finish with a cadence of boo-hoos.

7.   Wintergreen, in a recitative, says that his wife's love means more to him than the threat of impeachment, and Vice President Throttlebot-

tom proceeds to call the roll in a reprise of "The Senator From Minnesota." Suddenly, Mary halts the proceedings, singing "With your permission I must tell you of my husband's delicate condition.'

8. Now we are given a waltz by Mary, this one entitled "I'm About to be a Mother." Like "Jilted," it makes use of downward leaps. But here the tumbles are a bit ungainly (there is a major seventh fall between "a" and "moth" in "a mother"). Gershwin, having marked the song a là Viennoise, is parodying the luftpause and, while this number is not blatantly comic, it is very far from Diana's forlorn waltz. (Oscar Levant described "I'm About to be a Mother" as "a lusty and infectious waltz with satiric overtones.") It is thirty-six bars in length and this includes a short but inventive release ("I must tell it") based on an arpeggiated E-ninth chord with an added sixth, a coda made from an extension of that arpeggio idea ("to have a baby/A baby!"), and a final line that quotes the "who could ask for anything more" finish from Gershwin's own "I Got Rhythm." When Mary concludes his song the ensemble joins her in a second chorus, just as they did for Diana in "Jilted." "I'm About to be a Mother" then continues as an instrumental as Wintergreen asks, "Mary, is it true? Am I to have a baby?"

9. As Diana's "I was the Most Beautiful Blossom" lament is played unaccompanied in the bass, the senators vote "not guilty" and the President's impeachment is called off. Diana then sings "I Was the Most Beautiful Blossom." She is followed by the Atlantic City girls who, to the tune of "Who is the Lucky Girl to Be?," sing "strike up the cymbals, drum and fife. One of us was to be the President's wife." At this point the scene seems headed for an emphatic cadence in E-major (the key of "I'm About to be a Mother"). But it comes to an abrupt halt in E-minor.

Recordings: This music can be heard in the recording made of the 1952 Broadway revival of *Of Thee I Sing* (Capitol S-350, reissued on Capitol T-11651), on the recording of the 1972 television presentation of the show (Columbia S-31763), and in a 1987 recorded version of the show featuring Jack Gilford, Jack Dabdoub, Paige O'Hara, Maureen McGovern, the New York Choral Artists and the Orchestra of St. Luke's conducted by Michael Tilson Thomas (CBS S2M 42522).

243. POSTERITY IS JUST AROUND THE CORNER

Lyricist: Ira Gershwin
Key: D
Time: 2/4
Tempo: Allegro moderato
Introduced by: William Gaxton and Lois Moran in *Of Thee I Sing* at the Music Box Theatre in New York City on December 26, 1931.

Lore: For the 1952 revival of *Of Thee I Sing* Ira updated this song, calling it "The President is Going to Be a Daddy."

Analysis: The title, a takeoff on the Depression-era palliative, "prosperity is just around the corner," refers to the impending birth of a child to the President and his lady. It is they and the ensemble who sing this catchy, seventy–two-bar long gospel-style march. For the first thirty–six bars the music is through-composed, with President Wintergreen, Mary and the ensemble taking turns developing an initial four-bar dotted note phrase. The song ends with a wacky coda built around a pun—"Oomposterity." The melody here is a series of up-ward octave leaps: from A to A, then from B-flat to B-flat and so on. By the time we get to C-sharp, Wintergreen and the others are oom-pahing together. They end the song with a final repetition of the title phrase.

Recordings: The revised ("The President is Going to Be a Daddy") version of this song can be heard in a recording of the 1952 Broadway revival of *Of Thee I Sing* (Capitol S-350, reissued on Capitol T-11651). This music can also be heard in a 1987 recording of the show, featuring Larry Kert, Maureen McGovern, the New York Choral Artists, and the Orchestra of St. Luke's conducted by Michael Tilson Thomas (CBS S2M 42522).

244. TRUMPETER BLOW YOUR GOLDEN HORN

Lyricist: Ira Gershwin
Key: Various
Time: Various
Tempo: Various
Introduced by: Sam Mann, Harold Moffet, Edward H. Robins, George E. Mack in *Of Thee I Sing* at the Music Box Theatre in New York City on December 26, 1931.

Analysis: "Trumpeter Blow Your Golden Horn" is the final song in *Of Thee I Sing*; the rest of the music in the show consists of a collection of brief interconnected interludes. "Trumpeter" itself has no conclusive ending, but segues into the first of those interludes (called "On That Matter No One Budges" by Gershwin biographers). Breaking this scene down into its component musical parts, we get:

1. "Trumpeter Blow Your Golden Horn," sung to hail the impending birth of the presidential baby, and marked Allegro maestoso. It is a broad and confident tune, one with real nobility. In the seventh bar (on "horn") the music, having been in F, develops an unexpected play between D and G chords and the effect is not unlike that of the energizing "I got no car, got no mule" section of "I Got Plenty of Nuthin'" from *Porgy and Bess*. A short and sarcastic, four-bar release is sung by a group called the Flunkeys ("With a hey-nonny-nonny and a ha-cha-cha!") and then the main idea returns with a concluding twelve-bar coda. At this point things become quieter and the music moves to the relative minor (A-minor) as the presiding physician is asked for a progress report on the First Lady's labor. The Flunkeys repeat their "hey-nonny-nonny" material. And there is a final repetition of "Trumpeter Blow Your Golden Horn," including a reprise of its coda.
2. At this point the Supreme Court justices respond to a question raised in "Trumpeter"—namely, will the new baby be a girl or a boy? Their conclusion ("On that matter no one budges for all cases of the sort are decided by the judges of the Supreme Court") is sung in a quasi-recitativo patter style, first in the key of F and then in A. Then the judges, whose presence has been announced by a character called

the Chief Flunkey, proceed to introduce themselves. This music, heard first in the Finale Act I, is sometimes referred to as "Entrance of the Supreme Court Judges." For four bars the judges sing in unison using a whole note scale while, underneath, augmented chords add to the strangeness and the satire. The "hey-nonny-nonny" music from "Trumpeter" follows this and then it is back to the "on that matter no one budges" patter.

3.   Now it is the Secretary of Agriculture who is announced, and he sings a version of "The Farmer in the Dell" ("The farmers in the dell/The farmers in the dell/They all keep a-asking me A boy or a gel?"). The judges follow this with "on that matter no one budges," and then it is the Secretary of the Navy who is introduced. To the tune of "The Sailor's Hornpipe" he says that no one in the U.S. Navy will eat and that no one will "Jib an anchor" until it is determined whether the new baby is a boy or a girl.

The judges respond again with "on that matter no one budges" and then it is Senator Carver Jones who is introduced. To the tune of "Rainbow" (by Percy Wenrich) he states that all the cowboys on the prairie keep asking him if it is a girl or a boy ("For a baby boy or girl they are keen/But they want nothing in between"). The judges punctuate this with another chorus of "on that matter no one budges" and then Senator Robert E. Lyons is introduced. Named for the Confederate general, he sings to the tune of "Old Folks at Home," his point being that people on the Swanee also want to know the sex of the new baby. Again, the judges reply that "on that matter no one budges."

Thus, Gershwin, in drawing *Of Thee I Sing* to its conclusion, ends the show as he began it in "Wintergreen For President"—weaving quotations from old and mainly American tunes around his own original music.

4.   The music concludes with a chorus of "Trumpeter Blow Your Golden Horn." As a full chorus holds the final note, the tune turns up in the bass line of the accompaniment where, extended, it becomes the coda. Then comes the final cadence, which is somewhat startling: A major to F.

Recordings: This music can be heard in the recording of the 1952 Broadway revival of *Of Thee I Sing* (Capitol S-350, reissued on

Capitol T-11651). In a 1987 recorded version of the show, it is performed by George Dvorsky, Merwin Goldsmith, Frank Kopyc, Mark
Zimmerman, Walter Hook, the New York Choral Artists, and the Orchestra of St. Luke's conducted by Michael Tilson Thomas (CBS S2M
42522).

245. OF THEE I SING: FINALE ULTIMO

Lyricist: Ira Gershwin
Key: Various
Time: Various
Tempo: Various
Introduced by: Ralph Riggs, Florenz Ames, Grace Brinkley and
William Gaxton in *Of Thee I Sing* at the Music Box Theatre in
New York City on December 26, 1931.

Analysis: The finale begins with a reprise of "On That Matter
No One Budges" from the "Trumpeter Blow Your Golden Horn" section. Here, the Supreme Court judges declare again that it is within
their purview to determine the sex of the presidential baby. Then, after
a fanfare made from the refrain of "Of Thee I Sing" (heard before in
the Finale Act I and in "The Senate"), the Chief Justice, in recitativo-
style, delivers a verdict: "Where-as: The judges of the Supreme Court
have been sent to determine the sex of the aforesaid infant. Where as:
By a strict party vote it has been decided that It's a boy."
    Now to music first heard in "The Senate" (section three), the
French ambassador loses his temper and threatens war. Shortly thereafter, Diana Devereaux reprises "I Was the Most Beautiful Blossom."
Her predicament is finally solved when she becomes betrothed to Vice
President Throttlebottom. After two more fanfares (the first is the one
based on "Of Thee I Sing" and the second, four bars long, is marked
Grandioso) and a four–bar snatch heard previously in the overture
(section eight) and in section fourteen of the Finale Act I, principals
and ensemble join in a final rendition of the "Of Thee I Sing" refrain.

Recordings: A 1987 recording of *Of Thee I Sing*, featuring

Larry Kert, the New York Choral Artists, and the Orchestra of St. Luke's conducted by Michael Tilson Thomas (CBS S2M 42522).

246. YOU'VE GOT WHAT GETS ME

Lyricist: Ira Gershwin
Key: F
Time: Alla breve
Tempo: Moderato
Introduced by: Eddie Quillan and Arline Judge in *Girl Crazy*, released by RKO in 1932.

Lore: George and Ira were given $2,500 to write this song for the first film version of their 1930 Broadway hit, *Girl Crazy*.

Analysis: The twenty-bar verse ("I've got a secret") has an easygoing soft-shoe quality plus a few hard-to-hit notes. Particularly difficult is a high E in the fifth bar (on "And" and "you're" in "And you're the one") which is not only a major seventh leap up from the previous note, an F, but the major seventh of its supporting chord, F-major. The thirty–two–bar refrain ("You've got what gets me") has some fun with amen or plagal cadences, using them continuously and mostly on the off beat. The form is AA¹BA¹B¹A¹.

Recordings: The 1932 film version of *Girl Crazy* can be heard on JJA-19773. Another contemporary version was by Roy Fox and His Band (English Decca DLP 7002). The first modern recording of this song was by Ella Fitzgerald (Verve MGV-4027).

247. SECOND RHAPSODY

For orchestra with piano

Key: F
Introduced by: George Gershwin, piano, and the Boston Sym-

phony Orchestra conducted by Serge Koussevitzky in Symphony Hall in Boston on January 29, 1932.

Lore: The Gershwins first wrote for the movies in 1923, when they fashioned a song, "The Sunshine Trail," to promote a silent film of the same title. They did not actually go to Hollywood until November of 1930, when they began work on *Delicious*, a Fox film starring Charles Farrell and Janet Gaynor. For this film they wrote eight pieces: six songs and two extended works tailored to the needs of the screenplay. One of those longer compositions, sometimes called "Dream Sequence" or "Welcome to the Melting Pot" or "We're From the *Journal*," depicts, through instrumental and vocal sections, the arrival at Ellis Island of a Scottish immigrant (played by Gaynor). The other, called *Manhattan Rhapsody*, is an eight-minute work for piano and orchestra that depicts Gaynor wandering in her somewhat menacing new surroundings. Neither of these longish works was published. But, when George Gershwin found that he had finished his Hollywood assignment and that he was facing several weeks in California with nothing to do, he began to rework the *Manhattan Rhapsody* into a longer piece, one that was called, for a time, *Rhapsody in Rivets* and which he eventually named *Second Rhapsody* (his father suggested *Rhapsody in Blue #2* as a title).

Gershwin wrote the piece in his rented home on Chevy Chase Drive in Beverly Hills, at the Santa Monica residence of Aileen Pringle (a silent screen actress with whom, at the time, he was having a romance), and at his New York City residence when he returned there in early 1931. Sticking to the themes that had been in the screen version of the piece, he doubled its length, completed a two-piano draft, and then did the orchestration. The composition was completed on May 23, 1931 and the orchestration by the end of June.

On June 26, Gershwin hired a 55-piece orchestra to give the *Second Rhapsody* its first orchestral run-through. This took place at NBC's studio B in Radio City and it was recorded by Victor as a favor to the composer, who, after listening to the record, made some minor alterations in the score.

Then came a six-month delay while a conductor was sought for the first public performance. Gershwin very much wanted Arturo Toscanini to take the job and he and Oscar Levant auditioned the two-piano version of the rhapsody for the great Italian conductor. But, when the latter refused to commit himself, the first performance was assigned to Serge Koussevitsky and the Boston Symphony, who performed it in Boston's Symphony Hall on January 29, 1932 with Gershwin at the piano.

It was by now de rigueur for critics to write with perplexity about a new Gershwin concert work. Usually, the kudos was for the composer's energy and for the freshness of his melodies, harmonies and rhythms, while doubts were habitually expressed about his ability to create structure and instrumentation. This time, however, it was the other way around. H.T. Parker, for example, wrote in the Boston *Evening Transcript*: "Mr. Gershwin waxes in craftsmanship but at the cost of an earlier and irresistible élan."

As it turned out, the *Second Rhapsody* has never caught on with the public. In Gershwin's lifetime, only the two-piano version of the piece was published and, then, in 1953, when the orchestral score was put out by New World Music, the instrumentation had been revamped by Robert McBride at the behest of editor Frank Campbell-Watson. The latter made the dubious claim that Gershwin had approved of these revisions shortly before his death, sixteen years earlier. Actually, the first rescoring of the *Second Rhapsody* had occurred in 1933, four years before Gershwin's death, when Ferde Grofe tackled the job for Paul Whiteman. Only recently has Gershwin's original orchestration become the one most commonly used in performances and recordings of the piece. This is because it has been only recently that the public has had its appetite whetted for this most obscure of the composer's highbrow compositions—an appetite that, at the same time, has been growing for performances of these compositions as they were originally written, and as Gershwin himself played them.

Analysis: There are six main thematic ideas in the *Second Rhapsody*:

1.   An opening rivet theme, consisting mainly of repeated notes (the first eight notes are the same). It is followed by a four-note tag that makes use of a bluesy minor third interval. This idea is a Gershwin

oddity in that it is determinedly minimal and intentionally monotonous. Stranger still, it is the idea that recurs most often in and dominates the piece. But one should pay attention to its many transformations. For instance, when, toward the end of the rhapsody, the piano plays a march accompanied by snare drums, that march is derived from a tag that the composer had attached to a lighthearted, Latinesque variation on this rivet theme. Also, the final coda of the work—which employs an intriguing, jazzy sighing sound—is derived from a figure that Gershwin uses to accompany the rivet theme when, midway into the rhapsody, it is presented for full orchestra.

2.   An idea for solo piano in contrary motion, played just twice: once, immediately after the first statement of the rivet theme and then again to mark the line between the exposition and development sections of the piece.

3.   A syncopated rumba idea, presented immediately after themes one and two. During the first half of the rhapsody, this idea is juxtaposed with and often provides the rhythmic background to the rivet idea.

4.   A delicate and syncopted idea with a bluesy tag, played high in the treble. It has great charm and a nascent, understated nobility. Its syncopation (a series of off-the-beat quarter notes following an eighth note rest) figures throughout the piece.

5.   An A-major slow theme marked Sostenuto e con moto. It is related to (perhaps intentionally) the E-major Andantino moderato of the *Rhapsody in Blue*. Both melodies employ a three-note ascension and then a sudden octave fall. But the one in the *Second Rhapsody* has less forward motion and its repeated notes and poignant harmonies give it a more subdued and plangent feel than the affirmative grandeur of the slow theme of the first rhapsody. Where the *Rhapsody in Blue*'s slow theme begins with sonorous consonances, this one starts with a B-sharp over C-sharp clash. Then, the melody line is harmonized by slowly ascending tenths, which clash with it along the way. These attributes make the Sostenuto e con moto one of the most heartfelt of Gershwin's nstrumental themes and one of the most beautiful.

6.   A theme that appears on the heels of and is subsidiary to theme five. It is related to the airy theme four, but has the nobility and commanding air that was only hinted at in that earlier idea.

Recordings: Gershwin's June 21, 1931 run-through of this piece at Radio City, which features him conducting from the piano, has been issued on Mark 56 641. Pianist Oscar Levant recorded the *Second Rhapsody* with Morton Gould and His Orchestra and they kept to the original orchestration (Columbia ML 2073, reissued on CBS MLK-39454). More recently, the record by pianist and conductor Michael Tilson Thomas with the Los Angeles Philharmonic (CBS IM 39699) remains true to Gershwin's original intentions.

Other versions (in alphabetical order by pianist): Roy Bargy with Paul Whiteman's Orchestra (recorded October 23 1938—Decca 29052 8024), Sondra Bianca with the Pro-Musica, Hamburg conducted by Hans Jurgen Walther (MGM E-3307), Teodor Moussov with the TVR Orchestra conducted by Pancho Vladigerov (Monitor MCS-2153), Christina Ortiz with the London Symphony conducted by Andre Previn (Angel CDC-47021), Leonard Pennario with the Hollywood Bowl Symphony Orchestra conducted by Alfred Newman (Capital SP8581, Angel 36070), Jeffrey Siegel with the St. Louis Symphony conducted by Leonard Slatkin (Vox Box 5132), Ralph Votapek with the Boston Pops conducted by Arthur Fiedler (London 411835-1 LJ).

The composer's arrangement of this piece for two pianos, four hands has been recorded by Frances Veri and Michael Jamanis (Connoisseur Society CSQ 206).

248. CUBAN OVERTURE

For orchestra

Key: D
Introduced by: The New York Philharmonic-Symphony Orchestra conducted by Albert Coates on August 16, 1932 at Lewisohn Stadium in New York.

Lore: In the spring of 1932, Gershwin began studying with musical theorist Joseph Schillinger, who gave him lessons with such titles as "Rhythmic Groups Resulting from the Interference of Several Synchronized Periodicities," and who had him plotting music mathematically on graph paper. Gershwin was particularly anxious, in these studies, to gain some expertise in the use of counterpoint, and it was in the *Cuban Overture* that he first put what he had learned into a musical composition.

The new piece was written in July of 1932, after the composer returned from a visit to Havana. While there, a sixteen-piece rumba band had serenaded him late one night outside the window of his room at the Almendares Hotel and, intrigued by the sound and instrumentation of their music, he conceived of an orchestral piece that would incorporate both.

Originally called *Rumba*, it was written quickly, so that it could be included in the first all-Gershwin concert, which was to take place on August 16 at Lewisohn Stadium. Gershwin's initial draft was for one piano-four hands (that version has been published). Then came the orchestrated manuscript, whose first page sports the composer's sketch of the four Cuban instruments included in the instrumentation (Cuban sticks, bongo, gourd and maracas) as well as a note to the conductor directing that they be placed in front of the orchestra (Gershwin was anxious that the audience be able to see as well as hear them).

The premiere was conducted by Albert Coates, who also at this concert conducted *An American in Paris* and the *Second Rhapsody*. William Daly was the conductor for the *Of Thee I Sing* Overture, the *Concerto in F*, the *Rhapsody in Blue*, "Wintergreen For President," and a medley of Gershwin tunes. Oscar Levant played the *Concerto in F* and Gershwin was soloist in his two rhapsodies as well as the song medley.

After the concert, having decided that the title *Rumba* would make people think that the piece was a dance arrangement, Gershwin gave it the more symphonic title of *Cuban Overture*.

Analysis: This music, like all of Gershwin's orchestral compositions, is in a fast-slow-fast format. Gershwin's own analysis of these sections, written in the program notes for the Lewisohn Stadium concert, was as follows:

In my composition I have endeavored to combine the Cuban

rhythms with my own thematic material. The result is a symphonic overture which embodies the essence of the Cuban dance. It has three main parts.

The first part (moderato e molto ritmato) is preceded by a (forte) introduction featuring some of the thematic material. Then comes a three-part contrapuntal episode leading to a second theme. The first part finishes with a recurrence of the first theme combined with fragments of the second.

A solo clarinet cadenza leads to a middle part, which is in a plaintive mood. It is a gradually developing canon in a polytonal manner. This part concludes with a climax based on an ostinato of the theme in the canon, after which a sudden change in tempo brings us back to the rumba dance rhythms.

The finale is a development of the preceding material in a stretto-like manner. This leads us back once again to the main theme.

The conclusion of the work is a coda featuring the Cuban instruments of percussion.

The principal themes of the *Cuban Overture* are:

1.   Quick, high-pitched triplets which, making use of the tritone, have a tropical bird-call sound.
2.   An emphatic, syncopated tune presented first by the trumpets and employing harmony in sixths. This idea immediately follows theme one.
3.   An insistent staccato nine-note motive presented by the violins and oboe. It immediately follows the first statement of theme two.
4.   A bass line rumba motive that makes its first appearance as an accompaniment to theme three (these first four ideas have all appeared by the sixth bar of the piece).
5.   A singing, climbing melody introduced by strings to the insistent accompaniment of theme four.
6.   Another singing motive, this one in a minor key. It consists of a quarter-note rest and then four notes that rise yearningly before ending in the lively rhythms of theme two.
7.   A long and, as Gershwin put it, plaintive melody. It is introduced by the oboes and then, upon the entrance of the English horn, is

given a canonic treatment. In the background are peaceful harmonies played to Cuban rhythms, here made soothing and restful. One should note the presence in this section of the triplets of theme one and a bluesy secondary melody (the only bluesy moment in the piece). Also worth noting is the fact that the contrapuntal workings here serve to make the music heartfelt, rather than severe.

Recordings: (In alphabetical order by conductor) Riccardo Chailly and the Cleveland Orchestra (London 417326-1 LH), Arthur Fiedler and the Boston Pops (RCA Victor LSC-2586), Howard Hanson and the Eastman-Rochester Orchestra (Mercury 90290), Andre Kostelanetz and His Orchestra (Columbia ML 4481), Louis Lane and the Cleveland Pops Orchestra (Epic BC-1047, LC-3626), Lorin Maazel and the Cleveland Symphony Orchestra (London 414067 LJ, 417716-2 LM), Eduardo Mata and the Dallas Symphony (RCA ARC1-4551), Andre Previn and the London Symphony (Angel CDC-47021), Edo de Waart and the Orchestra National de l'Opera de Monte Carlo (Philips 6500-290), Hans Jurgen Walther and the Pro Musica, Hamburg (MGM 3-El), Paul Whiteman (recorded October 21, 1938—Decca 29053 and 29054).

The composer's arrangement for one piano, four hands has been recorded by Frances Veri and Michael Jamanis (Connoisseur Society CSQ 206, Book of the Month Club Records 61-5426).

249. MISCHA, YASCHA, TOSCHA, SASCHA

Lyricist: Arthur Francis (Ira Gershwin)
Key: G
Time: Common
Tempo: Moderato
Introduced by: George and Ira Gershwin at social gatherings in the early 1920s.

Lore: In his 1929 *New Yorker* profile of the composer, S.N. Behrman claimed that the Gershwin brothers had written this for a party given by Jascha Heifetz. Behrman did not say just when that party took place, and the birthdate of the song is open to some discussion. A New York *Times* sheet music compilation called *Gershwin Years in Song* gives 1919 as the year of composition but Warner Bros.' 1973 list of Gershwin's published works says that 1922 was the year. The latter seems the more likely date, since Ira did not begin using the pseudonym Arthur Francis (after his youngest brother and sister) until 1920.

"Mischa, Yascha, Toscha, Sascha" was always a parlor song. It never appeared in any Broadway or Hollywood vehicle (although it was almost inserted into the 1931 film *Delicious*) and it did not see publication until 1932 when it was included in the deluxe, autographed limited edition of *George Gershwin's Songbook*. It was written to poke fun at four contemporary Russian-born violin virtuosos (Mischa Elman, Jascha Heifetz, Toscha Seidel and Sascha Jacobsen) and the Gershwins loved to sing it at parties—especially if any of that foursome was on hand. That George was consistent in his fondness for this song is attested to by stage and film director Reuben Mamoulian. Mamoulian first met the composer in 1923 and it was on the day they met that Gershwin first played him this song. He last heard Gershwin play it in 1937, a few days before the composer's death. As to Gershwin's style of performing "Mischa, Yascha, Toscha, Sascha," we have biographer Isaac Goldberg's eyewitness account:

> You must hear George pronounce the word *sour*, with an upward inflection that is precisely enough off-pitch to emphasize the point without becoming merely incorrect. More: you must see him raise his chin to follow the inflection, and thrust it forward, as if to curl around the acidity of the tone.

In 1941 Ira returned to his fascination with Russian names when he wrote "Tschaikowsky (and Other Russians)" with Kurt Weill for *Lady in the Dark*—the idea was from a poem that he had penned in 1924 and the goal was to give Danny Kaye a nightly chance to say the names of forty-nine Russian composers in record-breaking, if not jaw-breaking, time.

Analysis: The piano introduction begins, with a chromatic treatment of Dvorak's "Humoresque." Then comes a light-hearted sixteen-bar verse ("We really think you ought to know") whose main idea is a lazy dotted note motive that uses the notes of the pentatonic scale. This music becomes sing-songy and almost light-headed at the phrase "darkest Russia." The refrain ("Tempr'amental Oriental Gentlemen are we"), a brief twenty bars, is basically a string of eight straight quarter notes against a descending bass line. In bars five and six, as the names of the four violinists are sung, there are parallel fifths in the accompaniment—the sound of a violin tuning up.

Recordings: Paul Whiteman did this song in a July 10, 1938 George Gershwin memorial broadcast (Mark 56 761). Bobby Short recorded it on November 14, 1971 (Penzance 43).

250. GEORGE GERSHWIN'S SONGBOOK

For solo piano

Introduced by: There was no formal, public premiere of this work. Leonid Hambro made the first recording (see below).

Lore: By the early 1920s, Gershwin was famous for his ability to sit at the piano and improvise variations on his own song themes. In 1929, representatives of Simon and Schuster asked him to put some of these impromptu works on paper but, although intrigued by the idea, three years would pass before he got down to the task, composing solo piano arrangements of eighteen tunes. In May of that year there appeared a Random House limited edition, signed by Gershwin and the illustrator, Constantin Alajalov, which contained these transcriptions, as well as standard piano/vocal arrangements of the songs and, as a bonus, the first piano/vocal publication of "Mischa, Yascha, Toscha, Sascha." The general edition (minus "Mischa") was published by Simon and Schuster in September of 1932.

Gershwin contributed an introduction to this book and, in it, he fondly recalled the piano stylists who had influenced his own playing. These pianists included Lucky Roberts, Zez Confrey, pianists Phil Ohman, Victor Arden, and Mike Bernard. The latter, Gershwin wrote,

289

had a "habit of playing the melody in the left hand, while he wove a filigree of counterpoint with the right"—an effect that appears at the beginning of the "Somebody Loves Me" transcription.

The *Songbook* is dedicated to Kay Swift.

These transcriptions were the basis of George Balanchine's 1970 ballet *Who Cares?* (although Balanchine had the pieces orchestrated).

Analysis: In these variations, Gershwin treats only the refrains, not the verses. The songs appear in chronological order and they contain the following tempo markings:

1. "Swanee"—Spirited
2. "Nobody But You"—Capriciously
3. "I'll Build a Stairway to Paradise"—Vigorously
4. "Do it Again"—Plaintively
5. "Fascinating Rhythm"—With agitation
6. "Oh, Lady Be Good!"—Rather slow (with humor)
7. "Somebody Loves Me"—In a moderate tempo
8. "Sweet and Low-Down—Slow (in a jazzy manner)
9. "That Certain Feeling"—Ardently
10. "The Man I Love"—Slow and in singing style
11. "Clap Yo' Hands"—Spirited (but sustained)
12. "Do-Do-Do"—In a swinging manner.
13. "My One and Only"—Lively (in strong rhythm)
14. "'S Wonderful"—Liltingly
15. "Strike Up the Band"—In spirited march tempo
16. "Liza"—Languidly
17. "I Got Rhythm"—Very marked
18. "Who Cares?"—Rather slow

Recordings: Richard Rodney Bennett (EMI EMD 5538), William Bolcom (Nonesuch 71284), Leonid Hambro (Walden 200), Leonard Pennario (Angel DS-37359), Andre Ratusinski (Trax Classique TRXCD-111), Frances Veri (Book of the Month Club Records 61-5426). François-Jöel Thiollier (RCA Red Seal RL 37590).

251. TILL THEN

Lyricist: Ira Gershwin
Key: F
Time: Common
Tempo: Moderato
Introduced by: Don Bestor and His Orchestra on a recording made on September 25, 1933 (see below).

Lore: This song was written in 1933 at the request of Jerome Kern, who had just bought T.B. Harms, a music publishing company.

Analysis: The brief twelve-bar verse ("'Forever and a day is a long time,' I've heard it said") has a slow, measured pace. A gradually descending bass and regular diminished chords give it a sad and resigned demeanor. The refrain ("Till black is white") is thirty-two bars long and contrastingly playful. Its melody has a "Looking For a Boy" dotted note pattern and it makes consistent use of blue notes as leading tones and suspensions to create a kittenish effect. The release ("I don't know just what it is about you") is a grittier idea, presented in A-minor, then C.

Recordings: Don Bestor and His Orchestra recorded this on September 25, 1933 (vocal by Neil Buckley—Victor 24462). Another version is by the Longines Symphonette Society (Longines Symphonette LW 227). In 1985 there was a solo piano version by Kevin Cole (Fanfare DFL 7007).

252. ISN'T IT A PITY?

Lyricist: Ira Gershwin
Key: A-minor (verse)
      C (refrain)
Time: Common (verse)
      4/4 (refrain)
Tempo: Moderato (verse)
      Not fast, with expression (refrain)

291

Introduced by: George Givot and Josephine Huston in *Pardon My English* at the Majestic Theatre in New York City on January 20, 1933.

Analysis: This is one of the most beautiful of Gershwin's ballads. Its sixteen-bar verse ("Why did I wander") has a hushed quality, an atmosphere of intimacy and calm. In its seventh and eighth bars the title phrase is stated—something that does not often happen in a verse. The refrain ("It's a funny thing"), like the refrains of "The Man I Love" and "Someone to Watch Over Me," relies on a repeating pattern sung in successively lower registers. In this case, the pattern is created by a series of eighth note triplets. In the lyric, Ira Gershwin is once again able to inject humor in a ballad without destroying its romantic mood. In the verse, for example, he has the female singer (a male singer is given his own stanza) do a quick rundown on her former German boyfriends ("Sleepy was Herman/Fritz was like a sermon"). And in the refrain he manages to get away with "My nights were sour/Spent with Schopenhauer."

Recordings: Recorded in December of 1932 by Victor Arden-Phil Ohman and Their Orchestra (Victor 24206), and a month later by Eddy Duchin and His Central Park Casino Orchestra (Brunswick 6476). Frances Gershwin, sister of the writers, has also released her rendition (World Records SH-208, Monmouth-Evergreen MES 7060).
Other choices: Kaye Ballard (Walden 302), George Byron with piano accompaniment by Dick Hyman (Atlantic ALS 410), Michael Feinstein (Parnassus PR 0100), Ella Fitzgerald (Verve 2-2525), Mitzi Gaynor (Verve MGV 2115), Teddi King (Inner City 1044), Helen Merrill (Inner City 1080), Joan Morris/William Bolcom (Nonesuch 71358), and Sarah Vaughan (Mercury MG-20310).

253. I'VE GOT TO BE THERE

Lyricist: Ira Gershwin
Key: A-flat
Time: 2/4
Tempo: Moderato

Introduced by: Carl Randall and Barbara Newberry in *Pardon My English*, at the Majestic Theatre in New York City on January 20, 1933.

Analysis: The heart of this song lies in its funny and sudden switch from waltzlike triplets in the first four bars of the refrain ("When music is playing") to a staccato double time in measures five through eight ("I've got to be there!"). Another oddity is the length—thirty–five bars—due to a note that is held for three measures near the end (on "fair" in "the women are fair"). The verse ("When I keep seeing things") has an unusual length too—twenty–eight bars—and an appealing melody atop a rich sequence of chord changes. Alternating between major and minor thirds, this melody harkens back to the days of "The Man I Love." As for the lyric, it expresses the singer's love of parties.

Recordings: Bobby Short's recording was released in 1973 (Atlantic SD 2-608).

254. LORELEI

Lyricist: Ira Gershwin
Key: F (verse)
      B-flat (refrain)
Time: Common (verse)
      Alla breve (refrain)
Tempo: Moderato
Introduced by: Carl Randall and Barbara Newberry sang this in the Broadway premiere of *Pardon My English* at the Majestic Theatre in New York City on January 20, 1933. But the first performance belonged to Lyda Roberti, who sang it during the out-of-town tryout.

Analysis: In this song the Gershwins returned to a theme they had first tackled in 1924 in "The Four Little Sirens" from *Primrose*. But here the imagery is more explicit ("I'm treacherous—Ja, Ja!/ Oh, I just can't hold myself in check./I'm lecherous—Ja, Ja!/ I want to bite

293

my initials on a sailor's neck."). Musically, the song is interesting for two quotations. The first occurs in the introduction, where the piano plays the rumba theme from the composer's *Second Rhapsody* ("Lorelei" and *Second Rhapsody* were both written in 1932). Then, as the singer concludes the refrain, the accompaniment quotes the German folk song "Die-Lorelie." In between we are given a twenty-bar verse ("Back in the days of Knights in Armor") that is all but through-composed and whose predominant note is a whiny D-flat—the diminished fifth of a G9 chord (on "Knights"). And then we get a rowdy refrain ("I want to be like that gal on the river") that is similar in spirit to "My Cousin in Milwaukee" from the same show, although, this melody has more of an innate, natural pulse.

Recordings: Doris Rhodes and the Joe Sullivan Orchestra recorded this on March 26, 1940 (Columbia 35548). Other versions have been by Carol Burnett (Decca DL/DL7-4049), Ella Fitzgerald (Verve MGV-4028), George Byron with piano accompaniment by Dick Hyman (Altantic ALS 410), Cleo Laine (Jazz Man 5033), Joan Morris/ William Bolcom (Nonesuch H-71358, Ross and Sargent (Columbia 31190), Bobby Short (Atlantic SD 2-608), and Sarah Vaughan (Mercury MG-20310).

255. LUCKIEST MAN IN THE WORLD

Lyricist: Ira Gershwin
Key: E-flat
Time: 2/4
Tempo: Allegretto moderato
Introduced by: George Givot in *Pardon My English* at the Majestic Theatre in New York City on January 20, 1933.

Analysis: This is an "I don't need anything else as long as I've got you" lyric. The oddly topical verse ("I may never have the fame of Mussolini"), a full thirty-two-bar song in itself, has, despite a lightness of touch, something sad in it—perhaps it is the sprinkling of blue notes or the mildly unsettling E-flat augmented chord upon which it comes to its first rest (on "prize" in "Nobel prize"). The refrain ("I'm about

294

the luckiest man in the world") has several points of interest. It begins in E-flat, reaches a climax in bar five (on "world") with an A-flat ninth chord, and then inner voicings change that chord to Fm/A-flat, G7/A-flat, and G-flat major seventh/E-flat, before the final resolution in E-flat. At this point ("I've met") we are led to expect a repetition of the first idea, but get instead an extension of the melody. In fact, our hopes are falsely raised on two other occasions before, at bar twenty-five, the tune repeats for the first and only time. That repetition quickly leads into the coda, bringing this refrain in at thirty-six bars.

Recordings: None

256. MY COUSIN IN MILWAUKEE

Lyricist: Ira Gershwin
Key: E-flat
Time: Common
Tempo: Moderato
Introduced by: Lyda Roberti in *Pardon My English* at the Majestic Theatre in New York City on January 20, 1933.

Lore: Lyda Roberti had been born in Warsaw and was a former circus performer, but she made it on Broadway as a no-holds-barred comedienne and this song, sung to a group of policemen, was her show-stopper in *Pardon My English*. Unfortunately for her, the show was stopped permanently for lack of patronage after only forty-six performances.

Analysis: The singer extolls the talents of her cousin, who is another singer—one with the ability to get "boyfriends by the Dozen" by belting out numbers in a voice that is sometimes hot, sometimes blue. The sixteen-bar verse ("Once I visited My Cousin in Milwaukee") begins unhurriedly, almost recitativo-style, lulling the audience before the storm of the bump and grind refrain ("I got a cousin in Milwaukee"). The latter is AABAC in form and thirty–four bars long— the extra two bars being an extension in the coda (at "because she taught me") where half notes in the melody are punctuated by quarter note chords in the accompaniment—not unlike what would happen at greater length in "A Woman Is A Sometime Thing."

Recordings: There are two versions by Lyda Roberti (dates unknown—Epic LZN-6072, Totem 1026), and there is one by Frances Gershwin (World Records SH-208, Monmouth-Evergreen MES 7060). In addition, this song was recorded in December 1932 by duo pianists Victor Arden and Phil Ohman (Victor 24206), in January of 1933 by Eddy Duchin and His Central Park Casino Orchestra (Brunswick 6476), in March of 1933 by Ramona and Her Grand Piano (Ramona Davies and Ray Bargy—Victor 24260), in 1942 by Hildegarde (Decca 23426), in 1959 by Ella Fitzgerald (Verve V/V9-29-5), and circa 1960 by Nancy Walker (Dolphin 2).   A more recent version is by Joan Morris with piano accompaniment by William Bolcom (Nonesuch H-71358).

257. SO WHAT?

> *Lyricist:* Ira Gershwin
> *Key:* B-flat (verse)
>   G (refrain)
> *Time:* 2/4
> *Tempo:* Moderato
> *Introduced by:* Jack Pearl and Josephine Huston in *Pardon My English* at the Majestic Theatre in New York City on January 20, 1933.

Analysis: It is possible that the brothers had their father in mind when they wrote this song. The elder Gershwin had died on May 15, 1932 and the opening lines of the verse ("I once had a father/Worry didn't bother;/He had been around,/He knew what it was all about") could well be a description of him. This verse, which is a full thirty-two-bar song in itself, has a happy-go-lucky, polka-style gait to match its philosophy. The refrain ("You sigh—So what/") expresses the same verbal and musical thoughts but in a more punchy, clipped style. Harmonically, there are several dramatic moments. For instance, the melody of the release ("If you take philosophy") begins on an F-sharp and is supported by a C9 chord, making for a sudden, crying sound. Later, in the coda (at "might as well be happy now") an F-natural is juxtaposed with a C9 chord, creating a less strident, more forgiving dissonance.

Recordings: None

258. WHERE YOU GO, I GO

Lyricist: Ira Gershwin
Key: E-flat
Time: 2/4
Tempo: Moderato
Introduced by: Lyda Roberti and Jack Pearl in *Pardon My English* at the Majestic Theatre in New York City on January 20, 1933.

Analysis: A man and a woman trade lines in the verse ("Lady, let me go!"), the upshot being that he wants to get away and she won't let him. In the refrain ("Where you go, I go") they are given separate choruses but she is still chasing him and he is still backing off. As for the music, the two-bar piano introduction begins with a "Shave and a haircut" quote, the twenty-bar verse is a series of easygoing, descending imitative phrases, the thirty-two-bar refrain is a bright Latinesque melody that is through composed for twenty-four bars, and the first piano ending again quotes "Shave and a haircut" (we never do get to hear the "two bits").

Recordings: None

259. BLUE, BLUE, BLUE

Lyricist: Ira Gershwin
Key: C
Time: 4/4 (verse)
     Alla breve (refrain)

Tempo: Moderato (verse)

Moderato (slowly, with expression) (refrain)

Introduced by: The ensemble (the wives of John P. Wintergreen's supporters) in *Let 'Em Eat Cake* at the Imperial Theatre in New York City on October 21, 1933.

Lore: The second act of *Let 'Em Eat Cake* was staged entirely in blue and this song was its opening number. The tune had existed for some time in one of Gershwin's notebooks and, had the composer had his way, it would not have been used in this show. He believed that it had the makings of something special and would have liked to have worked on it for its own sake. But Ira thought it perfect for the second act opener of the new show and George gave in.

Analysis: This is a most unusual song. The introduction consists of four oddly constructed chords that sound a bit like the chimes from Act II of *Porgy and Bess*. Then comes an eleven-bar verse ("it's off with the old") in which the singer has only two notes to sing. The first, F-sharp, is repeated twenty times. The second, A, is repeated nineteen. The supporting harmony, however, is chromatic, dissonant, constantly shifting, and written in what must be the most difficult piano accompaniment in American pop song history. As for the refrain ("Blue, Blue, Blue!"), it is a twenty–four-bar ballad whose lyrical first eight bars are followed by a jumpy four-bar section ("The country clamored for somebody new"). Though "Blue, Blue, Blue" was one of five songs from *Let 'Em Eat Cake* to be chosen for individual publication (the rest of the score has not been published), it really was tailored for the specific needs of the show. The lyrics of the verse talk about "painting the White House blue" while those of the refrain refer to Wintergreen's presidential victory.

Recordings: Zubin Mehta and the New York Philharmonic with pianist Gary Graffman (as part of a medley—Columbia JS-36020), Marni Nixon with piano accompaniment by Lincoln Mayorga (Reference RR-19), Michael Tilson Thomas conducting the Orchestra of St. Luke's and the New York Choral Artists (CBS S2M 42522).

298

260. LET 'EM EAT CAKE

Lyricist: Ira Gershwin
Key: D-minor (verse)
  C (refrain)
Time: Alla breve, 6/8
Tempo: Con spirito (verse)
  Tempo di marcia (with spirit) (refrain)
Introduced by: William Gaxton in *Let 'Em Eat Cake* at the
Imperial Theatre in New York City on October 21, 1933.

Analysis: This number is well beyond the usual pop song format. Although it is not particularly lengthy—the verse is thirty-two
bars and the refrain is forty—it contains many more ideas than usual,
all of them interrelated and carefully juxtaposed.

It begins with a slinky, chromatic two-bar instrumental motive.
Then comes the verse ("Oh, comrades you deserve your daily bread")—
a minor key march sung by John P. Wintergreen. He had been President in *Of Thee I Sing* but here he is out of office and leading a
revolution against the government. This march, though played up-
tempo, has a trudging, Russian quality. After a short and lyrical release
(the ensemble singing "We've always wanted cake") it returns ("With
drums a-booming"), but with D-major instead of D-minor chords. Another lyrical interjection by the ensemble ("Comrades, it is clear—The
millenium is here!") leads into the refrain.

This refrain is in eight sections:

1. The main idea ("Let 'Em Eat Cake!") is a spirited four-bar C-major
fanfare in alla breve time.
2. An instrumental G-major motive in 6/8 time.
3. A repeat of section 1.
4. A repeat of section 2 but in the key of E.
5. A subsidiary fanfare in A-minor, this one pure Broadway in feel
("Now is the time to be waking!").
6. A repeat of section 1.
7. A repeat of section 2 but in the key of C.
8. A coda in the grand style ("Let it be known the whole world over").

299

Recordings: In October of 1933, this was recorded by Emil Coleman and His Riviera Orchestra (Columbia 2831-D), Leo Reisman and His Orchestra (Victor 24429), Paul Whiteman and His Orchestra (Victor 39003), and by Victor Young and His Orchestra (Brunswick 6691). In 1987 it was recorded by Larry Kert, Haskell Gordon and Michael Tilson Thomas (CBS S2M 42522).

261. MINE

Lyricist: Ira Gershwin
Key: C
Time: Alla breve
Tempo: Moderately slow (with much expression)
Introduced by: William Gaxton and Lois Moran in *Let 'Em Eat Cake* at the Imperial Theatre in New York City on October 21, 1933.

Lore: Gershwin took an unusually academic approach in discussing this—his last as it turned out—Broadway musical. But it shows where he was headed—opera:

> I've written most of the music for this show contrapuntally, and it is this very insistence on the sharpness of a form that gives my music the acid touch it has—which points the words of the lyrics, and is in keeping with the satire of the piece. At least, I feel that it is the counterpoint which helps me to do what I am trying to do.

Analysis: No verse is included in the published sheet music, although there was a recitativo verse in *Let 'Em Eat Cake*. At one point in that verse (on "Why, when I think how we suffered together, worried together, struggled together") the music presages the recitative style of *Porgy and Bess*. (This music can be heard on a recent recording issued on the Turnabout label—see below). The refrain ("Mine, love is mine") is Gershwin's most notable entry into the field of multiple-tune songs—that is, songs with contrasting tunes that are played separately at first and then in counterpoint ("Some Girls Can Bake a Pie" from *Of Thee I Sing* has three melody lines). The initial melody in "Mine" is unusual in that it consists of a number of held notes which last long enough to allow the words of the countertune ("The point they're making in the song") to be heard and understood.

At the heart of the song is a four-chord vamp. It is a variation on that most familiar of chord progressions, the "Heart and Soul" I–vi–ii7–V7. Here we get I6–VI7–II7–v7+. In other words, three of the chords have been given color notes and the two minor chords have been made major. This results in a strange but bouncy effect. There is no release but, after eight bars, the idea is repeated a fourth higher, in F. Then it comes back to C to conclude with a brief coda ("Mine, more than divine"). At this point the counter melody is sung. It is a tap dance tune—notier than the first but played to the same vamp harmony. It is insouciant rather than flowing and its lyric is a humorous commentary on the earnest declaration of love that makes up the first tune. The two melodies are then sung simultaneously.

Recordings: "Mine" was played by the orchestra on an April 30, 1934 radio broadcast ("Music By Gershwin") hosted by the composer (Mark 56 Records 641). In October of 1933, the song was recorded by Emil Coleman and His Riviera Orchestra (Columbia 2831-D), Leo Reisman and His Orchestra (Victor 24429), Paul Whiteman and His Orchestra (Victor 39003), and Victor Young and His Orchestra (Brunswick 6691).

There were versions in 1939 by Shirley Ross (Decca 2878), in 1947 by Bing Crosby and Judy Garland (Decca 23804), in 1948 by Skitch Henderson (Capitol 15136), and in 1973 by Bobby Short (Atlantic SD 2-608). In 1976, "Mine" was performed by Thomas Bogdan, Priscilla Magdamo and the Gregg Smith Singers as part of a scene from *Let 'Em Eat Cake* (Turnabout TV S-34638). In 1987 it was done by Larry Kert, Maureen McGovern and Michael Tilson Thomas in a more complete recording of the show (CBS S2M 42522).

Others: Jackie Cain/Roy Kral (Concord Jazz 186), Al Caiola (Bainbridge 1012), Jane Froman (Capitol 2154), Dorothy Kirsten (Columbia 4620-M), Zubin Mehta conducting the New York Philharmonic (Columbia JS-36020).

262. ON AND ON AND ON

Lyricist: Ira Gershwin

Key: D (verse)
G (refrain)
Time: 2/4 (introduction and refrain)
Alla breve (verse)
Tempo: Vigoroso (introduction)
In strict rhythm (verse)
Tempo di Marcia (refrain)
Introduced by: William Gaxton, Lois Moran and a squad of troops in *Let 'Em Eat Cake* at the Imperial Theatre in New York City on October 21, 1933.

Analysis: The introduction is a four-bar fanfare with a mocking, off-key sound. It leads into two marches: the eighteen-bar verse ("Left! Right!") and the thirty-six-bar refrain ("On! And on! And on!"). In the former, Ds and As played in octaves alternate in the bass, keeping time, while the melody and treble harmony rise steadily by half steps, creating an increasingly dissonant and noisy crescendo. The refrain is contrastingly consonant and lyrical.

Recordings: In October of 1933 this was recorded by Paul Whiteman and his Orchestra (Victor 39003). In 1987 it was done by Jack Dabdoub, Larry Kert and Michael Tilson Thomas (CBS S2M 42522).

263. UNION SQUARE

Lyricist: Ira Gershwin
Key: E-flat
Time: Common (refrain)
2/4 (interlude)
Tempo: Moderato con moto (refrain)
Allegro agitato (interlude)

Introduced by: Philip Loeb in *Let 'Em Eat Cake* at the Imperial Theatre in New York City on October 21, 1933.

Lore: According to Oscar Levant, Gershwin became fond of Schubert's *C-major Quintet* (the one with two cellos) at the time that he was composing *Let 'Em Eat Cake*, and the "Our hearts are in communion" portion of "Union Square" is influenced by the second theme of the Schubert piece.

Analysis: This music is in three sections. The first, marked "Refrain," is a credo sung by down and out revolutionaries in the happy-go-lucky, sing-songy style that Gershwin had used previously in *Strike Up the Band* and *Of Thee I Sing* when setting nihilistic or absurd sentiments to music. This is the "Our hearts are in communion" section to which Levant was referring. It is twenty-six bars long. The sixty-eight-bar middle section, sometimes referred to as "Down with Everything That's Up," is marked "Interlude." In it, Ira tries his hand writing couplets for a street mob—a mob with evolved and idiosyncratic hatreds (examples are "Let's tear down the House of Morgan!/ Let's Burn up the Roxy organ!" and "Down with Balzac! Down with Zola!/Down with pianists who play 'Nola'!"). The music is cheerful here too, but more insistent. It is introduced by a four-bar instrumental vamp (alternating E-flat sixth and D-flat sixth chords) that sets up a pace and feel similar to that in "Wintergreen For President," although minor chords dominated in that piece and major chords dominate here. When minor chords do come, they are slipped in and quickly whisked away, creating an almost subliminal effect. Gershwin could not resist throwing in two bars of "Nola" after that piece is mentioned in the above-quoted line.

The final section is a repeat of the first. It ends with a brief coda.

Recordings: In October of 1933 this was recorded by Paul Whiteman and His Orchestra (Victor 39005). In 1987 it was done by David Garrison and Michael Tilson Thomas (CBS S2M 42522).

264. "I GOT RHYTHM" VARIATIONS

For piano and orchestra

Key: F

Introduced by: George Gershwin, piano, and the Reisman Symphonic Orchestra, Charles Previn conducting, in Symphony Hall in Boston on January 14, 1934.

Lore: In January and February of 1934 Gershwin allowed an old friend, Harry Askins, to manage him on a twenty-eight city tour commemorating the tenth anniversary of the *Rhapsody in Blue.* Askins was the man who, in recommending Gershwin to publisher Max Dreyfus, had been instrumental in getting him his first big break.

Also on this tour was the Leo Reisman Band (billed as the Reisman Symphonic Orchestra). Reisman was another old friend, one with whom Gershwin had palled around in Paris in 1928 (together, they had made a determined hunt for New York-style lox in Parisian shops). Unfortunately, Reisman was not able to accompany his band on the tour, having suffered a leg injury. His place was taken by yet another longtime Gershwin friend, Charles Previn. The latter had conducted the composer's *La La Lucille* in 1919 and *Of Thee I Sing* in 1931.

The *"I Got Rhythm" Variations* was a new work for piano and orchestra, composed by Gershwin for this tour. His initial manuscript, for two pianos (it has been published), was written while he stayed at the Palm Beach, Florida home of Emil Mosbacher. The orchestrated version was completed on January 6, 1934, after Gershwin returned to New York. The tour began eight days later in Boston and proceeded to twenty-seven other cities in as many days. Inasmuch as the program featured Gershwin as piano soloist in the *Concerto in F,* the *Rhapsody in Blue,* and the *"I Got Rhythm" Variations,* and, as some 12,000 miles were covered visiting cities from Maine to Ontario to Nebraska, it was, for Gershwin, significant as a physical as well as a musical accomplishment. He was pleased, too, with the reception that he received from the audiences. But Askins had booked him into small-to-mid-sized auditoriums (ie., the one at Technical High School in Omaha) and ticket sales could not recoup expenses, much less turn a profit.

The new orchestral work had some of the zip, but none of the brooding or majesty of the *Rhapsody In Blue* and the *Concerto in F*. However, it gave Gershwin the chance to continue the experiments he had been making based on his studies with Joseph Schillinger—experiments that had commenced in 1932 with the *Cuban Overture*. Oscar Levant, in his book *A Smattering of Ignorance*, noted that, in the *"I Got Rhythm" Variations*, Gershwin used Schillinger's "theories of cyclical harmonic progressions, with an intricate leading of bass notes...[and a] scheme of rhythmic permutations." Another Gershwin friend, Vernon Duke, noted that Gershwin's orchestration in this piece used instrumental devices recommended by Schillinger. In that regard, Gershwin biographer Charles Schwartz has speculated that the pizzicato glissandos and the back of the bridge playing by the violins may have been Schillinger suggestions.

Unfortunately, the *"I Got Rhythm" Variations* have never been published in the composer's orchestration. In his lifetime, only the two-piano version was made publicly available. Then, in 1953, came an orchestral version, published by New World Music, in which Gershwin's instrumental intentions were doctored by William C. Schonfeld.

The *"I Got Rhythm" Variations* are dedicated to Ira Gershwin.

Analysis: This piece consists of the following continuous sections:

1.   An introduction in F in which a solo clarinet plays the first four notes of the tune and then repeats the phrase a couple of times, giving it a tone row effect. The orchestra then toys with the theme, playing its first and last few notes, but skipping the rest. It should be noted that only the "I Got Rhythm" refrain is used in this work, not the verse.

2.   A straightforward solo piano rendition of the full theme in F.

3.   A variation in F based on syncopated, broken arpeggios, played high in the treble.

4   A waltz variation in D that, although marked Valse triste, has a comic edge, made especially evident by little descending sneers played by the first violins.

5.   A "Chinese Variation" in B and G, marked Allegretto giocoso.

In this section, as Gershwin described it, "The left hand plays the melody upside down and the right plays it straight, on the theory that you shouldn't let one hand know what the other is doing."

6.   A jazz variation in F, featuring a walking slap bass sound against a gritty blues tune for flutes and clarinets. "I Got Rhythm" is used here for punctuation.

7.   The finale begins in D-flat with trills played first by the solo piano, with trumpets and horns joining in. Below, the cellos and basses play a driving, syncopated ostinato—one that continues (with other instruments joining in) as the piano plays a forte full-tilt "I Got Rhythm."

Recordings: A recording made with Gershwin at the piano exists, taken from an April 30, 1934 radio broadcast (Mark 56 #641).

An October 8, 1944 performance by pianist Morton Gould and conductor Artur Rodzinski is on Penzance 43.   Other versions (listed alphabetically by pianist): Sondra Bianca and the Pro Musica, Hamburg conducted by Hans Jurgen Walther (MGM 3-El), Werner Haas with the Monte Carlo Opera Orchestra conducted by Edo de Waart (Philips 6500-118), Oscar Levant with Morton Gould and His Orchestra (Columbia ML 2073), Teodor Moussov and the TVR Orchestra conducted by Pancho Vladigerov (Monitor MCS-2153), David Parkhouse and the London Festival Orchestra conducted by Stanley Black (London 417098-4), Leonard Pennario with the Hollywood Bowl Symphony Orchestra conducted by Alfred Newman (Capitol P8581),   Jeffrey Siegel and the St. Louis Symphony conducted by Leonard Slatkin (Vox C-T2122, Vox Box CBX-5132), Buddy Weed with Paul Whiteman's Orchestra (Coral 57021), Alexis Weissenberg and the Berlin Philharmonic conducted by Seiji Ozawa (Angel CDC-47152), Earl Wild and the Boston Pops conducted by Arthur Fiedler (RCA-VCS-7097).

The composer's arrangement for two pianos, four hands has been recorded by Anognoson and Kinton (Pro Arte CDD-367) and by Frances Veri and Michael Jamanis (Connoisseur Society CSQ 206, Book of the Month Club Records 61-5426).

265. PORGY AND BESS

Opera in three acts

Librettist: DuBose Heyward
Lyricist: DuBose Heyward and Ira Gershwin
Introduced by: Todd Duncan (Porgy), Anne Wiggins Brown (Bess), Warren Coleman (Crown), Ruby Elzy (Serena), Abbie Mitchell (Clara), Georgette Harvey (Maria), Eddie Matthews (Jake), John W. Bubbles (Sporting Life), Ford L. Buck (Mingo), Henry Davis (Robbins), Gus Simons (Peter), the Eva Jessye Choir, the Charleston Orphans' Band, Alexander Smallens (conductor), Rouben Mamoulian (director) at the Alvin Theatre in New York City on October 10, 1935.

Lore: DuBose Heyward, the son of a still proud but financially fading Southern family (Thomas Heyward had signed the Declaration of Independence), was, for a time, a bale-checker on the Charleston, South Carolina wharves. It was there that he came into close contact with poor black dockworkers and fishermen and it was in that milieu that he learned of a local beggar named Goat Sammy—a legless cripple whose means of locomotion was a cart pulled by a goat. Heyward himself had been a polio victim and that may have accounted for at least part of his fascination with and empathy for Sammy. In 1925 he wrote a best-selling novel, *Porgy*, about a crippled beggar who wanted to be able, like other men, to fall in love and be loved.

When George Gershwin picked up the book one evening in September of 1926 he became so absorbed that he finished it at one sitting and then, at four a.m., wrote Heyward proposing that they turn *Porgy* into an opera. The two men met to discuss the idea later that year but then Gershwin backed off, having decided that he was not yet musically sophisticated enough to tackle such a formidable project.

Six years later, Gershwin revived the idea in a March, 1932 letter to Heyward. The latter was receptive but there was a new problem: Al Jolson was keen on doing his own musical *Porgy* and he had gotten Jerome Kern and Oscar Hammerstein II (the authors of *Show Boat*) to agree to write the score. Heyward wanted to write the opera with

Gershwin but, having been hit hard by the Depression, he was sorely tempted to sign onto Jolson's undertaking. Gershwin sympathized with Heyward's dilemma and said that he would not stand in his way, thereby demonstrating a graciousness that not only endeared him to Heyward but made their collaboration all the smoother when the Jolson project fell through in September of 1933.

But there were more delays. The composer spent December of 1933 in Florida writing the *"I Got Rhythm" Variations* and then came six weeks of touring with the Leo Reisman Orchestra. When, at last, he and Heyward did get to work it had to be by long distance, as Gershwin was tied to a radio program ("Music By Gershwin") in New York and Heyward was loathe to leave South Carolina. To facilitate their collaboration, Ira Gershwin was brought in to help with the lyrics.

By mid-June of 1934 the opera was finally taking shape and Gershwin, freed from his duties at NBC, traveled to Charleston, where he and his cousin Henry Botkin, an artist, stayed in a four-room cottage on Folly Beach—a tiny island ten miles off the coast. There they tucked their suitcases under their cots and got to work: Gershwin at the piano and Botkin at his easel. Heyward and his wife, Dorothy, rented a cottage nearby and they introduced Gershwin to the locale: the churches, the harbor, the once aristocratic but now lowly Cabbage Row section of the old city. It was while visiting a church on a nearby island that Gershwin joined so enthusiastically in some congregational singing (called "shouting") that he, according to Heyward, "stole the show" from the champion shouter.

It took all of 1934 for him to write his new work and the better part of 1935 to orchestrate it. Then, on September 2, 1935, he wrote "finished" on his manuscript.

Before the first public performance there was a full-scale run-through of the opera at Carnegie Hall, attended only by family and friends. This production, which was done without scenery or staging, was the first presentation of the work in its entirety—and, as things turned out, the last such presentation for more than forty years. By the time of the first public performance—at Boston's Colonial Theatre on September 30, 1935—the "Buzzard Song," the opening piano music and the trio section of "Oh, Bess, Oh Where's My Bess?" had been cut. Critics and opera-goers greeted this production with great enthusiasm but when the show began its run at the Alvin Theatre in New York City the reception was mixed. After 124 performances it closed, as it was not earning enough money to cover expenses.

In the remaining year and a half of his life, Gershwin did what he could to keep *Porgy and Bess* alive. In an article for the New York *Times* he answered two questions that were being asked persistently at the time—questions that seemed important then but which now seem beside the point: why had *Porgy and Bess* been produced by the Theatre Guild and not by an opera company? Why had Gershwin filled it with songs? The composer explained that the work was produced on Broadway to ensure many more performances than would otherwise have been the case. As for having put songs into an opera, he pointed out that many great operas contained wonderful songs and proudly insisted that he was not ashamed of writing songs as long as they were good ones. Then he created an orchestral suite (see *Catfish Row*), hoping that the music could be kept alive at symphony concerts. Shortly before his death in July of 1937, he was involved in plans to produce the opera on the West Coast (a production that was mounted in 1938).

But it was not until 1941-1942, when *Porgy and Bess* was given under the auspices of Cheryl Crawford, that financial success and critical kudos became the norm. However, Crawford's production eliminated all of the recitative, and future triumphant productions, which occurred with increasing frequency in the United States and abroad, were always made with cuts and with reduced or changed orchestration. It would not be until 1976, with the Houston Grand opera's production, that the work would be presented as on that first occasion in Carnegie Hall and as Gershwin had written it, every note of his intact.

The slow, grudging, evolutionary acceptance of *Porgy and Bess* as an opera has an operatic sweep and silliness and grandeur all its own. But now it seems that the world, after more than fifty years, has at last concluded that it is, indeed, an opera—and a great one at that.

Perhaps the wisest commentary about all of this came in a statement made by Todd Duncan some fifty years after he originated the role of Porgy in the first production:

The communication, the strength, the drama, the passion
that come in the grand operas is in *Porgy and Bess* and the

309

main ingredient that is in *Porgy and Bess* is the same ingredient that's in *Tosca*, the same ingredient that's in *Siegfried*, and that means performance, passion, communication, sheer heaven, excitement, theater.

Analysis: See individual scenes.

Recordings featuring Gershwin and original cast members:

On July 19, 1935 a recording was made of Gershwin rehearsing the *Porgy and Bess* principals. He can be heard conducting, coaching and singing from the podium. Featured are some of the "Jasbo Brown Piano Music" (Gershwin at the piano), "Summertime" (sung by Abbie Mitchell), "A Woman is a Sometime Thing" (Eddie Matthews), the orchestral finale from Act I, Scene I, "My Man's Gone Now" (Ruby Elzy), and "Bess, You is My Woman Now" (Todd Duncan and Anne Brown). This recording has been released on Mark 56 667.

Gershwin supervised another recording of excerpts, this one featuring Lawrence Tibbett and Helen Jepson with Alexander Smallens (who had the orchestra in the original Broadway production) conducting (Victor Red Seal 11878 through 11881 and RCA Camden CAL-400). At a September 8, 1937 George Gershwin memorial concert, Ruby Elzy sang "My Man's Gone Now"; Todd Duncan sang "Buzzard Song," "I Got Plenty O'Nuttin, " and "I'm On My Way"; Duncan and Anne Brown sang "Bess, You is My Woman Now"; Brown sang "Leavin' For the Promise' Lan'" (identified as "The Train Song")—Citadel CT 7025. In 1942, a record was made of that year's Broadway revival, featuring Duncan and Brown as well as others who had been in the 1935 production: Eddie Matthews, the Eva Jessye Choir and Alexander Smallens. Also heard is Avon Long, who was Sporting Life in the 1938 West Coast Production (Decca DL-8042, DL-9024, DL-79024, MCA-2035A).

Complete recordings: The first truly complete recording of *Porgy and Bess* was one made by conductor Lorin Maazel and the Cleveland Orchestra and Chorus in 1976. Featured are Willard White (Porgy), Leona Mitchell (Bess), McHenry Boatwright (Crown), Florence Quivar (Serena), Barbara Hendricks (Clara), Barbara Conrad (Maria), Arthur Thompson (Jake), and François Clemmons (Sporting Life). This three-record set was released on London OSA 13116.

310

So far, the only other complete recording of the opera is the one made in 1977 by the Houston Grand Opera and Chorus with John De Main conducting. It features Donnie Ray Albert (Porgy), Clamma Dale (Bess), Andrew Smith (Crown), Wilma Shakesneider (Serena), Carol Bryce (Maria), Alexander B. Smalls (Jake), Betty Lane (Clara), and Larry Marshall (Sporting Life). It too is a three-record set and it is available on RCA ARL 3-2109.

In 1951 a nearly complete recording was made by conductor Lehman Engel with the J. Rosamond Johnson Chorus. It features Lawrence Winters (Porgy), Camilla Winters (Bess), Inez Matthews (Serena), Warren Coleman (Crown), Eddie Matthews (Jake—he had appeared in the 1935 original cast), and Avon Long (Sporting Life—from the 1938 revival). This three-record set was released on Columbia SL-162 and reissued on Odyssey 32 36 0018.

Excerpt recordings: A recording of selected scenes from the opera features William Warfield, Leontyne Price, McHenry Boatwright and John W. Bubbles (Sporting Life from the 1935 original cast), and conductor Skitch Henderson (RCA Victor LSL-2679, RCA AGL 1-3654).

Other excerpt recordings: Rise Stevens, Robert Merrill and the Robert Shaw Chorale (RCA Victor LM-1124); Cab Calloway and Helen Thigpen (RCA Victor LPM-3158); Broc Peters, Margaret Tynes and Paul Belanger conducting the Opera Society Chorus and Orchestra (Musical Masterpiece Society M2035-OP22), Simon Estes and Roberta Alexander with Leonard Slatkin conducting the Berlin Radio Chorus and Berlin Symphony Orchestra (Philips 4127201), Robert Trendler and Orchestra (Pilotone 5121/23, 25, 27, 28).

Jazz recordings: Jazz interpretations of *Porgy and Bess* have been recorded by the following: Louis Armstrong and Ella Fitzgerald with orchestrations and conducting by Russell Garcia (Verve 64068); Miles Davis with orchestrations and conducting by Gil Evans (Columbia CS-8085); Sammy Davis, Jr. And Carmen McRae (Decca DL-78854); Bob Crosby and His Bobcats (Dot DLP 3193); the Modern Jazz Quartet (Atlantic SD 1440); Russ Garcia (Bethlehen EXLP-1); Harry Belafonte and Lena Horne with arrangements by Lennie Hayton and Robert Corman (RCA Victor LDP 1507); Ray Charles and Cleo Laine (Victor CPL 2-1831), Mel Torme and Frances Faye (Bethlehem 3BP1).

Recordings of individual numbers:

"Jasbo Brown Piano Music" has been recorded by George Gershwin (see above), Richard Rodney Bennett (EMI EMD 5538), William Bolcom (Nonesuch H-71284), Morton Gould (RCA Victor Red Seal 6033).

"Summertime" was recorded in July of 1936 by Billie Holiday and Her Orchestra (featuring Artie Shaw—Vocalion/Okeh 3288). In September of that year came a version by Casper Reardon, His Harp and His Orchestra (Liberty Music Shop L-199). In a September 8, 1937 George Gershwin memorial concert, "Summertime" was sung by Lily Pons with Alexander Steinert conducting the Los Angeles Philharmonic Orchestra (Citadel CT 7025). Guy Lombardo and His Royal Canadians recorded it in October of 1937 (Victor 25716). Then came versions in 1938 by Bing Crosby (accompanied by Matty Malneck and His Orchestra—Decca 2147 and 24542), Bob Crosby (Decca 2205), Morton Gould (Decca 18204), and Paul Robeson (Victor 26359); in 1939 by the Sidney Bechet Quintet (Blue Note 6) and Jerry Kruger and Her Orchestra (Vocalion 4927); in 1940 by Jane Pickens (Columbia 35580); in 1941 by Joan Merrill (Bluebird 11125) and Joe Sullivan (Commodore Music Shop 540); in 1942 by Nat Brandywynne and His Orchestra (Decca 24075) and Leo Reisman and His Orchestra (vocal by Helen Dowdy—Decca 18242); in 1945 by Boyd Raeburn (Guild 111).

Others: Ernestine Anderson (Concord Jazz 109), Mike Auldridge (Takoma TKM 7041), Sil Austin (SSS International 8, SSS International 14) Pearl Bailey (Roulette RE-101), Carlos Barbosa-Lima (Concord Jazz 2005), Ray Barretto (Fantasy 24713), Kenny Barron and Ted Dunbar (Muse 5140), Count Basie (Bulldog 2020), George Benson (CBS Associated 8031), Walter Bishop, Jr. (Muse 5151), the Art Blakey Quartet (MCA/Impulse 5648), Booker T and the MG's (Atlantic 81281-1-Y),

John Coltrane (Atlantic 1361), Concord Super Band (Concord Jazz 120), Chris Connor and Maynard Ferguson (Atlantic 143-1), Sam Cooke (Audio Fidelity SOS-5006, Victor AYL1-3863), Jim Cullum Jazz Band (Columbia MK-42517), Blind John Davis (Alligator 4709), Miles Davis (Columbia PC-8085), Duke Ellington (Dr. Jazz W2X-40012), Bill Evans (Riverside OJC-018), Gil Evans (Atlantic 90048-1), Tal Farlow (Prestige 7732, 24042), Ella Fitzgerald (Pablo 2308234),

Ella Fitzgerald and Louis Armstrong (Verve 827475), Bruce Forman Quartet and Bobby Hutcherson (Concord Jazz 251), Red Garland Trio (Prestige OJC-193), Erroll Garner (Atlantic 1227, Columbia PG-33424), Stan Getz Quartet (Verve UMV-2075), Dizzy Gillespie/Mongo Santamaria/ Toots Thielemans (Pablo 2308229), Urbie Green (Project 3 5087), Al Haig (Sea Breeze 1001, 1006), Herbie Harper (Sea Breeze D-101), Bill Hemmons (SSS International 25), Barbara Hendricks/Katia and Marielle Labeque (Philips 9500987),

Hi-Lo's (DRG Records SL-5184), Earl Hines (Classic Jazz 31, Quicksilver 9000), Richard "Groove" Holmes (Prestige 7485), Eddie Jefferson (Inner City 1033), Joe and Eddie (Crescendo 2032), Lonnie Johnson (Prestige 7724), Janis Joplin (Columbia PC-32168), Duke Jordan (Savoy 1169), Kamahl (Philips 6603001), Sammy Kaye (Victor VPM-6070), Barney Kessel and Red Mitchell (Jazz Man 5025), John Klemmer (MCA 1639),

Eric Kloss (Prestige 7627), L.A. 4 (Concord Jazz 63), Cleo Laine and Ray Charles (Victor CPL2-1831), Love Sculpture (EMI Manhattan SQ-17208), Herbie Mann (Atlantic 1380), Shelly Manne Quintet & Big Band (Discovery 909), Marcels (Eric 114), Toussaint McCall (Ronn 7527), Carmen McRae (MCA 2-4111), Yehudi Menuhin and Stephane Grappelli (Angel 37156), Mabel Mercer (Liberty Music Shop L-362), Helen Merrill (Inner City 1080), Julia Migenes-Johnson (Victor ARL1-5323),

Modern Jazz Quartet (Atlantic 2-301, 2-909), Mystic Moods Orchestra (Bainbridge 6204), Willie Nelson and Leon Russell (Columbia CG-36064), Marni Nixon with piano accompaniment by Lincoln Mayorga (Reference RR-19), 101 Strings Orchestra (Alshire ALCD-3, ALCD-12), Charlie Parker (Verve UMV-2562), Joe Pass (Pablo 2405-419, 2312109), Houston Person (Muse 5260), Oscar Peterson (Pablo 2625711), Oscar Peterson and Jon Faddis (Pablo 2310743), Oscar Peterson and Joe Pass (Pablo 2310779), Oscar Peterson and the Trumpet Kings (Pablo 2310817), Artie Shaw (Victor AXM2-5579),

Zoot Sims (Pablo 2310744), Derek Smith (Progressive 7002), Paul Smith (Outstanding 023), Soundtrack (Columbia OS-2016), Blaine Sprouse (Rounder 0155), Billy Stewart (Chess 91004, Allegiance CDP-72941, MCA MCAD-5805), Sylvester (Barner Bros. 1-2527), Buddy Tate (Muse 5249), Tijuana Brass (A&M 3268), Sarah Vaughan (Columbia CJ-40652), Joe Venuti (Flying Fish 035), Carla White (Milestone M-9147), Cedar Walton and the H. Mobley Quintet (Muse 5132), Dinah Washington (Emarcy 1013), Doc Watson (Liberty LN-10201), Gerald Wiggins (V.S.O.P. 31), Teddy Wilson (Classic Jazz 32), Zombies (Epic PEG-32861).

"A Woman is a Sometime Thing" was recorded by Paul Robeson in January, 1938 (Victor 26358) and by Leo Reisman and His Orchestra in March, 1942 (vocal by Avon Long—Decca 18281). Other versions are by Pearl Bailey (Roulette 42002), Ella Fitzgerald and Louis Armstrong (Verve 2-2507), Cleo Laine and Ray Charles (Victor CPL2-1831).

"My Man's Gone Now" has been recorded by Bob Crosby (Dot DLP 3193), Miles Davis (Columbia OC-8085, Columbia C2-38005), Bill Evans (Riverside 018, Riverside OJC-140, Verve 2-2509), Ella Fitzgerald and Louis Armstrong (Verve 2-2507), Gun Club (Animal 6006), Barney Kessel (Contemporary 7585), Cleo Laine and Ray Charles (Victor CPL2-1831), Shelly Manne (Discovery 909), Mabel Mercer (Liberty Music Shop L-361), Oscar Peterson and Joe Pass (Pablo 2310779), Buddy Rich (Pacific Coast Jazz 10089), Nina Simone (Victor AFL1-4374), Sarah Vaughan (and the L.A. Philharmonic conducted by Michael Tilson Thomas—Colubmia FM-37277).

"It Take a Long Pull to Get There" was recorded by Paul Robeson in January of 1938 (Victor 26359). There is also a version by Bob Crosby and His Bobcats (Dot DLP 3193).

"I Got Plenty O' Nuttin" was recorded in November of 1935 by Leo Reisman and His Orchestra (vocal by Edward Matthews—Brunswick 7562) and in December of 1935 by Guy Lombardo and His Royal Canadians (Victor 25204). It was recorded in March of 1936 by Bing Crosby with Victor Young and His Orchestra (Decca 806 and 25409) and in July of 1936 by Joe Reichman and His Orchestra (American Record Company 6-10-12). In May of 1940 Todd Duncan recorded this song with Alexander Smallens and The Eva Jessye Choir (Decca 29068). Other versions are by Bob Crosby (Dot DLP 3193), Sammy Davis, Jr. (MCA 2-4109), Ella Fitzgerald and Louis Armstrong (Verve 2-2507), Cleo Laine and Ray Charles (Victor CPL2-1831), Mabel Mercer (Liberty Music Shop L-360), Julia Migenes-Johnson (Victor ARL1-5323), Oscar Peterson and Joe Pass (Pablo 2310779), Soundtrack (Columbia OS-2016), Barbra Streisand (Columbia PL-9209), Lawrence Tibbett (Victor 18880), We Five (A&M 4111).

"Buzzard Song" was recorded by Todd Duncan with Alexander Smallens and the Eva Jessye Choir in May of 1940 (Decca 29068).

"Bess, You is My Woman Now" was recorded in May of 1940 by Todd Duncan and Anne Brown with the Eva Jessye Choir and Alexander Smallens (Decca 9069). In 1942 there was a version by Leo Reisman and His Orchestra with vocals by Helen Dowdy and Avon Long (Decca 18323). Others: Clifford Brown (Emarcy 1012), Bob Crosby (Dot DLP 3193), Miles Davis (Columbia PC-8085), Sammy Davis, Jr. (MCA 2-4109), Ella Fitzgerald and Louis Armstrong (Verve 2-2507), Tommy Flanagan (Inner City 1084), Al Haig (Seabreeze 1006), Cleo Laine and Ray Charles (Victor CPL2-1831), Mabel Mercer (Liberty Music Shop L 361), Paul Smith (Outstanding 023), Cal Tjader (Fantasy 8098, Prestige 24026), Teddy Wilson (Columbia CL603, 748, CL1318, Classic Jazz 32).

"Oh, I Can't Sit Down" was recorded by Bob Crosby and His Bobcats (Dot DLP 3193).

"It Ain't Necessarily So" was recorded in November of 1935 by the Leo Reisman Orchestra (vocal by Edward Matthews—Brunswick 7562) and in December of 1935 by Guy Lombardo and His Royal Canadians (Victor 25204). There was a March, 1936 recording by

315

Bing Crosby with Victor Young and His Orchestra (Decca 806 and 25409). In 1938 came recordings by Paul Robeson (Victor 26358) and Maxine Sullivan (Victor 26132). Martha Raye's version was released in 1939 (Columbia 35394). Todd Duncan recorded the song with the Eva Jessye Choir and Alexander Smallens in May of 1940 (Decca 29068). Others: Bronski Beat (MCA 25052), Cab Calloway (Glendale 9007), Classics IV/ Dennis Yost (Liberty LN-10221), Bob Crosby (Dot DLP 3193), Miles Davis (Columbia PC-8085), Ella Fitzgerald and Louis Armstrong (Verve 2-2507), Jascha Heifetz (RCA Red Seal LSC 3205), Ish (Geffen GHS-24095), Cleo Laine and Ray Charles (Victor CPL2-1831), Herbie Mann (Atlantic 1380), Joe Pass (Pablo 2312133), Oscar Peterson and Joe Pass (Pablo 2310779), Alec Templeton (Decca 18272), Lawrence Tibbett (Victor 11878).

"What You Want Wid Bess" was recorded in May of 1942 by Todd Duncan and Anne Brown (Decca 23250).

"I Loves You, Porgy" was recorded by Todd Duncan and Anne Brown in May of 1942 (Decca 23250). Other versions are by Stanley Clark (Elektra El-60021), Bob Crosby (Dot DLP 3193), Miles Davis (Columbia PC-8085), Sammy Davis, Jr. (MCA 2-4109), Buddy De Franco (Progressive 7014), Paul Ellingston (Ivy Jazz El-2), Frances Faye (Crescendo 92), Barbara Hendricks and Katia and Marielle Labeque (Philips 9500987), Billie Holiday (Jazz Man 5005), Cleo Laine and Ray Charles (Victor CPL2-1831), Mabel Mercer (Liberty Music Shop L 360), Helen Merrill (Inner City 1080), Phil Moore (Musicraft 15048), Oscar Peterson (Pablo 2625711), Oscar Peterson and Joe Pass (Pablo 231 0779), Paul Smith (Outstanding 023), Barbra Streisand (Columbia OC-40092), Dave Valentin (GRP 1016), Grover Washington, Jr. (Motown M5-189).

"There's A Boat That's Leaving Soon For New York" was recorded in October of 1941 by Jan Savitt and His Top Hatters (Victor 27706), in February of 1942 by Guy Lombardo and His Royal Canadians (Decca 18548) and in March of 1942 by Leo Reisman and His Orchestra (vocal by Avon Long—Decca 18282). Other versions: Bob Crosby (Dot DLP 3193), Miles Davis (Columbia PC-8085), Sammy

Davis, Jr. (MCA 2-4019), Ella Fitzgerald and Louis Armstrong (Verve 2-2507), Cleo Laine and Ray Charles (Victor CPL2-1831), Mabel Mercer (Liberty Music Shop L 362), Oscar Peterson and Joe Pass (Pablo 2310779), Andre Previn (RCA Victor LPM 1011), Ramona and Her Grand Piano (Liberty Music Shop L 19), Phoebe Snow (Columbia PC-33952).

"Oh, Bess, Oh Where's My Bess" was recorded in May of 1940 by Todd Duncan with Alexander Smallens and the Eva Jessye Choir (Decca 29068—the label reads "Porgy's Lament"). Others: Cannonball Adderly (Fantasy 9455), Bob Crosby (Dot DLP 3193), Miles Davis (Columbia PC-8085), Ella Fitzgerald and Louis Armstrong (Verve 2-2507), Andre Kostelanetz (Columbia MS6133), Cleo Laine and Ray Charles (Victor CPL2-1831), James Melton (RCA Victor Red Seal 11-9224), the Modern Jazz Quartet (Atlantic 90049-1).

"Oh, Lawd, I'm On My Way" was recorded in May of 1940 by Todd Duncan with Alexander Smallens and the Eva Jessye Choir (Decca 29068—the label reads "Finale").

265 (1-8). PORGY AND BESS: ACT I, SCENE I

Lyricist: Dubose Heyward wrote the lyrics for "Summertime," "A Woman is a Sometime Thing," "Here Come De Honey Man," "They Pass By Singin'," and "Oh, Little Stars."

Lore: In the play *Porgy*, which was written by DuBose Heyward and his wife, Dorothy Heyward, there is a passage that quotes the folk song "All My Trials." In working on the libretto for the opera, Heyward marked this section as one having musical potential and, toward that end, wrote the lyric for "Summertime" before any thought was given to the music. The music, apparently, was the first for *Porgy and Bess* that Gershwin composed. He inscribed a lead sheet of it to Gertrude Mosbacher that was dated Palm Beach 1934. (Gershwin was at the Mosbachers' residence in Palm Beach in December of 1933 and early January of 1934, working on his *"I Got Rhythm" Variations*.)

317

Rouben Mamoulian, director of *Porgy and Bess*, described the first time that George Gershwin played him the score:

> George played with the most beatific smile on his face. He seemed to float on the waves of his own music with the Southern sun shining on him. Ira sang—he threw his head back with abandon, his eyes closed, and sang like a nightingale! In the middle of the song George couldn't bear it any longer and took over the singing from him. To describe George's face while he sang "Summertime" is something that is beyond my capacity as a writer. Nirvana might be the word.

Verna Arvey, wife of composer William Grant Still, has pointed out the similarity between the opening notes of "Summertime" and those of the "St. Louis Blues" by W.C. Handy.

The contrapuntal "Crown cockeyed drunk" music that appears shortly before the "Crap Game Fugue" in Act I, Scene I, is a canon—a musical device that Gershwin was very proud of having mastered. As for the "Crap Game Fugue," it makes use of the techniques that were taught to Gershwin by musical theoretician Joseph Schillinger. Vernon Duke, discussing Schillinger with Gershwin in 1935, argued against the teacher's mathematicization of music. Gershwin, on the other hand, was delighted with the exercises that Schillinger had assigned him for homework. He liked the fact that the system gave order to the techniques that he had theretofore used only by instinct. After playing the "Crap Game Fugue" for Duke, Gershwin exclaimed, "Get this—Gershwin writing fugues! What will the boys say now?"

Analysis: The first scene of the opera takes place on Catfish Row on a summer evening. The music can be divided into the following sections:

1.   An orchestral "Introduction"—265(1)—whose first idea is a syncopated perpetual motion figure that moves in a continuous stream of sixteenth notes. The first six notes of this idea strongly resemble the "I ain't goin' nowhere" section of "Bess, You Is My Woman Now." The second subject is a seven-note percussive declamation harmonized in

318

fourths. As it is repeated, new combinations of fourths are added to make the harmony more complex and dissonant.

2. On stage a pianist, Jasbo Brown, plays what is usually referred to as the "Jasbo Brown Piano Music"—265(2). Its main idea comes from the second theme of the "Introduction," which is extended and harmonically altered. In the thirty-first bar we get, high in the treble, a portion of the music that will be Crown's motive. Then comes a barrelhouse piano-style section, followed by dancers who scat sing, while the piano music takes on ominous overtones. The seven-note motive from the "Introduction" reasserts itself and the orchestra joins in.

3. Lights fade on Jasbo Brown and the dancers, and another portion of the stage is lit, showing Clara, who is singing "Summertime"—265(3)—to her baby. This music is introduced by a gradually decrescendoing and increasingly restful orchestra, which alights on two minor sixth chords which alternate peacefully, suggesting the rocking of the baby in its mother's arms. The melody is one of those rare ones that can be beautiful a capella. On the other hand, the accompaniment would be beautiful without he tune. Together, they are heavenly. There is no verse or release, just sixteen bars. When "Summertime" is repeated, female voices join in, as does a delicate countermelody for solo violin. The peaceful orchestral coda is harmonized like a chorale.

4. The lights fade out on Clara and illuminate the crap game that is already in progress. The music here begins with a brief statement—a foreshadowing—of what will be the subject of the "Crap Game Fugue."

5. A recitativo invocation over the dice is sung in foreboding F-sharp minor by Mingo, Sporting Life and the chorus.

6. An orchestral interlude presents two of the opera's motives, both of them depicting the atmosphere of Catfish Row.

7. The crap game continues as Jake (Clara's husband) complains about unlucky dice. The music here is light and springy. it continues under much of the recitative of the gamblers and it will reappear in the second and third scenes of Act III. In the course of the game, Robbins enters and, against the protestations of his wife, Serena, joins the game.

8. A reprise of "Summertime," is sung by Clara against a countermelody by the crap shooters.

9. As a prelude to "A Woman is a Sometime Thing," a series of chords played in a crescendo (as Jake sings, "That chile ain't asleep yet") are the same chords that make up the initial swaying harmonies

of "Summertime." Jake sings "A Woman is a Sometime Thing"—265(4)—after taking the baby from Clara. Some of the extraordinary touches in this fifty-bar number: the way that the accompaniment, with rising hosannas, anticipates the entry of the chorus (on the long held note for "But"), the F-major to G-minor cadence on "sometime thing," the tranquil eight-bar release ("Yo' mammy is the first to name you"), and the extended coda on the title phrase, in which the chorus joins in, punctuated by powerful, exclamatory and polytonal chords in the orchestration.

10.   Peter, the honey man, announces his own entrance with "Here Come De Honey Man"—265(5). He is an elderly, beloved Catfish Row figure and this music is warm and consonant.

11.   Porgy's first entrance begins with the perpetual motion figure from the "Introduction." Then we hear his motive, played exultantly in E-major (the opening and closing key of the opera and the key that Gershwin associated with majesty). As Porgy sings his first words (the recitative that begins "Evenin' ladies") the orchestra gives a full reading of this motive.

12.   "They Pass By Singin'"—265(6), sung by Porgy, falls somewhere between recitative and aria and, in it, Porgy describes the loneliness of the life of a cripple. After the words "They pass by cryin'," there is a short, frenzied orchestral interjection which pressages the buzzard calls in "The Buzzard Song" of Act II. On "Night time, day time," we get the mournful music that will later introduce "Bess, You Is My Woman."

13.   Crown's and Bess's first entrance begins with a series of high energy runs. Then we hear Crown's motive—music that begins with furious high-pitched repeated notes that sound like a syncopated fire alarm and ends with a harmonically riveting and rhythmically thrilling chord sequence in the bass. With Crown's first words ("Hi boys!") the harmony somehow sums up his love of danger and, at the same time, contains a presentiment of doom. The six-note tag under "make it damn quick" will come in for much development in later scenes.

14.   Bess's first words are a contemptuous offer of Crown's liquor to the "God fearin' ladies." The music here is lush and sultry.

15.   Crown snatches the bottle away from Bess ("Oh no, you don't") and his syncopated, repeated note idea takes over as he joins the crap

game.

16. The nervous "Crap Game Fugue"—265(7)— as the gamblers start to play in earnest.

17. We hear a plaintive, sensuous cry from Bess ("Yo' woman is easy when you know the way").

18. A reprise of "A Woman is a Sometime Thing," with Porgy and Bess singing a few bars of it as a duet. Then the full chorus joins in.

19. The crap game and the "Crap Game Fugue" continue, interrupted by occasional incantations over the dice, such as Mingo's "Yo' mammy's gone and yo' daddy's happy." When Crown shoots ("Kiss rabbit foot") the six-note tag on his theme is developed in a manner marked "mysterioso." The fugue is also interrupted by the first appearance of the happy dust or "dope" theme as Sporting Life produces the powder from his hat band (at "Crown too cockeyed drunk to read 'em").

20. Peter, to a harmonically ominous reworking of his Honey Man music, cautions against the use of dope ("frien' and dice and happy dust ain't meant to associate").

21. The crap shooters tease Crown, singing a ditty as a canon ("Crown cock-eyed drunk").

22. Porgy's lyrical, somewhat ethereal "Oh, Little Stars" chant—265(8)—begins simply, in G, but it moves into E—the key that is associated with Porgy—at the end of the phrase "roll me some light." Then, on "'leven little stars come home, come home," we get the chord progression from the "got no misery" section of "I Got Plenty O' Nuttin'."

23. There is a brief return of the peaceful, cheerful dancelike music that was first heard at the beginning of the crap game, on Robbins' entrance.

24. An argument between Robbins and Crown develops when Robbins, winning a roll, sweeps up his earnings. Then, as four and sometimes five onlookers express their thoughts (each with a different melody line), the fight between Robbins and Crown begins. The orchestral accompaniment here is the "Crap Game Fugue."

25. At the moment that Robbins is killed the music stops but for a series of low, thudding E-flat dominant seventh chords over an A-natural bass, followed by a dramatic, eerie, disorienting, low F-sharp. Life has stopped—and then, suddenly, it begins again, as the fugue returns.

321

26.   Bess, in a nervous, bluesy recitative, tells Crown to get away before the police come. As she and Crown talk hurriedly about where he will go and what she will do when he is in hiding, the chord played upon the death of Robbins continues to sound low in the bass.

27.   Sporting Life tries to lure Bess to him, giving her happy dust, telling her that he can take her with him to New York. The music here, in G-minor and in alternating 5/4 and 2/4 time, is lyrical in a spooky way, with outbursts from the brass while the strings are given a haunting, compelling phrase.

28.   The fugue starts up again as Bess looks for shelter.

29.   When she is told which is Porgy's room, his motive appears briefly in the orchestra. Then, when Porgy takes her in, we are given a full orchestral version of "They Pass By Singing"—one that, passionate and emotional, still maintains its mournfulness.

265 (9-12). PORGY AND BESS: ACT I, SCENE II

Lyricist: DuBose Heyward wrote the lyrics for "Gone, Gone, Gone," "Overflow," "My Man's Gone Now," and "Leavin' For The Promise' Lan'".

Analysis: Act I, Scene III takes place in Serena's room. She is sitting at the foot of the bed and beside her are her fellow mourners. On the bed is the body of her husband, Robbins. The scene can be divided into the following musical sections:

1.   Four bars of funeral music marked Larghetto and consisting of a series of despairing, harmonically altered and enriched G-minor chords against a thudding D-note in the bass.

2.   "Gone, Gone, Gone"—265 (9)—is sung by those assembled in a slow and precise tempo—only quarter notes—like the in-sync steps of a funeral procession. The harmonies are a sequence of major and minor triads. The contrast between major and minor is particularly effective here. Note that the use of four quick chords after the first pause makes for a particularly eerie effect—just *because* all four of those chords are major. Later, at "an' he's sittin' in de garden by de

tree of life," there is a sudden, brief moment of harmonic calm via a peaceful D-flat major seventh chord. When Serena sings "Who's dat a-comin' climbin' up my steps?" the choral part becomes a slow harmonic undercurrent, rising higher and higher and continuously stoking the tension with a series of augmented chords. Porgy and Bess are coming up to Serena's room to add some money to the saucer, which has been put out for burial donations. On "Dis ain't Crown's money," the basses in the chorus begin singing "gone, gone gone" in a steady stream of quarter notes, doubling the drumbeat in the orchestra.

3.   An initial, brief version of "Overflow"—265(10)—is the first of the opera's spirituals. It is fashioned in a call and response format, with the call coming from a solo soprano (from the chorus) whose spirited singing (marked "fanatically") is an attempt to rouse the mourners out of their lethargy so that they will be more inclined to contribute toward Robbins' burial. The chorus' response of "Overflow" is built harmonically on fourths. A little later in this scene, there will be a more extended "Overflow": the two have a verse/refrain relationship.

4.   As Serena and Maria discuss the state of the burial kitty, the chorus again begins to sing "gone" with a slow, steady rising of pitch.

5.   After Serena wails, "What am I goin' do if we ain't got de money?" Porgy sings a determined recitative in which he expresses his conviction that there will beenough money to bury Robbins. In accompanying him here, the orchestra punctuates each of his phrases with a powerfully harmonized amen (D-flat seventh with an augmented ninth to D-minor).

6.   "Overflow" now becomes the opera's first full-length spiritual. Here, it is a G-minor melody that dances around the flatted fifth (D-flat)—a note that gives it its punch and its blue feel. The singing is by the chorus (written in six parts: the altos and basses are divided) and the contrapuntal interplay between the various parts creates forward motion and momentum. Above the spiritual, Porgy utters a prayer (although spoken, there are pitch indications for each of his words) to Jesus to take care of Robbins' soul.

7.   The detective enters. He, as all white people in the opera, uses the spoken rather than the singing voice. He bullies Peter into admitting that he saw Crown murder Robbins. Later, Peter is hauled off to jail as a material witness. But now, as he is being interrogated, the

uneasy underlying harmonies are the same as those chanted by the chorus on the word "gone" earlier in the scene. When Peter mentions Crown's name, the Crown motive appears low in the orchestra. Then, when the detective turns his attention to Porgy and begins to question him, we hear Porgy's theme.

8.   A recitative by Porgy ("I can't puzzle this thing out") is based on the extended version of his motive. This begins thoughtfully but, on "with his wife an' his fadderless chillen," Porgy's confusion and anger over Robbins' death and Peter's incarceration are expressed with a dramatic chord: an F–sharp dominant seventh with an augmented second. Then his rage grows steadily atop a D-minor tremolo.

9.   The chorus re-enters with its slowly crescendoing "gone"s, leading to the orchestral introduction to "My Man's Gone Now"—265(11), which is marked piu mosso ed appasionato. The melody of this aria opens with the plaintive minor third (in much the way Gershwin opened "The Man I Love" and the second piano prelude) and then makes use of the first, third, fourth, fifth and seventh notes of the E-minor scale. The meter is 3/4 but has nothing waltz-like in it. After the initial eight bars comes the first of Serena's wails. They always take her out of E-minor, as if her excessive grief has pulled her into different harmonic territory. The "Ain' dat I min' workin'" section is the first of two releases, this one with some major key relief. Upon repeating the main motive, at "Ole Man Sorrow," Serena is joined by the females in the chorus. Then comes the second release, at "Tellin' me de same thing." It is shorter than the first and leads into the concluding orchestral statement and the final, beautiful, harrowing cries of Serena with the full chorus (as the undertaker enters the room) and then of Serena alone. The spare beauty of Heyward's lyric, employing only two rhymes and making use of simple and evocative images ("Ole Man Sorrow sittin' by de fireplace") adds greatly to the effect.

10.   A recitative between the undertaker and Serena ("How de saucer stan' now my sister?") has, lying under it, the same unsettling tritone harmonies that were heard in the "Gone, Gone, Gone" music earlier in this scene.

11.   This is true also of the emphatic orchestral commentary after Serena's moving plea that Robbins' body not be allowed to end up in the hands of the medical students—and in the recitative leading up to

the spiritual, "Leavin' For The Promise Lan'."

12. "Leavin' For The Promise' Lan'"—265(12)—is introduced as a sudden break in the funereal mood. "Leavin'," the second spiritual in the opera, is begun slowly, almost tentatively, by Bess—who, as Crown's former consort, has not yet been accepted by the citizens of Catfish Row. As she sings, "Oh, the train is at the station," the orchestra delivers an amazingly train-like sound, made of harmonies built from fourths alternating with harmonies made from tritones. Like a train pulling out of a station, the music gradually accelerates. When the music come to its first pause (on "an' it's headin' for the Promise' Lan'") there is, for the first time in this scene, a feeling of serenity and well-being. After the tentativeness has disappeared and the joy of this music has swept the singers, there is an extended choral passage in which altos and basses first, then sopranos and tenors are given rhythmic variants of the main idea, followed by an ambitious contrapuntal statement by the entire chorus. When the orchestra joins them the mood has turned to exhilaration. The piece concludes orchestrally with another depiction of a train, this time as it slows down on arrival.

265 (13-19). PORGY AND BESS: ACT II, SCENE I

Lyricist: DuBose Heyward wrote the lyrics for "It Take A Long Pull to Get There." Ira Gershwin and DuBose Heyward wrote the lyrics for "I Got Plenty O' Nuttin'." Heyward wrote the lyrics for "I Hates Yo' Struttin' Style," "Woman to Lady," and "Buzzard Song." Heyward and Ira Gershwin wrote the lyrics for "Bess, You Is My Woman Now." Ira Gershwin wrote the lyrics for "Oh, I Can't Sit Down."

Lore: Re the genesis of "It Take a Long Pull to Get There": In March of 1934 Gershwin wrote Heyward:

> I would like to write the song that opens the Second Act, sung by Jake with the fish nets, but I don't know the rhythm you had in mind—especially for the answers in the chorus, so I would appreciate it if you would put dots and dashes

over the lyric and send it to me.

Heyward replied a few days later:

> If you will imagine yourself at an oar and write music to
> conform to that rhythm that will give you a better idea than
> anything I can write.

Re the creation of "I Got Plenty O' Nuttin'": A month or so
later, Gershwin, Heyward and Ira Gershwin were in the composer's
workroom in New York when Heyward said that Porgy needed something more cheerful to sing in Act I of the opera. With that in mind,
George went to the piano and in less than a minute had improvised the
main idea of what would become "I Got Plenty O' Nuttin'." Then, a
moment later, Ira blurted out a title—the title. Now it was Heyward's
turn. Up to this point, his lyrics for *Porgy and Bess* had preceded the
composer's musical settings. He asked Ira if it would be all right if he
tried his hand at fashioning words to an already existing melody. Two
weeks later, he sent the manuscript to the Gershwins from his home in
Charleston. Ira then smoothed out the rough edges.

Concerning "Bess, You is My Woman Now," some editions of
the sheet music credit Ira as co-lyricist while others credit only Heyward. That Ira did have a hand in the words is attested to by George
who, in a November 5, 1934 letter to Heyward, wrote: "Ira has written
the lyrics for Porgy and Bess' first duet and I really think this bit of
melody will be most effective." As for whether the melody did prove
to be effective, one can refer to two very opposing opinions, one expressed verbally, the other physically. The verbal opinion came from
New York music critic Lawrence Gilman, who wrote: "Listening to
such sure-fire rubbish as the duet between Porgy and Bess, 'You is My
Woman Now'...you wonder how a composer...could stoop to such easy
and such needless conquests." The physical opinion came from
Gershwin's music editor at Chappell's, Dr. Albert Sirmay. Prior to the
opera's premiere, Gershwin played the song for Sirmay and the latter,
in response, began to weep. "Doc," Gershwin said, "are you laughing?" When Sirmay said that he was not, George promptly phoned Ira
and told him to come over immediately (at that time, Ira lived across
the street). The phlegmatic lyricist, never one to bestir himself unnec-

essarily, asked why he was being summoned. "I just played the duet for the Doc," George replied, "and, Ira, he's crying!"

Analysis: Act II, Scene I of the opera takes place on Catfish Row, a month after the wake that took place at the end of Act I. This scene can be divided into the following musical sections:

1. An opening prelude that begins with decisive march rhythms. Above the march we hear one of the Catfish Row motives. This is followed by a frenetic idea, one that depicts the hustle and bustle of the wharf. The curtain still down, we hear the chimes of St. Michael's striking nine. Then the curtain rises to reveal Jake and the fishermen repairing their nets.

2. "It Take a Long Pull to Get There"—265 (13)—is a work song in which an optimistic verse in G ("Oh, I'm a goin' out to de Blackfish banks") alternates with a sorrowful and weighted down chorus in G-minor ("It Take a long pull"). It is sung by Jake, who is accompanied by a chorus of fishermen.

3. Annie reminds the fishermen about the upcoming picnic. Accompanying her is a development, mainly contrapuntal, of the Catfish Row motive heard in the opening prelude to this scene.

4. "I Got Plenty O' Nuttin" —265(14)—is called a banjo song in the score and its tempo is Moderato con gioja. It is an outburst of infectious joy—the first truly upbeat moment in the opera—and as Porgy sings it at his window, Bess is his and the gloom in his life is gone. Part of the good feeling of this song is the humor of the insistent, unchanging Gs in the bass as the simple harmonic pattern sounds above. Left out of most popular recordings, but enchanting in the opera, is the choral accompaniment, which is given its own distinctive and joyous release section ("Porgy change since dat woman come to live with he").

5. The "I Got Plenty" music continues in the orchestra as Serena tells Porgy that Bess is not the sort of woman who will stick with a cripple and that it takes a killer like Crown to keep her.

6. Sporting Life enters to a motive derived from "It Ain't Necessarily So" (which will not be heard until Act II, Scene III).

7. Maria confronts Sporting Life, blowing the white happy dust out

of his hands. When he says "Le's you and me be frien'" she launches into "I Hates Yo' Struttin' Style"—265(15)—a humorous tirade, partly spoken, with a minimal accompaniment that is mainly a jeering ostinato in the bass.

8. In a second comic sequence, a lawyer named Frazier convinces Porgy that he will have to pay extra to arrange to have Bess divorced from Crown—seeing as how they were never married in the first place. After Porgy agrees to this ("I'm a goin' to buy you a divorce") the orchestra plays, worriedly, a section from the Porgy motive. The same music appears later when Bess urges Porgy not to let the lawyer take him in. Then, as Porgy hands over his money to Frazier, the complete Porgy motive is plaintively played. "Woman to Lady"—265(16)—is the chorus' commentary on this divorce transaction.

9. The main Catfish Row motive is heard again as Alan Archdale, the only sympathetic white person in the opera, appears. Archdale tells Serena, Clara and Porgy that he is bailing Peter (the honey man) out of jail. Peter's theme is then played briefly as Porgy and the others thank Archdale for his help.

10. The "Buzzard Song"—265(17)—begins with a high-pitched trill backed by an angry clash of C-sharp and G major tonalities. A great bird has flown low and the people of Catfish Row have taken this as a portent. This is Porgy's most dramatic and despairing aria. The melody is a series of slow descents and the accompaniment consists of a dervish-like, swirling six-note grace figure that leads continually into strident, dissonant chordal pairs. It is at the "Two is strong where one is feeble" section that the aria becomes lyrical and particularly touching. Heyward's words, which express the desire of a poor and crippled man for the chance to love and be loved, is spare and powerful. There are no rhymes. Midway, there is an orchestral interlude in which the instruments give a fair imitation of a buzzard's cry. This leads to a section in which Porgy addresses the shadowy bird, angrily at first and then with pride ("Porgy who you used to feed on Don' live here no mo'"). At the conclusion, when the chorus joins Porgy in singing "Buzzard, keep on flyin'," the orchestra plays a theme that will be part of the hurricane music, to be heard later in Act II.

11. People leave the courtyard and Sporting Life and Bess are left alone. Sporting Life again tries to lure her to come with him to New

328

York, this time singing a tuneful piece ("Picnics is alright for these small town suckers") that lands midway between song and recitative. It is music that might easily have come from the *Rhapsody in Blue*.

12. When Sporting Life removes some happy dust from his hat band and tries to give it to Bess, the orchestra plays the serpentine happy dust motive against what will become the "Oh, my Porgy" section in "Bess, You is My Woman Now." Porgy then cuts off Sporting Life's persistent importuning, reaching from his window and grabbing him by the wrist.

13. "Bess, You Is My Woman Now"—265(18) —is introduced by a reprise of one of the main themes of Act I (where Jake sang, "Honey, we sure goin' strut our stuff today!") and by an instrumental passage first heard in "They Pass By Singing" in Act I. It is the principal duet between the two leads, sung first by Porgy in B-flat, then by Bess in D, then by both of them in D with Porgy given a most effective counter melody. The main melody is characterized by a minor third (on "wo" in "woman") that is made especially poignant by the B-flat grace note, which creates a catch-in-the-throat effect. It is also characterized by octave leaps down ("you is") and even greater leaps upward (a tenth on "because" in"because of sorrow of de past"). The harmony is lush and constantly in motion, making much use of suspensions. The form is A, A[1] (Porgy's solo), A (Bess' solo), B ("I ain't goin!"), A, C ("mornin' time"), A (duet), B, A, C, D ("Oh, my Porgy"), A.

14. "Oh, I Can't Sit Down"—265(19)—immediately follows "Bess, You Is My Woman Now." It is introduced by a rousing fanfare that is played not only by the pit orchestra but by an on-stage band. Then the chorus (the residents of Catfish Row) pours onto the stage singing this joyous march tune as they prepare to take a boat to Kittiwah Island for a picnic. This march is a lively rouser backed by simple, consonant harmony and its good spirits are quite infectious. There is real joy in this music, expressed at one point by a line given the piccolo, which is sent flying high above the rest of the orchestra.

15. Bess, now fully accepted on Catfish Row, is talked into leaving Porgy for the afternoon to accompany the others to the island. It is Maria who convinces her to go, in a charming recitative ("Sho'you goin'") that perfectly conveys her fondness for a woman she had previously shunned.

16.   Bess sings her goodbye to Porgy and he sings his to her. This is a brief reprise of the "Bess, You is My Woman" music. Their final goodbyes here are accompanied by tranquil orchestral triplets.
17.   As Porgy goes back to his room, he sings a reprise of "I Got Plenty O' Nuttin'."

265 (20-22). PORGY AND BESS ACT II, SCENE II

Lyricist: It was probably DuBose Heyward who wrote the brief lyrics for "I Ain't Got No Shame." Ira Gershwin was the lyricist for "It Ain't Necessarily So." Heyward wrote the lyrics for "What You Want Wid Bess."

Lore: In an early 1934 cover letter to George Gershwin (attaching two scenes from the libretto), Heyward wrote: "I have discovered for the first time a type of secular dance that is done here that is straight from the African phallic dance, and that is undoubtedly a complete survival." This was the basis for what would become "I Ain't Got No Shame," a dance that opens this scene.

As for "It Ain't Necessarily So," the music to this song came first and it demanded that the lyricist, Ira Gershwin, create an unusual limerick structure. Ira at first used "It Ain't Necessarily So" as his dummy title—a form-fitting set of syllables that had popped into his head. But then, after a couple of days spent trying to get a real title, he decided that the dummy had possibilities. George Gershwin is the one who came up with the "Wa-doo, zim bam boodle-oo" scat sounds. Ira's rhymes here ("He fought big Goliath/Who lay down and dieth") are probably the wittiest of his career. When he offered to let Heyward take credit for the song so that he could have a fifth published song (necessary for admission to ASCAP), Heyward, though touched, had to resist. "Ira," he said, "you're very sweet. But no one will ever believe that I had anything to do with that song."

John Bubbles, who played Sporting Life in the original production of *Porgy and Bess*, was one half of the famous vaudeville team of Buck and Bubbles (his partner, Ford L. Buck, played Mingo in that first production). Being a song and dance man and not a professional

330

musician, he was unable to read Gershwin's written score and that became a real problem when it came to the slow triplets of "It Ain't Necessarily So"—sung as they are against the 4/4 meter of the orchestral accompaniment. Finally, conductor Alexander Steinert came up with the idea of tap-dancing the rhythm. Quickly, then, Bubbles got the idea.

In Denmark during World War II, the Danish underground would interrupt Nazi victory claims on the radio with a recording of this song. The Nazis had closed down a 1943 production of *Porgy and Bess* in Copenhagen.

The lyrics to "What You Want Wid Bess," which contain no rhymes, preceded the music.

Analysis: Act II, Scene II takes place on Kittiwah Island, the same day. It can be divided into the following musical sections:

1.   Two African drums play an increasingly complex series of rhythms and cross-rhythms. The tempo marking is Allegretto barbaro and the time is a cross between 2/4 and 6/8. This music accompanies a wild and joyous dance by the Catfish Row residents, who have landed on the island to have a picnic.
2.   When the drum rhythms reach their highest intensity and complexity, the chorus sings "I Ain't Got No Shame"—265(20). This tune, with two prominent blue notes, is an unsubtle one and it is sung in unison by both the male and female members of the chorus.
3.   There follows a scat-sung (again, by the chorus in unison) dance in 5/4 time marked Con brio e molto barbaro, which leads directly to the amoral tenets of Sporting Life's "It Ain't Necessarily So."
4.   "It Ain't Necessarily So"—265(21)—features a catchy, serpentine melody with a comically insistent accompaniment (the continuous triplets of the melody against the determinedly 4/4 beat of the accompaniment is part of the humor). The limerick structure has the chorus taking the repetition of the opening phrase. There are two releases. The first is a wild bit of scat-singing ("Wa-doo") over an ingenious harmonic scheme that takes us into the relative major (E-flat) and through F-sharp minor, A-flat and F-minor among other tonalities, before the return to the key of the piece, G–minor. The second release

331

("To get into heaven"), also in E-flat, uses the same slow triplets that were heard in the main part of the song. This release is calmer than the first one, although its harmonic pattern is equally rich. At the end comes a melodic coda ("I'm preaching this sermon to show"), also sung in triplets.

5.   Following the song, Sporting Life dances to an orchestral reprise of the music and then he and the chorus sing the coda again. Before they can finish, however, they are interrupted by Serena, who sings "Shame on all you sinners"—a tirade against the hedonism and licentiousness that have characterized the behavior of the picnickers. In the bass of the accompaniment, as Serena is singing, we get another foreshadowing of the hurricane music.

6.   The music becomes urgent and increasingly agitated as the crowd makes haste to gather up their things and head for the boat that will take them back to the mainland.

7.   After Maria says, "Hurry up, Bess! dat boat's gettin' de whoopin' cough," there is an orchestral crescendo and then Crown whistles to Bess from the thicket. As he does so, the orchestra plays, basso, his staccato, ominous motive. What follows is Gershwin rising to the heights as the composer of a dramatic musical scene. There is the use and development of Crown's theme as an undercurrent to the interplay and rising sexual tension between Bess and Crown (as Crown sings "You bes' listen to what I gots to tell you"). There are Crown's boasts, expressed in a confident, jazzy manner ("You sho' got funny tas' in men"). There is Bess' great, moving recitative at "It's like dis, Crown, I's the only woman Porgy ever had." There is the orchestra mimicking Crown's laughter when he hears her plea.

8.   Bess, in her aria "What You Want Wid Bess"—265(22), tries to convince Crown that he should let her go back to Porgy, that she is older now, not so desirable. Yet, the sensuousness of the music tells us that she is trying to convince herself as much as she is trying to persuade Crown. The lyric here is written without rhymes. The principal melody line is based on the three notes of a B-minor triad. Because the music is in B–major, the D-natural (on "want" in the title phrase) has the quality of a blue note. But it is less that than the representation of a clash between major and minor. At "You know how it's always been with me," there is a new key, E-flat, and when the music moves

back into B (at the high note on "back" in "wanted me back"), it is a powerful moment. From this point on, including that point at which Crown joins in with a melody line of his own to make this a duet, this piece is mainly through-composed. Bess, in telling Crown that she wants to return to Porgy, does not say that she loves Porgy, only that he needs her. At the same time, the pulsating music indicates that she needs Crown.

9.   Bess finally relents and puts her arms around Crown. As he says, "Git in dat thicket," there is a return of his motive with its staccato bell-ringing and the powerful, quickening progression of chords below.

265 (23-27). PORGY AND BESS: ACT II, SCENE III

Lyricist: Ira Gershwin and DuBose Heyward wrote the lyrics for "Oh, Doctor Jesus." Heyward wrote the lyrics for the "Street Cries" ("Strawberry Woman," "Crab Man"). Ira Gershwin and DuBose Heyward wrote the lyrics for "I Loves You, Porgy."

Analysis: Act II, Scene III takes place on Catfish Row before dawn. It is a week after the Kittiwah Island picnic. The music in this scene can be divided into the following sections:

1.   The chimes of St. Michael's sound the half-hour. These are six-note chords built of fourths.
2.   A slow, contemplative and slightly ominous instrumental prelude is heard. Above it, Jake and the other fishermen say good-bye to their women as they take to their ships. The music here mixes placidity and tension, especially when one of the fishermen, Nelson, says, "It looks to me like it goin' storm today."
3.   As the fishermen move toward the gate they sing a reprise of "It Take a Long Pull to Get There." Again, at the end, there is a lovely, somewhat forlorn C to G-minor cadence, sung barbershop style.
4.   Bess, lying in Porgy's room with a fever, sings the very words ("Take yo' hands off me") that, when she was last seen, she sang to Crown. Apparently, Crown is the subject of her delirium.
5.   Peter (the Honey Man) has, per Mr. Archdale's promise, been let

333

out of jail. He sings a good natured tune ("De white folks put me in") in which he expresses his puzzlement as to why he was taken to and then released from jail.

6.   A recitativo section in which we hear Bess's feverish implorings, Peter's advice to Porgy that he take her to the white folks' hospital, and Porgy's agitated reaction to that suggestion. Running under these exchanges is a continuous return to and reshaping of the music from the instrumental prelude to this scene.

7.   Serena tells Porgy that there will be no need to send Bess to the hospital, that she, Serena, will pray for her. With that, she goes to her knees and sings "Oh, Doctor Jesus"—265(23)—not an aria or a song, but an extended recitative, sung a cappella but for a low trilled B-flat chord. Amens are sung by Porgy, Peter and Lily.

8.   After Serena confidently says, "By five o' clock dat woman goin' be well," there is another return to the tranquil, yet ominous, music of the scene's opening.

9.   The first of the street cries is "Strawberry Woman"—265(24). The words here ("Oh day's so fresh an' fine") lie above very still and spare hymn-like harmony. On the second "fine" the C-dominant seventh chord has, unobtrusively, been given a diminished fifth, making for an understated jazzy touch. Next up is Peter, whose cry ("Here come de Honey Man") was heard in Act I, Scene I. Peter, who is hard of hearing, fails to respond to the orders coming from his customers. Then comes "Crab Man"—265(25)—a cry supported by the same sort of calm, still harmony as was used to accompany "Strawberry Woman." But this tune is more assertive and confident.

10.   The chimes sound five o'clock in the morning (again, six-note chords made of fourths) and, true to Serena's promise, Bess is cured of her fever. We know that this is so when she sings a melodious eleven-note tune in C—one that is clear and sane and lyrical ("Porgy, Porgy, dat you there ain't it?").

11.   Bess appears in the doorway in her dressing gown as the orchestra wells with a few bars of "Bess, You Is My Woman." These few bars then become the basis for an exchange between Bess and Porgy in which he pre-empts her confession about having been with Crown by saying that he already knows this, that cripples such as he have an intuition where things like that are concerned, and that he forgives her.

334

The motive from "Bess, You Is My Woman" that is developed under this scene is, it becomes clear, very much the same as the perpetual motion idea of the "Introduction" to the opera.

12. A tense interchange between the two lovers in which Porgy tells Bess that she need not stay with him if she does not want to leads into "I Loves You Porgy"—265(26). The latter is a melody made from arpeggios, the first of them going up the notes of an F-eleventh chord. It is an unusually fashioned song, beginning with an eight-bar main section sung by Bess ("I wants to stay here") and then, against smokey "The Man I Love"-style harmonies, an eight-bar release ("Someday I know he's coming back"). Porgy then sings a four-bar question ("If dere war'nt no Crown, Bess, If dere was only jus' you an' Porgy, what den?"). Now comes a return of the first section, this time more fully harmonized—and this time when Bess sings it, she sings the title phrase. In the fifth section Porgy, with decisiveness and in a musical sequence that recalls the rumba theme of the *Second Rhapsody*, tells Bess that, having chosen him, she need no longer worry about Crown—but should leave Crown to him. In the final section, Porgy continues to sing this music while Bess again sings "I Loves You, Porgy."

13. A maestoso orchestral reading of Porgy's motive is followed by a return to the lyrical, contemplative music that was first heard at the beginning of this scene. As in the opening, this music becomes more and more worried and dissonant. Above it, Maria and Clara talk about the possibility of a storm.

14. Amidst trills and glissandos, the hurricane theme sounds, as does the hurricane bell. The scene concludes with the violent orchestral "Hurricane Music"—265(27).

265 (28-31). PORGY AND BESS: ACT II, SCENE IV

Lyricist: Dubose Heyward wrote the lyrics for "Oh, Hev'nly Father," "Oh, De Lawd Shake De Heavens," and "Oh, Dere's Somebody Knockin' at De Do'." Ira Gershwin wrote the lyrics for "A Red Headed Woman."

Lore: George Gershwin and Heyward were outside a Holy Rollers church in Hendersonville, South Carolina when they heard various portions of the congregation singing individual melody lines that were effective separately and even more effective together. This became the format for the six-part prayer, "Oh, Hev'nly Father," that opens this scene.

On March 19, 1934 Heyward wrote Gershwin:

> This scene [Act II, Scene IV] will give you the greatest musical opportunity of the show. I bank heavily on it to top the big effect of Act I, Scene II. The scene builds rapidly to Crown's jazz song being done against the spiritual of the crowd. I have made no effort to suggest words for these songs, because the music is the basic value. I should think that it would be best for you to work out the two tunes and musical effects, then get Ira to work with you on the words as this is a job calling for the closest sort of collaboration."

Analysis: The scene opens at dawn in Serena's room (the location of the wake in Act I) at dawn. Musically, it can be divided into the following sections:

1. The residents of Catfish Row are huddled together in Serena's room while the storm vents its fury and they sing "Oh, Hev'nly Father"—265(28)—a six–part prayer. In this music each of the solo voices sings a separate devotional recitative against the drone-like humming of the rest of the chorus. The prayers, which are in G-minor, conclude with an E chord.
2. Next comes "Oh, De Lawd Shake De Heavens"—265 (29)—another of the opera's choral spirituals and one that is as simple, melodic and homophonic as the prayer was complex and polyphonic. After this sixteen-bar melody is sung once by the chorus alone, Porgy, Clara and Sporting Life trade recitativo comments as the chorus sings it again.
3. The spiritual concludes abruptly upon a sudden burst of wind, lightning and thunder. Then comes a return of the instrumental hurri-

cane theme against strident, chromatic up and down runs.

4. Clara stands at the window with her baby in her arms, watching for her husband, Jake, who is out at sea. She sings a reprise of "Summertime"—calm music, but for a series of nervous punctuating trills.

5. At the conclusion of the lullaby the chorus continues with "Oh, De Lawd Shake De Heavens" while Porgy and Bess sing of Crown. The latter, on Kittiwah Island without shelter, will not, they conclude, survive this storm.

6. Another roar from the storm brings an orchestral frenzy which, in turn, introduces another choral spiritual, "Oh, Dere's Somebody Knockin' at De Do'"—265(30). This music is very similar to that of "Oh, De Lawd Shake De Heavens" in its consonance and lyricism. It is even simpler in form, being just thirteen bars long. As it is repeated, Peter suggests that it is Death who is knocking on the door. The others say that it may well be Death, since Peter is deaf and can hear no mortal sounds. Finally, Maria goes to the door and opens it to show Peter and the others that no one is there.

7. Now we hear Crown's music: the staccato, syncopated, bell-ringing idea above the quick drum-rolled chords. Crown enters. There follows a recitativo exchange between him, Bess, Serena and Porgy in which his singing is mocking, boastful and sometimes lightheartedly bluesy. Bess, as she tells Crown "Porgy is my man now," sings the main idea of "Bess, You is My Woman." Serena warns Crown not to insult God. Porgy stays in the background suffering Crown's insults ("Ain't dere no whole ones left?"), except to order Crown, who has grabbed Bess, to turn her loose. Beneath all this, the orchestra consistently refers to Crown's motive.

8. In the middle of Crown's boast that he and God are evenly matched ("If God want to kill me") the storm reasserts itself in a whirligig of chromatics. Then comes a reprise by the chorus of "Oh, De Lawd Shake De Heavens." Crown, continuing his bravado in the face of the storm and everyone else's fear of it, barks at them to stop their song. Then he interrupts them with one of his own.

9. This is "A Red Headed Woman"—265(31)—a lusty, bar–room ditty that is the most blatantly jazzy number in the opera (the tempo marking is tempo di Jazz). It is through-composed and quite brief—just eighteen bars long. Crown repeats it once ("But show me the red

head") and then sings it again, this time against the accompaniment of the chorus, which asks that God not make them all suffer for Crown's disrespect.

10. The sounds of the hurricane are heard again and the hurricane motive is played as Bess, having gone to the window, tells the others that Jake's boat has capsized. Clara screams Jake's name and rushes out into the storm after her husband, handing Bess her baby. Bess, against the continuous storm music, calls for someone to go after Clara and bring her back. Crown, to a stretto-style development of his motive, volunteers to do so, taking the opportunity to taunt the crippled and immobile Porgy ("Looks to me like dere ain' only one man roun' here!"). The Crown motive continues, gathering force, until the scene concludes as it began with the six-part prayer, "Oh, Hev'nly Father."

265 (32). PORGY AND BESS: ACT III, SCENE I

Lyricist: The lyrics for "Clara, Clara," were written by DuBose Heyward.

Analysis: Act III, Scene I takes place on Catfish Row the following night. It can be divided into the following musical sections:

1. "Clara, Clara"—265(32), sometimes referred to as "The Requiem," is a calm but doleful work in B-flat minor for chorus. The simple melody is made up of a series of perfect fourth falls and the accompaniment consists of a four-chord sequence, repeated over and over again in a pattern that calls to mind the left hand accompaniment that begins the composer's second piano prelude. This music is just sixteen bars long and is divided into two equal parts, the second ("Jesus is walkin' on de water") being particularly rich harmonically and eloquent. After the chorus sings this music for Clara, it proceeds to sing it for Jake who, like Clara, has been lost in the storm.

2. As the singers start to intone Crown's name to the "Clara, Clara" music—for he too is presumed lost in the storm—Sporting Life begins to laugh. Sporting Life's motive (made from "It Ain't Necessarily So") is then heard as Maria berates him for mocking the heartfelt sentiments of the mourners. His reply, to an effervescent accompanimental

338

figure, indicates that Crown is still alive. He correctly predicts what is about to happen: Porgy's slaying of Crown, Porgy's incarceration, and Bess' subsequent turn to the man who has been waiting for her all along—Sporting Life himself.

3. Bess appears at a window holding Clara's baby and she sings "Summertime." This is the last time that this music will be heard in the opera and, as if reluctant to leave it, Gershwin extends it contrapuntally.

4. Crown slips past the gate and there is the buzzing of ominous trills. Then comes the principal six-note portion of his motive and then the return of the "Crap Game Fugue" (which contains those six notes)—music first heard in Act I, Scene I. It was to this music that Crown killed Robbins and now it is heard again as Crown, who has paused under Porgy's window, is stabbed and choked to death by Porgy. With Porgy's exultant cry of "Bess, you got a man now, you got Porgy!", the orchestra plays the six notes of Crown's theme one last time and immediately follows them with a maestoso reading of Porgy's theme.

265 (33). **PORGY AND BESS: ACT III, SCENE II**

Lyricist: Ira Gershwin wrote the lyrics for "There's a Boat That's Leavin' Soon For New York."

Lore: On opening night, John Bubbles, who played Sporting Life, surprised everyone by wearing a flashy emerald-green suit in this scene. As it happened, the zipper was not working and the entrance music had to be played three times before he came out—and then he was forced to sing "There's a Boat That's Leavin' Soon For New York" with his back to the audience.

Analysis: The setting for this scene is Catfish Row on the afternoon of the day after Crown's death. The music can be divided into the following sections:

1. A flurry of frenetic sixteenth notes ushers in an instrumental introduction—one that mainly consists of music first heard in Act I, Scene I.

339

2.   The residents of Catfish Row are interviewed by the gruff, authoritarian detective (a white man) who is investigating Crown's murder. Serena's alibi for not having seen the killing is that she has been sick, and when she tells this to the detective a discordant snippet from "My Man's Gone Now"—her main aria—is quoted by the orchestra. Augmented chords are used to indicate her discomfort and they are used, in turn, to indicate the discomfort of everyone who speaks to the detective. Also effective in this recitativo section are the E-flat minor chords used for punctuation. They are tonally very distant from the keys of F-minor and F-sharp which otherwise dominate here (one of these E-flat minor chords can be heard just after Serena and the other women sing "Yes boss, we swear to that").

3.   As Bess helps Porgy to his doorstep (it is their turn to be questioned) a full reading of the Porgy motive is played by the orchestra. Porgy is not suspected of being the murderer but he is, against his protestations, taken into custody to identify Crown's body. Sporting Life tells Porgy that when a murderer confronts the body of his victim the dead man's wounds will bleed and give him away. Throughout this portion of the recitative, there is a development of Porgy's motive. When Bess advises Porgy to go with the detective but only pretend to look at Crown's body, there is a development of the "I ain't never" portion of "Bess, You is My Woman."

4.   After Porgy is taken away, Sporting Life laughingly plays on Bess' despair. Again (see section 11 of Act II, Scene I), his musical expression is melodically and harmonically reminiscent of Gershwin's writing in the *Rhapsody in Blue*, with its insouciant melancholy ("Sister, that Porgy ain't goin' be no witness now"). At one point (after "May be one year, may be two year, may be—") Sporting Life makes a gesture indicating that Porgy might be hanged. Here, the orchestra plays a weird C-ninth with a sixth and flatted fifth.

5.   As Sporting Life takes out some happy dust for Bess ("But cheer up sistuh") there is a rhythmically nervous and very twisting, winding variation on the happy dust motive. Then, as Bess succumbs to temptation, the music is derived from the triplets of "It Ain't Necessarily So."

6.   "There's a Boat That's Leavin' Soon For New York"—265(33)— is a fifty-five-bar song in AABA[1] form. It is the B section ("I'll buy

340

you de swellest mansion") that takes it beyond a thirty-two-bar format, in that this section is itself twenty-three bars long. Throughout it and the entire number are the slinky chromatic runs that characterize all of Sporting Life's music. At the conclusion of this song, a sprightly and joyful dancing figure is given to the xylophone. It, like the modal and bluesy notes of the melody, expresses the simple, amoral pleasure that Sporting Life takes in indulging in his scheme.

7.   To a sequence based on the triplets of "It Ain't Necessarily So," Bess tells Sporting Life to get away from her. Then, as she begins to reconsider his offer, we hear a discordant distortion of the opening bars of "Bess, You is My Woman Now."

8.   Sporting Life leaves the dope on Bess' doorstep and the slithering happy dust theme is played, followed by a maestoso orchestral reading of "There's a Boat."

265 (34-37). PORGY AND BESS: ACT III, SCENE III

Lyricist: It is unclear who, Ira Gershwin or DuBose Heyward or both, wrote the lyrics for "Good Mornin', Sistuh!" Ira Gershwin is credited for the lyrics to "Oh, Bess, Oh Where's My Bess" on sheet music issued separately from the score. Heyward wrote the lyrics for "Oh, Lawd, I'm On My Way."

Lore: On January 24, 1935 Gershwin wrote Todd Duncan (who had just been signed to sing the role of Porgy):

> I am leaving for Florida this weekend where I begin the task of orchestrating the opera. I just finished a trio in the last scene for Porgy, Serena, and Maria which I think will interest you very much.

According to Duncan, Gershwin wove into the counterpoint here themes from earlier sections of the opera. However, the trio section of "Oh, Bess, Oh Where's My Bess" was dropped from the show before its Boston opening.

Analysis: Act III, Scene III takes place a week later on Catfish Row. It can be divided into the following musical sections:

1. This, the final scene, begins with a long instrumental prelude, one that opens with a half-awake, dreamy nineteen-bar presentation of one of the Catfish Row motives. Then comes a reprise of the allegretto theme that was heard in Act I, Scene I and again in Act III, Scene II. It is developed here in a stretto manner. Next, in a section marked Allegretto semplice, is carefree, somewhat lethargic music meant to portray a "Sleeping Negro." It is followed by the depiction of a "man with a broom" via a jumpy but rhythmically symmetrical figure that is played against a more forceful version of the Catfish Row motive. After a brief return to the "Sleeping Negro" music, there is the portrayal of a "Man with hammer and man with saw" that contrasts a frisky idea high in the treble with a thudding, syncopated idea deep in the bass. This prelude is sometimes referred to as "Occupational Humoresque"—265(34).
2. "Good Mornin', Sistuh!"—265(35)—begins with a series of clipped phrases that travel in the chorus from the sopranos downward. The three-note "good morning" phrases sometimes sandwich an A chord between two C chords, sometimes a D chord between two B chords— and this produces a feeling of anticipation. Then, against the syncopated bass idea heard in "Man with hammer and man with saw," the chorus bursts into a lyrical "How are you dis very lovely mornin'?" A moment later, a group of children comes on stage to sing a partly puerile, partly mocking tune atop the same rhythm, "Sure to go to heaven." This music is taken over by the orchestra and becomes more exuberant. Then the chorus returns to "How are you dis mornin'?"
3. A five-bar reprise of the opera's opening introduction—the perpetual motion idea—leads to the entrance of Porgy, who has been released from jail. When he sings "Thank Gawd I's home again!" the chorus welcomes him, singing his motive in a variation made from a succession of major chords in root position. Porgy's theme is then taken up by the orchestra, as he crosses the courtyard and goes over to Maria.
4. Porgy, in his longest recitative of the opera, proceeds to hand out gifts to his friends (he won a lot of money shooting craps while in jail). This recitative begins with a harmonically modern, even atonal, sec-

tion that rises ever higher in pitch ("I keep des eyes shut in dat room"). Then comes music in a more lyrical vein ("Don't anybody let on I's home again"), leading into a presentation of Porgy's motive as his bundles are laid on Maria's table. The first of the gifts is a harmonica, which Porgy hands to one of the children, while the orchestra mimics a mouth organ. Toward the end of this section is a quote from the harmonica-like main idea of "Oh, I Can't Sit Down." The next gift is a new bonnet for Lily Holmes. It is at this point that "I Got Plenty O' Nuttin'" becomes the accompaniment to Porgy's recitative. When, unaccountably to him, his friends begin leaving (they know that Bess has left him), he tells the story of his jailhouse crap game to keep them crowding around. Porgy then calls out for Bess and now, against his recitative, the accompaniment is the "Bess You is My Woman" music. It is when Porgy sees Serena with the baby that Bess had been caring for, that he realizes that Bess is gone.

5.   "Bess, Oh Where's My Bess"—265(36), marked Andantino con molto calore, is sung solo at first by Porgy. He then sings it as a trio with Serena and Maria. As a solo it is just twenty-two-bars long. As a trio it is much extended. What is perhaps its most beautiful moment occurs at that point in the trio where Porgy sings "I counted the days"— when there is a sudden shift from E to B-flat minor that creates a great richness of feeling. This idea is developed at length and with much harmonic variety before the main idea returns, followed by an emphatic coda.

6.   In the concluding recitative of the opera, a rapid pulse develops in the orchestra via quick repeated chords and chordal patterns as Porgy learns that Bess is alive and as he states his determination to go to her.

7.   A maestoso sounding of Porgy's motive (at "Ain't you say Bess gone to Noo York?") leads into the perpetual motion theme of the opera's orchestral introduction—which, in turn, serves as the introduction to the final number, the spiritual "Oh, Lawd, I'm On My Way."

8.   The melody of "Oh, Lawd, I'm On My Way"—265(37)—begins with the notes of an E triad. The full, consonant harmony below is the same as Gershwin used for the noble slow theme of the second movement of the *Concerto in F*, also in E-major. Later, this spiritual makes effective use of the contrast between the keys of G and E (in the G-

natural to F-sharp progression under "to a heav'nly" in "to a heav'nly land" and on "there" in the concluding "you'll be there to take my hand"). After the first three bars, Porgy is joined by the chorus. There are just thirty-two bars in all.

9. The conclusion of the opera is a final grandioso orchestral statement of "Bess, You is My Woman," followed by a grandioso, reading of Porgy's motive.

266. KING OF SWING

Lyricist: Albert Stillman
Key: C
Time: Alla breve
Tempo: Moderato
Introduced by: Ford L. Buck and John W. Bubbles in *Swing is King* at Radio City Music Hall New York City on May 28, 1936.

Lore: Ira was on vacation in the West Indies and George wrote this and two other songs ("Doubting Thomas" and "I Won't Give Up Till You Give in to Me"—both as yet unpublished) with Albert Stillman. The latter was a staff lyricist at Radio City Music Hall. These were the last songs that Gershwin wrote with anyone other than his brother.

Analysis: This first post-*Porgy* Gershwin song has an atavistic, early 1920s feel in its verse ("Before what's known as the Jazz Age"), due to old-fashioned blue notes and syncopation with a ragtime feel. The refrain ("They're dancin' at the Coronation") is an outgoing rouser, one whose initial and principal idea is the harmonic jump from C to E-flat. At two points the composer may have been pointing back to *Porgy and Bess* (John Bubbles, who helped introduce "King of Swing," had played Sporting Life): In the sixteenth bar there is a major-to-minor amen phrase in the accompaniment that was heard in "The Lord Shake De Heavens," and at bar thirty-one there are accented staccato chords reminiscent of those at the conclusion of "A Woman is a Sometime Thing." In the lyric, Stillman humorously refers to a complaint that Richard Rodgers and other songwriters were making about the new swing bands ("He's got composers shoutin' murder/They say: He's killin' my song!'/But the King Of Swing can do no wrong").

Recordings: None

267. BY STRAUSS

Lyricist: Ira Gershwin
Key: F
Time: 3/4
Tempo: Tempo di Valse Viennoise
Introduced by: Gracie Barrie in *The Show is On* at the Winter Garden Theatre in New York City on December 25, 1936.

Lore: At a New York party director Vincente Minnelli heard the Gershwin brothers fooling around with a Strauss-like waltz. A few months later, in August of 1936, he wired them in Beverly Hills (they were staying at the Beverly Wilshire Hotel) with a request that they finish it up and send it to him, as he wanted to use it in a new revue. They did so, taking a day off from their work on "Hi-Ho!" for *Shall We Dance.* "By Strauss," therefore, was the last song written by George Gershwin for the Broadway stage.

Though well-received, it did not become popular until 1951 when it was sung by Gene Kelly in Vincente Minnelli's film *An American in Paris.* Some of the text was changed by the lyricist for that occasion. According to Minnelli, "By Strauss" was included in *An American in Paris* because Kelly wanted one of his dances to be a duet between himself and a little old lady and it seemed most fitting that the number be a waltz.

The song's unusually long verse (forty-three bars) disconcerted the publisher, who did not want to go to the expense of printing an extra page of music. An editor wrote Gershwin about the problem, asking if he would help her whittle the piece down. In a December 4, 1936 letter the composer replied: "It has always been my policy to give the public a lot for its money; and I think it would be a good idea to put on the title page—'This song has an extra long verse so you are getting more notes per penny than in any other song this season'...in other words, dear Selma, I would like the song printed as I wrote it, with no commas left over. Love and Kisses, George."

Analysis: The above-mentioned verse ("Away with the music of Broadway!") is a notable and melodic waltz in and of itself. Its lyric mentions a few of the great contemporary songwriters: Irving Berlin, Jerome Kern, Cole Porter and George Gershwin himself. Ira Gershwin had done something on this order before in "When Do We Dance" but then his list had only included Kern and Berlin. The phrase "Gershwin keeps pounding on tin" might be a reference to his brother's piano playing or to Tin Pan Alley or it may have been a handy way to come up with a rhyme for Berlin. The refrain ("When I want a melody lilting through the house") begins with Straussian luftpauses and continues throughout to parody its model with fond exuberance. It is thirty-six bars long and ABA^1B^1 in form, with the final section ("By Jo!") dipping for a moment into the distant key of D-flat for some extra push. It is interesting to note that "Hi-Ho!," which Gershwin was writing at this time, is also in F and also spends some time in D-flat.

Recordings: Gene Kelly's 1951 version is on the *An American in Paris* soundtrack album (MGM 93). Ella Fitzgerald's 1959 recording is on Verve 2-2525. Others: George Byron with piano accompaniment by Dick Hyman (Atlantic ALS 410), Kiri Te Kanawa (Angel DS 47454), the Longines Symphonette Society (Longines Symphonette LW 227), Shelly Manne (Discovery 909), Julia Migenes-Johnson (Victor ARL1-5323), Marni Nixon with piano accompaniment by Lincoln Mayorga (Reference RR 19-A), Joan Morris/William Bolcom (Nonesuch 71358), and Rosalind Rees/Oresta Cybriwsky (the truest to Gershwin's original piano/vocal setting—Turnabout 534638).

268. (I'VE GOT) BEGINNER'S LUCK

Lyricist: Ira Gershwin
Key: D (verse)
     G (refrain)
Time: Alla breve
Tempo: Moderato
Introduced by: Fred Astaire singing to Ginger Rogers in *Shall We Dance*, a film released by RKO on May 7, 1937.

Analysis: The words are a model of economical, memorable songwriting. In the verse ("At any gambling Casino From Monte Carlo to Reno") the singer gives two traditional examples of beginner's luck—at the gambling table and with a fishing pole. Then, in the refrain ("For I've got beginner's luck"), he gives a third and less conventional example—his own love life. The music in the verse is unhurried and sweet. Many repeated notes manage to become a graceful tune through harmonic change and a C-natural rather than the expected C-sharp on "From" in "From Monte Carlo to Reno." The melody of the refrain has a similar gentle quality; there is something lovable about it. When, in the sixth bar, the singer exclaims "Gosh I'm lucky!" the music is an exclamation too—it is outside of the key and tempo of what has been going on before. This aside then becomes the basis for the transition to the release ("Gosh I'm fortunate!"), itself a breezy, all's-right-with-the-world tune.

Recordings: Fred Astaire's version, taken from the *Shall We Dance* soundtrack, can be heard on Soundtrak STK-106. On March 19, 1937, Astaire recorded a studio version, accompanied by Johnny Green and His Orchestra (Brunswick 7855). Frances Gershwin's recording is on Monmouth-Evergreen MES 7060. Other versions recorded in March of 1937 were by Tommy Dorsey and His Orchestra (Victor 25444), Carl Fenton and His Orchestra (Variety 529), Shep Fields (Bluebird B-6878), Abe Lyman (Decca 1225), Dick McDonough and His Orchestra (American Record Company 7-05-18), and the Six Swingers (Columbia FB-1723). In April of 1937 came Artie Shaw's record (Thesaurus 389). Later versions include one made circa 1955 by Chris Connor (Atlantic 2-601), one in 1959 by Ella Fitzgerald (Verve MGV 4024), and one in 1973 by Bobby Short (Atlantic 2-608).

269. LET'S CALL THE WHOLE THING OFF

Lyricist: Ira Gershwin
Key: D (verse)
    G (refrain)
Time: Alla breve
Tempo: Allegretto
Introduced by: Fred Astaire and Ginger Rogers (on roller skates) in *Shall We Dance*, a film released by RKO on May 7, 1937.

Lore: This was the first George and Ira collaboration after *Porgy and Bess*. It was begun in New York before they left for Hollywood in August of 1936.

In *Lyrics on Several Occasions*, Ira recalled that, having worked with the sophisticated and classically trained Vernon Duke for much of 1935, he found George's new tune somewhat "thin and unimportant." Eventually, he changed his mind.

Ira Gershwin and his wife Leonore suffered the linguistic incompatibility featured in this song, Ira preferring the eether and Leonore the eyether.

Analysis: The eighteen-bar verse ("Things have come to a pretty pass") is written in a highly evolved but colloquial pop recitative style— one in which color notes are added to simple harmonic sequences to create transient and subtle emotional effects: for instance, instability, yearning and satisfaction in the "For you like this and the other/While I go for this and that" section. There is a joke in the fourth bar when on the word "flat" in "Our romance is growing flat" the singer is left stranded singing a C-sharp atop an unrelated G-ninth chord.

The refrain ("You say eether/And I say eyether") has a soft-shoe quality. Like many later Gershwin songs, it makes use of the I–vi–ii⁷–V⁷ "Heart and Soul" harmonic pattern. But Gershwin spruces this pattern up with color notes. Instead of a G-Em-Am⁷-D⁷ sequence we get G-

348

Em^9-Am^7-$D7^{-9}$. For the release ("But Oh!") he creates a sound that has real discomfort in it (a C#m7 with a diminished fifth) and it is only gradually resolved.

Recordings: Fred Astaire's *Shall We Dance* soundtrack recording is on Soundtrak STK-106. On March 19, 1937, he recorded a studio version accompanied by John Green and His Orchestra (Brunswick 7855). In later years, he recorded this song with the Grantz All-Stars (Mercury MG C-1001), with an orchestra conducted by David Rose (A/AS-1), and with an orchestra conducted by Elliot Lawrence (Daybreak DR 2009).

Other March 1937 versions were by Jimmy Dorsey (Decca 1204), Shep Fields (Bluebird B-6878), Joe Haymes and His Orchestra (Perfect 70514), Red Nichols and His Orchestra (Variety 502), and Adrian Rollini and His Orchestra (MAS 114). In April of 1937 there were recordings by Eddy Duchin (Victor 25569), Billie Holiday (Vocalion/Okeh 3520), and the Ink Spots (Decca 1251). In May of that year there was a version by Hildegarde (Columbia FB-1712), and in June there was one by Greta Keller and Brian Lawrence (Decca F-6461).

Other versions are by Michael Feinstein (Parnassus PR 0100), Ella Fitzgerald (Verve 2-2526), Ella Fitzgerald and Louis Armstrong (Verve 6-8811), Earl Hines (Classic Jazz 31), Marni Nixon with piano accompaniment by Lincoln Mayorga (Reference RR 19-A), Sarah Vaughan (Mercury MGP-2-101).

270. SHALL WE DANCE

Lyricist: Ira Gershwin
Key: C (verse)
      F (refrain)
Time: Alla breve
Tempo: Moderato (verse)
      Brightly and rhythmically (refrain)
Introduced by: Fred Astaire dancing with Harriet Hoctor in the film *Shall We Dance*, released by RKO on May 7, 1937.

Lore: George and Ira had already gone on to their next Hollywood assignment, *A Damsel in Distress,* when producer Pandro S. Berman asked them to write one more song for the just-finished film. That film, having had the tentative titles *Watch Your Step, Stepping Toes, Stepping Stones,* and *Stepping High,* was being rechristened again, this time as *Shall We Dance,* and Berman wanted a title tune.   The Gershwins complied and this song replaced "Wake Up, Brother and Dance" in the score.

A woman in Butte, Montana had apparently written a song with the same title and, though unpublished, it had received some local radio airplay.   Although RKO was not in much of a spot here (titles cannot be copyrighted) their legal department did think it best to make an out-of-court settlement: the lady was given permission to look for a publisher for her song; she was also given two free tickets to the RKO film.

In *Lyrics on Several Occasions* Ira Gershwin said that the melody of this song "brings to the listener (me, anyway) an overtone of moody and urgent solicitude."   And, in hindsight, the "time is short" theme of its lyric is poignant, inasmuch as its composer was embarking upon his last half year of life.

Analysis: The verse ("Drop that long face!") employs the syncopation pattern used in the refrain of "I Got Rhythm."   Here it is in the service of a sporty and melodic tune—one good enough to have made it as a refrain.   In the eleventh bar Ira refers to a 1932 Harold Arlen/ Ted Koehler song, "I've Got the World on a String."   The odd length of this verse, twenty-two bars, is the result of two final instrumental measures in which there is an exciting step-wise progression of chords from C to F over a C pedal point.

The thirty-two-bar refrain ("Shall We Dance") uses the same syncopation (a quarter rest followed by two dotted eighths) but it is darker and much more urgent.   Its syncopation is carried into the release ("Shall we give in to despair") while the harmony becomes more complex, even strident.   In the coda ("You'd better dance, little lady, Dance little man!") anxiety is replaced by resolve and there is strength in the final notes ("Dance whenever you can!")

350

Recordings: Fred Astaire's *Shall We Dance* soundtrack recording is on Soundtrak STK-106. On March 21, 1937 he recorded a studio version, accompanied by John Green and His Orchestra (Brunswick 7857). Other March 1937 recordings were by Abe Lyman (Decca 1225), Dick McDonough and His Orchestra (American Record Company 7-05-18), and Paul Whiteman (Victor 25552). In the early 1950s the song was done by David Craig (Citadel CT 7017). Ella Fitzgerald's version was made in 1959 (Verve 2-2525). Bobby Short's was made in 1973 (Atlantic SD 2-608). There is also a version by Frances Gershwin (Monmouth-Evergreen MES 7060).

271. SLAP THAT BASS

Lyricist: Ira Gershwin
Key: E-flat minor (verse)
      E-flat (refrain)
Time: Alla breve
Tempo: Moderato
Introduced by: Fred Astaire (tap dancing in the boiler room of an ocean liner) in *Shall We Dance*, a film released by RKO on May 7, 1937.

Analysis: The music begins with an instrumental four-bar vamp. In the film it was used as an extended prelude to this song. Then comes a vigorous twenty-two-bar verse ("Zoom-zoom! zoom-zoom! The world is in a mess!") whose arch and malevolent style recalls the "Come on, you children" verse of "Clap Yo' Hands," written a decade earlier. In the fourth bar, on the word "mess," there is a quote from "There's A Boat Dat's Leavin' Soon For New York" when the piano taps out three consecutive diminished fifths (in "There's a Boat" this moment occurs after "I'll buy you de swellest mansion").

After the verse comes an unexpected repeat of the introductory vamp. Its bass line then becomes the bass line of the refrain ("Slap that bass, slap it till it's dizzy"). This music has the same attitude as the verse but it relies more on old-fashioned blue notes, mostly minor thirds. The high point is a relaxed and very melodic release ("Dicta-

351

tors would be better off"). Other interesting moments are another self-quotation ("I Got Rhythm" is referred to in both the music and lyrics at bar twenty-four), and jazzy piano writing in both the first and second endings.

Recordings: The original performance, complete with Astaire's tapping and the ship's steam whistle, is available on Soundtrak STK-106. On March 21, 1937, Astaire recorded a studio version with John Green and his Orchestra (Brunswick 7856). Other March 1937 recordings were made by Jimmy Dorsey (Decca 1203), Joe Haymes and His Orchestra (Perfect 70514), Ike Ragon and His Orchestra (Vocalion 03513), Adrian Rollini and His Orchestra (MAS 114), and the Six Swingers (Columbia FB-1723). The Ink Spots did their version in April of 1937 (Decca 1251). Later renditions have been by Chris Connor (Atlantic 2-601), Ella Fitzgerald (Verve MGV 4027), Susannah McCorkle (Pausa 7195) and the Mike Wofford Trio (Discovery 778).

272. THEY ALL LAUGHED

Lyricist: Ira Gershwin
Key: G
Time: Alla breve
Tempo: Moderato
  (gracefully - verse)
  (happily - refrain)
Introduced by: Fred Astaire and Ginger Rogers (singing and dancing in the rooftop restaurant of a Manhattan hotel) in *Shall We Dance*, a film released by RKO on May 7, 1937.

Lore: This was one of the first of the *Shall We Dance* songs to be written and the only one written at the RKO studios. The Gershwins' office there had once been Lily Pons's dressing room.

When the brothers played this song for playwright George S. Kaufman he cut in after the references to Thomas Edison and Wilbur Wright, saying, "Don't tell me this is going to be a love song!" It was only with the line, "They laughed at me wanting you" that he realized how they had pulled it off.

Ira took the title from a famous 1920s correspondence school ad which read, "They all laughed when I sat down to play the piano."

Analysis: The verse ("The odds were a hundred to one against me") is in the pop recitativo style that characterized nearly all of Gershwin's post-*Porgy* verses. Beginning with a distinctive harmonic progression (B-flat7^{-5} to Am7 on "The odds"), it traverses twenty bars with melodic and rhythmic phrasings that take their cue from the natural inflections of speech. Its contemplative personality contrasts sharply with the brightness of the refrain ("They all laughed at Christopher Columbus"). That tune catches the ear by beginning on an eighth note after an initial eighth note rest, making for a comic effect—like stepping into rather than onto a stair. Gershwin then produces a very singable melody, backed by the elementary I-vi-ii-V7 progression that was the point of departure for so many of these, his final songs. This harmony becomes richer and more subtle as the refrain continues. Some other points of interest: the rhythmically tricky piano fill after bar six (after "recorded sound"), the smart progression of ninth chords in bars fifteen and sixteen ("It's the same old cry"), the surprise second ending ("He, He, He!") which begins abruptly in far-off E-flat and then, breezily, works its way back to a home key finish.

Recordings: Fred Astaire's original performance, taken from *Shall We Dance*, is on Soundtrak STK-106. On March 18, 1937 he recorded a studio version with Johnny Green and His Orchestra (Brunswick 7856). In later years, Astaire recorded this song with the Grantz All-Stars (Mercury MG C-1001), with an orchestra conducted by Pete King (Kapp KL-1165), with an orchestra conducted by David Rose (Choreo A/AS-1) and with an orchestra conducted by Elliot Lawrence (Daybreak DR 2009).

The week that Astaire was making his record with Johnny Green, a number of other bands were setting down their versions. On March 10, 1937 came a recording by Tommy Dorsey and His Orchestra (Victor 25544). On March 12 it was Ozzie Nelson and His Orchestra (vocal by Ozzie—Bluebird B-6873). On March 13 it was Nat Bran-

353

dywynne and His Stork Club Orchestra (American Record Company 7-05-16) and Tommy Dorsey and His Orchestra (Decca 1204). On March 14 it was Red Nichols and His Orchestra (Variety 502). Harry Richman recorded the tune in July (Columbia DB-1711).

Other versions have been by David Allyn (Discovery 916), Rosemary Clooney (Concord Jazz 112), Michael Feinstein (Parnassus PR 0100), Ella Fitzgerald (Verve 2-2525), Yehudi Menuhin/Stephane Grappelli (Angel DS-37860), Joan Morris/William Bolcom (Nonesuch 71358), Andre Previn (RCA Victor LPM 1011), Frank Sinatra (Reprise 3FS-2300), Sarah Vaughan (Mercury MGP-2-100).

273. THEY CAN'T TAKE THAT AWAY FROM ME

Lyricist: Ira Gershwin
Key: E-flat
Time: Alla breve
Tempo: Moderato (lightly) (verse)
Slowly, with warmth (refrain)
Introduced by: Fred Astaire (singing to Ginger Rogers on a ferry boat from New Jersey to Manhattan) in *Shall We Dance*, a film released by RKO on May 7, 1937. Astaire later danced it in the film with Harriet Hoctor; it was not until the 1949 picture *The Barclays of Broadway* that he danced it with Rogers.

Lore: On October 24, 1936 George Gershwin wrote a friend, "Ira and I have written a song called 'They Can't Take That Away From Me' which I think has distinct potentialities of going places." The composer's high opinion of this song was later attested to by conductor and fellow songwriter John Green:

> When George wrote the songs for *Shall We Dance*, I made arrangements of them and accompanied Fred Astaire's recordings for Brunswick with my orchestra. I remember vividly when I brought the test pressings for George and Ira to hear. I went to 1019 [North Roxbury Drive] and, as I recall, Lee [Ira's wife], Ira, George and George's mother

354

were there. I put the recordings on and when George heard "They Can't Take That Away From Me," he broke down, reached his hand out to me, and came close to tears. He kept saying "Thank you" and I don't know why. That song must have meant something special to him.

Deeply felt as it was as a finished composition, the song had begun as a playful parody of the victory motto from Beethoven's *Fifth Symphony*. Beethoven used three Gs and an E-flat and Gershwin had turned the theme upside down by playing three E-flats and a G. It was Ira who suggested that two additional E-flats be added for rhythmic variety. Thus, the opening phrase: five E-flats and a G.

During this period Gershwin was a frequent visitor at Harold Arlen's house and he invariably played this song at Arlen's piano. On one such occasion, he was especially delighted when Arlen's wife Anya sang an improvised eight-bar contrapuntal melody to the tune.

"They Can't Take That Away From Me" was nominated for an Academy Award in 1937 but lost out to "Sweet Leilani" (a song by Harry Owens).

Analysis: In the verse ("Our romance won't end on a sorrowful note") the singer acknowledges that he has lost his friend/lover for good and, although far from happy about this, he chooses not to pro-test—certainly an unusual attitude to take in a popular song. The music is urgent: in the fifteenth bar, on "though" in "But though they take you from me," the singer holds a D-natural against an A-flat ninth chord and the result is a disoriented other-worldliness, such as comes to one who is all of a sudden romantically adrift. There is no stated reason for the breakup but the choice of the word "they" as opposed to "he" or "she" implies that the singer's partner has been taken not by a rival but by some impersonal or collective force.

In the refrain ("The way you wear your hat") the singer proceeds to list the endearing quirks of his or her friend—the tilt of the hat, the smile—to music that possesses all of the verse's urgency and, in addi-tion, an innate, graceful swinging beat. It is filled with wonderful moments. For instance, in the first statement of the pick-up phrase ("The way you wear your") a lone bass note appears in the left hand of the accompaniment. The second time this pick-up phrase comes around there are two bass notes—making for a fledgling phrase that adds a little bit of momentum. Then, when the pick-up phrase comes around the third and final time, two more notes are added in the bass, and the phrase is now complete. In the same way, the second appearance of the "No, no! They" exclamation is made more powerful than the first by use of new chords (E-flat^{11}, E-flat^6, E-flat^7) that pack great cumulative power. Two bars later the title phrase is repeated one last time, to a pastoral chorale-like coda that is one of the most moving moments in pop song literature.

Recordings: Fred Astaire's original performance from *Shall We Dance* is on Soundtrak STK-106. On March 14, 1937, Astaire recorded a studio version with Johnny Green and His Orchestra (Brunswick 7855). In a September 8, 1937 George Gershwin memorial concert, Astaire sang the song to the accompaniment of the Los Angeles Philharmonic Orchestra, Victor Young conducting (Citadel CT 7025). In later years, he recorded this song with the Grantz All Stars (Mercury MG C-1004), with an orchestra conducted by Pete King (Kapp KL-1165), with an orchestra conducted by David Rose (Choreo A/AS-1), and with an orchestra conducted by Elliot Lawrence (Daybreak DR 2009).

On March 12 of 1937, two days before the above-mentioned Astaire/Green record, a version was set down by Ozzie Nelson and His Orchestra (vocal by Ozzie—Bluebird B-6873). On March 13 came one by Nat Brandwynne and His Stork Club Orchestra (American Record Company 7-05-16). Then came versions by Jimmy Dorsey and His Orchestra on March 17 (Decca 1203), Tommy Dorsey and His Orchestra on March 20 (Victor 25549), and Carl Fenton and His Orchestra on March 24 (Variety 529). On April 1, 1937 Billie Holiday and Her Orchestra did their rendition (Vocalion/Okeh 3520). Then came recordings by Hildegarde on May 20, 1937 (Columbia FB-1712), Greta Keller and Brian Lawrence on June 24, 1937 (Decca F-6461), and Count Basie and His Orchestra on June 30 of that year (CBS C3L-21).

There were recordings in 1938 by Herman Chittison (Swing 58), in 1939 by Connie Boswell (Decca 2879), in 1945 by Betty Jane Bonney (Victor 20-1678), in 1947 by Anita Ellis (Mercury 3068), in 1950 by Percy Faith (Columbia 38862), in 1953 by Billy Taylor (Prestige 796), in 1959 by Ella Fitzgerald (Verve 2-2525), and in 1973 by Bobby Short (Atlantic 2-608).

Others: Ruby Braff/George Barnes Quintet (Concord Jazz 5), Al Caiola (Bainbridge 1010), Carmen Cavallaro (MCA 2-4056), Rosemary Clooney (Concord Jazz 112), Chris Connor (Atlantic 2-601), Bing Crosby (Decca DC-5081), Ray Conniff (Columbia CK-40214), Michael Feinstein (Parnassus PR 0100), Ella Fitzgerald (Pablo 2308234 and 2310711), Ella Fitzgerald/Louis Armstrong (Verve 6-8811), Dizzie Gillespie (Crescendo 9006 and Savoy 2209), Barbara Hendricks and Katia and Marielle Labeque (Phillips 9500987),

Duke Jordan (Prestige 7849), Peggy Lee (MCA 2-4049), Yehudi Menuhin/Stephane Grappelli (Angel DS-37860), Julia Migenes-Johnson (Victor ARL1-5323), Anita O'Day (Glendale 6000), Charlie Parker (Verve VE-2512 and Verve UMV-2562), Joe Pass (Pablo 2312109), the Sonny Rollins Quintet (Prestige OJC-214), Artie Shaw (Victor AXM2-5580), Frank Sinatra (Capitol N-16112, Reprise FS-1005, and Reprise FS-1015)

Keely Smith (Fantasy 9639), Joanie Sommers/Bob Florence (Discovery 887), Supersax and L.A. Voices (Columbia FC-39925), Art Tatum (Pablo 2310789), Mel Torme (Glendale 6018), and Mary Lou Williams (Crescendo 9029).

274. WAKE UP, BROTHER, AND DANCE

Lyricist: Ira Gershwin
Key: D
Time: Alla breve
Tempo: Allegro moderato
Introduced by: Kevin Cole in a 1985 piano solo recording (see below).

Lore: This song was dropped from *Shall We Dance* in favor of the title tune (the title of the movie was arrived at late in the game, the film having been called *Watch Your Step* at first). It finally appeared in 1964 in the Billy Wilder film *Kiss Me, Stupid*. But now its title was "Sophia" and it had been rewritten lyrically and restructured musically (see "Sophia").

Analysis: The melody of the twenty-six-bar verse ("Crash those cymbals!") is characterized by sets of staccato repeated notes tapped out as if in Morse Code. These sets are interrupted by a jazzy instrumental motive that contrasts B-flat and D-flat sounds over a thumping D bass. The sound of B-flat is heard again in the second and concluding section ("That's what it takes") as the song heads back into D for the refrain ("If the goblins have got you"). The latter is syncopated in the "I Got Rhythm" style but it has a Latin flavor. When played at a moderate tempo it sounds a bit like mariachi music (the composer had vacationed in Mexico at the end of 1935).

Recordings: In 1985 pianist Kevin Cole made the first and, so far, the only recording of this piece. On his first run-through, he plays directly from the sheet music and with the breezy ragtime feeling of the Gershwin piano rolls (Fanfare DFL 7007).

275. A FOGGY DAY

Lyricist: Ira Gershwin
Key: F
Time: Alla breve
Tempo: Moderato (verse)
　　　　 Brighter but warmly (refrain)
Introduced by: Fred Astaire (in the fog on the grounds of Totleigh Castle) in *A Damsel in Distress*, a film released by RKO on November 19, 1937.

Lore: George had come back to his and Ira's Beverly Hills residence after a party and at about one in the morning he sat down at the piano and asked Ira if he had any song ideas. Since the movie they were working on was set in London, Ira suggested doing something about a foggy day in London town. Less than half an hour later, they had finished the refrain. The verse was written quickly too, but on the following day. Ira suggested doing something with a wistful Irish quality and George improvised the delicate and atmospheric verse.

Analysis: The music begins with the sound of early morning chimes, played quietly and up high in the treble. Then comes a sixteen-bar verse ("I was a stranger in the city"), one of the composer's finest and most expressive. It has the recitativo style of his late verses—which is to say that it has the intimacy of conventional speech and, at the same time, an insistent, graceful melody. In the tenth bar, on "blue" in "The outlook was decidedly blue," we are given not a blue note as such but a sound—a major ninth chord—that is blue by virtue of the stillness that it creates. In the refrain ("A foggy day in London town") Gershwin uses harmonic minutia to create subtle and cumulative emotional effects. For instance, on the third word he switches from the initial major tonality to a minor sixth chord. He returns to the major four syllables later (on "town") but chips away at it by flatting the ninth of the chord. Then the minor seventh on the third syllable of the next phrase ("low" in "had me low") is quickly altered, becoming a more disquieting minor sixth. Five bars later there is another little slide from major to minor on the word "alarm." The heart of the piece occurs in the twenty-fifth bar on the word "suddenly" where the melody, in reaching its highest note, all but cries out. The resolution is a simple chorale ("and through foggy London town"), as had been the case at the close of "They Can't Take That Away From Me." The song ends as it began: with a succession of five-note chords played high in the treble. They sound like a cross between wind chimes and the tolling of Big Ben.

Recordings: Fred Astaire's original rendition from *A Damsel in Distress* can be heard on Curtain Calls 100/19. On October 17, 1937, Astaire recorded a studio version with Ray Noble and his Orchestra (Brunswick 7982). Later versions by Astaire were with the Grantz All-Stars (Mercury MG C-1004), with an orchestra conducted by David Rose (Choreo A/AS-1), with an orchestra conducted by Pete King (Kapp KL-1165), and with an orchestra conducted by Elliot Lawrence (Daybreak DR 2009).

Preceding Astaire to the recording studio were Vincent Lopez and His Orchestra on September 7, 1937 (American Record Company 7-12-01), Hal Kemp on September 8 (vocal by Skinny Ellis—Victor 25685), and Shep Fields on September 15 (Bluebird B-7195). Bob Crosby recorded the song on November 5, 1937 (Decca 1539) and Gracie Fields did her version in January of 1938 (Rex 9237). There were subsequent recordings in 1950 by Les Brown (Columbia 38878) and Henry Jerome (London 359), in 1954 by Ralph Sharon (London 1453), in 1959 by Ella Fitzgerald (Verve 2-2525), and in 1973 by Bobby Short (Atlantic SD 2-608).

Others: Count Basie (MCA 2-4163), the Dave Brubeck Quartet (Milestone 24728), Charlie Byrd (Savoy 1131), Al Caiola (Bainbridge 1012), Rosemary Clooney (Concord Jazz 47), Chris Connor (Atlantic 2-601), Lenny Dee (MCA 2-4042), Roy Eldridge (Verve 2-2531), Ferrante & Teicher (Liberty LN-10261), Ella Fitzgerald/Louis Armstrong (Verve 6-8811), Ella Fitzgerald/Joe Pass (Pablo 2310702), Judy Garland (Carnegie Hall concert—Capitol SWBO-1569), the Red Garland Trio (Prestige OJC-126),

Corky Hale (Crescendo 9035), Earl Hines (Everest 356), Hank Jones (Jazz Man 5028), Barney Kessel (Contemporary OJC-238), Vic Lewis (Esquire 10-174), Jackie McLean (Prestige 7757), Marion McPartland (Savoy 22481), Yehudi Menuhin/Stephane Grappelli (Angel SQ-37533), Charles Mingus (Atlantic 8809, Fantasy 86009, Prestige 24010), Alfred Newman (Majestic 20010), Joe Pass (Pablo 2312133),

The Oscar Peterson Trio (Pausa 7059), Bud Powell (Verve 2526), Jimmy Rainey (Prestige OJC-1706), Artie Shaw (Victor AXM2-5579), Frank Sinatra (Capitol N-16112, Reprise FS-1001), Paul Smith/Bellson & Brown (Outstanding 009), Art Tatum (Pablo 2310887), Sarah Vaughan (Mercury MGP-2-101), John Williams (Columbia FM-42119), and Lester Young (Verve 2-2516).

276. I CAN'T BE BOTHERED NOW

Lyricist: Ira Gershwin
Key: G
Time: Alla breve

Tempo: Moderato con spirito

Introduced by: Fred Astaire (singing and dancing on a busy London Street—he does not sing the verse) in the film *A Damsel in Distress*, released by RKO on November 19, 1937.

Lore: Gershwin's manuscript books show that he wrote this tune twice, first on February 23, 1937 and again on March 28, 1937.

Analysis: For twelve bars the verse ("Music is the magic that makes ev'rything sun-shiny") expresses a simple joie de vivre. Then (at "turning" in "I don't care if this old world stops turning") a sudden gust of excitement is created by a series of I–V^7 cadences, first in the highly unexpected key of E-flat, then in F-sharp, and then in A. Eventually we are led to a D^7—the V7 chord of the home key of G.

The refrain ("Bad news, Go 'way!") uses step-wise writing to build gradually towards a climax, with each successive phrase coming to rest on a higher note. But this music is not out to express any great drive or forward propulsion. Instead, it has a carefree feel that is in keeping with the title and the lyric. This is especially so in the lilting release ("I'm up above the clouds"), in which the singer is given a high F-natural above a C-ninth chord—a dissonance that creates an appropriately ethereal sound. The refrain is AA^{1}BA^2 and thirty-eight bars long. The unusual length is due to the fact that each successive A section is two bars longer than the one before: eight, ten and twelve bars, respectively.

Recordings: Fred Astaire's original performance from the *A Damsel in Distress* soundtrack is on Curtain Calls 100/19. On October 19, 1937, Astaire made a studio recording with Ray Noble and his Orchestra (Brunswick 7982). Preceding Astaire in the studio were Art Kassell and His "Kassels-in-the-Air" on September 21, 1937 (Bluebird B-7196), and Gene Kardos and His Orchestra on October 15, 1937 (American Record Company 8-01-06). Ella Fitzgerald recorded this song in 1959 (Verve 2-2525). The New Rhythm Boys and Tommy Tune recorded it in 1983 (on the *My One and Only* cast recording—Atlantic 80110-1-E).

Other versions are by Chris Connor (Atlantic 2-601), Teddi King

(Inner City 1044), the New Mayfair Orchestra conducted by Ben Frankel (His Master's Voice B.D. 486) and Helen Merrill (Inner City 1080).

Analysis: For twelve bars the verse ("Music is the magic that makes ev'rything sun-shiny") expresses a simple joie de vivre. Then (at "turning" in "I don't care if this old world stops turning") a sudden gust of excitement is created by a series of I–V^7 cadences, first in the highly unexpected key of E-flat, then in F-sharp, and then in A. Eventually we are led to a D^7—the V7 chord of the home key of G.

The refrain ("Bad news, Go 'way!") uses step-wise writing to build gradually towards a climax, with each successive phrase coming to rest on a higher note. But this music is not out to express any great drive or forward propulsion. Instead, it has a carefree feel that is in keeping with the title and the lyric. This is especially so in the lilting release ("I'm up above the clouds"), in which the singer is given a high F-natural above a C-ninth chord—a dissonance that creates an appropriately ethereal sound. The refrain is AA^{1}BA^2 and thirty-eight bars long. The unusual length is due to the fact that each successive A section is two bars longer than the one before: eight, ten and twelve bars, respectively.

Recordings: Fred Astaire's original performance from the *A Damsel in Distress* soundtrack is on Curtain Calls 100/19. On October 19, 1937, Astaire made a studio recording with Ray Noble and his Orchestra (Brunswick 7982). Preceding Astaire in the studio were Art Kassell and His "Kassels-in-the-Air" on September 21, 1937 (Bluebird B-7196), and Gene Kardos and His Orchestra on October 15, 1937 (American Record Company 8-01-06). Ella Fitzgerald recorded this song in 1959 (Verve 2-2525). The New Rhythm Boys and Tommy Tune recorded it in 1983 (on the *My One and Only* cast recording—Atlantic 80110-1-E).

Other versions are by Chris Connor (Atlantic 2-601), Teddi King (Inner City 1044), the New Mayfair Orchestra conducted by Ben Frankel (His Master's Voice B.D. 486) and Helen Merrill (Inner City 1080).

277. THE JOLLY TAR AND THE MILK MAID

Lyricist: Ira Gershwin
Key: A-minor (verse)

F (refrain)
Time: 6/8
Tempo: Allegretto scherzando
Introduced by: Fred Astaire, Jan Duggan, Mary Dean, Pearl Amatore, and Betty Rone in *A Damsel in Distress*, a film released by RKO on November 19, 1937.

Lore: On May 12, 1937 Gershwin wrote a letter to Isaac Goldberg (the author, in 1931, of the first Gershwin biography). In it he complained that his and Ira's songs for *Shall We Dance* had been poorly showcased. He also complained that the only two singers in the film had been Fred Astaire and Ginger Rogers. "In our next picture," he wrote, "'Damsel in Distress,' we have protected ourselves in that we have a madrigal group of singers and have written two English type ballads for background music so the audience will get a chance to hear some singing besides the crooning of the stars." As it turned out, Astaire did join in the singing of this tune, although he was not involved in the performance of the other madrigal, "Sing of Spring."

In 1976 "Sing of Spring" saw publication for the first time. At that time it and "The Jolly Tar and the Milk Maid" were published by Lawson–Gould, Inc. (of New York) in Gershwin's original version, which was for a four–part chorus of mixed voices with piano accompaniment. This version of "The Jolly Tar," unlike the piano/vocal edition published in 1937, ends with an attractive five–bar *vocalise* (see recordings).

Analysis: The verse ("There was a Jolly British Tar who met a milk maid bonny") has two stanzas. In the first the sailor asks the lady to marry him, while in the second he changes his mind, having recalled that he already has wives in Kerry, Spain and Timbuctoo. The music has a convincing minstrel feel. It is a bouncy twenty-two-bar tune in 6/8 that is introduced by a pleasant high register piano introduction and vamp.

In the refrain ("'Our hearts could rhyme,' said she") the singers, again in separate stanzas, consider the possibility of a romance—but decide against it for the sake of their spouses and children. The music here has the same springy minstrel character as the verse, but it is in the relative major, F. Its structure is odd: after a brief, four-bar idea (ending with "'Tis flattered I'm,' said she") there comes a one-bar idea ("'But oh, ah me'") that goes through a fifteen-bar long series of false endings and hesitant extensions. This makes for a playfully indecisive quality, one that matches the attitude of the flirting couple. The second time around the refrain is not nineteen but twenty-five bars long, having been given a harmonically inventive coda.

Recordings: In 1976 Gershwin's original version for mixed chorus and piano was recorded by Catherine Aks and Jeffrey Meyer (Turnabout TV-S 34638). Other versions are by George Byron with piano accompaniment by Bobby Tucker (General 4014), and the New Mayfair Orchestra conducted by Ben Frankel (His Master's Voice B.D. 486).

278. NICE WORK IF YOU CAN GET IT

Lyricist: Ira Gershwin
Key: G
Time: Alla breve
Tempo: Moderato
Introduced by: Fred Astaire, Jan Duggan, Mary Dean, and Pearl Amatore in A Damsel in Distress, a film released by RKO on November 19, 1937.

Lore: George first jotted down the core of this tune in July of 1930. In his notebook it appears after "Garçon, S'il Vous Plait" and before "Posterity is Just Around the Corner" (both from *Of Thee I Sing*). At that time the tune was just nine bars long and it was fitted with the words, "If the truth you're telling, then I'm yelling there's no stopping us now." The last five words were the working title. Six years later the composer retrieved this from his notebook and got to work on it. As for a new lyric, Ira had seen a cartoon by George Belcher that had one woman telling another that a third lady's daughter had become a whore. To this the second had replied, "It's nice work if you can get it."

Analysis: In the twenty–bar verse ("The man who only lives for making money") we are told not to count on achieving wealth or fame, but to realize that "the only work that really brings enjoyment/Is the kind that is for girl and boy meant." The music begins playfully but, in the fifth bar (on "Likewise") we are given a B7$^{\#5}$ chord—the first of the strange sounds with which Gershwin will pepper this piece. This chord appears again at the beginning of the refrain ("Holding hands at midnight") and it is followed by a succession of weird sounds, a sequence based on the simple cycle of fifths pattern but with spooky alterations. Had this sort of harmony been allowed to continue much longer the effect would have been quite disconcerting. However, at the title phrase, the harmony becomes conventional and the melody turns frisky and playful. The release ("Just imagine someone"), beginning at bar seventeen, is a dark and rhythmic excursion into the harmonic minor and it presents additional eerie sounds when, on "some" in "someone," a diminished fifth and a ninth are added to a C7 chord, and at "more" in "Who could ask for anything more?", when we get an F#7^{-5} chord with the diminished fifth in the bass. In the latter phrase the Gershwins are referring to their "I Got Rhythm," as they had a few months earlier in "Slap That Bass."

Recordings: Fred Astaire's original performance from the *A Damsel in Distress* soundtrack is on Curtain Calls 100/19. On October 19, 1937, Astaire made a studio recording with Ray Noble and His Orchestra (Brunswick 7983). In later years, he recorded this song with the Granz All-Stars (Mercury MGC-1002) and with an orchestra conducted by David Rose (Choreo A/AS-1). In September of 1937 there were recordings by Shep Fields (Bluebird B-7195) and Vincent Lopez and His Orchestra (American Record Company 7-12-01). In October of that year there were versions by Tommy Dorsey (Victor 25695) and Maxine Sullivan (Vocalion/Okeh 3848). In November there were renditions by the Andrews Sisters (Decca 1562), Bob Crosby (Decca 1539), the Benny Goodman Trio (Columbia ML-4590), and Teddy Wilson and His Orchestra (Brunswick 8015).

There were recordings by Edythe Wright in 1938 (Victor 25695), May Ann McCall in 1949 (Discovery 512), Thelonious Monk in 1951 (Blue Note 1575), Bud Powell in 1951 (Roost 521), the Swedish All-

365

Stars in 1952 (Musica 9215), and by Ella Fitzgerald in 1959 (Verve 2-
Others: Ruby Braff/George Barnes Quintet (Concord Jazz 5),
Charlie Byrd (Concord Jazz 82), Al Caiola (Bainbridge 1012), Rose-
mary Clooney (Concord Jazz 112), Chris Connor (Atlantic 2-601), Vic
Dickenson (Vanguard VSD-99/100), Ella Fitzgerald (Columbia PG-
32557), Barbara Hendricks and Katia and Marielle Labeque (Phillips
9500987), the Hi-Lo's (MCA 2-4171), Earl Hines (Everest 246), Billie
Holiday (Columbia PG-32127, Columbia PC-36811, Verve 2-2515),
Art Lande (1750 Arch Records 1769), Peggy Lee (Glendale 6023),

Carmen McRae (51-West Records 16075, MCA 2-4111), Yehudi
Menuhin/Stephane Grappelli (Angel 37156), Julia Migenes-Johnson
(Victor ARL1-5323), Joan Morris/William Bolcom (Nonesuch 71358),
Marni Nixon with piano accompaniment by Lincoln Mayorga (Reference RR 19-A), Joe Pass (Pablo 2312133), Andre Previn (RCA Victor
LPM 1011), Arnold Ross (MoodMusic 9), Frank Sinatra (Reprise FS-
1015), Frank Sinatra/Count Basie (Reprise 1008), Paul Smith (Outstanding 004), Sonny Stitt (Prestige 7585), Twiggy (from the *My One
and Only* cast recording—Atlantic 80110-1-E).

279. STIFF UPPER LIP

Lyricist: Ira Gershwin
Key: E-flat
Time: Alla breve
Tempo: Moderato (with humor)
Introduced by: Gracie Allen in *A Damsel in Distress*, a film
    released by RKO on November 19, 1937.

Lore: In the film, Gracie Allen sings this after she, George
Burns and Fred Astaire arrive at the bottom of a fun house slide. In the
ensuing dance, Fred and Gracie do one of the manic and silly run-
around dances that had long been the trademark of Fred and Adele
Astaire (see "Swiss Miss" and "The Babbitt and the Bromide").

Analysis: The verse ("What made good Queen Bess/Such a
great success?") is a flip little survey of Britons who relied on the title

366

phrase. It is twenty bars long, through-composed, and it takes a not unexpected dip into G-minor before working its way back toward E-flat. The refrain ("Stiff Upper Lip! Stout fella!") is a compendium of British locutions (pip-pip, dash it all, keep muddling through) set to a jaunty and not very ambitious tune. Its main musical interest occurs in the release ("Carry on through thick and thin") where Gershwin provides an effective series of harmonic suspensions. The form is AA^1BA^2C and the length is thirty-two bars.

Recordings: The original performance from the *A Damsel in Distress* soundtrack is on Curtain Calls 100/19. Other versions are by Kaye Ballard (Citadel CT 7017), Ella Fitzgerald (Verve 2615063), the New Mayfair Orchestra conducted by Ben Frankel (His Master's Voice B.D. 486), John McGlinn and the New Princess Theater Orchestra (EMI Digital CDC-747977 2).

280. THINGS ARE LOOKING UP

Lyricist: Ira Gershwin
Key: D (verse)
      G (refrain)
Time: Alla breve
Tempo: Moderato e cantabile
Introduced by: Fred Astaire (on the downs of Totleigh Castle) in *A Damsel in Distress*, a film released by RKO on November 19, 1937.

Analysis: The lovely twenty-bar verse ("If I should suddenly start to sing") is in a free-form pop recitative style. Its initial idea is repeated in a new key (F-major) at bar twelve (at "The long, long ages of dull despair") but it is otherwise through-composed. The refrain ("Things are looking up!") begins with two ten–rather than eight–bar phrases, making for an overall length of thirty-six bars. It is a very graceful tune that, though more melodically defined and rhythmically emphatic than the verse, has some of the same attitude of free association. There is an extraordinary eight-bar release in B-minor ("See the sun beams!")—dark and rhythmic with a feeling of power and inevitability. And there is an unusual coda ("Oh, I'm happy as a pup")—one with a harmonic sequence that would be disorienting but for the downward, roosting path of the melody line.

Recordings: Fred Astaire's original performance, taken from the *A Damsel in Distress* soundtrack, is on Curtain Calls 100/19. On October 17, 1937 Astaire recorded a studio version with Ray Noble and His Orchestra (Brunswick 7983). In September of 1937 there were records by Art Kassell and His "Kassells-in-the-Air" (Bluebird B-7196) and Hal Kemp (Victor 25685). Gene Kardos and His Orchestra did their version in October of that year (American Record Company 8-01-06) and Teddy Wilson's came in November (Brunswick 8015). Other versions have been by Ella Fitzgerald (Verve 2-2525), Kiri Te Kanawa (Angel 0547454), Bernie Leighton (Key 643), and New Mayfair Orchestra conducted by Ben Frankel (His Master's Voice B.D. 486), Artie Shaw (Victor AXM2-5580), Sarah Vaughan (Mercury MGP-2-101).

281. I LOVE TO RHYME

Lyricist: Ira Gershwin
Key: G
Time: Alla breve
Tempo: Moderato con spirito
Introduced by: Phil Baker (accompanying himself on the accordion) and Edgar Bergen (and Bergen's puppet Charlie McCarthy) in *The Goldwyn Follies*, a film released by Goldwyn-United Artists on February 23, 1938. In the film, this performance is constantly interrupted by comic patter and the song is never sung all the way through.

Analysis: The title seems to promise a series of virtuoso rhyming stunts but, instead, we get something less ambitious. There are, however, a few four-syllable rhymes ("Variety, society") and there is a very charming conclusion ("I love to rhyme,/And wouldn't it be sublime/If one day it could be/That you rhyme with me?"). The music consists of a tuneful eighteen-bar verse ("There are men who, in their leisure, Love to fish for salmon") and a thirty-two bar AABA[1] refrain ("I love to rhyme") that is all happiness and simplicity, like a children's song.

Recordings: The original version, taken from *The Goldwyn Follies* soundtrack, is on Music Masters JJA-19773. A 1982 version by Sarah Walker and Roger Vignoles is on Meridian E-77056. Another, by George Byron with piano accompaniment by Bobby Tucker, is on General 4013.

282. I WAS DOING ALL RIGHT

Lyricist: Ira Gershwin
Key: G
Time: Alla breve
Tempo: Animato (verse)
　　　　Moderately (refrain)
Introduced by: Ella Logan (unseen, on the radio) in *The Goldwyn Follies*, a film released by Goldwyn-United Artists on February 23, 1938.

Lore: In June of 1937, a month before his death, Gershwin was asked to come into Samuel Goldwyn's office and play the score-in-progress for *The Goldwyn Follies*. Goldwyn had already been pressing the composer to write "hit songs you can whistle" and now he said, "Why don't you write hits like Irving Berlin?" So far, he had disliked all of the Gershwin score except for the release section of "I Was Doing All Right" which, in Goldwyn's judgment ought to have been repeated during the course of the song. Shortly after this meeting Gershwin told playwright S.N. Behrman, "I had to live for this, that Sam Goldwyn should say to me: 'Why don't you write hits like Irving Berlin?'"

Ira Gershwin wrote but never used some additional lines to this song. They were to have been sung in the film by the puppet Charlie

McCarthy who, with ventriloquist Edgar Bergen, was making his film debut.

Analysis: The fourteen-bar verse ("Used to lead a quiet existence") starts with the sound of G, A-flat, G-flat and F chords in the treble over a G-major bass, resulting in a tranquil, even ethereal sensation. The beat of the refrain ("I was doing all right") has a gentle swing and riding it happily is an unaggressive and singable tune. When this melody comes to its first pause it does so with a very unusual cadence: the singer must drop to a low B-natural—a tenth below his or her starting point. Also worth listening for is a marvelous release ("But now/Whenever you're away"). It is in a contrasting key (E-major) and in a contrasting attack (marcato as opposed to legato). It begins in a driven and propulsive manner but, through a series of quarter note triplets, loses some steam and makes the transition back to the more carefree style of the opening.

Recordings: The soundtrack recording is unavailable on record but the video cassette of the film is available from MGM/UA. Also, Ella Logan made a studio recording of this song on December 30, 1937 (Brunswick 8064). Another December 1937 recording was by Abe Lyman (Bluebird B-7369). In January of 1938 there were versions by Mildred Bailey with Red Norvo and His Orchestra (Brunswick 8068), Larry Clinton and His Orchestra (Decca 1660), Ella Fitzgerald and Her Savoy Eight (Brunswick 02605), and George Hall's Arcadians (Vocalion 3957).

Other choices are the Central Park Sheiks (Flying Fish 27026), Chris Connor (Atlantic 2-601), Ella Fitzgerald (Verve MGV-4027), Dexter Gordon (Manhattan/Blue Note BST-84077), Carmen McRae (MCA 2-4111), Oscar Peterson and Buddy De Franco (Verve MGV 2022), and Artie Shaw (Victor AXM2-5580).

283. LOVE WALKED IN

Lyricist: Ira Gershwin
Key: E-flat
Time: Alla breve
Tempo: Moderato (verse)

370

Slowly, with much expression (refrain)
Introduced by: Kenny Baker (making hamburgers in a diner) in The Goldwyn Follies, a film released by Goldwyn-United Artists on February 23, 1938.

Lore: George Gershwin called this tune his "Brahmsian" number (Ira described it as "churchy"). Though it was one of his last songs, the principal strain had entered his notebook in the fall of 1931 as a twenty-four-bar sketch (it followed "Jilted," which was dated September 16, 1931 and used in *Of Thee I Sing*). In 1937, when the tune was given words, no changes were made to the original sixteen bars (through "love said hello").

Ira always considered this lyric somewhat pompous.

Oscar Levant recalled singing this song to his psychoanalyst while thinking, "The S.O.B. is so unmusical that he doesn't realize what a great song it is!"

"Love Walked In" was on *Your Hit Parade* for fourteen weeks in 1938.

Analysis: The lyric is a rarity for Ira Gershwin in that in it his treatment of the subject of love is without humor. In fact, he gives love a poetic anthropomorphism, allowing it to walk and speak and knock on doors. The verse ("Nothing seemed to matter anymore") is a brief one—just sixteen bars. It is characterized by descending, sighing melody lines for both the singer and the accompanist. The refrain ("Love walked right in") is very spare—just eighty-five notes in thirty-two bars. In the second bar, on "drove the" in "drove the shadows away," the E-flat of an F-dominant seventh chord is played in the bass and it creates the feeling that something important is impending. In the sixteenth bar the use of a B-natural on "word" in "though not a word was spoken" gives the melody a catch-in-the-throat quality. The length is thirty-two bars and the form is ABAC.

Recordings: Kenny Baker's performance, taken from *The Goldwyn Follies* soundtrack, is on Music Masters JJA-19773. Baker also recorded a studio version (Decca 1795). There were versions in January of 1938 by Jan Garber (Brunswick 8060) and Gene Kardos and His Orchestra (American Record Company 8-03-05); in February of that year by Leo Reisman and His Orchestra (vocal by Felix Knight—Victor 25790, vocal by Jack Kilty—Victor 27627) and Dick Todd (Bluebird B-7446); in March by Jimmy Dorsey and His Orchestra (Decca 1724) and Sammy Kaye (Vocalion 4017); in May by Louis Armstrong (Decca 1842) and Una Mae Carlisle and Her Jam Band (Vocalion S-162); in July by Hildegarde (Columbia FB-1992); in August by Gracie Fields (Rex 9377); and in September by Freddy Gardner and His Swing Orchestra (Rex 7381).

There were versions in 1939 by Artie Shaw (Decca 24869), in 1942 by Bob Grant and His Orchestra (Decca 24087), in 1946 by Dave Tough (Jamboree 907), in 1949 by Erroll Garner (Savoy 701), in 1950 by the Dave Brubeck Octet (Fantasy 509), in 1959 by Ella Fitzgerald (Verve MGV-4027), and in 1973 by Bobby Short (Atlantic 2-608).

Others: George Benson (Accord SN-7163), Ruby Braff/George Barnes Quintet (Concord Jazz 5), Kenny Burrell (Prestige 7347), Chris Connor (Atlantic 2-601), Bing Crosby (Decca DL-508), Lou Donaldson (Blue Note BST-84108), Peter Duchin (Fortune 299), Herb Ellis (Concord Jazz 116), Art Farmer (Concord Jazz 179), the Frederick Fennell Orchestra (Mercury 75127), Ferrante and Teicher (Liberty LN-10242), the Flamingos (Roulette 59018), Pete Fountain (Capitol SN-16224),

Al Haig (Seabreeze 1005), the Hi-Lo's (Columbia PC-36980), Earl Hines (Classic Jazz 41), the L.A. 4 (Concord Jazz 199 and 1001), Joan Morris/William Bolcom (a beautiful version, true to the printed music—Nonesuch 71358), Jessye Norman/John Williams and the Boston Pops (Philips 412625-1), Andre Previn (RCA Victor LPM 1011), George Shearing (Pausa 2035), George Shearing and the Montgomery Brothers (Riverside OJC-040), Dinah Shore (Victor 20-1651), Frank Sinatra (Reprise FS-1002), Paul Smith (Outstanding 023), Rise Stevens (Columbia 4431-M), Warren Vache (Concord Jazz 98), Sarah Vaughan (Mercury MGC-2-101), Dinah Washington (Mercury 30091).

284. LOVE IS HERE TO STAY

Lyricist: Ira Gershwin
Key: F

Time: Alla breve

Tempo: Con anima

Introduced by: Kenny Baker (at the microphone during a radio broadcast) in *The Goldwyn Follies*, a film released by Goldwyn-United Artists on February 23, 1938.

Lore: At Gershwin's death, only a twenty-bar lead sheet of this song had been written down. But Oscar Levant remembered the piece well from the composer's piano renditions and his memory was indispensable when Vernon Duke was brought in to complete the score and reconstruct this song. Actually, it was at Levant's insistence that Gershwin had spent two days trying to put more breathing space into the long phrases—before realizing that the original version was best. Ira Gershwin also offered some musical advice during the composition of this number and his advice was taken. Ira's suggestion was that dotted eighth notes be placed in the ninth and tenth bars (these are the "and"s in "The radio and the telephone and").

As for the verse, it is not by George Gershwin. In fact, there is some question as to who did write it. In his autobiography, *Passport to Paris*, Duke claims that he wrote the verses for all of the Gershwin songs in *The Goldwyn Follies*. Ira later claimed that he, Ira, had come up with the music for this verse and that he had sung it to Duke, who wrote it down. As for the other Gershwin songs in the score, Ira, in his book *Lyrics on Several Occasions*, says only that he and Duke "fixed up a couple of missing verses."

The lyricist never did have a reason for the discrepancy between the title and the lyric. Upon including the song in his book he had wanted to change the title to "Our Love is Here to Stay" but balked, feeling that it was too late to alter such a well-known song.

"Love is Here to Stay" was not given an elaborate or even a prominent spot in *The Goldwyn Follies*. Only when Gene Kelly sang it to Leslie Caron in the 1951 film *An American in Paris* did it catch on.

Analysis: The eighteen-bar verse ("The more I read the papers, the less I comprehend") is not by George Gershwin but it is worthy of him and of the refrain that follows. It is in the same quiet, ruminative

373

and through-composed style that characterized so many of his last verses. In its ninth and tenth bars (on "Nothing seems to be lasting") it achieves a tender sound with a succession of major and minor seventh chords. The refrain ("It's very clear/Our Love is Here To Stay") begins with three pick-up notes, each supported by its own distinctive chord. In the second eight measures we get the long phrases that Oscar Levant objected to and for which Ira Gershwin suggested the connecting "and"s (at "The radio and the telephone"). These notes descend slowly and with a swaying motion, like a falling leaf. Gershwin never knew that he was dying. Nevertheless, this beautiful music, which is touched by resignation, seems quite uncanny.

Recordings: Kenny Baker's soundtrack recording is available on Music Masters JJA-19773. Baker did not record a studio version but Ella Logan, who was also in *The Goldwyn Follies*, did—on December 30, 1937 (Brunswick 8064). A day earlier, Abe Lyman had set down his version (Bluebird B-7369). Then came four recordings in January of 1938: by Jimmy Dorsey and His Orchestra (Decca 1660), George Hall's Arcadians (Vocalion 3957), Gene Kardos and His Orchestra (American Record Company 8-03-05), and Red Norvo and His Orchestra (Brunswick 8068). Frances Gershwin's version is on Monmouth-Evergreen MES 7060.

Gene Kelly's 1951 version, from the film *An American in Paris*, is on MGM 30402. The Jackie Gleason Orchestra did theirs in 1953 (Capitol 2438). Then came recordings by Ralph Sharon in 1954 (London 1438), Ella Fitzgerald in 1959 (Victor 2-2525), and Bobby Short in 1973 (Atlantic SD 2-608).

Others: Tony Bagwell (Starborne 2), Joe Bushkin (Atlantic 51621-1), Rosemary Clooney (Concord Jazz 112), Nat King Cole (Capitol SWK-11355), Chris Connor (Atlantic 2-6-1), Wild Bill Davison (Storyville 4029), Dewey Erney/Ron Eschete (Discovery 881), Booker Ervin (Prestige 7318), the Bill Evans Trio (Milestone 47068, Riverside 018), Michael Feinstein (Parnassus PR 0100), Mynard Ferguson (Emarcy 1026), Ferrante and Teicher (Liberty LN-10242), Ella Fitzgerald/Louis Armstrong (Victor 6-8811), Barbara Hendricks/Katie and Marielle Labeque (Philips 9500987),

Earl Hines (Classic Jazz 31), Billie Holiday (Verve 2V6S-8816),

Eddy Howard (Hindsight 405), Barney Kessel (Contemporary OJC-238), Cleo Laine (DRG 502), Shelly Manne (Discovery 909), Laurel Masse (Pausa 7165), Carmen McRae (MCA 2-4111), Yehudi Menuhin/Stephane Grappelli (Angel 36968), Julia Migenes-Johnson (Victor ARL1-5323, Victor ARL1-7034), Hugo Montenegro (Bainbridge 1028), Joan Morris/William Bolcom (Nonesuch 71358), Jessye Norman/John Williams and the Boston Pops (Philips 412625-1), Joe Pass (Pablo 2312133), Oscar Peterson (Pausa 7080), Bud Powell (Manhattan Blue Note BST-84430),

Andre Previn (RCA Victor LPM 1011), Bob Ralston (Ranwood 8088), Diana Ross (Motown MCDO-6133), Jimmy Roselli (M&R 1002), Artie Shaw (RCA Victor AXM2-5580), Frank Sinatra (Capitol ST-11309), Singers Unlimited (Pausa 7076), Toni Tennille (Mirage 90162-1), Lucky Thompson (Inner City 7016), Cal Tjader (Fantasy 8083), the George Wallington Quintet (Prestige OJC-1704), Ben Webster (V2-2530).

285–P. DAWN OF A NEW DAY

Lyricist: Ira Gershwin
Key: C
Time: Alla breve
Tempo: Tempo di Marcia
Introduced by: This song was written in 1938 and played by Paul Whiteman that year (see below). Ethel Merman sang it at the 1939 New York World's Fair. It was the Fair's official march.

Lore and Analysis: Composer Kay Swift, an intimate friend of the Gershwin family, was on hand to help Ira with the musical construction of this song. For the verse ("Leave those cares and furrows!") they chose the music for "Come, Come, Come to Jesus"—a George and Ira Gershwin song written circa 1930 for a show that was never produced. As one might expect from such origins, this music has a gospel flavor. Its melody, spare of notes, is harmonized simply, like something from a church hymnal. In the course of twenty-four

375

bars, Ira manages to refer to New York City's five boroughs and to racial harmony, democracy, and the colors of both the city and the federal government. The thirty-two-bar refrain ("Sound the brass! roll the drum!") was made from two other previously unused Gershwin tunes. It is not clear which ones those were. Perhaps they were two of the discarded marches from *Strike Up the Band*. In any event, this is a straightforward march based on a three-note (one of them blue) bugle call. It is thirty-two bars in length and its form is ABAC.

Recordings: Paul Whiteman did this song in a July 10, 1938 George Gershwin memorial broadcast (Mark 56 761). Johnny Messner and His Orchestra recorded it on January 6, 1939 (Blue Bird B-10101). Another version was made that year by Horace Heidt and His Musical Knights with Charles Goodman, vocal (Brunswick 8313). There has also been a recording by the Longines Symphonette Society (Longines Symphonette LW 227).

286–P. TREAT ME ROUGH

Lyricist: Ira Gershwin
Key: In the 1954 piano/vocal score of *Girl Crazy*, "Treat Me Rough" is published in E-flat. In separately published sheet music it is in C.
Time: In the piano/vocal score the time signature is 2/4. In the sheet music it is alla breve.
Tempo: In the piano/vocal score there is no tempo marking. In the sheet music the marking is Bright Tempo.
Introduced by: William Kent in *Girl Crazy* at the Alvin Theatre in New York City on October 14, 1930.

Lore: This song was first published in 1943 in conjunction with the second film version of *Girl Crazy*.

Analysis: This is the credo of a fellow who, having been privileged and pampered from birth, wants to become "a man among men." He realizes that, in order to do so, he will have to undergo a bit of manhandling and he is willing to suffer such an initiation if it is at the hands of the right woman.

The thirty-two-bar verse ("When I was born they found a silver spoon in my mouth") has a blithe and charming melody—there is a feeling of weightlessness about it. Its release ("Women and head-waiters fawned on me") uses descending inner voices to create a contrasting sense of resignation—although here the singer is less sincere in his self-pity than was the case in the verse to "But Not For Me" (from the same show), which uses a similar technique.

The thirty-two-bar refrain ("Treat me rough") is one of *Girl Crazy*'s three raunchy numbers (the others being "Sam and Delilah" and "Boy! What Love Has Done to Me!"). Its main idea concerns the blue note on "rough": it starts out as the top of a dominant-seventh chord but, while held across the bar line, changing harmony makes it part of a diminished chord. This refrain has no release.

On pages 117-118 of the *Girl Crazy* score, there is a piano arrangement of this song.

Recordings: "Treat Me Rough" was sung by June Allyson in the 1943 film version of *Girl Crazy* and her performance can be heard on Curtain Calls 100/9-10. Mickey Rooney and Judy Garland, also in that film, made a studio version in 1944 (Decca 23309). Other recordings are by Ruby Braff and the Shubert Alley Cats (Warner Bros. WS 1273), Eddie Chappell (Columbia OS-2569, OL 7060), Ella Fitzgerald (Verve MGV 4027), Mitzi Gaynor (Verve MGV 2115), Jackie Cain and Roy Kral (Roulette R-25278).

287–P. AREN'T YOU KIND OF GLAD WE DID?

Lyricist: Ira Gershwin
Key: E-flat
Time: Common
Tempo: Moderato
Introduced by: Dick Haymes and Betty Grable in *The Shocking Miss Pilgrim*, a film released by 20th Century Fox in January of 1947.

377

Lore: George and Ira wrote this song circa 1934 without any specific venue in mind. Reflecting the times, it concerned a man and a woman who decide to marry despite their poverty. The song was not used until twelve years later—nine years after George Gershwin's death—and then Ira had to rework the lyric, as it was now intended for a nineteenth century Boston locale, rather than Depression-era Manhattan.

This new lyric was one of Ira's more risqué efforts. He made some changes so as to tame it a bit prior to publication but, even so, the song was banned from radio play. When heard in the context of the plot of the film, however, the sexual innuendoes are greatly diminished. All the couple in the film actually "did" was see the sights of Boston without benefit of a chaperone.

Ira's real source of satisfaction with regard to this song was that he had begun it with a polysyllabic adverb ("honestly").

Analysis: A twenty-bar verse ("Oh it really wasn't my intention"), marked "in conversational style," is peppered with bluesy moments. One of them, appearing in both the first and ninth bars, has, because it juxtaposes a major and a minor third within a dominant seventh chord, a sound that recalls the blues from *An American in Paris*. The refrain ("Honestly I thought you wouldn't") is a standard thirty-two-bar AABA ballad. In it Gershwin moves the main melody along above increasingly complicated versions of an E-flat chord (from a triad to a sixth to a major seventh to a ninth) and then, for contrast, gives us a chromatically descending rush of unrelated chords (on "And probably we shouldn't").

Recordings: The original Haymes/Grable version, taken from the soundtrack of *The Shocking Miss Pilgrim*, can be heard on Classic International CIF-3008. In 1947, Dick Haymes also recorded this with Judy Garland (who was not in the film) on Decca 23687. In 1946 there was a record by Gene Krupa (Columbia 37158). Other versions are by Kaye Ballard and David Craig (Citadel CT 7017), Peggy Lee with Dave Barbour and His Orchestra (Capitol 292), the Longines Symphonette Society (Longines Symphonette LW 227), Vaughn Monroe (RCA Victor 20-1946), Sarah Vaughan (Mercury MGP-2-101).

288–P. THE BACK BAY POLKA

Lyricist: Ira Gershwin
Key: C
Time: 2/4
Tempo: Moderato (with humorous emphasis)
Introduced by: Allyn Joslyn, Charles Kemper, Elizabeth Patterson, Lillian Bronson, Arthur Shields and Betty Grable in *The Shocking Miss Pilgrim*, a film released by 20th Century Fox in January of 1947.

Analysis: The four separate stanzas, all about repressed human passion amongst the upper crust of old Boston, make for one of Ira Gershwin's lengthiest lyrics. It is also one of his best comedic efforts ("Laughter goes up the flue/Life is one big taboo no matter what you do/it isn't being done in Boston"). The music is a very simple dance tune in the relentless 2/4 of a polka. There is no verse. That the refrain ("Give up the fond embrace") was written by the composer as a single piece and not stitched together from different entries in his notebook, is attested to by the fact that the release ("Painters who paint the nude") is clearly a minor key variation on the major key main idea. It is ABACD in form, the last of those sections being an eight-bar instrumental dance marked "Optional Interlude." In all, the piece is forty-four bars long.

Recordings: The original version, taken from the soundtrack of *The Shocking Miss Pilgrim*, can be heard on Classic International CIF-3008. More recent versions are by George Byron with piano accompaniment by Dick Hyman (Atlantic ALS 410) and by Anthony Perkins, Barbara Cook, Bobby Short and Elaine Stritch (Painted Smiles 1357).

289–P. CHANGING MY TUNE

Lyricist: Ira Gershwin
Key: C
Time: Common

Tempo: Moderato (conversationally) (verse)
With a rocking rhythm (refrain)
Introduced by: Betty Grable in *The Shocking Miss Pilgrim*, a
film released by 20th Century Fox in January of 1947.

Lore: This, along with the rest of the score for this film, was
derived by Ira Gershwin and Kay Swift from unpublished George Gershwin manuscripts.

Analysis: The graceful lyric is in the "Things Are Looking Up"
category. The music consists of a ten-bar verse ("Yesterday the skies
were black") that is in the composer's later, ruminative style. The
thirty-two-bar refrain ("Castles were crumbling") is based on a
syncopated *Kitten on the Keys* sort of idea. But here the rhythm is
restrained and mild. As in other posthumous Gershwin pieces, the
harmony is very simple. The main idea is backed by the I–vi–ii–V⁷
progression that, in the composer's last works, was used as a point of
departure for subtle invention. Here it is presented as is. There is a
fine release ("At last the skies are bright and shiny") that begins in A-
minor but stops in a number of other minor keys as well. The appearance of G-minor (on "It's a human world") makes for an unusual and
heartfelt sound.

Recordings: Betty Grable's original version, taken from the
soundtrack of *The Shocking Miss Pilgrim*, can be heard on Classic
International CIF-3008. In 1946, this song was recorded by Judy Garland (Decca 23688). In 1947, there was a rendition by Mel Torme and
His Mel-Tones with the Artie Shaw Orchestra (Musicraft 412). Other
versions are by Anthony Perkins (Painted Smiles PS-1357), Ted Heath
and His Music (London LL 1217), and Vaughn Monroe (RCA Victor
20-2009).

290–P. FOR YOU, FOR ME, FOR EVERMORE

Lyricist: Ira Gershwin
Key: E-flat

380

Time: 4/4

Tempo: Moderato

Introduced by: Dick Haymes and Betty Grable in *The Shocking Miss Pilgrim,* a film released by 20th Century Fox in January of 1947.

Lore: This music may have been composed circa 1936-1937. Kay Swift played it for Ira Gershwin from George's manuscript and they both liked it well enough to give it the temporary title "Gold Mine." It was the principal ballad of *The Shocking Miss Pilgrim* but was, in the opinion of the lyricist, sung too slowly by Dick Haymes.

Analysis: The lyric is a conventional declaration of love without a humorous or offbeat angle. The music consists of a romantic, somewhat operetta-like sixteen-bar verse ("Paradise cannot refuse us") and a standard thirty-two-bar ABAC refrain ("For You, For Me, For Evermore"). That this refrain was originally all of a piece and not derived from separate Gershwin melodies is made apparent by the release ("It's plain to see"), which is a development of the initial idea. It and the childlike simplicity of the coda ("What a lovely world this world will be")—which contrasts with the romantic nature of the rest of the song— are the highlights.

Recordings: The original version by Dick Haymes and Betty Grable, taken from the soundtrack of *The Shocking Miss Pilgrim,* can be heard on Classic International CIF-3008. In 1947, Dick Haymes recorded this song again, this time with Judy Garland (Decca 23687). In 1946 there were versions by Henry Busse (4-Star 1139), Jane Froman (Majestic 1086), and Benny Goodman and His Orchestra (Columbia 37149). In 1947 there were recordings by Larry Green (Victor 20-2009), and by Artie Shaw and Mel Torme (Musicraft 412).

Others: George Chakiris with the Ted Heath Band (Horizon WP 1610), Chris Connor (Atlantic 2-601), Percy Faith (Columbia C2L-1), Coleman Hawkins (Prestige 24083), Teddi King (Inner City 1044), Dave McKenna (Inner City 1044), Vaughn Monroe RCA Victor 20-2009), Margaret Whiting (Capitol 294).

291–P. ONE, TWO, THREE

Lyricist: Ira Gershwin
Key: C
Time: 3/4
Tempo: In strict Waltz rhythm
Introduced by: Dick Haymes in *The Shocking Miss Pilgrim*, a
film released by 20th Century Fox in January of 1947.

Analysis: Those of Gershwin's posthumous works that were
reconstructed from his notebooks are uncharacteristicly simple in both
their melodies and harmonies. "One, Two, Three" is one of the more
extreme examples of this. Its long thirty-two-bar verse ("One, two,
three") is made up mainly of tonic and dominant harmony, although
there is a brief excursion from the key of C to that of E. This music
has the quality of a prim old country landler. The thirty-six-bar refrain
("When we go waltzing") is also made up a few elementary, unaltered
chords. It is quicker and more of a dancing waltz.

Recordings: Dick Haymes' original version, taken from the
soundtrack of *The Shocking Miss Pilgrim*, is on Classic International
CIF-3008. A brief orchestral rendition can be heard by The Symphony
of the Air Pops Orchestra, conducted by D'Artega (Epic LN 3651)

292–P. GIRL CRAZY OVERTURE

Instrumental

Key: Various
Time: Various
Tempo: Various
Introduced by: George Gershwin conducting the *Girl Crazy* pit
orchestra (which included the Red Nichols Band) at the Alvin
Theatre in New York City on October 14, 1930.

Lore: On October 16, 1930 Gershwin wrote the following to his
biographer, Isaac Goldberg:

382

I am just recuperating from a couple of exciting days. I worked very hard conducting the orchestra and dress rehearsal and finally the opening night, when the theater was so warm that I must have lost at least three pounds, perspiring. The opening was so well received that five pounds would not have been too much. With the exception of some dead head friends of mine, who sat in the front row, everybody seemed to enjoy the show tremendously, especially the critics. I think the notices, especially of the music, were the best I have ever received.

This piece, as part of the complete *Girl Crazy* piano/vocal score, was published in 1954.

Analysis: Although mainly a medley, there is some thematic development in this composition. The construction is as follows:

1. "I Got Rhythm" played against a long, percussive, melody line marked sempre marcato
2. "Embraceable You"
3. An eight-bar transition based on "Embraceable You"
4. "I Got Rhythm"
5. An instrumental motive from "Land of the Gay Caballero"
6. "But Not For Me"
7. "Broncho Busters" in E-major, repeated in F-major.
8. A twelve-bar coda based on "I Got Rhythm"

Recordings: The Buffalo Philharmonic with Michael Tilson Thomas conducting recorded this piece (Columbia M34542). They are faithful here to the printed score. So is pianist Kevin Cole in his recording (Fanfare DFL 7007).

293–P. THE LONESOME COWBOY

Lyricist: Ira Gershwin

Key: F (verse)
      B-flat (refrain)
      E-flat (trio)
Time: 6/8
Tempo: Tempo di marcia
Introduced by: The Foursome in *Girl Crazy* at the Alvin Theatre in New York City on October 14, 1930. It was published in 1954 as part of the *Girl Crazy* piano/vocal score.

Analysis: Here a group of cowboys sings proudly about having saved up enough money to get married. Ira's simple lyric has some cowboy locutions ("There's a gal that I'm a-dying for to see") and George's music is appropriately sanguine and guileless. There is a twenty-six-bar verse in F ("If you wonder why I am dressed up in my best"), a thirty-six-bar ABAC refrain in B-flat ("Oh, the lonesome cowboy won't be lonesome now"), and a sixteen-bar trio in E-flat ("Hee-haw!"). The song concludes with a repetition of the final twenty bars of the refrain.

Recordings: This was recorded in October of 1930 by Bill Simmons (Victor 23533) and in January of 1933 by Dwight Butcher (Victor 23772). The chorus sings it in a latter-day recreation of *Girl Crazy* (identified on the jacket and label as "Opening Chorus"—Columbia COS-2560).

294–P. BRONCHO BUSTERS

Lyricist: Ira Gershwin
Key: F (verse)
      E-flat (refrain)
Time: 2/4
Tempo: Moderato (verse)
      Ritmato (refrain)
Introduced by: The ensemble in *Girl Crazy* at the Alvin Theatre in New York City on October 14, 1930. It was published in 1954 as part of the *Girl Crazy* piano/vocal score.

Analysis: This is a takeoff on the feckless easterner vs. hearty westerner theme. In the long fifty-one-bar verse ("In town we used to fret away"), easterners readily admit that they are not as manly as their western counterparts. This verse is ABA in form and in the B section ("Before we're at the ranch another week") an intriguing melodic pattern grows out of an odd, almost grotesque succession of tritones.

Between the verse and refrain comes a ten-bar march, one that accompanies the entrance of the cowboys. This is really a vamp—two alternating, thumping chords in the deep bass region. The fact that, in accompanying the cowboys, it continues the grotesqueness introduced in the verse might indicate that Gershwin was having his own say about the contest between New York and Arizona. An even more telling moment in this respect occurs when the cowboys begin to sing the refrain ("We are broncho busters"). Composer Jules Styne, when asked to analyze the tempo and meter of this music, said, "It's simple. It's time is Broadway." Thus, when the cowboys are singing lines such as "On Western prairies we shoot the fairies/Or send them back to the East," they are doing so to music that summons up images of a chorus line on the Great White Way.

A solo piano arrangement of the "Broncho Busters" refrain appears on pages 40-42 of the *Girl Crazy* piano/vocal score. On page 90 the refrain and release are presented with a new introduction and third-person lyrics.

Recordings: This song is sung by the chorus on a studio recording of *Girl Crazy* (Columbia OS-2560 and OL-7060). It can also be heard in an outtake from the 1943 MGM film of the show with Judy Garland, Mickey Rooney and Nancy Walker (Out Take Records OTF-2), and in a medley by Zubin Mehta and the New York Philharmonic with pianist Gary Graffman from the soundtrack to Woody Allen's film *Manhattan* (Columbia JS36020).

295–P. BARBARY COAST

Lyricist: Ira Gershwin
Key: C
Time: Alla breve
Tempo: Vigoroso
Introduced by: Peggy O'Connor and Olive Brady in *Girl Crazy* at the Alvin Theatre in New York City on October 14, 1930. It was published in 1954 as part of the *Girl Crazy* piano/vocal score.

Analysis: In this song about a sordid section of old San Francisco, Ira Gershwin is especially inventive in the verse ("Let me take you to a place/Where humming birds sing bass!"). The music of the verse ("If you ask me what place") is made up of two sections. The first is in C-minor and it hearkens back to the early 1920s with a Charleston motive and unsubtle blue notes. The second, marked poco a poco crescendo, consists of an eight-bar melodic and harmonic climb that ends with a beautiful and unexpected G chord. The refrain ("Oh, the minute that you strike it") is most interesting musically for the contrary motion that appears in bars five and six ("Where baa-baa, black sheep/Baa, baa, baa the most") and, altered, at the end of the song ("at the bar-bar-barbarous Bar-Bar-Barbary Coast!").

A series of piano solo versions of "Barbary Coast" appears on pages 46-53 of the *Girl Crazy* piano/vocal score. They take the song through various keys and provide it with some new material: an alternate release, an extension of the contrary motion idea, and a different ending. The arrangement on pages 52-53 is interesting enough to have merited inclusion in *George Gershwin's Songbook*. On page 95 there is another piano rendition of the refrain (see "Girl Crazy Act Two Entr'acte").

Recordings: Ruby Braff and the Shubert Alley Cats (Warner Bros. WS 1273).

296–P. GIRL CRAZY FINALETTO/GOLDFARB! THAT'S I'M

Lyricist: Ira Gershwin
Key: G
Time: 6/8
Tempo: Tempo di Marcia
Introduced by: Willie Howard in *Girl Crazy* at the Alvin The-
atre in New York City on October 14, 1930. It was published
in 1954 as part of the *Girl Crazy* piano/vocal score.

Analysis: This is a comedy number in which a fellow named
Gieber Goldfarb, who is sheriff of Custerville, Arizona, brags about
his prowess as a lawman in such a way as to make it very clear that he
is thoroughly and unabashedly corrupt. The piece is forty-eight bars
long and AABACA in form. The music is simple, good-natured, and,
in the C portion ("So vote for Goldfarb"), bluesy. Some of the lines
are sung not by Goldfarb but by the chorus and by a character named
Slick Fothergill.

Recordings: None

297–P. GIRL CRAZY ACT II ENTR'ACTE (SPECIALTY)

Lyricist: Ira Gershwin
Key: Various
Time: Alla breve
Tempo: Various
Introduced by: George Gershwin conducting the *Girl Crazy* pit
orchestra at the Alvin Theatre in New York City on October
14, 1930. It was published in 1954 as part of the *Girl Crazy*
piano/vocal score.

Analysis: This is a collection of five musical interludes:

1. An instrumental version of "Barbary Coast."
2. A highly syncopated sixteen-bar melody in C-major. This music

is untitled and is not heard elsewhere in the score.

3.　　An instrumental version of "Embraceable You."

4.　　Another piece of new material, also untitled. Here, in a jazzy recitativo style, an unnamed singer asks a cornet player to do "a number from the show."

5.　　An instrumental version of "I Got Rhythm" for trumpet. Marked "Swing," at first it is a reading of that song without syncopation. Then it gently eases into the real rhythm.

Recordings:　None

298–P. LAND OF THE GAY CABALLERO (MEXICAN HOTEL SCENE)

Lyricist:　Ira Gershwin
Key:　Various
Time:　Various
Tempo:　Various
Introduced by:　The ensemble in *Girl Crazy* at the Alvin Theatre in New York City on October 14, 1930. It was published in 1954 as part of the *Girl Crazy* piano/vocal score.

Analysis:　This music is in five sections:

1.　　A twenty-eight-bar instrumental consisting of an Andante introduction in 3/4 time and then a Valse Allegro in 3/8 and 6/8 time. The Andante, with its triplet flourishes and its juxtaposition of major and minor modes, resembles the opening of the *Cuban Overture*. The Valse Allegro begins with a burst of emphatic and staccato E-minor chords which become Em9, E6, and then E7 chords. After this a melody appears—one in which long held notes are punctuated by quick triplets.

2.　　A sixteen-bar crooning south-of-the-border style tune in E and in 4/4 ("Romantic land of the gay caballero/Romantic land of guitar and sombrero"). Here the triplet motive is achieved via grace notes.

3.　　A twelve-bar instrumental section marked Dance. It consists of

388

a staccato rhythmic figure in E-minor and, high above it, a melody made up of a double-dotted half note followed by double sixteenth notes (another variation on the triplet idea).

4. A twenty-four-bar instrumental section in 3/4 time. B-flats are added to alternating C and G7 chords and then the two principle chords become E-flats and B-flat sevenths. The ending is a rhythmically and harmonically exciting crescendo. It is this section of "Land of the Gay Caballero" that was included in *Girl Crazy*'s overture.

5. A fifty-six-bar instrumental composition called Solo Dance Specialty. It is based on section two but it is in 6/8 rather than the 4/4 of that section. As written in the *Girl Crazy* score, it is complete enough to deserve consideration as another Gershwin instrumental or piano work.

Recordings: As part of the *Girl Crazy* overture this was recorded by Andre Kostelanetz (Columbia CS-8933) and by Michael Tilson Thomas leading the Buffalo Philharmonic (Columbia M34542). It can also be in a medley by Zubin Mehta and the New York Philharmonic with pianist Gary Graffman, recorded as part of the soundtrack to the Woody Allen film *Manhattan* (Columbia JS-36020).

299–P. WHEN IT'S CACTUS TIME IN ARIZONA

Lyricist: Ira Gershwin
Key: B-flat minor (verse)
D-flat (refrain)
Time: 2/4
Tempo: Lively
Introduced by: Ginger Rogers in *Girl Crazy* at the Alvin Theatre in New York City on October 14, 1930. It was published in 1954 as part of the *Girl Crazy* piano/vocal score.

Analysis: In the verse the singer expresses love for several Western states and then settles on Arizona as the one of choice. The refrain says little more than the title phrase, although Ira does come up with a couple of fair rhymes for Arizona in "Ramona" and "own a."

389

The music of the verse ("New Mexico, I love you"), though bouncy in tempo, is melodically and harmonically dark-hued. Its melancholia comes to a head in the seventeenth bar (on "but of all the states in the West") where the music seems to be on the verge of becoming a Russian march. In the refrain ("When it's cactus time in Arizona") we move to the relative major for a tune that, like "Bidin' My Time," relies for its effectiveness on some barbershop-style harmonies. The first occurs in bar one where the home key chord of D-flat alternates with the very distant sound of C-major. In bar three (on the "zo" in "Arizona") an unexpected A-natural does what the sudden C7 chord on "dizzy" did in "Bidin' My Time"—it becomes the hook.

A piano arrangement of the refrain of "Cactus Time" can be found on page 135 of the *Girl Crazy* piano/vocal score.

Recordings: Although used in the 1943 film of *Girl Crazy*, this song was not included on the soundtrack album. It is included in a studio recreation of *Girl Crazy*, where it is sung by Louise Carlyle (Columbia OS-2560, OL 7060).

300–P. JUST ANOTHER RHUMBA

Lyricist: Ira Gershwin
Key: E-minor (verse)
  G (refrain)
Time: Common
Tempo: Moderato (Rhumba rhythm)
Introduced by: Ella Fitzgerald in her 1959 album *Ella Fitzgerald Sings the George and Ira Gershwin Songbook.* Although written in 1937, the song was first published in conjunction with this recording.

Lore: The Gershwins had Fred Astaire in mind when they first began working on this song. But, by the time they got around to submitting it to a movie studio, they were working on *The Goldwyn Follies* and Astaire was not in that picture. Ella Logan rehearsed it for that film but it was not included.

390

The line "The rhumba that blighted my life" is a play on one of Al Jolson's big vaudeville numbers, "The Spaniard That Blighted My Life."

No reason has been offered as to why it was decided, in this song, to spell rumba "rhumba."

Analysis: In this lyric Ira voices the same complaint against the rumba that he had lodged against "Fascinating Rhythm" some thirteen years earlier—and, in so doing, gets off rhymes such as "At first it was divine-ah/But it turned out a Cuban Frankenstein-ah!" and "It's got me by the throat-ah/Oh what's the antidote? Ah." The music has an adventuresome spirit, employing cross-rhythms, recurring instrumental motives, and an elaborate 116-bar structure. It begins with a twenty-three-bar verse that contrasts a brittle syncopated central idea ("It happened to me/On a trip to the West Indies") with a lyrical second theme ("It isn't love"). Of harmonic interest here is the way the occasional F7 chord is played off against the E-minor background (on "since that trip" and, later, on "It's a very funny trouble"). Then comes the ninety-three-bar refrain ("It's just another rhumba"). It is ABACA in form, with A and B being in strict and forceful rhythms while C is a less taut, more comic twenty-five-bar trio ("Ah! Ah!"). The second two A sections end with an ingeniously harmonized coda ("Why did I have to sucumbah to that rhumba?"). There is a constant use of quick triplets (on "rhumba," for instance), a trait characteristic of all of Gershwin's Latin pieces.

Recordings: Ella Fitzgerald (Verve MGV-4024), Joan Morris with piano accompaniment by William Bolcom (Nonesuch H-71358).

301–P. THE REAL AMERICAN FOLK SONG

Lyricist: Ira Gershwin
Key: C
Time: 6/8 (verse)
   Alla breve (refrain)
Tempo: Allegretto (verse)

Tempo di Fox Trot (refrain)

Introduced by: Nora Bayes in 1918 on the tryout tour of *Ladies First* prior to the New York opening of that show. On the New York stage it was sung by Hal Ford in *Ladies First* at the Broadhurst Theatre on October 24, 1918.

Lore: Ira Gershwin wrote this lyric under a pseudonym, Arthur Francis (made from the names of his two other siblings), and it was the first of his lyrics to appear in a show. It was dropped from *Ladies First* shortly after that show's Broadway premiere and it received no further attention until 1958, when it was discussed by Edward Jablonski and Lawrence D. Stewart in their book *The Gershwin Years* (Doubleday & Co., 1958). Publication in 1959 and a first recording by Ella Fitzgerald quickly ensued.

Analysis: In the verse, while the lyric speaks about folk song styles near Barcelona, the music bounces along in the 6/8 time of not too distant Naples. Then, in the refrain, when Ira says that "The Real American folk song is a rag," the tempo becomes alla breve and the composer writes a ragtime. Another witty moment occurs in the eleventh bar of the refrain when, just before the lyric speaks of critics changing their tune, the music jumps keys—from C to A-flat. One ought to note too that this song is through-composed; that is, there are no repeated sections. This may have been due to the fact that in this, the first instance of the brothers' partnership, the words came first. Later, George almost always started things off with a tune.

Recordings: Ella Fitzgerald's premiere recording is on Verve MG V-4025. More recent versions are by Travis Hudson (Monmouth-Evergreen MES 7061), Jeanne Baxtresser and Julius Baker (flutes), Andrew Davis (piano), and Dave Young (bass) (Fanfare DFL-6006), and Shelly Manne (Discovery 909).

392

302–P. PROMENADE

For chamber orchestra with two pianos

Key: C
Time: Alla breve
Tempo: Allegretto moderato
Introduced by: Nathaniel Shilkret conducting an RKO studio orchestra for the film *Shall We Dance,* released in May of 1937.

Lore: This instrumental composition was written for the ship-board dog-walking scene in *Shall We Dance.* According to witnesses, Gershwin quickly improvised the tune on the set. He then scored it himself so as to make sure that it would not be bloated beyond recognition by a hired Hollywood orchestrator. The composer's orchestration was for a chamber group with two pianos and it was called "Walking the Dog." But, when published in 1960, it was for piano solo and called "Promenade" (at Ira's suggestion). It was thought, at that time, that the original score had not survived, and the piano piece was written from memory by Hal Borne who, in 1936, had been rehearsal pianist for *Shall We Dance* (it is Borne's piano playing that is heard on the soundtrack). Then, in 1978, Gershwin's original arrangement was found in an RKO warehouse. In 1981 it was for the first time played in concert as originally written—by Michael Tilson Thomas and the Los Angeles Philharmonic Orchestra.

Analysis: Promenade is a sixty-eight-bar composition in ABC form. It begins with an eight-bar vamp consisting of the harmonic progression that will lie under the A sections. As Gershwin did so often during this period, he constructs here a take-off on the elementary I–vi–ii–V^7 pattern: I is given an added major seventh, vi a minor seventh, ii a ninth, and V^7 a sixth and a diminished ninth. This pattern is then used to support a whimsical and somewhat jazzy tune. The B section is a lyrical dotted-note theme, one that travels farther and farther from the home key until it gets to D-flat, when a neat one-bar modulation takes us back to C.

Recordings: The original version can be heard on the sound-track recording of *Shall We Dance* (Soundtrak STK-106) and in a 1985 recording by the Los Angeles Philharmonic conducted by Michael Tilson Thomas (CBS IM 39699). The piano version has been recorded by Richard Rodney Bennett (EMI EMD 5538), William Bolcom (Nonesuch H-71284) and Leonard Pennario (Angel DS-37359). Non-Gershwin orchestral arrangements include one by Nelson Riddle that was part of the deluxe edition of *Ella Fitzgerald Sings the George and Ira Gershwin Songbook* (Verve MG V-4029-5), recorded in 1959; and one by Andre Kostelanetz, done at about the same time (Columbia CS-8933).

303–P. ALL THE LIVELONG DAY (And the Long, Long Night)

Lyricist: Ira Gershwin
Key: G
Time: Common
Tempo: Moderato (verse)
　　　　Leisurely (refrain)
Introduced by: Ray Walston in *Kiss Me, Stupid*, a film released by United Artists in December of 1964.

Lore: This song was written for but rejected by Dean Martin. Martin's decision may have had something to do with the schizophrenic nature of the material. Because the plot of the film concerned amateur songwriters, Ira's assignment from director Billy Wilder was to write like a neophyte—and nothing else could have been more against the grain of this lyricist, especially with regard to "All the Livelong Day," which he wanted to turn into another, perhaps final, standard ballad from the Gershwin brothers. How to write a great Gershwin ballad that could double as the dumb product of novice songwriters was Ira's quandary and it shows up in this song, for his solution was to write a fairly puerile lyric to some interesting, if not overly sophisticated, material by George.

The music was put together Frankenstein-fashion from the remains of two old Gershwin melodies. The verse came from "Phoebe"—

394

a number written by the brothers and Lou Paley in August of 1921 while they were vacationing in the Adirondacks—and the refrain was taken from a 1920s sketch called "Livelong Day." Roger Edens, who had been rehearsal pianist for *Of Thee I Sing*, helped Ira with the musical stitching and, in doing so, managed to take a musical phrase from the verse and slip it into the refrain.

For a time, Ira considered using the phrase "Lovelong Night" but then decided against it, thinking it a bit vulgar.

Analysis: The verse ("You've really got me") is sixteen bars long and made of ten repetitions of a five-note motive that is similar to the motto of "That Certain Feeling." The refrain ("All the livelong day and the long, long night") is a slow, wistful melody, made forlorn by a descending chromatic pattern in the bass. Its release ("You'll find I'm perfect casting") has a touch of pathos, due in part to the fact that Gershwin has written it in D-minor—an unusual choice inasmuch as the main idea is in G (E-minor would have been more expected). Lyrics like "Dream about you-oo-oo!" and harmonic cliches such as the D-augmented chord leading to the restatement (at "You're my one and all time") may have been planted to, per the exigencies of *Kiss Me, Stupid*, keep things from becoming too professional.

Recordings: None

304–P. I'M A POACHED EGG

Lyricist: Ira Gershwin
Key: F (verse)
  C (refrain)
Time: Alla breve (verse)
  Common (refrain)
Tempo: Moderato (verse)
  Brightly (refrain)
Introduced by: Cliff Osmond and Ray Walston in *Kiss Me, Stupid*, a film released by United Artists in December of 1964.

Lore: For decades Ira had been toying with what he considered a perfect metaphor for loneliness: a poached egg without a piece of toast. Because of the requirements of this film (*Kiss Me, Stupid* was about a fledgling songwriter and, thus, director Billy Wilder asked the lyricist to come up with songs that could pass for the work of an amateur), Ira wrote two sets of lyrics: one, somewhat simple, was sung; the other, more clever, was published. The music for the refrain was drawn from an eight-bar tune that Ira, recalling his and George's first pass at the poached egg idea in the 1920s, had whistled to Kay Swift in 1945. The release came from another Gershwin tune from the 1920s, "Are You Dancing?"

After all of this, Billy Wilder asked Ira if he would give the song a more conventional title, "When I'm Without You." But Ira, who had been waiting nearly forty years to use his poached egg line, refused.

Analysis: The verse ("Way back in Noah's ark") is a simple twenty–bar tune with a mindless sing–songy quality. The refrain ("I'm a poached egg") is a ditty too, one whose most distinctive feature is the way the main musical phrase stops suddenly, as if it has crashed into the bar line (this first happens in bar seven at "when I'm without you"), leaving the listener hanging for three long beats until the next note appears. Another oddity is its length: thirty bars. An eight–bar section A is repeated, then comes a brief four–bar release, and then A returns, this time for ten bars.

Recordings: None

305–P. SOPHIA

Lyricist: Ira Gershwin
Key: C
Time: 3/4
Tempo: Tempo di valse moderato
Introduced by: Ray Walston in *Kiss Me, Stupid*, a film released by United Artists in December of 1964.

396

Lore: A front page article in the February 17, 1964 edition of the New York *Times* declared that Ira Gershwin was about to release a number of previously unpublished Gershwin melodies including three that would be heard in the forthcoming Billy Wilder film *Kiss Me, Stupid*. It was at this time that Ira sent George Balanchine fourteen unpublished tunes by his brother for use as the basis of a new ballet (George Gershwin and Balanchine were to have collaborated on a ballet for *The Goldwyn Follies*, a project that was halted by the composer's sudden death). These fourteen pieces were not used by Balanchine, who said that they would be better served by a Broadway musical. A Balanchine ballet called *Who Cares?*, using Gershwin standards, did appear in 1970.

As for the Wilder project, it posed an interesting problem for Ira. The plot of the film had singer Dean Martin stranded in a Nevada desert town where he was besieged by two persistent but decidedly second rate songwriters. As it was their compositions that would make up the score, the Gershwin songs had to be both amateurish and memorable.

"Sophia" was derived from a completed George and Ira song, "Wake Up, Brother, and Dance," which had been written for but not used in the 1937 film *Shall We Dance*. In keeping with the needs of *Kiss Me, Stupid*, "Sophia" became a simplified version of the earlier song.

Analysis: "Sophia" is "Wake Up, Brother and Dance" made into a waltz. Its verse ("Ev'ry day I sit and pray") lacks the jazzy instrumental idea of its predecessor and it is harmonically simpler (the musical rewriting here was done by Roger Edens, composer of "In-Between," "You'll Never Know," and other songs). Its refrain ("Listen to me, Sophia") is simpler too, although it retains a staccato instrumental motive that was present in the earlier song. But the Latin flavor is at least as apparent here as it was in "Wake Up, Brother."

Recordings: None

306-P. **HI-HO!**

Lyricist: Ira Gershwin
Key: F
Time: Common
Tempo: Moderately
Introduced by: Tony Bennett in a 1968 recording (see below).

Lore: This is the first song that George and Ira finished upon arriving in Los Angeles in August of 1936. It was written in their suite at the Beverly Wilshire Hotel. It must have taken some daring, even defiance, to begin their work on *Shall We Dance* with such an unorthodox work, since the studio chiefs in Hollywood had been openly worried about the composer's "highbrow" inclinations—so worried that the brothers had to lower their salary requirements from $100,000 plus a percentage of the film's profits to not much more than half of that. Still, the movie executives reacted favorably to "Hi-Ho!," *Shall We Dance* director Mark Sandrich saying "this is real $4.40 stuff" (the price of a good seat on Broadway). "Hi-Ho!" was to have accompanied a sequence—devised by the Gershwins—that would have had Astaire dancing around the streets of Paris singing the praises of a celebrity (Ginger Rogers) whom he knew only from Parisian posters.

The song was first heard publicly in the late 1940s in an S.N. Behrman play, *Let Me Hear the Melody*, which was based on the author's memories of George Gershwin and F. Scott Fitzgerald. But the play and the song got nowhere. Publication did not come until 1967, when the composition was made part of an exhibition of Gershwin works at the Museum of the City of New York.

Analysis: "Hi-Ho!" resembles Gershwin's one published 'art' song, "In the Mandarin's Orchid Garden," in its adventurous length, its unhurried flow and its abundant and interconnected ideas. But, unlike "Mandarin," "Hi-Ho!" is completely in the vernacular, both musically and lyrically. It is also more than twice as long, coming in at 118 bars. Yet, it is more simply constructed than the other song, being ABAC in form.

It begins with a piano introduction—a light, evanescent motive that comes and goes throughout (Harold Arlen and Kay Swift play it in

398

their respective recordings—see below). There is no verse. Section A ("Hi-Ho!"), which has a low-keyed joyousness, is forty-two bars long and, except for the two-note title phrase, does not repeat. Like the refrain of "Let's Call the Whole Thing Off," it is based on a I–ii–vi^7–V^7 sequence. But here, atop a gentle swinging beat, the melody gradually surges; it has a lighthearted grandeur. The B section ("Please, pardon me, sir") begins suddenly in the far-off key of D-flat. It is a wonderful melody, as singable as it is unusual, and it finishes with a joyous and unexpected little tag ("She's lovely"). Section A is then repeated in F until, in the 109th bar of the song, we come to the coda ("Hi-Ho! I've got it"). Here the melody speaks in asides while the accompaniment dances about in a pleasing progression of unusual chords.

The lyric is entirely in the spirit of the music and it contains such deft wordplay as "Will I ever be her Romeo, me, oh my!"

Recordings: The first and best recording of "Hi-Ho!" was a homemade version from late 1937 or early 1938 by Ira Gershwin (vocal) and Harold Arlen (piano). It is available on Mark 56 Records 641. The first commercial recording was made in 1968 by Tony Bennett (Columbia CS 9678). A more recent and very fine version was done by Bobby Short with Gershwin friend Kay Swift at the second piano (Atlantic SD 2-608).

307-P. DEAR LITTLE GIRL

Lyricist: Ira Gershwin
Key: A-flat
Time: 2/4
Tempo: Brightly
Introduced by: Oscar Shaw in *Oh, Kay!* at the Imperial Theatre in New York City on November 8, 1926.

Lore: Ira Gershwin said that this, of all of his Broadway songs, received the least applause—that, in fact, it got none. Consequently, it was dropped from *Oh, Kay!* after opening night. It was to have been the third song of Act I, Scene I with the main character (a rich Long

399

Islander) singing it to all the ladies who had tidied up his house in preparation for his homecoming.

"Dear Little Girl" was first published in 1968—forty-two years after its premiere. The occasion was its inclusion in the Gertrude Lawrence film biography *Star!*

Analysis: The first four bars of the twenty-four-bar verse ("It's good to see familiar faces") make for a deeply felt and very affecting beginning. The answering four bars ("Rosie, Posie, Josie") are more lighthearted, but the overall effect is one of quiet intensity. In the refrain ("I hope you've missed me") Gershwin lets the bass stay with a steady A-flat chord while, in the treble and in quasi-triple meter, he alternates three harmonies: F-minor, G-minor and E-flat. When bass and treble are played together the chords become more complicated—A-flat sixth, A-flat major seventh with a ninth, and A-flat major seventh—and this conjoining produces a lovely, shimmering effect. The melody, made mostly from quarter notes, can seem static if sung in too foursquare a fashion—and the piano accompaniment is no help here, being inappropriately up-pahish. The form is AA¹BB¹A² and the length is forty-eight bars (due to the choice of 2/4 time).

Recordings: The soundtrack of *Star!* was released on 20th Century Fox DS-5102. Jack Cassidy sings this song in a studio version of *Oh, Kay!* (Columbia OS-2550 and OL-7050).

308-P. HARLEM RIVER CHANTY

Lyricist: Ira Gershwin
Key: Various
Time: Various
Tempo: Moderate 2
Introduced by: This was written for but not used in *Tip-Toes*, a
    show that premiered at the Liberty Theatre in New York City
    on December 28, 1925.

Lore: Ira Gershwin published the lyrics to this song in his 1959 book *Lyrics on Several Occasions*. The music was not published until 1968, when it appeared in an arrangement by Ross Hastings for piano and four-part chorus (SATB).

Analysis: Ira pokes fun at Prohibition here by writing a sailor's chanty that praises soft drinks. To boot, the sailor/singer proclaims his preference for a Central Park rowboat over more manly types of vessels. The music is simple and unpretentious in its melody and harmony, but is relatively elaborate in its structure. The form is ABCDEBCDE[1]. Section A ("When our supply of pieces of eight") is a cheerful sixteen-bar ditty in D and in 6/8 time. B is a four-bar instrumental in the same key and meter. C ("It's great to be a sailor"), eight-bars long and in A, is given some substance by a chromatic countermelody. D ("Yo-ho-ho, and a bottle of milk shake"), an eight-bar tune in D and in 2/4, is also a ditty but it is a little more emphatic. E, a twelve-bar instrumental dance in G and 2/4, has the feel of a Clementi sonatina. It moves into D-minor the first time around. In its second appearance, it is just eight bars long and it begins in D-minor, becoming the coda.

Recordings: None

309–P. LULLABY

String Quartet in one movement

Key: D
Time: 4/4
Tempo: Molto moderato e dolce
Introduced by: The Juilliard String Quartet at the Library of Congress on October 29, 1967.

Lore: It was in 1923 that Gershwin, having failed to prepare a harmony exercise for his third lesson with Rubin Goldmark (nephew of Hungarian composer Karl Goldmark and a pupil of Antonin Dvorák), turned in this composition, written several years earlier. As Gershwin

401

later told it with some glee, Goldmark, upon looking at *Lullaby*, told the young composer, "It's plainly to be seen that you have already learned a great deal of harmony from me!" This, as it turned out, was Gershwin's last lesson with this particular teacher.

Lullaby was actually written in 1919 or 1920 as a harmony exercise for teacher Edward Kilenyi. Gershwin wrote it both as a string quartet and as a piano piece although, as a piano work, it remained unfinished and has not been published. In the months following its composition, it was played as a string quartet by the composer's friends at private musicales. But it was not until 1922 that any of the music was heard publicly. The occasion was Gershwin's one-act opera *Blue Monday*, which turned the main idea of *Lullaby* into an aria entitled "Has Anyone Seen My Joe?" For the next forty years, *Lullaby* remained unheard (except in revivals of *Blue Monday*). Then, in 1962, harmonica virtuoso Larry Adler mentioned to Ira Gershwin that, in recording a film score, he was going to overdub himself four times. The word "four" reminded Ira of *Lullaby* and he showed the manuscript to Adler. On August 29, 1963, Adler premiered his transcription of the piece (for harmonica and string quartet) in an appearance with the Edinburgh String Quartet at the Edinburgh Festival. Adler later recorded Morton Gould's arrangement for harmonica and string orchestra (see below).

On October 29, 1967 *Lullaby* was finally performed publicly as Gershwin had written it. The occasion was a concert by the Juilliard String Quartet at the Library of Congress. As to its place in the Gershwin oeuvre, Ira Gershwin, upon publication of the score in 1968, wrote, "It may not be the Gershwin of *Rhapsody in Blue, Concerto in F*, and his other concert works, but I find it charming and kind."

Analysis: Lullaby, 165 bars long and sweet and tranquil throughout, can be divided into the following six sections:

1. A brief introduction, in which the first violin, using artificial harmonics, introduces the principal accompanimental idea.
2. A songlike AABA section in which the melody rises and falls tranquilly, like the rocking of a cradle, and then ends with an insistent B-flat, which makes for a bluesy/Hebraic sound.

402

3.   A second AABA section, in which the same music is arranged differently, the melody going now to the second and not the first violin. The second violin plays it double stopping.

4.   A contrasting section employing a simple rocking figure, one based on alternating notes, usually a whole or a half tone apart.

5.   A forte restatement of section 2.

6.   A coda consisting of a restatement of the main idea (all four instruments using artificial harmonics) and a three-note pizzicato phrase, given in turn to the cello, viola, second violin and first violin.

Recordings: Larry Adler's recording with Morton Gould of the Gould transcription for harmonica and string orchestra (entitled *Lullabye Time*) was released on RCA Victor LSC-2986. Other versions are by the Dickermann Quartet (Thorofon MTH-275) and the Juilliard String Quartet (Columbia M-32596). Transcriptions for string orchestra can be heard by the Cleveland Orchestra conducted by Riccardo Chailly (London 417326-1) and the St. Louis Symphony conducted by Leonard Slatkin (Vox QSVBX 5132).

310–P. TWO WALTZES IN C

For solo piano

Key: C
Time: 3/4
Tempo: Various
Introduced by: Earl Busby conducting the pit orchestra for *Pardon My English* on January 20, 1933 at the Majestic Theatre in New York City.

Lore: George Gershwin and Kay Swift would play this music at two pianos and Ira Gershwin referred to it as "Her Waltz, His Waltz, Their Waltz." The first of the waltzes is based on the song "Tonight" from *Pardon My English*. For a time, Ira refused to allow it to be published, as he did not want it confused with the song of the same title that appeared in the 1956 Broadway show *West Side Story*. In

403

1971, however, he relented and this music was published for piano solo and called *Two Waltzes in C*. The sheet music indicates that it was adapted by Saul Chaplin (he had re-orchestrated *An American in Paris* for the 1951 film of that title by Vincente Minnelli) and edited by Ira Gershwin.

Analysis: There are four sections. The first presents the main ideas of the piece in a continuous flow—they are not yet pitted one against the other contrapuntally. The "Tonight" music is stated as a waltz in the grand style and it is played in a very full and lush manner. Also introduced here are the series of somewhat dissonant augmented chords that will figure throughout. They are very much the same as the chord sequence underlying the "Once I visited my cousin" section of the verse to "My Cousin in Milwaukee" (also from *Pardon My English*).

The second section, labeled Waltz I, is a simple, lyrical statement of the "Tonight" theme, although midway through, things take a chromatic turn.

The third section, labeled Waltz II, is a broad and romantic melody, one that is full of yearning, and sentimental suspensions.

The fourth section is labeled Waltzes I and II and they are played simultaneously. The chromatics of the first give a more modern sound to the old fashioned sentimentality of the second.

Recordings: Richard Rodney Bennett (EMI EMD 5538), Leonard Pennario (Angel DS-37359), duo-pianists Veri and Jamanis (Book of the Month Club Records 61-5426).

311–P. IMPROMPTU IN TWO KEYS

For solo piano

Key: C and D-flat
Time: 4/4
Tempo: Moderato
Introduced by: William Bolcom in a recording made in 1973

(see below).

Lore: A manuscript of this piece was found after Gershwin's death. Per Gershwin biographer Edward Jablonski, it was originally written in 1929 as a song, "Yellow Blues," for the unproduced Ziegfeld musical *East is West.* It was published as a piano solo in 1973.

Impromptu in Two Keys has also been called "Blues in Two Keys."

Analysis: This charming piece is more easygoing than the *Preludes for Piano* of 1926 and it is not quite so difficult to play. It is thirty-three bars long. There is a main four-bar melody in C and it is accompanied by alternating D-flat and A-flat bass notes—hence, the two keys. This motive is repeated verbatim and then moved up a fourth before it is repeated again in C and D-flat. There is an eight-bar release in which the phrases tailgate one another. Then the first theme reappears for two bars, leading into a six-bar coda.

Recordings: Richard Rodney Bennett (EMI EMD 5538), William Bolcom (Nonesuch H-71284).

312–P. THREE-QUARTER BLUES

For solo piano

Key: C
Time: 3/4
Tempo: Andante con moto
Introduced by: It is not clear just when this music was first publicly performed.

Lore: Three-Quarter Blues was written sometime in the 1920s. After the composer's death it was listed by Ira Gershwin as Melody #32. He also referred to it as "Irish Waltz." It was first recorded in the early 1960s by harmonica virtuoso Larry Adler (on the same disc as his premiere recording of Gershwin's string quartet *Lullaby*). Publication came in 1974.

Analysis: This thirty-seven-bar waltz is written like a beginner's piano piece. Its likable tune is full of minor thirds and its form is a simple AA¹.

Recordings: Larry Adler's recording was released on RCA Victor LSC-2986. As a work for solo piano, the piece has been recorded by Richard Rodney Bennett (EMI EMD 5538), William Bolcom (Nonesuch H-71284) and Leonard Pennario (Angel DS-37359).

313–P. MERRY ANDREW

For solo piano

Key: A
Time: Alla breve
Tempo: Allegretto
Introduced by: Marilyn Miller and Jack Donahue danced to this in *Rosalie*, which premiered on January 10, 1928 at the New Amsterdam Theater in New York City.

Lore: This was written in 1927 for Fred Astaire in *Funny Face* but was dropped from that show. A place was then found for it in *Rosalie* the next year when it was entitled "Setting-Up Exercises." In 1936 its first five notes became the basis of the refrain in "They All Laughed." After the composer's death, Ira Gershwin listed this as "Melody #43 - Comedy Dance." It finally saw publication in 1974 as a piano piece.

Analysis: As its title suggests, this music has a happy-go-lucky quality. It is in ABA form. A is twenty-six bars long and begins with an "on the banks of the Mississippi" feel. Then, at bar twelve, the melody takes an intriguing, Gershwinesque turn with minor playing against major in a succession of unexpected keys. These twists and turns of melody and harmony continue in the sixteen-bar B section

406

which returns to the playful opening mood.

Merry Andrew has been published in a folio with *Promenade* and *Three Quarter Blues*. Together, they are Gershwin's only published compositions for beginning and intermediate piano.

Recordings: Richard Rodney Bennett (EMI EMD 5538), William Bolcom (Nonesuch H-71284), Leonard Pennario (Angel DS-37359)

314–P. SING OF SPRING

Lyricist: Ira Gershwin
Key: E-flat
Time: 4/4
Tempo: Andantino pastorale
Introduced by: Jan Duggan and ensemble in *A Damsel in Distress*, a film released by RKO on November 19, 1937.

Lore: Because much of *A Damsel in Distress* was set in the English countryside, Gershwin wrote two English-style madrigals ("The Jolly Tar and the Milkmaid" and "Sing of Spring") and arranged them for four-part chorus with piano accompaniment. The idea was to have them done in the film by a genuine madrigal group—which was how things worked out except that "Sing of Spring" was given short shrift. It was not sung in its entirety. Not until April 15, 1969, at a concert by Abraham Kaplan and the Collegiate Chorale at the Whitney Museum of Modern Art, was it finally heard as intended. And not until 1976 were it and "The Jolly Tar" published in the composer's original choral settings ("The Jolly Tar" had appeared in a piano/vocal arrangement in 1937).

Analysis: In keeping with the Andantino pastorale tempo marking, the music begins with a two-bar bird call introduction. Then comes the main melody, sung by the soprano and consisting of held notes which end in steep but graceful downward leaps. Against these notes are beautiful descending chordal patterns given to the alto, tenor and bass. They have a cascading effect.

407

This music maintains a determinedly pure, antiquarian style (it was originally entitled "Back to Bach") until measure eleven (at "tra la li lo"), when the sudden incursion of an F^7 chord gives it a touch of Broadway that is obvious enough to be funny but subtle enough not to break the mood. This happens again at bar fifteen (at "pi-mi-ny mo")—at which point the bluish C-natural sung by the bass is a little more obviously and emphatically a joke.

The length is thirty-two bars and the form is AA¹.

Recordings: In 1976, the Gregg Smith Singers recorded Gershwin's setting for piano and chorus (Turnabout TV-S 34638).

315–P. IN THE SWIM

Lyricist: Ira Gershwin
Key: Various
Time: 2/4
Tempo: Allegretto giocoso
Introduced by: The ensemble in *Funny Face* at the Alvin Theatre in New York City on November 22, 1927.

Lore: This production number was first published in 1983, the year of Ira Gershwin's death. He had suggested its inclusion in *My One and Only*, a new Broadway show featuring old Gershwin songs.

Analysis: "In the Swim" is one of the few published production numbers from Gershwin musicals (see "Bride and Groom") and it, like the others, is musically more freewheeling than a typical verse/refrain song. Its ninety-nine measures can be divided into the following sections:

1. A ten-bar instrumental fanfare in G.
2. A twenty-four-bar apostrophe on lakeside romance addressed by chorines to an unnamed party ("If you will take our tip, you'll join us in a dip"). Here, a simple bugle-call style tune is suddenly pushed upward, only to begin a giddy descent, as if it has been pushed off a

408

diving board. When it comes up to the surface, it is in the key of E.

3.   A sixteen-bar section ("One thing that we lack here"), marked un poco meno, and in the key of A. It is characterized by a melody with nervous and truncated phrases, and by the strange sound of an E-minor seventh chord with a diminished fifth supported by A octaves in the bass.

4.   A sixteen-bar version of section two ("The sun is on the lake").

5.   A thirty-two-bar refrain ("Swimming, swimming, what a sport!") marked by odd melodic leaps and unusual, almost random harmonies. It makes its quasi-atonal way toward one climax and then another before reaching a sudden, bluesy ending.

Recordings: The chorus sings this in the original cast recording of *My One and Only*, but only up to and not including section 5 (Atlantic 80110-1-E).

316–P. BRIDE AND GROOM

> *Lyricist:* Ira Gershwin
> *Key:* E, A
> *Time:* 2/4
> *Tempo:* Allegro
> *Introduced by:* Sascha Beaumont, Oscar Shaw and Frank Gardiner in *Oh, Kay!* at the Imperial Theatre in New York City on November 8, 1926.

Lore: "Bride and Groom" was not published until 1984, when it appeared in a Warner Bros. folio featuring vocal selections from *Oh, Kay!*

Analysis: This production number can be divided into the following sections:

1.   A sixteen-bar instrumental fanfare in E.

2.   A thirty-two-bar refrain in E ("It's never too late to Mendelssohn") that incorporates and becomes a variation on Felix Mendelssohn's "Wedding March." This very distinctive music contains a release in G-

409

sharp minor ("Two fond hearts") and a restatement that begins in C-sharp minor rather than in the original key of E. Ira Gershwin's inventive and funny rhyme scheme combines Mendelssohn's name with the subject of love and marriage to produce combinations such as "two hearts at journey's endelssohn," "Two fond hearts will always blendelssohn," and "a gay honeymoon they'll spendelssohn." And there is a final if indirect nod to Wagner's wedding march in "we hope they Lohengrin and bear it."

3.   A tranquil eight-bar instrumental transition.

4.   A twenty-bar through-composed section in E ("This is my wedding day"), made from imitative phrases and accompanied by chords that change in increments, mournfully, as in the "I ain't going" section of "Bess, You is My Woman."

5.   An up-tempo section in A ("We'd love to take a picture") whose melody consists of high leaps, then winding chromatic descents. There are four oddly proportioned seven-bar phrases, then a transitional bar made of a quick succession of ninth chords,

6.   A repeat of section four but with a six-bar extension.

7.   A repeat of section five.

Recordings: Barbara Ruick and Jack Cassidy sing this in a studio version of *Oh, Kay!* (Columbia OS-2550, OL-7050).

317–P. **DON'T ASK!**

> *Lyricist:* Ira Gershwin
> *Key:* E-flat
> *Time:* 2/4
> *Tempo:* Allegro
> *Introduced by:* Harlan Dixon and the Fairbanks Twins in *Oh, Kay!* at the Imperial Theatre in New York City on November 8, 1926.

Lore: This song was not published until 1984, when it appeared in a Warner Bros. folio featuring vocal selections from *Oh, Kay!* For a 1960 revival of that show, P.G. Wodehouse wrote new words to this

410

tune and called it "Home."

Analysis: If you can't figure out who the wonderful guy is that I'm singing about, then don't even ask, sings the wonderful guy himself in this number. The verse ("If you're looking for a playmate") is a jaunty twenty-four-bar tune that takes a brief dip in G-minor (at "You'll be feeling dizzy"). The refrain ("Who is the guy"), written for eccentric dancer Harlan Dixon, has a nervous melody, one that keeps starting and then abruptly stopping, like a series of interrupted takes. The release ("Moon and stars") continues the same rhythmic idea but is melodically different and is in a new key, G-major. The length is thirty-two bars, the form AABA.

Recordings: Allen Case and Roger White sing this in a studio recording of *Oh Kay!* (Columbia OS 2550, OL 7050).

318–P. THE WOMAN'S TOUCH

Lyricist: Ira Gershwin
Key: A, F
Time: 2/4
Tempo: Allegro
Introduced by: Betty Compton and Constance Carpenter in *Oh, Kay!* at the Imperial Theatre in New York City on November 8, 1926.

Lore: This number was not published until 1984, when it appeared in a Warner Bros. folio featuring vocal selections from *Oh, Kay!*

It was the show's opener and, in setting up the following situation, integral to the plot: A wealthy fellow named Jimmy Winter is returning to his home on Long Island. Unbeknownst to him, the house is being used by bootleggers to store their wares. "The Woman's Touch" is sung by Jimmy's girlfriends, who are tidying the place in anticipation of his homecoming.

Analysis: This is a production number in four contiguous sections:

411

1.   A sixteen-bar instrumental introduction in A major. It contains material not otherwise used in the song. The melody is a flourish high in the treble and it rests atop fanfare-style chords and an energizing ostinato bass.

2.   An enjoyable and ingratiating forty-six-bar ABA[1] refrain in A major ("Oh my goodness") whose hook is the regular use of a C-diminished chord over an E bass (at "this" in "what a mess this place is").

3.   An eight-bar transition in F ("Whoop it up!") that begins with a stately procession of descending chords and finishes with jazzy ninths.

4.   A lively thirty-two-bar foxtrot ("We must get everything all set"), also in F. The form is ABA.

Recordings: This number is sung in the 1960 *Oh, Kay!* revival cast recording (20th Century Fox 4003/SFX-4003). Barbara Ruick and Jack Cassidy do it in a studio version of the show (Columbia OS-2550, OL-7050).

A GERSHWIN COMPANION
PART TWO
UNPUBLISHED WORKS

1913

SINCE I FOUND YOU
Lyricist: Leonard Praskins
Lore: This was Gershwin's first composition.

RAGGING THE TRAUMEREI
Lyricist: Leonard Praskins

1914

TANGO
Work for solo piano
Lore: It was with this piece that Gershwin made his first public appearance as a pianist. This was at a social thrown by the Finlay Club (a literary society of City College of New York). Ira was on its entertainment committee.
Recordings: Gershwin is said to have recorded this tune with Fred Van Eps, a banjo player.

1916

GOOD LITTLE TUNE
Lyricist: Irving Caesar
Lore: This was an uninterpolated pop song.

MY RUNAWAY GIRL

Lyricist: Murray Roth

Lore: This song was accepted for but not used in *The Passing Show of 1916*, a Sigmund Romberg musical. Although Romberg was given credit as co-composer, he really had nothing to do with the writing of the song. A playful wrestling match between Gershwin and lyricist Roth suddenly turned serious and it ended both their partnership and friendship.

WHEN THE ARMIES DISBAND

Lyricist: Irving Caesar

Lore: Copyrighted on October 21, 1916, this was written for Henry Ford's Peace Ship (lyricist Caesar had worked as Henry Ford's secretary). It was interpolated into *Hitchy-Koo of 1918*.

1917

WE'RE SIX LITTLE NIECES OF OUR UNCLE SAM

Lyricist: Lou Paley

Lore: Gershwin and Paley sang this patriotic number at parties during World War I. It contains musical quotes from "Over There" and "The Marseillaise."

WHEN THERE'S A CHANCE TO DANCE

Lyricist: Unknown

Lore: This may have been written in 1918.

YOU ARE NOT THE GIRL

Lyricist: Ira Gershwin

Lore: Not used in any production.

1918

A CORNER OF HEAVEN WITH YOU

Lyricist: Lou Paley

Lore: Not used in any production.

CUPID
Lyricist : Edward B. Perkins
Introduced by: Sibyl Vane in *Half Past Eight* at the Empire Theatre in Syracuse, New York on December 9, 1918.

HONG KONG
Lyricist: Edward B. Perkins
Introduced by: Sibyl Vane in *Half Past Eight.*

THERE'S MAGIC IN THE AIR
Lyricist: Ira Gershwin
Introduced by: Sibyl Vane in *Half Past Eight.*
Lore: With different lyrics, this music became "The Ten Commandments of Love," used in *La La Lucille* in 1919.

LITTLE SUNBEAM
Lyricist: Unknown
Lore: Another number from *Half Past Eight.*

OUR LITTLE KITCHENETTE
Lyricist: Arthur J. Jackson and B.G. DeSylva
Lore: Written for but not used in *La La Lucille.*

THE TEN COMMANDMENTS OF LOVE
Lyricist: Arthur J. Jackson and B.G. DeSylva
Introduced by: John E. Hazzard and Janet Velie in *La La Lucille.*
Lore: This is the same music as "There's Magic in the Air."

WHEN YOU LIVE IN A FURNISHED FLAT
Lyricist: Arthur J. Jackson and B.G. DeSylva
Introduced by: Janet Velie, Clarence Harvey, and M. Rale in *La La Lucille.*

BABY DOLLS
Lyricist: B.G. DeSylva and John Henry Mears
Introduced by: Helen Shipman in *Morris Gest Midnight Whirl* at the Century Grove (atop the Century Theatre) in New York City on December 27, 1919.

DOUGHNUTS
Lyricist: B.G. DeSylva and John Henry Mears
Introduced by: Annette Bade in *Morris Gest Midnight Whirl.*

I'LL SHOW YOU A WONDERFUL WORLD
Lyricist: B.G. DeSylva and John Henry Mears
Introduced by: Helen Shipman and Bernard Granville in *Morris Gest Midnight Whirl.*

1919

O, LAND OF MINE, AMERICA
Lyricist: Michael E. Rourke
Lore: This won a $50 runner-up prize in a contest for a national anthem sponsored by the New York *American.* It was published in the March 2, 1919 edition of that paper, but has not appeared since and has never been formally published.

IT'S GREAT TO BE IN LOVE
Lyricist: Arthur J. Jackson and B.G. DeSylva
Introduced by: Helen Clark and John Lowe in *La La Lucille* at the Henry Miller Theatre in New York City on May 26, 1919.

IT'S HARD TO TELL
Lyricist: Arthur J. Jackson and B.G. DeSylva
Introduced by: Janet Velie, John E. Hazzard, Sager Midgely, Cordelia MacDonald and Maurice Cass in *La La Lucille.*
Lore: Added after the show's opening.

KISSES
Lyricist: Arthur J. Jackson and B.G. DeSylva
Lore: Written for but not used in *La La Lucille*.

MONEY, MONEY, MONEY!
Lyricist: Arthur J. Jackson and B.G. DeSylva
Introduced by: Janet Velie, John E. Hazzard, J. Clarence Harvey, Sager Midgely, Cordelia MacDonald, and Maurice Cass in *La La Lucille*.
Lore: Replaced by "It's Hard to Tell."

THE LEAGUE OF NATIONS
Lyricist: B.G. DeSylva and John Henry Mears
Introduced by: Annette Bade in *Morris Gest Midnight Whirl*.

LET CUTIE CUT YOUR CUTICLE
Lyricist: B.G. DeSylva and John Henry Mears
Introduced by: Annette Bade in *Morris Gest Midnight Whirl*.

1920

BACK HOME
Lyricist: Irving Caesar
Lore: Accepted for but dropped from *Dere Mabel*.

I DON'T KNOW WHY
Lyricist: Irving Caesar
Lore: Accepted for but dropped from *Dere Mabel*.

I WANT TO BE WANTED BY YOU
Lyricist: Ira Gershwin
Lore: Used in *Dere Mabel*.

EVERYBODY SWAT THE PROFITEER
Lyricist: Arthur Jackson
Introduced by: Myra Cullen, Anna Green, Sascha Beaumont,

Eleanor Dana, Ruth Grey, and Vera Colburn in *George White's Scandals of 1920* at the Globe Theatre in New York City on June 7, 1920.

MY OLD LOVE IS MY NEW LOVE
Lyricist: Arthur Jackson
Lore: Written for but not used in *George White's Scandals of 1920.*

QUEEN ISABELLA
Lyricist: Arthur Jackson
Lore: Written for but not used in *George White's Scandals of 1920.*

THE BABY BLUES
Lyricist: E. Ray Goetz
Introduced by: This was sung in *Piccadilly to Broadway*, a show that closed out of town. It is unclear who sang it in that production but Delyle Alda did it in *Selwyn's Snapshots of 1921* at the Selwyn Theatre in New York City in June of 1921.

ON THE BRIM OF HER OLD FASHIONED BONNET
Lyricist: E. Ray Goetz
Introduced by: It is unclear who sang this in *Piccadilly to Broadway*, a show that closed out of town, but Delyle Alda sang it in *Selwyn's Snapshots of 1921.*

1921

BEAUTIFUL BIRD
Lyricist: Ira Gershwin and Lou Paley
Lore: Gershwin first worked on this tune in 1917. Early the next year Ira expressed the hope that it would become a second "Poor Butterfly." The completed tune appeared in George's 1921 sketchbook, but it was never publicly performed.

ANYTHING FOR YOU
Lyricist: Ira Gershwin
Introduced by: Vinton Freedley and Juanita Fletcher in *A Dangerous Maid* in Nixon's Apollo Theatre in Atlantic City on March 21, 1921.

EVERY GIRL HAS A WAY
Lyricist: Ira Gershwin
Lore: Written for but not used in *A Dangerous Maid.*

PIDGEE WOO
Lyricist: Arthur Francis (Ira Gershwin)
Lore: Written for but not used in *A Dangerous Maid.*

TRUE LOVE
Lyricist: Arthur Francis (Ira Gershwin)
Introduced by: Juliette Day and Vinton Freedley in *A Dangerous Maid.*

FUTURISTIC MELODY
Lyricist: E. Ray Goetz
Introduced by: Leo Henning, Ruth White, Gertrude McDonald, Violet Vale, Inez and Florence Courtney, and Gilda Gray in *Selwyn's Snapshots of 1921* at the Selwyn Theatre in June of 1921.

MOTHER EVE
Lyricist: Arthur Jackson
Introduced by: It is unclear who sang this when it was introduced in *George White's Scandals of 1921* at the Liberty Theatre in New York City on July 11, 1921.

AIN'T LOVE GRAND
Lore: This tune, without lyrics, appears in Gershwin's 1921 sketchbook.

HE'S GONE
Lore: This melodic fragment appears in Gershwin's 1921 sketch book.

MOLLY-ON-THE-SHORE
Lore: This song (the identity of the lyricist is uncertain) was written circa 1921 and was not used in any production.

MOONLIGHT
Lore: This is the name of a tune in Gershwin's 1921 sketchbook.

PHOEBE
Lyricist: Ira Gershwin and Lou Paley
Lore: Not used in any production until 1964, when it became the basis for "All the Livelong Day" in the film *Kiss Me, Stupid.*

IN THE HEART OF A GEISHA
Lyricist: Fred Fisher
Introduced by: It is not clear who sang this when it was interpolated in *The Perfect Fool* at the George M. Cohan Theatre on November 7, 1921.

1922

ALL TO MYSELF
Lyricist: Arthur Francis (Ira Gershwin)
Introduced by: It is not clear who sang this in *For Goodness Sake* at The Lyric Theatre on February 20, 1922.

I CAN'T TELL WHERE THEY'RE FROM WHEN THEY DANCE
Lyricist: B.G. DeSylva and Arthur Francis (Ira Gershwin)
Introduced by: George White sang this and Mary Reed and Myra Cullen danced it in *George White's Scandals of 1921* at the Globe Theatre in New York City on August 29, 1922.

JUST A TINY CUP OF TEA
Lyricist: B.G. DeSylva
Introduced by: Pearl Regay and Richard Bold in *George White's Scandals of 1921.*

THE COONEY COUNTY FAIR
Lyricist: Brian Hooker
Introduced by: Olin Howland and Emma Haig in *Our Nell* at the Bayes Theatre in New York City on December 4, 1922.
Lore: Gershwin biographer Isaac Goldberg referred to this as a complex and satirical choral number.

THE CUSTODY OF A CHILD
Lyricist: Brian Hooker
Lore: Written for but not used in *Our Nell.*

GOL-DURN!
Lyricist: Brian Hooker
Introduced by: Jimmy Barry in *Our Nell.*
Lore: This music is by Gershwin and William Daly.

LITTLE VILLAGES
Lyricist: Brian Hooker
Introduced by: John Merkyl and Mrs. Jimmy Barry in *Our Nell.*
Lore: This music is by Gershwin and William Daly.

MADRIGAL
Lyricist: Brian Hooker
Introduced by: The ensemble in *Our Nell.*
Lore: This music is by Gershwin and William Daly.

MY OLD NEW ENGLAND HOME
Lyricist: Brian Hooker
Introduced by: It is not clear who sang this in *Our Nell.*

NAMES I LOVE TO HEAR
Lyricist: Brian Hooker

Introduced by: Olin Howland, Emma Haig, Mr. and Mrs. Jimmy
Barry, and Guy Nichols in *Our Nell.*
Lore: This music is by Gershwin and William Daly.

OH, YOU LADY!
Lyricist: Brian Hooker
Introduced by: Lora Sanderson in *Our Nell.*
Lore: This music is by Gershwin and William Daly.

WE GO TO CHURCH ON SUNDAY
Lyricist: Brian Hooker
Introduced by: The ensemble in *Our Nell.*

THE FLAPPER
Lyricist: B.G. DeSylva
Lore: This was an uninterpolated song, music by Gershwin and
William Daly.

1923

ALL OVER TOWN
Lyricist: Clifford Grey
Introduced by: It is unclear who sang this in *The Rainbow* when
that show premiered at the Empire Theatre in London on April
3, 1923.
Lore: This is the same melody as "Come to the Moon."

ANY LITTLE TUNE
Lyricist: Clifford Grey
Introduced by: Fred A. Leslie in *The Rainbow.*

GIVE ME MY MAMMY
Lyricist: Clifford Grey
Lore: Written for but not used in *The Rainbow.*

MIDNIGHT BLUES
Lyricist: Clifford Grey
Introduced by: Lola Raine in *The Rainbow*.

GARDEN OF LOVE
Lyricist: B.G. DeSylva
Introduced by: Helen Hudson and the Tip Top Four in *George White's Scandals of 1923* after that show, which premiered in New York City on June 18, 1923, went on the road.

KATINKA
Lyricist: B.G. DeSylva, E. Ray Goetz, and Ballard MacDonald
Introduced by: Lester Allen in *George White's Scandals of 1923*.

LAUGH YOUR CARES AWAY
Lyricist: B.G. DeSylva, E. Ray Goetz, and Ballard MacDonald
Introduced by: The ensemble in *George White's Scandals of 1923*.

LITTLE SCANDAL DOLL
Lyricist: B.G. DeSylva, E. Ray Goetz, and Ballard MacDonald
Introduced by: Olive Vaughn in *George White's Scandals of 1923*.

LOOK IN THE LOOKING GLASS
Lyricist: B.G. DeSylva, E. Ray Goetz, and Ballard MacDonald
Introduced by: Helen Hudson in *George White's Scandals of 1923*.

1924

BE THE LIFE OF THE CROWD
Lyricist: B.G. DeSylva
Lore: This was written for but not used in *Sweet Little Devil*, a show that premiered at the Astor Theatre in New York City on January 21, 1924

HURRAY FOR THE U.S.A.

Lyricist: B.G. DeSylva

Introduced by: Franklyn Ardell and Ruth Warren in *Sweet Little Devil.*

JUST SUPPOSING

Lyricist: B.G. DeSylva

Introduced by: Irving Beebe in *Sweet Little Devil.*

THE MATRIMONIAL HANDICAP

Lyricist: B.G. DeSylva

Introduced by: Marjorie Gateson, Ruth Warren, William Wayne, and Irving Beebe in *Sweet Little Devil.*

MY LITTLE DUCKY

Lyricist: B.G. DeSylva

Introduced by: This was written for but not used in *Sweet Little Devil* but Cyril Ritchard and Madge Elliott sang it in the *Midnight Follies* at the Hotel Metropole in London in 1926.

QUITE A PARTY

Lyricist: B.G. DeSylva

Introduced by: The ensemble in *Sweet Little Devil.*

THE SAME OLD STORY

Lyricist: B.G. DeSylva

Introduced by: Constance Binney in *Sweet Little Devil.*

STRIKE, STRIKE, STRIKE

Lyricist: B.G. DeSylva

Introduced by: Marjorie Gateson and Rae Bowdin in *Sweet Little Devil.*

SWEET LITTLE DEVIL

Lyricist: B.G. DeSylva

Lore: Written for but not used in *Sweet Little Devil.*

SYSTEM
Lyricist: B.G. DeSylva
Introduced by: Constance Binney, Marjorie Gateson, and Ruth Warren in *Sweet Little Devil.*

YOU'RE MIGHTY LUCKY
Lyricist: B.G. DeSylva
Lore: Written for but not used in *Sweet Little Devil.*

I LOVE YOU, MY DARLING
Lyricist: B.G. DeSylva
Introduced by: Will Mahoney in *George White's Scandals of 1924* at the Apollo Theatre in New York City on June 30, 1924.

I'M GOING BACK
Lyricist: B.G. DeSylva
Introduced by: Will Mahoney in *George White's Scandals of 1924.*

JUST MISSED THE OPENING CHORUS
Lyricist: B.G. DeSylva
Introduced by: The Williams Sisters in *George White's Scandals of 1924.*

LOVERS OF ART
Lyricist: B.G. DeSylva
Introduced by: The Elm City Four in *George White's Scandals of 1924.*

ISN'T IT TERRIBLE WHAT THEY DID TO MARY, QUEEN OF SCOTS?
Lyricist: Desmond Carter
Introduced by: Leslie Henson and Claude Hulbert in *Primrose* at the Winter Garden Theatre in London subsequent to the premiere of that show at the Winter Garden Theatre in London on September 11, 1924.

425

Lore: This song was added to the show for comedian Henson and, according to one critic, it made the biggest impression, having "rocked the house."

Recordings: Henson and Hulbert recorded this on English Columbia 9002 (reissued on Monmouth-Evergreen MES 7071).

THE LIVE WIRE
Lyricist: Desmond Carter
Lore: This was written for but not used in *Primrose*.

PEP! ZIP! AND PUNCH!
Lyricist: Desmond Carter
Lore: This was written for but not used in *Primrose*.

THE BAD, BAD MEN
Lyricist: Ira Gershwin
Lore: This was written for but not used in *Lady, Be Good!* In a November 26, 1924 letter to Lou and Emily Paley, Ira expressed his disappointment that this song was not included in the show.

CARNIVAL TIME
Lore: It is unclear if this is a song or an instrumental. In a November 26, 1924 letter to Lou and Emily Paley, Ira Gershwin referred to it as "Carnival Dance." It was performed by the ensemble in the Philadelphia tryout of *Lady, Be Good!* at the Forest Theatre on November 17, 1924, but dropped before the New York opening.

THE END OF A STRING
Lyricist: Ira Gershwin
Introduced by: The ensemble in *Lady, Be Good!* at the Liberty Theatre in New York City on December 1, 1924.

EVENING STAR
Lyricist: Ira Gershwin
Lore: Written for but not used in *Lady, Be Good!*

426

JUANITA
Lyricist: Ira Gershwin
Introduced by: Adele Astaire in *Lady, Be Good!*

LADDIE DADDY
Lyricist: Ira Gershwin
Lore: Written for but not used in *Lady, Be Good!*

LEAVE IT TO LOVE
Lyricist: Ira Gershwin
Introduced by: Fred and Adele Astaire, Alan Edwards, and Kathlene Martyn in the Philadelphia tryout of *Lady, Be Good!*
Lore: This song briefly replaced "The Man I Love" and then it, too, was dropped.

LINGER IN THE LOBBY
Lyricist: Ira Gershwin
Introduced by: The ensemble in *Lady, Be Good!*

RAINY DAY GIRLS
Lyricist: Ira Gershwin
Lore: Written for but not used in *Lady, Be Good!*

THE ROBINSON HOTEL
Lyricist: Ira Gershwin
Introduced by: It is unclear who sang this in *Lady, Be Good!*

SEEING DICKIE HOME
Lyricist: Ira Gershwin
Lore: Written for but not used in *Lady, Be Good!*

SINGIN' PETE
Lyricist: Ira Gershwin
Lore: Written for but not used in *Lady, Be Good!*

WEATHER MAN
Lyricist: Ira Gershwin

Lore: Written for but not used in *Lady, Be Good!*

WE'RE HERE BECAUSE
Lyricist: Ira Gershwin
Introduced by: Patricia Clark and Gerald Oliver Smith in *Lady, Be Good!*
Lore: This music appeared in Gershwin's sketchbook, dated July 26, 1921.

WILL YOU REMEMBER ME?
Lyricist: Ira Gershwin
Lore: Written for but not used in *Lady, Be Good!*

A WONDERFUL PARTY
Lyricist: Ira Gershwin
Lore: Written for but not used in *Lady, Be Good!*

1925

THE HE-MAN
Lyricist: B.G. DeSylva and Ira Gershwin
Lore: Written for but not used in *Tell Me More*, which premiered at the Gaiety Theatre in New York City on April 13, 1925.

HOW CAN I WIN YOU NOW?
Lyricist: B.G. DeSylva and Ira Gershwin
Introduced by: Emma Haig and Andrew Toombes in *Tell Me More.*

I'M SOMETHING ON AVENUE A
Lyricist: B.G. DeSylva and Ira Gershwin
Lore: Written for but not used in *Tell Me More.*

IN SARDINIA
Lyricist: B.G. DeSylva and Ira Gershwin
Introduced by: Lou Holtz in *Tell Me More.*

LOVE IS IN THE AIR
Lyricist: B.G. DeSylva and Ira Gershwin
Introduced by: The ensemble in *Tell Me More.*

MR. AND MRS. SIPKIN
Lyricist: B.G. DeSylva and Ira Gershwin
Introduced by: Lou Holtz in *Tell Me More.*

ONCE
Lyricist: Ira Gershwin
Introduced by: This was written for but not used in *Tell Me More.* William Kent and Betty Compton sang it in *Funny Face*, which premiered at the Alvin Theatre in New York City on November 22, 1927.

THE POETRY OF MOTION
Lyricist: B.G. DeSylva and Ira Gershwin
Introduced by: Willie Covan and Leonard Ruffin in Tell Me More.

SHOP GIRLS AND MANNIKINS
Lyricist: B.G. DeSylva and Ira Gershwin
Lore: Written for but not used in *Tell Me More.*

UKELELE LORELEI
Lyricist: B.G. DeSylva and Ira Gershwin
Introduced by: Emma Haig in *Tell Me More.*

WHEN THE DEBBIES GO BY
Lyricist: B.G. DeSylva and Ira Gershwin
Introduced by: Esther Howard in *Tell Me More.*

LOVE, I NEVER KNEW
Lyricist: Desmond Carter
Introduced by: Elsa MacFarlane in the London production of *Tell Me More* at the Winter Garden on May 26, 1925.

DANCING HOUR
Lyricist: Ira Gershwin
Lore: This was written for but not used in *Tip-Toes*, a show that premiered at the Liberty Theatre in New York City on December 28, 1925. It was also dropped from *Funny Face* in 1927.

GATHER YE ROSEBUDS
Lyricist: Ira Gershwin
Lore: This was written for but not used in *Tip-Toes*. The lyric is quoted on page 30 of the January 17, 1988 edition of the New York *Times*.

HARBOR OF DREAMS
Lyricist: Ira Gershwin
Lore: Written for but not used in *Tip-Toes*.

LADY LUCK
Lyricist: Ira Gershwin
Introduced by: The ensemble in *Tip-Toes*.

LIFE'S TOO SHORT TO BE BLUE
Lyricist: Ira Gershwin
Lore: Written for but not used in *Tip-Toes*.

OUR LITTLE CAPTAIN
Lyricist: Ira Gershwin
Introduced by: Queenie Smith in *Tip-Toes*.

TIP-TOES
Lyricist: Ira Gershwin
Introduced by: Queenie Smith in *Tip-Toes*.

WAITING FOR THE TRAIN
Lyricist: Ira Gershwin
Introduced by: The ensemble in *Tip-Toes*.

WE

Lyricist: Ira Gershwin
Lore: Written for but not used in *Tip-Toes*.

FAR AWAY

Lyricist: Otto Harbach and Oscar Hammerstein II
Introduced by: Greek Evans and the Russian Art Choir in *Song of the Flame* at the Forty-Second Street Theatre in New York City on December 30, 1925.
Lore: Gershwin wrote this music with Herbert Stothart.

TAR-TAR

Lyricist: Otto Harbach and Oscar Hammerstein II
Introduced by: Greek Evans and the Russian Art Choir in *Song of the Flame*.
Lore: Gershwin wrote this music with Herbert Stothart.

WOMEN'S WORK IS NEVER DONE

Lyricist: Otto Harbach and Oscar Hammerstein II
Introduced by: Dorothy Mackaye in *Song of the Flame*.
Lore: Gershwin wrote this music with Herbert Stothart.

1926

BUY A LITTLE BUTTON

Lyricist: Desmond Carter
Introduced by: The ensemble in the London production of *Lady, Be Good!* at the Empire Theatre on April 14, 1926.

AIN'T IT ROMANTIC?

Lyricist: Ira Gershwin
Lore: Written for but not used in *Oh, Kay!*, a show which premiered at the Imperial Theatre in New York City on November 8, 1926.

BRING ON THE DING DONG DELL
Lyricist: Ira Gershwin
Lore: Written for but not used in *Oh, Kay!*

THE MOON IS ON THE SEA (THE SUN IS ON THE SEA)
Lyricist: Ira Gershwin
Lore: Written for but not used in *Oh, Kay!*

STEPPING WITH BABY
Lyricist: Ira Gershwin
Lore: Written for but not used in *Oh, Kay!*

WHAT'S THE USE?
Lyricist: Ira Gershwin
Lore: Written for but not used in *Oh, Kay!*

WHEN OUR SHIP COMES SAILING IN
Lyricist: Ira Gershwin
Lore: Written for but not used in *Oh, Kay!*

1927

FLETCHER'S AMERICAN CHEESE CHORAL SOCIETY
Lyricist: Ira Gershwin
Introduced by: Herbert Cortheil, Max Hoffman, Jr. and Robert Bentley in *Strike Up the Band* at the Shubert Theatre in New York City on September 5, 1927.
Lore: This later became "Fletcher's American Chocolate Choral Society Workers" in the 1930 production of *Strike Up the Band* and it was so published.

THE GIRL I LOVE
Lyricist: Ira Gershwin
Introduced by: Morton Downey in *Strike Up the Band.*
Lore: This is the same tune as "The Man I Love."
Recordings: Michael Feinstein (Parnassus PR 0100).

HOMEWARD BOUND
Lyricist: Ira Gershwin
Introduced by: Morton Downey in *Strike Up the Band.*

HOPING THAT SOMEDAY YOU'LL CARE
Lyricist: Ira Gershwin
Introduced by: Vivian Hart and Roger Pryor in *Strike Up the Band.*

HOW ABOUT A MAN LIKE ME?
Lyricist: Ira Gershwin
Introduced by: Herbert Corthell, Lew Hearn, and Edna May Oliver in *Strike Up the Band.*

MEADOW SERENADE
Lyricist: Ira Gershwin
Introduced by: Vivian Hart and Roger Pryor in *Strike Up the Band.*
Recordings: Kiri Te Kanawa and the New Princess Theater Orchestra (Angel DS 47454).

O, THIS IS SUCH A LOVELY WAR
Lyricist: Ira Gershwin
Introduced by: It is unclear who sang this in *Strike Up the Band.*

THE WAR THAT ENDED WAR
Lyricist: Ira Gershwin
Introduced by: The ensemble in *Strike Up the Band.*

ACROBATS
Lyricist: Ira Gershwin
Lore: Written for but not used in *Funny Face*, a show that premiered at the Alvin Theatre in New York City on November 22, 1927.

AVIATOR
Lyricist: Ira Gershwin
Lore: Written for but not used in *Funny Face.*

BIRTHDAY PARTY
Lyricist: Ira Gershwin
Introduced by: Betty Compton and Gertrude McDonald in *Funny Face.*

BLUE HULLABALOO
Lyricist: Ira Gershwin
Introduced by: Betty Compton and Gertrude McDonald in *Funny Face.*

COME ALONG, LET'S GAMBLE
Lyricist: Ira Gershwin
Lore: Written for but not used in *Funny Face.*

THE FINEST OF THE FINEST
Lyricist: Ira Gershwin
Lore: Written for but not used in *Funny Face.*

IF YOU WILL TAKE OUR TIP
Lyricist: Ira Gershwin
Lore: Written for but not used in *Funny Face.*

SING A LITTLE SONG
Lyricist: Ira Gershwin
Introduced by: The Ritz Quartet in *Funny Face.*

TELL THE DOC
Lyricist: Ira Gershwin
Introduced by: William Kent in *Funny Face.*
Analysis: This is one of Ira's great lyrics.
Recordings: Leslie Henson and a male quartet recorded this during the London production of *Funny Face* in 1928 (English Columbia 9592, reissued on Monmouth-Evergreen MES 7037).

THOSE EYES
Lyricist: Ira Gershwin
Lore: Written for but not used in *Funny Face*.

WE'RE ALL A-WORRY, ALL AGOG
Lyricist: Ira Gershwin
Lore: Written for but not used in *Funny Face*.

WHEN YOU SMILE
Lyricist: Ira Gershwin
Lore: Written for but not used in *Funny Face*.

WHEN YOU'RE SINGLE
Lyricist: Ira Gershwin
Lore: Written for but not used in *Funny Face*.

1928

FOLLOW THE DRUM
Lyricist: Ira Gershwin
Lore: Written for but not used in *Rosalie*, a show which premiered at the New Amsterdam Theatre in New York City on January 10, 1928.

I FORGOT WHAT I STARTED TO SAY
Lyricist: Ira Gershwin
Lore: Written for but not used in *Rosalie*.

LET ME BE A FRIEND TO YOU
Lyricist: Ira Gershwin
Introduced by: Marilyn Miller and Jack Donahue in *Rosalie*.

NEW YORK SERENADE
Lyricist: Ira Gershwin
Introduced by: Bobbe Arnst in *Rosalie*.

TRUE TO THEM ALL
Lyricist: Ira Gershwin
Lore: Written for but not used in *Rosalie*.

WHEN CADETS PARADE
Lyricist: Ira Gershwin
Lore: Written for but not used in *Rosalie*.

WHEN THE RIGHT ONE COMES ALONG
Lyricist: Ira Gershwin
Lore: Written for but not used in *Rosalie*.

YOU KNOW HOW IT IS
Lyricist: Ira Gershwin and P.G. Wodehouse
Lore: Written for but not used in *Rosalie*.

A-HUNTING WE WILL GO
Lyricist: Ira Gershwin
Lore: Written for but not used in *Treasure Girl*, a show that premiered in the Alvin Theatre in New York City on November 8, 1928.

ACCORDING TO MR. GRIMES
Lyricist: Ira Gershwin
Introduced by: Ferris Hartman in *Treasure Girl*.

DEAD MEN TELL NO TALES
Lyricist: Ira Gershwin
Lore: Written for but not used in *Treasure Girl*.

GOOD-BYE TO THE OLD LOVE, HELLO TO THE NEW
Lyricist: Ira Gershwin
Lore: Written for but not used in *Treasure Girl*.

I WANT TO MARRY A MARIONETTE
Lyricist: Ira Gershwin
Lore: Written for but not used in *Treasure Girl*.

PLACE IN THE COUNTRY
Lyricist: Ira Gershwin
Introduced by: Paul Frawley and Norman Curtis in *Treasure Girl.*

SKULL AND BONES
Lyricist: Ira Gershwin
Introduced by: The ensemble in *Treasure Girl.*

THIS PARTICULAR PARTY
Lyricist: Ira Gershwin
Lore: Written for but not used in *Treasure Girl.*

TREASURE ISLAND
Lyricist: Ira Gershwin
Lore: Written for but not used in *Treasure Girl.*

WHAT CAUSES THAT?
Lyricist: Ira Gershwin
Introduced by: Clifton Webb and Mary Hay in *Treasure Girl.*
Recordings: Pianists Michael Feinstein and David Ross (Parnassus PR-0100).

LOOK AT THE DAMN THING NOW
Lyricist: Ira Gershwin
Introduced by: Leslie Henson and Rita Page in the London production of *Funny Face*, which premiered at the Princess Theatre on November 8, 1928.

1929

CHINA GIRL
Lyricist: Ira Gershwin
Lore: Written for the unproduced show *East is West.*

LADY OF THE MOON
Lyricist: Ira Gershwin
Lore: Written for the unproduced show *East is West*, this became "I Just Looked at You" in the 1929 production *Show Girl* and "Blah, Blah, Blah" in the 1931 film *Delicious*.

SING SONG GIRL
Lyricist: Ira Gershwin
Lore: Written for the unproduced show *East is West*.

UNDER THE CINNAMON TREE
Lyricist: Ira Gershwin
Lore: Written for the unproduced show *East is West*.

WE ARE VISITORS
Lyricist: Ira Gershwin
Lore: This was written for the unproduced show *East is West*. Some of the music in this number was used in "Love is Sweeping the Country" from the 1931 show *Of Thee I Sing*.

ADORED ONE
Lyricist: Ira Gershwin and Gus Kahn
Lore: Written for but not used in *Show Girl*, which premiered at the Ziegfeld Theatre in New York City on July 2, 1929.

AT MRS. SIMPKIN'S FINISHING SCHOOL
Lyricist: Ira Gershwin and Gus Kahn
Lore: Written for but not used in *Show Girl*.

BLACK AND WHITE
Lyricist: Ira Gershwin and Gus Kahn
Introduced by: The ensemble in *Show Girl*.

FOLLOW THE MINSTREL BAND
Lyricist: Ira Gershwin and Gus Kahn
Introduced by: Eddie Jackson and His Band in *Show Girl*.

HAPPY BIRTHDAY
Lyricist: Ira Gershwin and Gus Kahn
Introduced by: The Ensemble in *Show Girl.*

HOME BLUES
Lyricist: Ira Gershwin and Gus Kahn
Introduced by: Joseph Macauley in *Show Girl.*
Lore: This music is derived from the blues theme of *An American in Paris.*

HOME LOVIN' GAL (MAN)
Lyricist: Ira Gershwin and Gus Kahn
Lore: Written for but not used in *Show Girl.*

HOW COULD I FORGET
Lyricist: Ira Gershwin and Gus Kahn
Introduced by: The ensemble in *Show Girl.*

I JUST LOOKED AT YOU
Lyricist: Gus Kahn and Ira Gershwin
Lore: This is a revision of "Lady of the Moon," a song written for the unproduced *East is West.* Slotted for but unused in *Show Girl,* it later evolved into "Blah, Blah, Blah," sung in the 1931 film *Delicious.*

I'M JUST A BUNDLE OF SUNSHINE
Lyricist: Ira Gershwin and Gus Kahn
Lore: Written for but not used in *Show Girl.*

I'M OUT FOR NO GOOD REASON TONIGHT
Lyricist: Ira Gershwin and Gus Kahn
Lore: Written for but not used in *Show Girl.*

LOLITA
Lyricist: Ira Gershwin and Gus Kahn
Introduced by: Joseph Macaulay in *Show Girl.*

MINSTREL SHOW
Lyricist: Gus Kahn and Ira Gershwin
Lore: Written for but not used in *Show Girl*.

MY SUNDAY FELLA
Lyricist: Ira Gershwin and Gus Kahn
Introduced by: Barbara Newberry in *Show Girl*.

SOMEBODY STOLE MY HEART AWAY
Lyricist: Ira Gershwin and Gus Kahn
Lore: Written for but not used in *Show Girl*.

SOMEBODY'S ALWAYS CALLING A REHEARSAL
Lyricist: Ira Gershwin and Gus Kahn
Lore: Written for but not used in *Show Girl*.

TONIGHT'S THE NIGHT
Lyricist: Ira Gershwin and Gus Kahn
Lore: Written for but not used in *Show Girl*.

ASK ME AGAIN
Lyricist: Ira Gershwin
Lore: This was written in the late 1920s and never used in any production, although it was considered for the 1938 film *The Goldwyn Follies*.

1930

THERE NEVER WAS SUCH A CHARMING WAR
Lyricist: Ira Gershwin
Lore: Written for but not used in *Strike Up the Band* (second version), which premiered in the Times Square Theatre in New York City on January 14, 1930.

UNOFFICIAL MARCH OF GENERAL HOLMES
Lore: It is unclear if this is an instrumental piece or if it has

lyrics by Ira Gershwin. It was used in *Strike Up the Band* (second version).

TODDLIN' ALONG
Lyricist: Ira Gershwin
Introduced by: Nan Blackstone in *9:15 Review*, a show that premiered on February 11, 1930.
Lore: This is the same melody as "The World is Mine."

AND I HAVE YOU
Lyricist: Ira Gershwin
Lore: Written for but not used in *Girl Crazy*, a show that premiered at the Alvin Theatre in New York City on October 14, 1930.

THE GAMBLER OF THE WEST
Lyricist: Ira Gershwin
Lore: Written for but not used in *Girl Crazy* .

SOMETHING PECULIAR
Lyricist: Ira Gershwin and Lou Paley
Lore: This song was originally written circa 1921. It was slated for but not used in *Girl Crazy*.

YOU CAN'T UNSCRAMBLE SCRAMBLED EGGS
Lyricist: Ira Gershwin
Lore: Written for but not used in *Girl Crazy*.

THE DYBBUK
Lore: On October 30, 1929 Gershwin received a contract from the Metropolitan Opera Company to write an opera based on *The Dybbuk*, a Jewish folktale that had become a play by S.A. Ansky (whose real name was Solomon Rappaport). When Gershwin learned that Italian composer Lodovico Rocca had already secured the musical rights to the play, he had to bow out of the project. By that time, he had written some music—but the whereabouts of these sketches is unknown. Isaac Goldberg, Gershwin's first biographer, said that Gershwin played him some of what he had composed: a prayer scene, a

Chassidic dance. Many years later, Ira Gershwin wrote Charles Schwartz, a more recent Gershwin biographer, to say that there was no *Dybbuk* manuscript.

1931

THANKS TO YOU
  Lyricist: Ira Gershwin
  Lore: Written for but not used in the film *Delicious*.

WELCOME TO THE MELTING POT
  Lyricist: Ira Gershwin
  Introduced by: Raul Roulien and Marvine Maazel in the film *Delicious*.
  Lore: This has also been referred to as "Dream Sequence" and "We're From the Journal."

YOU STARTED IT
  Lyricist: Ira Gershwin
  Lore: This song was used as background music in the film *Delicious*.

CALL ME WHATE'ER YOU WILL
  Lyricist: Ira Gershwin
  Lore: Written for but not used in *Of Thee I Sing*, a show that premiered at the Music Box Theatre in New York City on December 26, 1931.

1932

FOR LILY PONS
  Sketch for piano
  Lore: Ira Gershwin recalled that his brother had begun writing a piece of music for soprano Lily Pons. On the asumption that this three-page fragment was it, he gave it this title.

Recordings: Michael Tilson Thomas on CBS 1M 39699.

1933

BAUER'S HOUSE
Lyricist: Ira Gershwin
Lore: Written for but not used in *Pardon My English*, a show that opened at the Majestic Theatre in New York City on January 20, 1933.

DANCING IN THE STREETS
Lyricist: Ira Gershwin
Introduced by: The ensemble in *Pardon My English*.

THE DRESDEN NORTHWEST MOUNTED
Lyricist: Ira Gershwin
Introduced by: Jack Pearl in *Pardon My English*.

FATHERLAND, MOTHER OF THE BAND
Lyricist: Ira Gershwin
Lore: Written for but not used in *Pardon My English*.

FREUD AND JUNG AND ADLER
Lyricist: Ira Gershwin
Lore: Written for but not used in *Pardon My English*.

HAIL THE HAPPY COUPLE
Lyricist: Ira Gershwin
Introduced by: Carl Randall and Barbara Newberry in *Pardon My English*.

HE'S NOT HIMSELF
Lyricist: Ira Gershwin
Introduced by: The ensemble in *Pardon My English*.

IN THREE-QUARTER TIME
Lyricist: Ira Gershwin
Introduced by: Ruth Urban and John Cortez in *Pardon My English*.

NO TICKEE, NO WASHEE
Lyricist: Ira Gershwin
Introduced by: It is uncertain who sang this in *Pardon My English*.

PARDON MY ENGLISH
Lyricist: Ira Gershwin
Introduced by: Lyda Roberti and George Givot in *Pardon My English*.

TOGETHER AT LAST
Lyricist: Ira Gershwin
Lore: Written for but not used in *Pardon My English*.

TONIGHT
Lyricist: Ira Gershwin
Introduced by: George Givot and Josephine Huston in *Pardon My English*.

WHAT SORT OF WEDDING IS THIS?
Lyricist: Ira Gershwin
Introduced by: The ensemble in *Pardon My English*.

CLIMB UP THE SOCIAL LADDER
Lyricist: Ira Gershwin
Introduced by: Lois Moran in *Let 'Em Eat Cake*, a show that opened at the Imperial Theatre in New York City on October 21, 1933.
Recordings: Maureen McGovern and Michael Tilson Thomas on CBS S2M 42522.

CLOISTERED FROM THE NOISY CITY
Lyricist: Ira Gershwin
Introduced by: Ralph Riggs in *Let 'Em Eat Cake.*

COMES THE REVOLUTION
Lyricist: Ira Gershwin
Introduced by: Victor Moore in *Let 'Em Eat Cake.*
Recordings: Bobby Short recorded this in 1973 (Atlantic SD 2-608). A 1987 recording was made by Jack Gilford and Michael Tilson Thomas (CBS S2M 42522).

FIRST LADY AND FIRST GENT
Lyricist: Ira Gershwin
Lore: Written for but not used in *Let 'Em Eat Cake*, this song was reconstructed by Kay Swift for the 1978 Berkshire Theatre Festival revival of that show.
Recordings: Paige O'Hara and David Garrison with Michael Tilson Thomas on CBS S2M 42522.

HANGING THROTTLEBOTTOM IN THE MORNING
Lyricist: Ira Gershwin
Introduced by: The ensemble in *Let 'Em Eat Cake.*
Recordings: New York Choral Artists on CBS S2M 42522.

A HELL OF A HOLE
Lyricist: Ira Gershwin
Introduced by: William Gaxton in *Let 'Em Eat Cake.*

I KNOW A FOUL BALL
Lyricist: Ira Gershwin
Introduced by: Victor Moore in *Let 'Em Eat Cake.*
Recordings: Jack Gilford, Larry Kert, and Michael Tilson Thomas on CBS S2M 42522.

LET 'EM EAT CAVIAR
Lyricist: Ira Gershwin
Introduced by: Phillip Loeb in *Let 'Em Eat Cake.*

NO BETTER WAY TO START A CASE
Lyricist: Ira Gershwin
Introduced by: It is uncertain who sang this in *Let 'Em Eat Cake.*

NO COMPRENEZ, NO CAPISH, NO VERSTEH!
Lyricist: Ira Gershwin
Introduced by: The ensemble in *Let 'Em Eat Cake.*
Recordings: David Garrison, Larry Kert, and Michael Tilson Thomas on CBS S2M 42522.

OYEZ, OYEZ, OYEZ
Lyricist: Ira Gershwin
Introduced by: It is unclear who sang this in *Let 'Em Eat Cake.*

SHIRTS BY THE MILLIONS
Lyricist: Ira Gershwin
Introduced by: Lois Moran and Florenz Ames in *Let 'Em Eat Cake.*
Recordings: The New York Choral Artists and Michael Tilson Thomas on CBS S2M 42522.

THAT'S WHAT HE DID
Lyricist: Ira Gershwin
Introduced by: Victor Moore and Philip Loeb in *Let 'Em Eat Cake.*
Recordings: David Garrison, Larry Kert, Jack Gilford, and Michael Tilson Thomas on CBS S2M 42522.

THROTTLE THROTTLEBOTTOM
Lyricist: Ira Gershwin
Introduced by: Philip Loeb in *Let 'Em Eat Cake.*
Recordings: David Garrison, Larry Kert, and Michael Tilson Thomas on CBS S2M 42522.

TWEEDLEDEE FOR PRESIDENT
Lyricist: Ira Gershwin

Introduced by: The ensemble in *Let 'Em Eat Cake.*

Analysis: This song, complete with its own quotes from patriotic songs, is sung in counterpoint to "Wintergreen For President" and *its* patriotic quotes (the quotes too are sung in counterpoint).

Recordings: The New York Choral Artists and Michael Tilson Thomas on CBS S2M 42522.

THE UNION LEAGUE

Lyricist: Ira Gershwin

Introduced by: The ensemble in *Let 'Em Eat Cake.*

Lore: The lyrics to this song are published in Ira Gershwin's book, *Lyrics on Several Occasions.*

Recordings: The New York Choral Artists and Michael Tilson Thomas on CBS S2M 42522.

UP AND AT 'EM! ON TO VICT'RY

Lyricist: Ira Gershwin

Introduced by: Ralph Riggs in *Let 'Em Eat Cake.*

Recordings: Casper Roos and Michael Tilson Thomas on CBS S2M 42522.

WHAT MORE CAN A GENERAL DO?

Lyricist: Ira Gershwin

Introduced by: It is unclear who sang this in *Let 'Em Eat Cake.*

Recordings: This selection, under the title "I've Brushed My Teeth," is performed by Jack Dabdoub and Michael Tilson Thomas on CBS SZM42522.

WHEN THE JUDGES DOFF THE ERMINE

Lyricist: Ira Gershwin

Introduced by: Ralph Riggs in *Let 'Em Eat Cake.*

WHO'S THE GREATEST?

Lyricist: Ira Gershwin

Introduced by: William Gaxton in *Let 'Em Eat Cake.*

Recordings: Larry Kert and Michael Tilson Thomas on CBS S2M 42522.

447

WHY SPEAK OF MONEY?
Lyricist: Ira Gershwin
Introduced by: The ensemble in *Let 'Em Eat Cake.*
Recordings: The New York Choral Artists and Michael Tilson Thomas on CBS 42522.

1934-1935

LONELY BOY
Lyricist: DuBose Heyward
Lore: This was written for but dropped from Act III, Scene III of *Porgy and Bess*, which premiered at the Alvin Theatre in New York City on October 10, 1935.

1936

CATFISH ROW
For orchestra
Introduced by: The Philadelphia Orchestra conducted by Alexander Smallens at the Academy of Music in Philadelphia on January 21, 1936.
Lore: Catfish Row is the title given by Ira Gershwin in 1958 to what his brother had originally called *Suite From Porgy and Bess.* This piece of music was the composer's own orchestral synthesis of the opera, written in the wake of *Porgy's* cool reception on Broadway. He hoped that it would keep the music alive. As it turned out, *Porgy and Bess* kept itself afloat while the suite was forgotten. By 1958, when Ira rediscovered it, another orchestral synthesis—Robert Russell Bennett's *Symphonic Picture*—had achieved great popularity; hence, the new title.
Analysis: There are five movements:

1. The first, entitled "Catfish Row," contains the opening "Introduction," the "Jasbo Brown Piano Music," "Summertime," and bits of the "Crap Game Fugue."

448

2. Part two, entitled "Porgy Sings," consists of "I Got Plenty O'Nuttin'" and "Bess, You is My Woman Now."
3. Part three, entitled "Fugue," is a complete rendering of the "Crap Game Fugue."
4. Part four, entitled "Hurricane," presents instrumental music from Act II, Scene III, beginning with the quiet and dreamy depiction of pre-dawn and ending with the "Hurricane Music."
5. Part five, entitled "Good Morning, Brother," presents the orchestral introduction to Act III, Scene III, "Good Morning, Brother" (entitled "Good Mornin', Sistuh!" in the piano/ vocal score), and "Oh, Lawd, I'm On My Way."

Recordings: The first recording of this piece was made by Maurice Abravanel conducting the Utah Symphony (Westminster XWN 18850). Subsequent versions have been by Erich Kunzel and the Cincinnati Pops (Telarc CD-80086), Seiji Ozawa and the Berlin Philharmonic (Angel CDL-47152), and Leonard Slatkin with the St. Louis Symphony (Vox QSVBX 5132).

DOUBTING THOMAS
Lyricist: Albert Stillman
Lore: This pop song was not used in any production.

I WON'T GIVE UP TILL YOU GIVE IN TO ME
Lyricist: Albert Stillman
Lore: This pop song was not used in any production.

SLEEPLESS NIGHT
For solo piano
Lore: This exists as a piano piece, although it was to be a song. Its first appearance was in Gershwin's 1924 tune book. He finished the music after arriving in Beverly Hills in 1936.
Recordings: Michael Tilson Thomas recorded this in 1985 on CBS IM 39699.

1937

FRENCH BALLET
Instrumental

Lore: This is one of several instrumental numbers written by Gershwin for *Shall We Dance*, an RKO film released in May of 1937. The film's cue sheets credit Nathaniel Shilkret as co-composer or arranger.

DANCE OF THE WAVES
Instrumental

Lore: An instrumental written for *Shall We Dance*, Nathaniel Shilkret credited as co-composer or arranger.

GINGER RHUMBA
Instrumental

Lore: An instrumental written for *Shall We Dance*, Nathaniel Shilkret credited as co-composer or arranger.

GRACEFUL AND ELEGANT
Instrumental

Lore: An instrumental written for *Shall We Dance*, Nathaniel Shilkret credited as co-composer or arranger.

BALLOON BALLET
Instrumental

Lore: An instrumental written for *Shall We Dance*, Nathaniel Shilkret credited as co-composer or arranger.

HOCTOR'S BALLET
Instrumental

Lore: Gershwin, working quickly and under deadline, wrote this ballet for *Shall We Dance*. He used new themes as well as snatches of "Shall We Dance," "Wake Up, Brother and Dance," "They Can't Take That Away From Me," and "They All Laughed" and was assisted by Nathaniel Shilkret and Robert Russell Bennett in the orchestrations and in creating the medley.

PAY SOME ATTENTION TO ME
Lyricist: Ira Gershwin
Lore: This was written for but not used in the 1937 RKO film *A Damsel in Distress.*

PUT ME TO THE TEST
Lyricist: Ira Gershwin
Introduced by: Fred Astaire, George Burns and Gracie Allen, who danced to this tune with whisk brooms in *A Damsel in Distress.*
Lore: Ira's lyrics were not sung in *A Damsel in Distress.* In 1944, he applied the title and lyric to a new melody by Jerome Kern and it was used in the Columbia picture *Cover Girl.*

1946-P

DEMON RUM
Lyricist: Ira Gershwin
Introduced by: The ensemble in *The Shocking Miss Pilgrim*, a 20th Century-Fox film released in January of 1947.

STAND UP AND FIGHT
Lyricist: Ira Gershwin
Introduced by: Ann Revere, Betty Grable, and Dick Haymes in *The Shocking Miss Pilgrim.*

SWEET PACKARD
Lyricist: Ira Gershwin
Introduced by: The ensemble in *The Shocking Miss Pilgrim.*

TOUR OF THE TOWN
Lyricist: Ira Gershwin
Lore: Written for but not used in *The Shocking Miss Pilgrim.*

WALTZING IS BETTER THAN SITTING DOWN
Lyricist: Ira Gershwin

Introduced by: Dick Haymes and Betty Grable in *The Shocking Miss Pilgrim.*

WELCOME SONG
Lyricist: Ira Gershwin
Lore: Written for but not used in *The Shocking Miss Pilgrim.*

A Gershwin Companion
Part Three
Indexes

457

INDEX OF RECORDING ARTISTS

465

INDEX OF RECORDING ARTISTS

470

471

General Index

Aarons, Alex, 103, 111
Adler, Larry, 402, 405
Aeolian Company, 2, 4
Alajalov, Constantin, 289
Alda, Delyle, 66, 418
Alda, Robert, 118
Allen, Gracie, 366, 451
Allen, Lester, 49, 51, 69, 423
Allen, Woody, 179, 385, 389
Amatore, Pearl, 363, 364
An American In Paris (film), 49, 134, 183, 184, 345, 346, 373, 374, 404
Americana, 155, 156
Ames, Florenz, 269, 273, 279, 446
Ansky, S.A. (Solomon Rappaport), 441
Ardell, Franklyn, 424
Arden, Victor, 289
Arlen, Anya, 355
Arlen, Harold, 350, 355, 398, 399
Armitage, Merle, 160
Arndt, Felix, 3
Arnst, Bobbe, 164, 187, 435
Arvey, Verna, 241, 318
Askins, Harry, 5, 304
Astaire, Adele, 8, 39, 111, 114, 115, 117, 121, 124, 152, 153, 154, 174, 177, 178, 180, 182, 187, 366, 427
Astaire, Fred, 8, 39, 111, 113, 114, 115, 152, 153, 154, 174, 175, 177, 179, 180, 181, 347, 348, 349, 351, 352, 354, 358, 360, 361, 363, 364, 366, 367, 390, 398, 427, 451
Atteridge, Harold, 2
Auer, Mischa, 248
Bade, Annette, 416, 417
Bailey, Pearl, 144
Baker, Kenny, 371, 373
Baker, Phil, 368
Balanchine, George, 290, 397
Ballet Russe de Monte Carlo, 112, 172
Balzac, Honore de, 303
Barclays Of Broadway, 354
Bargy, Roy, 134
Barrie, Gracie, 345
Barry, Jimmy, 421, 422
Barry, Mrs. Jimmy, 421, 422
Bartok, Bela, 41
Bayes, Nora, 5, 6, 392

Beaumont, Sascha, 409, 417
Beebe, Irving, 78, 424
Beethoven, Ludwig van, 82, 355
Behrman, S.N., 287, 369, 398
Belcher, George, 364
Bennett, Robert Russell, 448, 450
Bennett, Tony, 398
Bennison, Louis, 14
Bentley, Robert, 210, 220, 432
Berg, Alban, 199
Bergen, Edgar, 368, 370
Berkeley Square Orchestra, 117
Berlin, Irving, 13, 24, 125, 147, 261, 346, 369
Berlioz, Hector, 199
Berman, Pandro S., 350
Bernard, Mike, 289
Bernstein, Leonard, 37
Berson, Beulah, 71
Bessinger, Frank, 119
Bestor, Don, 291
Big Charade, 251
Big Chief Muddy Waters, 218
Binney, Constance, 78, 79, 424, 425
Blackstone, Nan, 185, 441
Blake, Eubie, 3, 51, 241
Bolcom, William, 404
Bold, Richard, 43, 46, 51, 66, 67, 68, 69, 76, 88, 92, 421
Bolitho, William, 172
Bolton, Guy, 157
Bordoni, Irene, 40-41, 72
Borne, Hal, 393
Boswell Sisters, 205
Botkin, Henry, 308
Bowdin, Rae, 424
Boyle, Jack, 2
Brady, Olive, 386
Brahms, Johannes, 139, 371
Brendel, El, 246
Brinkley, Grace, 253, 256, 262, 269, 273, 279
Broadway Brevities Of 1920, 26-27
Bronson, Lillian, 379
Brown, Anne, 307
Bryan, Al, 6
Bubbles, John W., 307, 330, 339, 344
Buchanan, Jack, 187
Buck, Ford L., 307, 330, 344
Burke, Billie, 11

481

483

READER'S NOTES

READER'S NOTES

READER'S NOTES

READER'S NOTES

READER'S NOTES

READER'S NOTES

READER'S NOTES

READER'S NOTES

READER'S NOTES

READER'S NOTES